To David —
Thanks for t.
day for our Fre
values. May you, like the zealots,
have the strength — spiritual, mental,
and physical — to "fight the good fight.
TOM 5/30/13

MW01047599

Founding Zealots

How Evangelicals Created America's First Public Schools, 1783-1865

Thomas W. Hagedorn

xulon
PRESS

Founding Zealots
How Evangelicals Created America's First
Public Schools, 1783-1865
by Thomas W. Hagedorn

Printed in the United States of America

Cataloging Data
Hagedorn, Thomas W.
Founding zealots: how evangelicals created America's first public schools, 1783-1865 / Thomas W. Hagedorn.
    p.   cm.
Includes bibliographic references and index.
ISBN 9781625098696
1. Public Schools--United States--History--19th century. I. Title.
LA215 2013   371.973

www.xulonpress.com

To God, who inspired me with an idea;
To Mary, who nurtured me with encouragement;
To Heather and Allison, who reassured me with understanding;
To countless others, who patiently listened to me for twenty years.

Contents

Preface

*M*y fascination with the creation of our public schools began in a most unusual way. Twenty years ago, while conducting research on an unrelated topic, I stumbled upon the following words in Ohio's first Constitution (1802):

> Religion, morality, and knowledge being essentially necessary to good government. . ., schools. . .shall forever be encouraged. . .

At the time, I found it both curious and ironic that from its very beginning Ohio promoted traditional religion and morality as core missions for education, while today it and other states operate schools that are at best indifferent to such values and at times even hostile to them. After all, it seemed to me that almost every month a new dispute was erupting somewhere over issues like vouchers for parochial schools, the posting of the Ten Commandments on school property, and the spiritual content of classroom assignments or graduation addresses. My accidental discovery caused me to wonder if the Buckeye State, or other states for that matter, had ever actually established schools with such spiritual objectives. That question led me to examine hundreds of 19th century letters, reports, histories, and biographies, many of which had long been neglected by historians. After many years I concluded that the leaders of the first public schools—from Connecticut to California, from Michigan to Missouri—were almost always New Englanders, Calvinists, or both. And not surprisingly, I found that those zealots felt that the teaching of religion and morality was more important than any other school activity. That result made sense to me, given the plain meaning of those words in the Constitution, but my next discovery puzzled me even more. For as I read the work of educational historians, the efforts of the Calvinists, many of whom were ministers and missionaries, were often ignored, minimized, or distorted. For well over a hundred years most historians, with a few notable exceptions, have told this story from a secular and sometimes even a Marxist perspective. In addition to minimizing the role of faith, they have overemphasized and condemned the influence of capitalism and overstated the contributions of the nation's first labor movement. *Founding Zealots* attempts to correct their accounts by profiling the Calvinist reformers, describing what they did, and placing them in their proper religious, demographic, and political context. Like those Calvinists, I am an evangelical, and I believe that my personal perspective has enabled me to better understand their motives, which may have caused difficulty for those historians who viewed this story through a totally secular lens. At the same time, I have tried to resist my own biases. I will leave it to the reader and the critics to decide if I have succeeded.

My two discoveries have taken me on a twenty-year odyssey that sent me across the nation to many historical sites and research libraries, but that mostly demanded long hours alone in my office. I have only been able to complete this work by clinging to the belief that five groups will find it both entertaining and useful. First, evangelicals will discover, probably for the first time, that their spiritual ancestors were responsible for one of our nation's most important institutions. Second, avid readers of American history will learn about the dramatic, five-decade-long struggle of a dedicated group of reformers who time after time refused to accept defeat. Third, educators will be exposed to a very different account of this story than the one they studied in teachers college. Fourth, historians of education will have the opportunity to consider a new interpretation of a movement that has been subjected to little study over the last three decades. And finally, students and librarians will appreciate the book's identification of the leaders and their story by state: in the text, in the index, and at the website, www.foundingzealots.com.

Introduction

*M*ost historians of the movement that created America's first public schools follow a similar storyline. Enlightenment ideals inspire Horace Mann and like-minded New Englanders to try to build a secular heaven on earth through their unrelenting application of reason. Starting in the urban Northeast and later in the rural West, the new institutions quickly become monuments to Rousseau and Jefferson and in the process gradually overcome the fading influence of religion, the Puritans, and the Reformation. But my research, using many long-neglected sources, reveals that it was not reason but faith—sparked by Western evangelicals during the Second Great Awakening—that played the dominant role in the origins of free education for the nation's children.

Founding Zealots tells how a small group of Calvinist preachers and laymen established schools that stressed religion, morality, and Bible-reading, while underemphasizing secular subjects like writing, arithmetic, and geography. Throughout this compelling drama it is clear that the zealots had a singular goal—providing a free education for every child in America. Further, they had an overriding motive—spreading Christianity and its message of salvation to every person on the continent, irrespective of their gender, race, class, or location. Unfortunately, the historical record also shows that they faced significant obstacles in the form of cultural groups and frontier conditions that often successfully stymied their frenzied efforts.

The common school movement spanned five decades and engaged several generations of Protestant leaders. This book traces the fight for universal schooling in four parts. Part I describes the opening context and the philosophical and religious thinking that inspired reform. Parts II, III, and IV each represent a distinct phase of the struggle. Except for Part I, which begins with a chapter providing background for the story, each part opens with a biographical chapter that introduces the main actors for that time period. A narrative chapter then follows, which reveals a pattern that is duplicated throughout all three phases of this struggle. First, a small group of single-minded crusaders overcome discouraging initial conditions, only to see their work partially undone by equally-determined opponents or unfavorable conditions. During the next phase, their project is taken up by a new, larger corps of reformers, who build on the limited progress achieved by their predecessors. This cycle repeats itself until the Republicans finally achieve a series of political victories in the 1850s and 1860s, resulting in a system of free, universal schooling in every state outside of the South. The Epilogue details the many ways in which this story has been misunderstood by historians in academia, explains their causes, and, in the spirit of the zealots, offers a needed reform.

Part I begins with the new nation in crisis. During the winter of 1783 Army officers demanded back pay from Congress in the form of western land grants and a territorial government that supported education and religion. After Washington, Jefferson, and Hamilton all failed to get Congress to enact a workable plan, we learn about Rev. Manasseh Cutler, a "Franklin-esque" figure who fortuitously possessed every skill necessary to break the impasse. In the historic summer of 1787 Cutler traveled to New York City and Philadelphia, where we learn about his efforts to achieve success where the three Founders had failed. Part I ends with an explanation of the Christian philosophy that inspired Cutler and others throughout their long struggle for the schools.

Part II introduces four new leaders, including Manasseh's son, Ephraim. Exploiting a narrow window of opportunity after the Panic of 1819, they exhibited impressive political skills, which helped them overcome several obstacles to pass the first significant school laws in Ohio and Illinois in the mid-1820s. Unfortunately, their joy quickly turned to sorrow as their opponents reversed some of their hard-fought gains. In this part we examine at length one group that consistently fought for public education, the New Englanders, and one that generally opposed it, the Appalachians. Both groups moved westward during the greatest internal migration in American history and their preferred destinations would become either areas of support for education, in the case of the Yankees, or opposition to it, in the case of the Appalachians. Further, this part of the book explains that persistent low population density and inadequate community and individual wealth also worked to frustrate the reformers.

Part III starts with profiles of the three most important figures of the late 1830s, Rev. Samuel Lewis of Ohio, Horace Mann of Massachusetts, and Henry Barnard of Connecticut, who led their states' movements during an era when professionalism began to take root. Like their predecessors, they seized upon a brief political opening during the Panic of 1837 to pass landmark legislation, but soon found themselves defending it against fierce opposition. Largely due to differing political conditions in their states, Mann succeeded while Lewis and Barnard did not. So once again, progress was followed by a partial retreat. Interestingly, evidence laid out in this part proves that Mann can no longer be considered the preeminent "Father" of America's public schools.

Part IV opens with a survey of the Western Literary Institute, an organization of evangelical activists that was instrumental in spreading the gospel of free education throughout fourteen states in the Ohio and Mississippi valleys. In this, the last part of our story, one sees that the structural barriers faced earlier by the reformers had weakened considerably by the 1850s. Population growth made the formation of schools feasible in more places, Yankee migration boosted the cause in places like Illinois, and the maturity of frontier communities left them with more resources for education. But perhaps just as important, outside the South the highly emotional issues of antislavery, temperance, and nativism had a destabilizing effect on politics, which gave the opportunistic crusaders in the North the ability to finally complete their project. On the West Coast a different set of reformers took advantage of the political turmoil caused by the Civil War to claim victory by the late 1860s. Then, over the next few decades the dominance of the Republican Party and the weakness of the Democrat Party assured that reform would not be reversed, as it had during earlier phases.

Founding Zealots has several features that set it apart from most histories of the origins of the public schools. First, it uses primary sources from scores of people in numerous states and it utilizes many older histories, which contain a great deal more detail than accounts that have been written in the last fifty years or so. Next, relying upon Aristotle's Dictum, it accepts the literal meaning of the zealots' writings, in contrast to many of the other treatments of this topic, which seem to presume that the reformers were pursuing a hidden agenda of exploitation. Further, it carefully attempts to place the story within its proper religious, demographic, intellectual, and state political context. Moreover, for the Midwest, Texas, and the West Coast, it provides more in-depth discussion of the cause than any account published in a long time. Finally, its special features, in conjunction with the book's website, www.foundingzealots.com, provide support for those committed to further study of local and state educational history.

The results of my research and the conclusions of this book could not be more ironic for even the most casual observer of American culture and society. For I found that evangelicals, who today seem to be so at odds with many of our nation's secular institutions, 150 years ago created one of its most revered organizations, the public school. Even more remarkably, their conservative educational vision stressed a form of religious and moral training that would be unthinkable in today's public schools. For the first time, *Founding Zealots* explains how those two surprising outcomes came to pass.

Part I

Laying the Foundation, 1783-1787

George Washington

Rev. Manasseh Cutler

Martin Luther

Rev. Timothy Dwight

Chapter 1

Obstacles at the Starting Line

Ｔhe story begins with a military conspiracy. In March 1783 Gen. George Washington unexpectedly strode into The Temple of Virtue, a large meetinghouse in Newburgh, New York that was packed with officers of the Continental Army. Moving quickly to the front, he seized the podium from a startled Gen. Horatio Gates, whose associates had just circulated two papers that threatened Congress and challenged the Commander in Chief's authority. Though historians argue over how far the mutineers would have gone, Washington had signaled his concern by staying close to the Army that winter. He knew that for three years sporadic rebellions had erupted in units from Connecticut, New York, New Jersey and Pennsylvania; commanders had used lethal force, court martial, and even execution to restore order. Still broad-shouldered and vigorous at 51, the 6'3" Washington possessed the command presence to quiet the battle-hardened crowd. Normally calm and reserved, on this day he appeared visibly agitated.[1]

Washington began by scolding the anonymous author of what came to be known as the Newburgh Addresses. "Gentlemen, by an anonymous summons, an attempt has been made to convene you together. How inconsistent with the rules of propriety, how unmilitary and how subversive of all order and discipline, let the good sense of the Army decide." Appealing to their sense of shared sacrifice, he reminded them that he had been "a faithful friend to the Army. . . . I was among the first who embarked in the cause of our common country." Washington recounted the plotters' threat that "If war continues, remove [yourselves] into the unsettled country. . .and leave an ungrateful country to defend itself." The general railed "My God! What can this writer have in view, by recommending such measures? Can he be a friend to the Army? Can he be a friend to this country? Rather is he not an insidious foe?" Washington pleaded with his men "to express your utmost horror and detestation of the man. . .who wickedly attempts to open the flood-gates of civil discord, *and deluge our rising empire in blood* [emphasis added]."[2]

Washington implored the audience to trust the Confederation Congress to make good on its promises of back pay, pensions, and allowances for food and clothing. He pledged to make their case before Congress. Then, gauging that he had not yet convinced them, he began to read a letter from Virginia Delegate Joseph Jones that tried to explain Congress' challenges in meeting the Army's demands. Struggling with the small script, he paused, fumbled for his reading glasses and pleaded, "Gentlemen, you must pardon me. I have grown gray in your service and now find myself growing blind." His emotional appeal transformed the mood of the crowd, even eliciting tears from some. As soon as he left the room, the officers voted unanimously to endorse their Commander in Chief's condemnation of the plotters and his plea for patience with Congress. Lawmakers would test the officers' forbearance for four more years, but the veterans' demands would eventually lead to the first government attempt to fund schools. This happened despite the reality that the mutineers cared much more about their pay grievances than universal education. This established an oft-repeated pattern in which other, more popular causes drove advances in public schooling. But before the veterans witnessed even modest success in either endeavor, many obstacles would have to be removed.[3]

Washington kept his promise to lobby Congress for the Army. He informed them of the Addresses, recounted his angry speech to the officer corps, and described the current mood of the Army, while urging immediate action. On the day Congress received his letter (April 18), they passed a tax on imports to fund long overdue pensions and bonuses. But the tax required collection by the states, and the Articles of Confederation stipulated that every state must ratify the law, a tedious and usually futile process. The quick response of Washington and Congress calmed the officers, but the enlisted men were not so easily mollified. In June, after two months of increasing defiance, hundreds of Continental recruits and Pennsylvania militia, their courage braced with alcohol, fixed bayonets and demanded answers about their back pay from Congress, which was meeting in Philadelphia. When Congress quietly relocated to the safety of Princeton, New Jersey, the troops dispersed and violence was avoided. Since the peace treaty with Great Britain had been signed in March, eliminating the need for a large army, Congress furloughed most of the Army in late June, which made protests far more difficult to organize. Within a year, the Army would number less than 1,000 men, down from 10,000 at the time of the Newburgh Addresses. Mutinies, threats, assemblies, and letters had produced many promises but little compensation for the soldiers or their families, who were suffering from a severe post-war economic depression.[4]

Yet, as Joseph Jones explained in his letter to Washington, Congress had few financial options. In addition to overdue Army pay, it had foreign and domestic debts so large that it could only afford minimal repayments. Yet Congress' main sources of cash, the states, were beset with their own financial problems, so they repeatedly spurned legislative attempts to raise revenues. As a last resort, Congress sent the states "requisitions," but since it had no power to collect them, it was essentially asking for voluntary payments. Ultimately, only fifteen cents came in for every dollar requested, so Congress had to borrow even more, using the proceeds to pay off prior obligations.[5]

But if the new nation had accumulated liabilities from the War, it had also acquired assets — millions of acres of land west of the Appalachians. Since the 1750s, thousands of Americans, including Washington himself, became familiar with this country while trading, hunting, and fighting two wars along the frontier. During most of the Revolutionary War neither the Americans, British, nor Indians had controlled this region, but that did not deter Congress from offering pieces of it to pacify the Army or attract new recruits. The Continental Army was losing men to state militias, which offered better pay and enlistment bounties. Some men, known as bounty jumpers, even deserted Continental units to join militias for cash. With little else to offer, Congress enticed them with the promise of property if they won the War. In September 1776 without any land to give, Congress nonetheless granted bounties for colonels (500 acres), lieutenant colonels (450 acres), majors (400 acres), captains (300 acres), lieutenants (200 acres), ensigns (150 acres), and privates (100 acres). Four years later Congress added bounties for brigadier generals (850 acres) and major generals (1,100 acres). Congress' failure to fulfill those promises would continue to anger the veterans for several years after the Newburgh Conspiracy.[6]

While some officers hoped to get wealthy from speculation, most simply wanted to settle on good farmland or to pass it along to their sons. Many were Yankees who, in addition to wanting to leave behind their region's barren soil, also yearned to plant their culture in a new land, just as their Puritan forefathers had done almost two centuries earlier. In fact, not long after their arrival in America, some of them began migrating away from the coast due to the failure of New England's farmland to accommodate their growing numbers. Congress favored their settlement in the West over the upland Southerners or Appalachians, who, without benefit of title, had already begun to squat there. They moved in small groups of extended families, which produced an isolated pattern of settlement, while the Yankee custom of dense settlement offered advantages to both the pioneers and the government. First, a few carefully-designed towns allowed for more efficient defense than the numerous villages and isolated homesteads common to the mountains of Virginia and North Carolina. Further, Congress believed that the rectangular surveying system practiced in New England, which measured property boundaries using straight lines at right angles to one another, produced relatively clean titles and high sales prices. On the other hand, the metes and bounds system preferred by the Appalachians, which yielded meandering lines that followed natural features, invited lawsuits and lower sales proceeds. However, delegates from New

England convinced Congress that some intangibles were even more important to draw pioneers to the West.[7]

Yankees desired a community that shared a common culture and faith and they believed that a good system of schools was the best way to reach that goal. Since the 1640s their ancestors had backed their commitment to education with money and mortar, with more enthusiasm than any other region in British North America. Their zeal was fueled by the Puritan conviction that moral education, grounded in the Bible, should be at the heart of schooling. Typically, the town's minister would use his congregation's meetinghouse to teach a curriculum stressing literacy, morality, and religion. Each colony's (and later each state's) laws and constitutions supported these local practices. For example, the people of Massachusetts, after having failed to adopt a Constitution in 1778 because it lacked such guarantees, approved one drafted by John Adams in 1780 that insisted on funding for "the support and maintenance of public Protestant teachers of piety, religion and morality." Interestingly, it also called for state support for "the public worship of God." Though some dissented from this mixing of church and state, such views were quite common throughout New England and beyond. Nevertheless, it would take two determined Army officers from Massachusetts, aided by the events at Newburgh, to advance the causes of land for the soldiers and schools for the children.[8]

In April 1783, Col. Timothy Pickering drafted what historians now call the Army Plan on behalf of the protesting officers at Newburgh. Since he served as Quartermaster General from 1780 to 1785, Pickering understood better than most the discontent that ran deep in the Continental Army, from some of the top generals down to the lowest privates, as well as the suffering and deprivation that drove it. Despite the risks and losses they had endured—one in five were killed or seriously injured—they were still due back pay, pensions, and bonuses, enlistees had been poorly fed, clothed, and housed during the war, and conditions back home were a grave concern. The British Army had inflicted massive destruction on private property, and both armies had appropriated livestock and other supplies from civilians. The War had generated severe shortages and hyper inflation that was destroying the value of the currency. With so

7

many married men off fighting the War, wives had often performed the hard physical labor of running the family farm. Despite some public and private charity, the soldiers' families were desperate and looked to the new government for relief. Yet Pickering was not the best choice to promote their plan. Often hot-tempered and loose-tongued, he would later involve himself in two other conspiracies that threatened the secession of New England from the Union. He was also the only officer known to publicly resist Washington's plea for patience at Newburgh and he did not particularly like the Virginian. Wisely then, the veterans chose another officer to sell the Army Plan to Washington.[9]

In June Brigadier Gen. Rufus Putnam sent Washington a petition signed by 288 officers, accompanied by a letter arguing for the Plan. The officers trusted Putnam, who they had selected to convey other grievances, as did Washington, who was grateful for his help in driving the British Army from Boston in 1776. Putnam, a self-taught engineer, had fortified the Dorchester Heights, making the British position untenable. The petition he carried requested that the land grants be satisfied in the Ohio country and that this region be established as "a distinct Government (or Colony of the United States)" before being admitted as a single state. His own letter argued that this new settlement was a military necessity and that it should consist of a series of forts, twenty miles apart, which would link the Ohio River valley with the Great Lakes. The forts and settlement would discourage foreign encroachment from Great Britain on the Great Lakes and Spain west of the Mississippi River and would also neutralize the Indians. Putnam hoped that trade would convert the tribes into allies, but if that failed to develop they would be "encircled" by the forts. He assured Washington that many of the soldiers receiving grants would "remove themselves to this country." It is not surprising that this letter between two senior Army leaders dwelt almost exclusively with military concerns.[10]

Putnam waited until the end of the letter to reveal how the petitioners intended to shape their frontier communities, proposing "townships of six miles square, allowing to each township 3,040 acres for the *ministry, schools*, waste lands, rivers, ponds and highways [emphasis added]." His concept of using land grants to support education and religion copied practices that were popular in both "old" and New England. Indeed, his proposal helped set a precedent that would tie public school funding to federal land policy well into the 20th century. On the surface, the reservation of 13% of each township seemed like a generous gift, but no one knew how much of the land was comprised of "waste lands, rivers, [and] ponds" and how much had to be reserved for "highways." As an experienced surveyor, Putnam knew that preparing this land for sale would be a challenge, but he had no way to know that his call to support the ministry and the schools would only be achieved after considerable delay and vigorous debate.[11]

The next day, Washington forwarded the petition to Congress along with Putnam's letter and his own endorsement. He knew the frontier well, from his trip to Lake Erie on behalf of Virginia's governor in 1753 and his campaign during the French and Indian War two years later. Repeating Putnam's argument for the advantages of forts and settlements, Washington noted that the veterans who settled there would provide security from the Indians and "our other neighbors" (England, France, and Spain). But while his endorsement of this plan lay in his desire for justice for his men, others were driven by the hope that their own plan would alleviate the nation's financial problems.[12]

On June 5 Theodorick Bland of Virginia and Alexander Hamilton of New York introduced a proposal in Congress that historians have called the Financiers Plan. Washington had corresponded with them in April, stressing the need to address the Army's complaints quickly. While the financiers also hoped to use the land to satisfy bounties and pay owed veterans, they had another goal that far overshadowed the others. These merchants, lawyers, and planters were determined to greatly expand the meager authority that the Articles of Confederation had granted to the national government. In their view, Congress needed expanded powers in order to stabilize the nation's shaky finances, strengthen its defense, and improve the private sector's ability to collect debts. At the same time their changes would also increase the value of government bonds, which many of them held, thereby increasing their personal wealth.[13]

Despite the impression left by their public talks with the officers, the financiers may not have been very eager for an early sale of western lands. Superintendent of Finance Robert Morris had estimated that property sales alone would never produce enough revenue to fund the government and his colleagues worried that once sales began they might lessen the pressure to find more productive sources of funds. The financiers' tepid support of these proposals helps explain the failure of both plans to advance through Congress, a fact that was becoming quite frustrating to Putnam and Washington by late spring, 1784. Putnam had promised Washington that he and three other officers would settle in the "Ohio Country" once a plan was approved, but with both Massachusetts and New York offering competitive land for homesteading, their patience was rapidly coming to an end. Washington offered no hope, even complaining about his own efforts to sell property he owned in Western Pennsylvania. The failure of Congress to address the revenue issue meant that foreign debt could not be serviced, causing some to fear for the future of the Confederation. Adding to everyone's misery, a depression began that year. While a finger of blame can be pointed at the financiers, there were three other groups with designs on the Ohio Country that stood squarely between the veterans and their new home. While these groups placed a roadblock in the path of settlement, their claims, paradoxically, also created a sense of urgency that was needed to solve the problem.[14]

Though Washington had mentioned all three groups in his letter to Congress the previous year, his primary concern rested with the Indians. Most of the tribes had fought for the British in the War, and the Americans felt they should pay reparations. In the first of a series of treaties, signed at Ft. Stanwix in 1784, Congressional commissioners convinced the Iroquois Confederacy, known as the Six Nations, to cede all claims to lands beyond the Ohio River. Over the next five years, negotiators used threats, food, and whiskey to acquire the southern portion of the Ohio Country from the Wyandot, Ottawa, Delaware, Chippewa, and Shawnee tribes. For their part, the Americans promised to stay out of the northerly areas reserved for the tribes, a commitment that the weak government and its tiny, 700-man Army could never hope to keep.[15]

Moreover, a wide cultural gap separated the two parties. First, the Indians had little understanding of the white concepts of the purchase, ownership, and sale of property: in their world, the Great Spirit gave the region to the entire tribe, for all time. Second, government negotiators did not understand the fluid nature of authority within the tribes. Assuming that the tribes followed a simple, hierarchical structure of governance, agents often overestimated, perhaps intentionally, the authority of Indian signatories. As a consequence, treaties signed with lesser chiefs were later rejected by those not present during negotiations. These misunderstandings and the difficulties of negotiating through translators made the first treaties ineffective, yet in a perverse way they still proved helpful in the settlement of the West. Congress, under the American concept of ownership, felt an obligation to acquire title to the area from the Indians before sale or transfer to others. Prospective buyers, ignorant of Indian ways, presumed that since the Ohio Country had been purchased from the Indians, they were safe from attack. By the mid-1780s the Indian obstacle to Western settlement seemed to be well on its way to a resolution, but it would be several decades before this became a reality. Meanwhile, another group threatened the peace the treaties had hoped to bring to the Ohio Valley.[16]

Washington alluded to this second, troublesome group in his 1783 letter to Congress when he referred to "those who have heretofore extended themselves beyond the Appalachian Mountains." Since 1774, hunters and subsistence farmers had migrated across the mountains from Virginia, North Carolina, and Western Pennsylvania into the areas that would later become the states of Kentucky and Tennessee. This migration defied the Proclamation of 1763, which prohibited any settlement in the region "to the westward of the sources of the rivers which |sic| fall into the sea from the west and northwest." The end of the Revolution brought a surge of this illegal homesteading. Attracted by rich soils, lush forests, and abundant water, the number of pioneers soared from 8,000 in 1782 to 50,000 in 1787. This de-facto land rush pressured Congress to legalize settlement in Ohio in three ways.[17]

First, it undermined treaties, leading to violent confrontations between the Indians and the squatters, causing the former to plead to the government for adherence to the treaties and the latter to beg for protection. As a result of these conflicts, the settlers developed a visceral hatred for the Indians, an attitude that would poison relations for decades. Second, the squatters did not have the character considered desirable for citizens of a republic. Most were Scotch-Irish, who were famous for their independence of spirit, loyalty to clan, and defiance of government. Both Northern and Southern elites in Congress considered their backwoods culture crude, violent, and lawless, so much so that they derisively called them "banditti." Congress felt that these squatters lacked "virtue," a classical concept that was considered essential for the survival of any republic. People with virtue sacrificed their personal interests for the good of the community, including their state and nation, but this was anathema for the Scotch-Irish, who avoided government, ignored it, or even at times fought it. It would not be the first or the last time that this proud people confounded the plans of government and the will of elite leaders.[18]

But the squatters' most serious challenge resulted from their effect on the market for land. If large numbers of people simply moved across the Appalachians and occupied land without payment, why couldn't others do the same? Worse, these migrants carefully scouted the country, choosing the most promising lots for themselves. If this continued, it would erode both the marketability and the price of this land. So the value of millions of acres of property, the only real asset of the impoverished government, was imperiled by every wagon that creaked through the Cumberland Gap and every flatboat that drifted down the Ohio River.

Washington's third concern in 1783 was "how far the district of unsettled country, which is described in the petition, is free from the claim of every state, or how far this disposal of it may interfere with the views of Congress. . . ." New York, Virginia, Connecticut, and Massachusetts had all claimed territory in the Ohio Country by virtue of their royal charters. Maryland, a state without such rights, had refused to ratify the Articles of Confederation until New York and Virginia agreed to cede their claims to the Confederation in 1780 and 1781, respectively. Virginia's Cession law reserved areas for the redemption of bounties by its citizens who had been members of its militia and the Continental Army, while leaving the remainder for the common benefit of the United States. These reservations delayed Congressional acceptance of the Cession because they invalidated the title of powerful investors who had already speculated in western land. Virginia had made these provisions because many Virginians, including its governor, Thomas Jefferson, harbored the Southern vision of a country settled by many independent yeomen farmers, not one controlled by a few large, absentee speculators.[19]

Despite the pessimism of Washington and Putnam, progress was finally made on March 1, 1784, when Congress, abandoning the interests of the speculators, accepted Virginia's Cession. But while Congress had removed one obstacle to Western settlement, it still had to devise a system of government for the first settlers and create an effective plan to sell the land. On the day the Cession was approved, Jefferson and two committee members submitted a recommendation, The Report of Government for the Western Territory, which followed principles set out in the Cession and reflected Jefferson's trust in the hard-working, yeoman farmer: small units of government gave the farmers maximum influence, and suffrage was open to all adult males, without qualification. At first, a "temporary government" could adopt the constitution and laws of any of the original states. Later, when the population reached 20,000, the voters could form a "permanent government" by writing their own territorial constitution. Finally, when the population equaled that of the smallest of the original states, they could apply for statehood. Congress passed the Report on April 23, 1784 and Jefferson immediately introduced a proposal to market the land, but within two weeks it lost its chief sponsor when the Virginian resigned in order to serve as envoy to France. Jefferson's influence on national land policy (and education) would be greatly diminished during the next five years, which he would spend in Paris. Without his presence the states never ratified the Report and the committee never approved his recommendation for land sales.[20]

Yet there is a more significant reason for the failure of Jefferson's two initiatives than his absence from the country. The founder of the University of Virginia and the father of the notion of separation of church and state had omitted government support for education and religion from both plans. These were very important features for the Yankees, who Congress favored to settle the West. As a result, delegates from New England, influenced by the Army and Financier Plans, would have a much greater impact on land policy and the religious and educational future of the schools than Jefferson.

By 1785, Congress found itself under intense pressure to resolve the western land question. The depression was deepening and the banditti continued settling in Ohio, provoking the Indians and upsetting the veterans, and Congress' financial problems were not improving. Finally, in March Congress appointed a special committee to deal with the issue. Comprised of one member from each state, the committee began to make major revisions to the stalled legislation. Monitoring the debate closely, Pickering complained to Massachusetts Delegate Rufus King that no provisions had been made for education and religion. King soon reported that Congress had addressed Pickering's complaints and that the bill had been changed to set aside land to support schools and the ministry. This key revision assured New Englanders that they could transplant the educational, moral, and religious structure of their society into the West. In particular, the land grants for religion made this region more attractive to Congregationalists, who had inherited many of the precepts of their faith from the Puritans. Even Southerners in Congress supported the grants, despite their absence from Jefferson's 1784 proposals. Abandoning the Virginian's vision of an agrarian countryside populated by yeomen farmers for a plan they believed would be more successful, they endorsed one with towns, centered on government-funded churches and schools, and populated by industrious Yankees.[21]

Yet on April 22, even though a clear majority favored public funding for both schools and religion, Congress stripped support for ministers from the bill. This action reveals more about the difficulties facing proposed legislation under the Articles of Confederation than it does about opposition to state support for religion. Chronic low attendance and arcane voting rules made the passage of any legislation problematic. Each state had one vote, determined by a poll of its delegation at the legislative session, with the stipulation that two members be present for a quorum. So a state could forfeit its vote due to low attendance, either because its delegation was split evenly on the proposition (the lower the attendance, the greater the likelihood of a tie within the delegation), because it failed to have a quorum of two, or because it had no delegates present. Yet as difficult as it was for a state to register its vote, the Articles made the passage of legislation even less likely with its requirement of the affirmative votes of nine of thirteen states to approve measures dealing with important military or financial matters. As a consequence, most Congressional legislation failed, whether it was designed to increase Confederation revenue or meant to assist religion.[22]

While the draft legislation had appeared headed for passage, a clause asking that a lot in each township be dedicated "for the support of religion" provoked some protests. Congress held a series of three votes to defeat motions that sought to remove the land grant for religion. Yankee delegates from Massachusetts, New Hampshire, and Connecticut unanimously voted "aye," but Connecticut's affirmative vote did not count because only William Johnson was present. Two-man delegations from Pennsylvania and Delaware both voted "aye." Virginia, South Carolina, and Georgia delegates all voted "aye," but the votes of the lone delegates from South Carolina and Georgia were voided for lack of quorum. The votes of New York and North Carolina were nullified by a tie of the vote of their two-man delegations. Two of Maryland's three delegates voted "no," possibly reflecting that state's religious diversity and fear of the intolerance of religious minorities that could be produced by public funding for ministers. Rhode Island's two delegates predictably voted "no," reflecting that state's historic embrace of the separation of church and state. New Jersey had no delegates present that day. The final tally was: five states voting "aye," two states voting "no," three states voting "aye," but without sufficient quorum, two states with a divided delegation, and one state absent. So even though seventeen of twenty-three delegates (73%) approved the land grant, due to Congress' unusual voting rules, the motions fell far short of the required nine votes and religious funding was stripped from the bill.[23]

Analysis of the vote indicates that a majority of the American people favored government support for religion, if you assume that the delegates' votes represented the views of their constituents. The "one state, one vote" rule in Congress gave the "no" vote of Rhode Island, which had a population of 52,946 in 1780, the same weight as the "aye" vote of Virginia, which had a population of 538,004 that year. Yet if we examine the 1780 census, we see that the states voting "aye" (including those with insufficient quorum) had a population of 1,709,895 (61% of national population), including three of the four largest states (Virginia, Pennsylvania, and Massachusetts). States voting "no" contained a population of only 298,420 (10% of national population), including the second-smallest state (Rhode Island). Still, while critics of state support for the ministry were in a distinct minority, they were determined to be heard.[24]

The dispute between the opposing sides of this question is best seen in Virginia. Though the Virginia Statute of Religious Liberty would separate church from state in the Commonwealth in less than a year, all three of Virginia's Delegates had voted in favor of the land grants. Soon after being advised of the vote, James Madison scolded future president and Delegate James Monroe: "How a regulation so unjust in itself, so foreign to the authority of Congress, so hurtful to the sale of the public land, and smelling so strongly of an antiquated Bigotry, could have received the countenance of a Committee is truly matter of astonishment." And there is little doubt that Madison's friend Jefferson, who had the Virginia Statute inscribed on his epitaph as one of his greatest achievements, would have joined him in this criticism had he been in America at the time. But most Americans were Christian believers, and many felt no compunction about a marriage of church and state, as evidenced by the five states that retained public funding for the church and the twelve states that still maintained religious tests for public office. As a consequence, this victory for separation could not stand for long. Critics of the religious use of public land would soon be overwhelmed by their opponents, setting a precedent that would also be reflected in the curriculum of the nation's first public schools.[25]

A year of debate on the western land legislation finally concluded on May 20, 1785, with the passage of the Land Ordinance of 1785, which famously reserved lot 16 in every township "for the maintenance of public schools. . . ." The grant for education was likely inserted to appeal to potential buyers, on the grounds that it would increase the marketability and value of the land. In a pattern that would be repeated many times throughout the battle for public schools, a provision for education resulted from a concern over another issue—the resolution of the western land question—that was more important to legislators than the schools themselves. Though its flaws would quickly be exposed, this provision of the act laid down a template for education funding that would be followed by almost every new state admitted to the Union. Starting with California in 1850, a second lot (#36) was added to the grant for schools. Finally, to allow for the low value of land in the desert Southwest, the grant was expanded to four sections in Arizona, New Mexico and Utah. Yet while the grants initially inspired much hope for education, they would ultimately prove disappointing to 19th century school promoters.[26]

But the promotion of education was only a secondary consideration for most of the advocates of the Land Ordinance. Financiers sought to stabilize the nation's finances and friends of the Army to give veterans their pay, but it soon became apparent that the act would also be unable to meet those goals. To prepare the land for sale, the act ordered surveyors in the Ohio Country to "divide the said territory into townships of six miles square, by lines running due north and south, and others crossing these at right angles. . . ." Just as the grant of lot 16 would affect school funding in every new state, so too, the method of survey would profoundly impact land surveying and property development.[27]

The traces from this template are best observed from a small airplane. On a clear summer day the land appears as a rectilinear quilt of fields in every shade of green and yellow, interrupted by ropes of dark green trees that betray the streams meandering below. Though not immediately visible on the ground, the grid's influence is also felt by the motorist, who is forced to make ninety degree turns every few minutes. County plat maps in most states formed after the original thirteen illustrate the rectilinear nature of property lines and roads. But while the method of survey prescribed in the Land Ordinance would have a lasting effect on the American landscape, the survey itself would prove to be a difficult and dangerous task.

Surveyors were supposed to report in when they had completed seven "ranges," beginning at the Ohio River near present-day East Liverpool, Ohio, running due west for forty-two miles, or six miles across for each range, then due south to the Ohio River. Each range was a column comprised of townships stacked on top of one another that were six miles square. Every township was to include thirty-six lots, each measuring one square-mile, including the reserved lots, with the boundary lines oriented along lines running north to south and east to west.[28]

Work began soon after passage of the Land Ordinance, led by the newly-appointed Geographer of the United States, Thomas Hutchins, and supported by a forty-man survey team. Each state was expected to supply a surveyor, but only eight complied. From the outset the pace was slow, for several reasons. First, the surveyors could not follow the more easily traversed natural trails and streams used in metes and bounds but had to trace out straight lines that sometimes went through trees, over cliffs, or across lakes. Second, the Delaware and Miami tribes were upset by what they perceived as an unauthorized encroachment on their land and they repeatedly threatened the surveyors. Neither tribe had signed the Treaty of Ft. Stanwix and, though some minor Delaware chiefs had ceded the survey land to the United States in the Treaty of Ft. McIntosh in January, 1785, most Delaware refused to honor it because it had been signed by lesser chiefs. Lastly, local variations in magnetic north made it difficult to determine true north. In October 1785 Hutchins and his team left the field after completing just four miles.[29]

Meanwhile, as the survey team struggled with natural obstacles, Congress was removing an artificial one. In 1785 and 1786 Massachusetts and Connecticut finally surrendered their western land claims to the United States, though Connecticut retained ownership of some land, called the Western Reserve, which was located west of Pennsylvania and along Lake Erie. This area soon attracted large numbers of Yankee settlers, whose passion for education and religion would later play an important role in the shaping of Ohio's first schools.[30]

With pressure mounting from Congress, squatters, and veterans, a larger team of surveyors returned in 1786, under the protection of

Lt. Col. Josiah Harmar, the most senior officer in the Continental Army. Just as the previous survey team was pulling out, Harmar had begun constructing a fort (modestly named Ft. Harmar) opposite the future site of Marietta, Ohio in order to protect the surveyors and discourage squatters. While the Indian threat seemed to diminish, his anti-squatter efforts proved futile, since illegal settlers forced from one location would simply relocate to another.[31]

Congress now felt that survey of the entire territory would take too long, so it ordered the team to complete just seven ranges, in an act that would give the area its name, the Seven Ranges. But even this reduced workload would exceed the abilities of the over-matched team. They only completed four ranges by the end of 1786 and would not complete their new task until June 1787. Worse, the work was shoddy, often failing to produce the expected right angles at the intersection of survey lines. Beyond the physical challenges of the survey, two other explanations might explain the sub-standard work. First, the introverted Hutchins proved inept as a supervisor. And second, the work of the team may have been sabotaged. Andro Linklater, noting that three surveyors were affiliated with private land companies, has suggested that their principals would not have wanted government land to go on the market before their own ventures were ready.[32]

Though only four ranges were available, a desperate Congress moved ahead with its first land sale, using terms that were largely set by the act. Land could be purchased at a New York City office, for $1 per acre. One-half the townships were offered in 640-acre lots (36 lots per township) and one-half were to be sold in their entirety. But buyers balked at the $1 per acre price: individual lot sales were disappointing and not one intact township sold. In an effort to boost sales, credit was soon extended to purchasers, who could pay two-thirds of the cost three months after sale, but this did little to spur sales.[33]

So despite progress made against some of the impediments to western expansion, several large hurdles still remained in 1787. Though Congress desired compact settlement, it had sold only scattered, individual sections that were spread across many townships. New Englanders, who lawmakers preferred as pioneers, may have been bothered by the absence of guarantees of civil liberties, schools, and churches they felt necessary for a Christian republic. Then too, Jefferson's plan in 1784 had promised immediate suffrage to citizens, while placing few restrictions on the design of government. This radical democracy frightened Yankees and others in Congress, who were just now experiencing the disorder caused by Shays' Rebellion in Massachusetts, a revolt many felt was made possible by too much freedom for the masses. The conservative New Englanders favored colonial rule for the West at first, then a gradual movement toward self-government as citizens became educated for that responsibility. They were also concerned that the Land Ordinance failed to provide assistance for religion, which was a long-established New England tradition. While Congress rightly understood that people with common religious beliefs wanted to migrate together, they had failed to use this to attract buyers and settlers. So at the beginning of 1787, veterans remained largely unpaid, the national debt was dangerously high, squatters continued to move west, and the Indians still threatened frontier security. It would take a Congregational minister with the heart of a Christian but the mind of a poker player to create solutions where others had found only frustration.[34]

Chapter 2

The First Yankee Leader — Rev. Manasseh Cutler

*O*n the clear, hot summer day of June 24, 1787, Rev. Manasseh Cutler climbed into his sulky and set out on the 250-mile trip from Ipswich Hamlet, Massachusetts, to New York City. The jarring bounce of the light, single-passenger wagon and the heat, dust, and odors along the road that day could have easily overwhelmed his senses, but mercifully his thoughts soon turned elsewhere. As was his practice, the minister started his journey with a brief prayer for the Lord's protection, but his attention then shifted to his dual purposes: lobbying Congress for land in the Ohio Country for his Yankee friends and guaranteeing those would-be pioneers that they could bring their government and their culture with them. Cutler dwelt on the righteousness of their cause, reflecting on his deep emotional connections with his partners, most of whom had served as officers in the just-completed War for Independence. As one of their chaplains, he was all too familiar with their suffering, and as one of their pastors, he knew full well the strong pull that Calvinism and community had on his fellow New Englanders. So like the Old Testament heroes, Moses and Joshua, he felt it was his calling to remove the remaining obstacles to western settlement and lead his people to the Promised Land in the West.[1]

While these tasks had proven too challenging for several of the Founding Fathers, the minister-turned-lobbyist possessed an array of skills so useful for this effort that someone in his circle might have presumed they had been provided by Divine Providence. Much like Franklin, Jefferson, and other leaders in the Revolutionary Era, his inquisitive mind was drawn to science, education, and politics, all of which were subordinated to his life-long devotion to Christianity. He pursued these passions with such intensity that they aided his mission in three ways. First, several technical skills that developed from them were of direct help on his journey. Perhaps even more valuable were the many friendships they helped him develop, which opened doors for him that might have been shut for others. Yet the greatest benefit of all was rooted in his religious beliefs. He possessed a high level of confidence, since he believed that God had given him this calling and that He had also equipped him with all the tools needed for success.

It is difficult for us in the 21st century to comprehend the breadth of Cutler's intellectual activity. Today, it seems that every avocation, ranging from the elite to the mundane, demands years of specialization and credentials. Professions require an advanced degree and even skilled trades call for formal, classroom training. But this was hardly the case in late-18th century New England. The body of knowledge in any field was much smaller than it is today, allowing even a part-time enthusiast like Cutler to master it and in the process to make significant contributions to our understanding of the world. In fact, in a time and place when mankind was unprotected from the vagaries of life by a safety net of social services, survival often required that men acquire several practical skills over their lifetime. At times they would practice two or more vocations at the same time. The specialized knowledge necessary was either self-taught or acquired through formal or informal apprenticeships. The slower pace of life meant those elites blessed with some assurance of life's necessities had more time for learning, whether they were developing marketable skills or simply pursuing personal interests.

Yet even in this environment, Manasseh Cutler's *curriculum vitae* was remarkable: pastor for fifty-two years, educator for four decades, and even brief stints as doctor and lawyer. The recipient of an undergraduate degree from Yale and a Master of Arts from Harvard, he was a charter member of the American Academy of Arts and Sciences (AAAS) and a member of the prestigious American Philosophical Society. Cutler published papers in learned journals in botany and astronomy and was also a serious student of medicine. When not otherwise engaged, he found time to invent a corn-shelling machine and serve two terms in the US Congress. While none of the later advocates for education could match the extent of his accomplishments, most of them would, like him, earn a college degree, participate in more than one profession, and practice the beliefs of evangelical Calvinism.[2]

Much of what we know about Manasseh comes from his personal journals, which span fifty years of his life. Two of his grandchildren published journal excerpts and selected correspondence in an 1887 biography, extensively editing their sources so as to avoid embarrassments for the family and regrettably leaving us with a flat, sanitized portrait of the vibrant minister. They were, of course, correct that he was very interested in farming, theology, science, the military, and politics. And he lived a very active, purposeful, and productive life. But their biography robs him of his passions and pleasures. Fortunately, 20th century historical research reveals a more human, less saintly person who literally loved "wine, women, and song."[3]

Manasseh loved life. Though serious about his faith, he was certainly not a stereotypical Puritan. While attending Yale in the 1760s, he was part of a student body that was often wild, noisy, drunk, and even destructive at times. But we have no evidence the young farmer's son indulged in the campus mayhem, since his only known infraction there was a fine for card-playing. Throughout their long marriage, he and his wife enjoyed good food, fine wine, and the company of many friends. A gregarious and ambitious man, his breadth of interests and prominence as a pastor yielded a large number of friends and acquaintances, opening the way to positions of social and political prominence in Essex County and Massachusetts. Beautiful women rarely escaped his roving eyes, though the historical record contains no hint of infidelity. Despite the efforts of his grandchildren to burnish his image, we know he launched sharp, sarcastic barbs at his political and religious opponents. This was no meek Puritan, hiding behind a pulpit or shuttered in his study. Rather, he was a man of this world as well as the next, just as comfortable lifting a cup to his lips as raising his voice in sacred song.[4]

Portraits of this lover of food and wine show him as "tall and portly," though one artist mercifully reduced his girth. The self-confidence of a Calvinist who is certain of his salvation is easily read on his lips, which struggle to conceal a smile. His grandson tells us he had a "florid complexion; a good-humored expression. . .a full-proportioned, well-set frame of body. . . remarkably slow and deliberate in all his motions." Several accounts describe him in the garb of a Congregational divine: "a black velvet suit, with black silk stockings and silver knee-and shoe-buckles." His life-long obsession with organization showed in the tidy way he kept his third floor study. No papers, books, or furniture were ever out of place or in disarray. Perhaps this was the cleric's unconscious tribute to a God who created the order of the cosmos. God had made an orderly world and it seemed that Manasseh was determined to keep it that way.[5]

Cutler was a very busy man. While his ponderous body moved at a glacial pace, his sharp mind always seemed to be in hyperdrive. Pastoral duties included church meetings, a Thursday evening lecture, and the preparation and delivery of a two-hour sermon on Sunday. Weddings, funerals, and visiting the sick consumed still more time. Then, of course, there were the many ministerial, political, and military matters that regularly pulled him away from Ipswich. Yet his parsonage, located adjacent to the meetinghouse, was no refuge from work. Within this sprawling building he and his wife frequently hosted community meetings, ran a boarding school, and managed their farm. Yet somehow his curiosity about the world helped him find the time to research botany, medicine, and astronomy and later in life to work on projects like the invention of a corn-shelling machine. This fascinating man was driven by his passions for science, education, the military, and politics, but above all, the Almighty.[6]

Manasseh loved God. Large parts of his childhood centered on the study and worship of God, which is not surprising for a descendant of Puritans who had migrated to Massachusetts Bay Colony in

1634. Two services each Sunday were the norm in his home town of Killingly, Connecticut and his father, Hezekiah, a leader in the local Congregational church, likely encouraged much prayer and bible study in their home. Later, his spiritual formation continued under their pastor, Rev. Aaron Brown, who tutored him successfully for admission to Yale.[7]

Calvinist theology, leavened by the Great Awakening, dominated Yankee thought and was seamlessly woven into Cutler's curriculum at Yale. Three aspects of the Yale experience would have important implications for Manasseh and many other students. First, Yale professors enthusiastically welcomed the scientific method of Sir Isaac Newton and the philosophy of John Locke, since they felt that God's Word could not conflict with either science or reason. Following an established tradition among Puritan scholars, they held that our observations of the physical world, the creation, enhanced our understanding of the Creator. Next, the Congregational college fully supported the concept that man is saved by faith alone. Finally, in what foreshadowed its activism in the first half of the 19th century, Yale advocated social concern for others, including minorities like oppressed Indians and enslaved Blacks. This naturally followed from Jesus' admonition to the apostles in the Gospel of Matthew to "go and make disciples of all nations, baptizing them. . .and teaching them. . ."[8]

Yale Rector Thomas Clap, a legalistic authoritarian, laid out what was essentially a classical curriculum, including Greek, Latin, logic, ethics, and rhetoric, but also the reading of Locke for philosophy. More practical courses of study included modern languages, mathematics, and geography. And, in an important innovation and a nod to Puritan tradition, Clap introduced natural philosophy (science), which helped to kindle Cutler's lasting interest in natural phenomena. Meanwhile, theology, Bible, and divinity studies helped the college carry out its primary purpose, the preparation of young men for the ministry and for eternity. Clap made clear to his students that the overriding goal of their program was "to obtain the Clearest Conception of Divine Things and to lead you to a Saving Knowledge of God in his Son JESUS CHRIST."[9]

But while religion permeated Manasseh's education at home, in his community and at Yale, his journal revealed little of his personal spirituality until a tragedy rocked his world in 1766. On May 21, his brother's horse, startled by a pig that had blundered into its path, reared up, threw him to the ground, and then crushed him with all of its weight. Twenty-two year-old Ephraim, barely clinging to life, was carried to the Cutler home. His death the next day and Manasseh's ensuing search for meaning in the loss of his only brother would change his life forever. The boys, separated by only two years, had studied and prayed at their farm and worked many hours in its fields, but they also had ample time to hunt and ride through its woods and fish and skate on its lake. It is easy to picture them wrestling after a playful insult, laughing over their latest misadventure, or sharing teenage "wisdom" about girls. But now the inseparable were separated forever. Tragedies like this either turn a believer away from God in anger or send him closer for consolation. For Manasseh, after much prayer, reflection, and study, it was the latter.[10]

Manasseh took Ephraim's loss very hard. His journal entry for May 22 ended with the appeal: "God grant that this may be an *awakening* to all to be always ready for so important a change, more especially those who are nearly *concerned* [emphasis added]." Though he is cryptic concerning whom should be awakened and concerned, he clearly is worried about someone's salvation—his brother's, his own, or all of humanity. That summer he sought comfort from his parents and his God. Secluding himself in his parents' home, he lost himself in the Bible, Bible commentaries, and sermons, including "Dr. Doddridge's Proofs of the Christian Religion" and "Mr. [Jonathon] Edwards on the Freedom of the Will." This spasm of study and reflection led the grieving young man to develop a deeper faith in God, putting him on a path that would change his life forever.[11]

In July, Manasseh became a full member of the church, after giving testimony to his personal relationship with Christ and responding to questions from an elder and a deacon. His membership signified his public commitment to a new life in Christ and his resolve to grow in it for the rest of his time on earth. Now officially one of the "elect," he had not only been set apart by God for his own salvation, but also personally tasked with the evangelical calling to help others find eternal life. Though his journal fails to reveal whether he yet understood how that mission was to begin, its seeds had already been planted the prior December when he met Miss Mary Balch.

Manasseh had courted Mary the previous winter, while teaching in Dedham, Massachusetts. Mary was the daughter of Rev. Thomas Balch, pastor of the Congregational church there and the sister of his good friend, Benjamin Balch, a future pastor and chaplain. While his brother's death led him to seek comfort in Christ, it also seems to have moved him to find comfort of a more earthly sort that summer, as he and Mary wed in September. During the couple's courtship in Dedham, he had spent a lot of time with her father and brother, a circumstance that must have contributed to his later decision to study for the ministry with his father-in-law in 1769, thereby discovering what would become the central focus of his multi-faceted life. Cutler underwent two years of apprentice-like training under Reverend Balch, who likely was serving as part of the extended faculty for Harvard, his alma mater. He drafted his first sermons and delivered them at Balch's church, as well as others in Essex County. After receiving his Master of Arts in 1770 he was licensed and ordained and he began searching for a pastorate.[12]

Reverend Cutler's call in 1771 to the parish in Ipswich Hamlet commenced a remarkable fifty-two years of service to that church, which ended only with his death. His vocation was much more than a job; rather, it was a way of life and its central feature was the Sunday sermon. Fifteen hundred of his carefully written lessons have survived and are preserved at the Dawes Memorial Library at Marietta College in Ohio. Betraying his penchant for order, each one is numbered, and since he gave many more than once and in more than one church, he carefully noted on the first page where and when it had been delivered to avoid excessive repetition. This system saved the faithful from boredom and Cutler from embarrassment. In a method similar to what is known today as expository preaching he selected a passage from the Bible, explained it, and then used it to construct the theme of his talk. When taken as a whole, these messages provide a unique window into his spiritual beliefs.[13]

The pious Yankee's theology reflected the radical evangelical reforms of the Great Awakening and embodied the philosophies of Jonathan Edwards and George Whitefield, two of the most recognized figures in 18th-century America. These men held that a "covenant of grace" existed between God and man. No matter how man strived, he could not earn his way to heaven through good works. Further, and in what was viewed as a direct challenge to more traditional clergy, mere church attendance or membership was insufficient for salvation. Man could enter heaven only by placing his trust in God during a life-changing conversion experience. Once he was saved, an increasingly close, personal relationship with God would begin to grow within the new Christian. Manasseh fully absorbed the teachings of Edwards and Whitefield at Yale and continued to study both after graduation.[14]

While Edwards' famous sermon "Sinners in the Hands of an Angry God" has been used to perpetuate the myth of Calvinist ministers obsessed with God's punishment for an undeserving humankind, he and New Light followers like Manasseh Cutler delivered a much more positive message for humankind. While they certainly confronted men with their sins, as did Edwards in "Sinners," their dominant themes dealt with the glory and greatness of God and His seemingly limitless grace and mercy. Cutler's lessons dealt far more with the path to salvation than the road to hell and that trend intensified as he aged. For example, on nine occasions he delivered a sermon based on Romans 8:32 that focused on God's redeeming grace and six times he taught Romans 15:13's strong words of hope. So, it is not surprising that this man, who taught positive lessons about life in the next world, was so hopeful about the potential of this one.[15]

The Ipswich pastor also taught from Biblical texts that emphasized the inclusiveness of the Gospel, reflecting his training at Yale. The apostle Paul, in several places in his letters, resisted the inclination of some of Christ's Jewish followers to exclude Greeks from the early Church. Like Paul, New Light Calvinists strove to touch all with their message of salvation. Great Awakening revivals had reached out to all social classes, to Indians, and to Blacks, with Edwards leading the way when he established a mission to the

Indians late in life. Picking up Edwards' torch, Cutler preached from Col. 1:27, which offers salvation to all who will listen and believe. In the years before the Civil War this evangelical heritage bore fruit in the abolitionist and women's movements and made a lasting impact on the drive for free public schools. If all could be saved and share in the glory of heaven in the next life, if all were made in the image of God, then why shouldn't all be accorded more dignity in this life? The inclusiveness of the gospel also meant that sinners or heretics, even those you disagreed with politically, were to be engaged rather than shunned. This commitment to outreach sometimes led to religious conversion, but it also encouraged political compromise, a tactic that would prove invaluable for educational zealots. Interestingly, the openness of New Light Calvinists towards the world of other people was often matched by their curiosity for the world of nature and both were major themes of Manasseh's life.[16]

Manasseh loved learning and science. Though his grandchildren excluded most of his scientific work from his biography, his journals disclose a broad range of interests in science, no doubt encouraged during his years at Yale. He read research in several fields of study and frequently discussed technical matters with the presidents of Harvard and Yale, corresponded with leading international scientists, and conducted personal research. Appropriately, his life-long motto was a quote from Virgil "*Felix, qui potuit rerum cognoscere causes*" (Happy is he who is able to know the causes of things). Just as Manasseh studied the Bible to seek out God's thoughts, he examined the physical world to understand God's works. While several disciplines fascinated him, he made notable contributions to advances in the fields of botany, astronomy, and medicine.[17]

The Yale graduate's greatest scientific accomplishments came in botany, a very practical science in an era when large groups of people were migrating into strange new lands. The identification of plant types and their uses was potentially life-saving information for migrants to a new area, such as the Ohio Country. The pioneers' welfare and even their survival depended on finding food sources, trade items, and medicinal plants. After years of study and field work, Cutler published "An Account of some of the Vegetable Productions naturally Growing in this part of America," in the AAAS journal in 1785. The "Account" was a detailed classification of New England's plants according to Linnaeus' new system of taxonomy, one of its first serious applications in America, and an important early contribution to our understanding of plants. The order of Linnaeus' system must have appealed to his near-obsession with neatness and organization. His botanical work continued for the rest of his life and included corresponding with leading European botanists as well as the most renowned American in the field, Henry Muhlenberg, who praised his work lavishly.[18]

But on clear evenings the polymath often lifted his gaze to the stars in the sky from the plants on the ground, since darkness precluded that work. Every few days he detailed his observations in his journal, sometimes accompanying them with an illustration. Astronomy was especially popular in New England, since knowledge of the night sky was necessary to determine longitude, thereby greatly improving navigation at sea, which not only saved lives but also helped the region's economy. Manasseh had mastered the complex mathematics and physics necessary for understanding celestial mechanics (the movement of bodies in space) after intense study at Yale under Dr. Ezra Stiles. While Cutler usually worked by himself, he sometimes made observations with two close friends: Stiles, who had become the President of Yale, and Dr. Joseph Willard, the President of Harvard and one of the most respected scientists in America. At one point, Cutler sent Stiles a paper challenging an explanation for the aurora borealis and arguing for a new theory that he had developed. His explanation that the northern lights have electrical origins is quite close to our current understanding of the mysterious phenomenon. While this paper impressed Stiles, the AAAS never published it, though it did publish two other Cutler treatises on astronomy.[19]

Unlike his interests in botany and astronomy, which grew out of his scholarly curiosity, his pursuit of the healing arts sprang from necessity during one of the bleakest periods of the Revolution. Manasseh decided to study and practice medicine upon his return from the disastrous Rhode Island Campaign in 1777. While he might have been moved to alleviate human suffering by the horrors he witnessed on the battlefield, he confesses to his journal that he was "driven to the practice of physic" by his compromised financial condition. With his cleric's salary unpaid, he was gradually liquidating his estate to survive the hyperinflation brought on by the War. Though medicine was always a part-time pursuit, he continued to assist at operations and autopsies for many years. His new occupation allowed him to not only minister to people's physical needs but it also helped sate his endless appetite for knowledge.[20]

As if his parish, family, farm, and other scientific pursuits were not enough to fill his days and nights, Cutler made two important contributions to public health during the 1780s. His first effort was inspired by his inoculation of hundreds of people in Essex County for smallpox, a life-saving practice for which he was much-beloved. Once again driven by a compulsion "to know the causes of things," he prepared a technical paper in 1781 sketching a theory explaining the effectiveness of the smallpox vaccine. He wrote the paper to overcome community objections to vaccination, which, though it prevented a serious disease that killed many, could also bring on short-term illness. His second initiative was an important early step in the collection of vital statistics, essential data for the practice of epidemiology. Once again displaying his compulsion for organization, Cutler methodically developed a system to classify diseases and in 1784 urged the collection of mortality statistics in Massachusetts according to his scheme. His proposal was enacted into law and in recognition of his contributions to medicine and public health he was awarded an honorary membership in the Massachusetts Medical Society. This work as well as his research in other areas was increasing his notoriety and his circle of friends, which would prove to be important assets in the work still ahead.[21]

In addition to the disciplines in which he conducted research meaningful to scholars, Manasseh also maintained life-long interests in archaeology, agriculture, cartography, history, literature, and weather. Perhaps because he and other New England ministers were so interested in science, they were also committed to passing on their knowledge to others, which established a tradition that would have profound implications for future generations of children. Manasseh spread the gospel of education in three ways that were quite typical for Yankee clergy. First, in 1782 he began operating a boarding school, both as a source of income and to fulfill his Christian obligation to educate students from his congregation and community. The parsonage had to be renovated to accommodate the school, which had as many as eighteen students during the day, and to board those students who stayed overnight. (The school placed a huge burden on his wife, who had to manage a house full of strangers in addition to her seven children!) Students were a diverse lot, including the sons of wealthy businessmen, sea captains, foreign-speaking West Indies merchants, his Black household servants, and even a few girls. He customized the curriculum for each student, who could be preparing for college, the ministry, or a life at sea.[22]

Second, for several years he served on the committee that inspected the local community school, an institution that was a forerunner of the first public schools. Such practices were widespread in New England and they would soon spread across the nation and become standard procedure in education. Lastly, in 1811 he formed a Sunday school in Ipswich, just as that movement began to sweep across the nation. The new institutions provided free instruction for children whose parents could not pay tuition or run their farm during the week without their children's help. But while Manasseh's dedication to learning and science followed from his curiosity about the world, his devotion to veterans evolved from his personal observation of the hardships they endured during the War.[23]

Manasseh's love for his Band of Brothers began at the very onset of the War, at Lexington and Concord. He wrote on April 19, 1775 that he traveled to Cambridge "with our people just after they fired their last gun" as the British completed their long, bloody retreat back to Boston. After staying with Doctor Willard that night, the next day "we went to Metomeny to see the dead. The regulars [Redcoats] lay principally in the streets, but our men in houses and barns." Historian David Hackett tells us that the fighting there was "intense," "bitter," and "hand to hand." By the time the British had reached Metomeny its officers had lost control of the enlisted men, enraged by what they perceived as the dishonorable tactics of the colonists, who sought cover behind trees and walls instead of fighting out in the open like European forces. Even more maddening for them, the carnage that resulted from this unanticipated strategy was horrendous. British anger and the close proximity of the combatants along the narrow village street combined to produce the heaviest casualties of any phase of the retreat that day. The Redcoats decided that any colonist they saw in Metomeny was a rebel and they either shot or bayoneted their hapless victims, including four men caught tippling in a tavern. The British suffered forty dead and eighty wounded, while the Americans lost twenty-five men but only nine wounded. Their unusually high ratio of killed-to-wounded reflected the merciless British rules of engagement. The War had indeed begun and Cutler had witnessed firsthand its bloody aftermath. Neither he nor anyone else could imagine that the sacrifices of blood and treasure that began that day would continue for seven years.[24]

The Massachusetts Provincial Council responded quickly to this challenge, calling up 13,600 of its militia to lay siege to the British in Boston. By the beginning of the summer Cutler was serving as one of its first chaplains, in a unit commanded by Col. Ebenezer Francis. For the rest of the War, he would serve the cause enthusiastically in many ways, some spiritual and some material. Though he only served full-time during two brief periods, he often visited with, prayed for, and preached to soldiers in Greater Boston. As a pastor, he cooperated with the Continental Congress and the Massachusetts Council by conducting Fast Days and Days of Thanksgiving, which asked for God's blessing on the Revolution, and by reading communications from Congress and Council to his congregation. Pastoral care was also important to the struggling families in his community who had men serving in the Continental Army and the militia. Yet he also made more material contributions, for example, using his scientific knowledge to manufacture saltpeter, an important ingredient of gunpowder.[25]

Cutler's commitment typified Calvinist ministers, derisively called the "black regiment" by loyalists for their black attire. Their motivation had its genesis in the struggles between the Puritans and the Crown during the English Civil War in the middle of the 17th century. Like many Congregational and Presbyterian divines, Cutler studied and admired Oliver Cromwell, the Calvinist revolutionary who led the fight to dethrone King Charles I. Cromwell and the Puritans eventually convicted the king of treason and cut off his head following the end of that war. These preachers and their followers saw the revolution against King George III as a just war and as simply one more battle in an ongoing campaign to resist an illegitimate government and a corrupted religion that were both perpetuated by the monarchy. Their efforts, along with those of other ministers sympathetic to the War, were critical in rallying public opinion for the Revolution.[26]

As Cutler shows, they helped that effort in several ways. In an era before the mass distribution of newspapers, sermons were one of the most common forms of public discourse. They were not only heard by church-going people, but they were often printed and distributed to others, playing an important role in forming public opinion. As the crisis deepened, ministers' lessons dealt increasingly with politics and their rhetoric began to merge with and reinforce that of secular revolutionaries, like Thomas Paine. For example, in January, 1777 Cutler gave a particularly hopeful sermon, perhaps encouraged by recent patriot victories at Trenton and Princeton, based on 2 Cor. 4:8-9: "We are hard pressed on every side, but not crushed; perplexed, but not in despair; persecuted, but not abandoned; struck down, but not destroyed." The clerics also used the rhetoric of others to make an important contribution to the cause. From 1775 to 1784 Congress issued six national proclamations calling for Fast Days and seven for Days of Thanksgiving, while state legislatures issued many similar statements, all of which were intended to be read from pulpits on Sundays. The divines' distribution and support of these messages strengthened political communication and national unity. Cutler's journal shows that he enthusiastically read to his Ipswich congregation at least fifteen of these statements, which seamlessly mixed political and spiritual language.[27]

These "Days" were based on covenant theology, a belief that was associated with the Puritans, and during revolutionary times with their theological descendents, the Congregationalists and Presbyterians. But in fact, most other Protestant sects in this era also professed this belief. Rooted in the history of the Jews as told in the Old Testament, covenant theology held that God and man had a contract. These Protestants saw themselves and their nation as a modern day Israel. If they, like God's chosen people the Israelites, confessed their sins and turned to God their land would be blessed, their storehouses filled with grain, and their enemies defeated. But on the other hand, if they disobeyed His commands they would face famine, defeat in battle, and slavery, suffering the same fate as the Jews. So these special Days resonated with most Protestants, encouraging a national response to God's promise that "if my people. . .will humble themselves and pray and seek my face and turn from their wicked ways, then. . .I. . .will forgive their sin and will heal their land (2 Chron. 7:14)."[28]

Many ministers also served as chaplains, comforting men who were separated from their loved ones while facing physical hardship and the risk of dismemberment or death. Cutler's journal described many pastoral visits with the men and social gatherings with the officers. At times, these trips could be dangerous. Describing one such visit to Boston just two days after the Battle of Bunker Hill, he noted that "a shot from a twelve pounder came very near us. . .another shot from the same cannon fell within the breastwork at Ran's Hill. I was very near where it fell." Later that week, he prayed with the troops, calling them a "very attentive congregation." Until the siege of Boston ended when the British fled on March 17, 1776 Cutler noted eleven different times when he traveled to pray, worship, or socialize with the soldiers and their officers. While Cutler may not have actually fired a weapon against the British, he did much to see that those who did so were properly armed. Throughout 1776 he collaborated with others to make gunpowder, a vital resource that was in short supply. In what might shock some 21st century sensibilities, many in the Black Regiment actually took up arms during the Revolution, including Rev. John Cleaveland, pastor of one of the other churches in Ipswich. But whether armed with bullets or Bibles, Calvinists proved to be more important to the rebel effort than any other religious group.[29]

Manasseh loved people, which is usually a prerequisite for success in politics. Relatives and acquaintances tell us he was "gentlemanly" and "courtly," and "there was no air of stiffness or reserve, but, on the contrary, the utmost frankness and cordiality." They note "he was very fond of society" and his journal left ample proof that he was an eager and charming host. In January 1767 only four months after moving to Martha's Vineyard to operate a whaling business, the sociable young newly-wed began a community singing group, the first of its kind in Edgartown, and he hosted its bi-weekly meetings. And soon after accepting the call to Ipswich, the gregarious minister began hosting parish and town meetings in his busy parsonage. For many years, he worked assiduously at turning acquaintances into friends, writing over thirty letters per week. Most of these relationships, which proved so helpful in his political activities, grew naturally out of his love for the ministry, science, education, and the military.[30]

Manasseh's position as a Congregational minister opened up many opportunities for friendship and influence. First, the parsonage and the meetinghouse, often the largest buildings in town, were popular gathering places for both the parish and the community, which Cutler exploited in Ipswich. Second, clerics were accorded great respect, given their religious authority and high level of education. Certainly, few in his village could match Manasseh's degrees from Yale and Harvard. Third, ministers frequently preached for one another, when they were sick, traveling, serving in the military, or just to give a congregation a fresh perspective. Cutler's journal and sermon notes document many such visits, providing him with exposure far beyond the boundaries of Ipswich. Lastly, and perhaps most helpful for his political influence, in addition to the frequent meetings of local ministers, each May their annual conference in Boston was always scheduled to begin immediately after the election of the Council. Cutler's journal shows that he attended both meetings in six of the ten years from 1772 to 1781. Gala receptions, including at least two at Faneuil Hall, and dinners usually accompanied these meetings, affording the preacher with unique opportunities for networking with the religious and political elites of Massachusetts. Apparently, he took full advantage of them; for example, in 1776 Manasseh and his wife found themselves at a dinner party with John Adams, who had just returned from a session of Congress.[31]

But in addition to their common interests in religion, many of these influential Yankees were, like Cutler, also quite interested in science. Two of his closest friends in science, Presidents Stiles and Willard, were also ministers with whom he exchanged pulpits. While the primary purpose of both colleges was the production of an educated ministry, many graduates also moved into law and government, so these two men constituted another important connection to New England's political leaders. Another path to political influence was his regular participation in the quarterly meetings of the AAAS. Beginning with its inaugural meeting in January 1781, he attended six consecutive meetings, and delivered papers at three sessions. While he met many leaders through this association, none were more important than James Bowdoin, the first President of the AAAS. Bowdoin was central to the leadership of Massachusetts from the revolution all the way through Shays' rebellion in 1786-1787 and, like many of his other friends, would play an important part in Cutler's plans for the Ohio Country. And of course, his voluminous scientific correspondence also gained him many acquaintances. But he developed his most loyal friends, not through his curiosity about the world, but from his associations with those who risked their lives for their new country.[32]

In addition to Varnum, Hancock, and the other officers Cutler befriended during the Rhode Island Campaign, he met many other soldiers and officers during his frequent visits to minister to their spiritual and human needs. These opportunities occurred throughout the War, but he had round-the-clock contact from September through November 1776, when he was activated to serve with Colonel Francis' unit during the Siege of Boston. The unit saw no action, but this afforded him ample time to circulate among the troops and socialize with their officers. Three years later, in September 1779 he fed and lodged some of the officers and men of Col. Henry Jackson's 16th Massachusetts Regiment at his expense, despite his strained financial position. As happened with many other people Manasseh met during the War, Colonel Jackson would later become one of his allies in his plan to settle the West. But whether they came from the military, the ministry, or the world of science, he and his friends often shared two common beliefs: faith in the patriot cause and in the Calvinist religion. By the mid-1780s Manasseh counted among his friends some of the most powerful leaders in New England. These relationships proved even more valuable than the formidable technical skills he took on his mission.[33]

So as Reverend Manasseh Cutler rattled along the Boston-to-New York Post Road in June 1787 he carried a traveling trunk with clothing and books, but he also brought along a bag of intangible tools that were just as indispensable. The affable cleric shared an interest in religion, science, and the military arts with many members of Congress, both those Yankees that he knew personally and others that he knew indirectly through his research. And for those to whom he was a stranger, he carried letters of introduction from some of his powerful friends. But perhaps even more important, this rosy-cheeked optimist had the ability to connect with anyone, an essential virtue for any lobbyist. Calvinists, both then and now, believe that when God sends you on a mission, He either equips you with gifts that are equal to the task or He alters circumstances so that victory is assured. In Cutler's case, his resume seemed more than adequate for the mission that awaited him at the end of the dusty road to New York City.

Chapter 3

Miracle at New York City

*A*s he pointed his sulky south in that historic summer of 1787, Manasseh Cutler focused on two objectives: a western land deal for his friends and a framework of government for their new territory. He was neither irritated by the sweat clinging to his clothes nor distracted by the shocks radiating through his bones on that hot, rough ride, for the man who felt he was God's agent was focused on his mission. If his plans were successful they would have an important impact on the future of the West. First, his fellow Yankees would be guaranteed civil liberty, support for their religion, and protection from radical democracy. And second, Congress would alleviate its problems with angry veterans, towering debt, uncontrolled squatters, and menacing Indians.

But while the rewards were enticing, the challenges were sobering. For four years now, Washington, Jefferson, Hamilton, and countless others had failed to execute an effective land sale, which was painfully clear from the tiny revenues and sparse settlement generated by the Seven Ranges project. Worse, efforts for a plan of government had been even less successful, as evidenced by reams of unfruitful correspondence, reports, and minutes. Yet Cutler was not discouraged by these earlier failures, since he was possessed by the need to help himself, his family, and his friends.

Prosperity had eluded him during the War's chaos and the depression that ensued. Those events made the father of seven worry about the kind of life his children would experience in the harsh climate and stingy soil of New England. His study of the Ipswich census records in 1783 had revealed a disquieting trend of westward migration among the young. They were voting with their feet, which convinced him that his family could also find a better life in the West, in his words, "the best part of the United States," as opposed to the "frozen regions" of their homeland. His profound admiration for the Revolution's soldiers, who had risked their lives and fortunes for freedom, helped him overcome any lingering doubts about his current mission. That respect was reciprocated and would be reflected in his leadership role in their continuing struggle to get fair compensation. Cutler's extensive social network also included many speculators, but while both groups were necessary for his plan's success, his Band of Brothers proved indispensable.[1]

The veterans' plans began to take shape in January 1786 at the Rutland, Massachusetts home of Rufus Putnam. He and his guest, Benjamin Tupper, both knew the region well and were impressed with its potential. Putnam had passed through it in 1773 as a leader of a failed migration to Mississippi, while Tupper was sent there to survey the Seven Ranges in 1785. Putnam's experience in Mississippi shaped his desire for government guarantees, since that settlement had collapsed when a grant from King George failed to materialize. Circumstances beyond their control were working in favor of the two former brigadier generals, as crushing debt problems fomented a collapse of local authority in western Massachusetts and the absence of a land policy tempted squatters, which threatened the value of the nation's only asset. The proposed settlement on the frontier promised to solve these problems for the nation and finally offered Putnam, Tupper, and their fellow veterans fair compensation for their service and a new life as pioneers. So the two men plotted by the fire for two days, hoping to craft a blueprint for migration that met the needs of New England and the new nation.[2]

The migration of veterans to Ohio would place hundreds of capable, armed men on the frontier, ready to thwart any threat, as Putnam had argued in his 1783 letter and petition to Washington.

In addition to discouraging squatters, it would also strengthen the western border against foreign powers. If anything, challenges had worsened in the last three years as Great Britain, in violation of the Treaty of Paris, still kept forts on the northern fringes of those lands and Spain occupied country west of the Mississippi and in Florida. Indians presented a dangerous obstacle by themselves, which could grow quickly if they formed an alliance with either European power. Meanwhile, with only 700 men the US Army could not oppose any of these forces without the assistance of a strong militia. It would not take long for the wisdom of the Army Plan to prove itself.[3]

Moving quickly, Putnam and Tupper organized meetings in eleven Massachusetts counties of veterans, who in turn elected representatives to the organizational meeting of the Ohio Company of Associates (OCA) at the *Bunch of Grapes Tavern* in Boston on March 1, 1787. By March 3, the Articles of Agreement were in place that set the cost of a share at $1,000 in Continental certificates and $10 in gold or silver specie (hard currency) to pay for surveying and other costs. Article Six assured the OCA would not be dominated by a few wealthy individuals by limiting the number of shares owned by any one individual to five. And in an improvement on the Seven Ranges plan, a system of agents was established to sell and administer shares. By this arrangement Congress would make one large sale, leaving the task of administering what was hoped would be a large number of small sales to the OCA and its agents. Yet despite this provision, sales in the first year reached only one-quarter of their $1,000,000 goal. It is likely that potential shareholders were bothered by the struggles of the Seven Ranges, the absence of a government deal, and the lack of a plan of government. But help was on the way, as armed rebellion in western Massachusetts would propel the OCA project forward in 1787.[4]

Beginning in the previous August, mobs had shut down several courts, which they saw as tools of wealthy Eastern creditors. Since paper money became almost worthless due to the high levels of state and national borrowing, lenders demanded payment in specie and used the courts to foreclose on the homes and farms of those unable to pay. What became known as Shays' Rebellion finally ended in February 1787, but not before Congress authorized 1,340 troops and Gov. Bowdoin called out 4,400 militiamen, including Tupper, who commanded the defenses around Springfield. The uprising frightened the political and economic elite, forcing them to look for solutions to what they saw as the root causes of the crisis. First, it underscored the need to quickly reduce the burden of government obligations. Second, it dramatized the fears of the coastal elite that these common folk in the interior needed more control and that the uneducated squatters of the Ohio Country might need similar attention. Washington, John Jay, and Henry Knox all urged Congress to act quickly on the western question, in part to prevent similar problems there. Meanwhile, OCA's plan offered hope, since it promised to reduce the debt and seed the frontier with trustworthy, law-abiding citizens.[5]

By the OCA's second annual meeting, held March 8, 1787 at the *Sign of Oliver Cromwell* tavern in Boston, the secretary was recording in the minutes that sales were going poorly due to "the Uncertainty of obtaining a sufficient tract of Country." In response to this urgent need, Cutler, Putnam, and Gen. Samuel Parsons were appointed to a committee to negotiate the purchase of a large tract from Congress. The inclusion of Connecticut resident Parsons illustrates how OCA's plans expanded to take on this challenge. While the first Associates all hailed from Massachusetts, by 1787 membership grew to include New Hampshire, Rhode Island, and Connecticut. The last state's veterans quickly came to dominate the Company, with Parsons along with Cutler forming the core of its leadership. It appears OCA was popular in Connecticut because its proposed purchase mimicked practices long-established in that state. For a century the Connecticut General Assembly had sold public property on its frontier, typically selling a large tract to a few dozen large investors, who in turn subdivided it into smaller tracts for resale. Just like the Associates, some of these investors planned to move west while others simply hoped to profit from their speculation.[6]

It should be noted that some modern historians have charged that greed moved the Associates to use their political power to build their personal wealth, yet in the late-18th century there was no bright shining line of ethical practice that separated government operations from private ventures. In fact, government was so weak that it could only hope to fulfill its mission through partnerships with the private sector. Certainly, the Associates possessed the political power to influence government policy, but it stretches credulity to describe these men as greedy, since many had exhausted their personal assets—not to mention risked their lives—during the War. Officers held land bounties that represented empty promises and continental certificates that were worth just one-tenth their original value. Some had even supplied their units out of their personal funds. So this was not so much an exercise in greed as it was a search for justice and an answer to their pleas at Newburgh.[7]

As for the other Associates, some planned to migrate, while others were pure speculators, planning to purchase certificates, use them to get land through the OCA, and then sell at a much higher price. What the critics fail to appreciate is that the speculators played an important role in the laissez-faire mercantile capitalism of that era. Their investment in the Ohio Country helped to improve the market for other western lands, thereby increasing the value of the nation's only asset. And while their venture succeeded, it might well have failed, as did several others, leaving their investment worthless. But the heart and soul of the OCA was the veterans, not the speculators.

The military background of its membership is exemplified by the eleven men who had been elected as delegates to the organizational meeting in 1786. Nine had served extended terms of duty as officers in the War and four had signed the Newburgh Petition. Their deep military ties were strengthened through religious and fraternal associations. First, given the religious environment of New England at that time, it is likely that most were Congregationalists. Further, six were members of the Society of the Cincinnati, a quasi-aristocratic fraternal organization formed at Newburgh, while three were masons. While these allegiances were important to the members, it was their military associations, forged during the misery of war, which created this inseparable Band of Brothers.[8]

Courageous is an apt description of several veterans who invested in the OCA. One of the more interesting was surgeon Eliphalet Downer, who fired at the British during their deadly retreat from Lexington in 1775, then treated their wounds and provided food and clothing to ease their suffering. Known as "the fighting surgeon of the Revolution," he served on three different ships during the War, was imprisoned twice, escaped twice, and received a severe combat wound. On his last ship, the *Lexington*, he volunteered to fight, in his words, in a "furious engagement" that left him with a serious arm wound and ended in his capture by the British. Escaping for the second time, he and fifty-six Americans dug a narrow tunnel to freedom, but not before it was widened to accommodate Downer's generous girth! Downer would also serve as an agent for the OCA. Other investors included John Paul Jones, the Father of the American Navy, Brig. Gen. Nathaniel Freeman, Commodore Abraham Whipple, and Lt. Col. William Barton. The last three served with great distinction, including suffering injuries or imprisonment at the hands of the British. Putnam, Sargent, Tupper, Brig. Gen. James Varnum and Lt. Col. Return Jonathan Meigs, Sr. rendered meritorious service during the War, beginning with the British retreat from Lexington. All five men were destined to become important pioneers in the West.[9]

If soldiers constituted the backbone of the OCA, then politicians provided its food (money) and its voice (advocacy). A 1796 shareholder list brims with politicians, some of whom also served important roles in the Continental Army. Alexander Hamilton and Elbridge Gerry (inspiration for the infamous term "gerrymandering") were delegates to the Constitutional Convention in Philadelphia. Five members of the 1787 Congress were owners, including its President, Arthur St. Clair. Arthur Lee and Walter Livingston were members of the three-man United States Board of Treasury, responsible for negotiating contracts for the government. Governors James Bowdoin (Massachusetts) and William Greene (Rhode Island), Deputy Governor Jabez Bowen (Rhode Island), future Governor Jonathan Trumball, Jr. (Connecticut), and Postmaster General Ebenezer Hazard all became investors, as did heroes of the Revolution Samuel Adams and Henry Knox. Yet despite its impressive list of owners, things were not going well for the OCA in 1787.[10]

In May Parsons made an offer to Congress, but Putnam and Cutler were unhappy that he proposed buying in central and western Ohio rather than a tract just west of the Seven Ranges, land that would include today's Marietta. They were convinced that the area was fertile, since both Tupper and Sargent had been impressed by it during surveys, and they feared that Congress might sell it to another buyer if they failed to act soon. Deciding to get directly involved, Cutler resolved to succeed where Parsons had failed.[11]

So on June 24, 1787, as Cutler set out for New York he was a man who was very focused on his mission. Along the way he met and discussed strategy with Putnam and Parsons, the other two members of the committee, since their venture seemed to be floundering. And he visited with Drs. Willard and Stiles and with Governors Bowdoin and Bowen to secure letters of introduction, since that was the way that one obtained access to elites in the late 18th century. But as much as he was dedicated to his mission, he still set some time aside to visit with friends, discuss science, and participate in Sunday worship. Throughout his trip he mixed the personal with the professional, as evidenced by five meetings with friends who became OCA investors. Along the Post Road Cutler took in the beautiful seascape of Long Island Sound on his left and the rolling hills of green on his right, but, as he recorded in his journal, he also experienced "extreme heat" and roads that were "wretchedly out of repair" and "excessively bad." When not staying with friends, many of his lodging experiences ranged from "indifferent" to "miserable" to "wretched." Even with two side trips to quench his thirst for science, he made good time, often traveling more than twenty miles a day, once making forty-five miles a day. When the tired lobbyist finally pulled into the *Plow and Harrow* tavern in the Bowery on Thursday, July 5, he had completed a journey of 300 miles in just twelve days.[12]

Despite the toll the trip must have taken, the energetic lobbyist walked the streets of the city that afternoon to begin to deliver some of the forty-two letters of introduction he carried with him, including some addressed to at least nine members of Congress. The lobbyist got a warm welcome when he visited Congress the next morning on Friday, July 6. He delivered more letters, including one to Edward Carrington of Virginia, chair of the committee responsible for land sales and soon to be named to a new committee on western government. Cutler must have charmed him because the Virginian introduced him to many members on the floor of Congress during its 11:00 a.m. session, giving him the opportunity to lay out the details of OCA's offer. He dined with Massachusetts Congressman Nathan Dane, who like Carrington also served on the two key committees and was the only other member of the land committee who was present in Congress during July, since James Madison and Rufus King were busy serving as delegates in Philadelphia and Egbert Benson of New York was absent. Dane fully supported OCA's plans and would work hard to push them through Congress. Cutler's journal tells us he spent the evening with unidentified members of Congress.[13]

Cutler continued his lobbying over the weekend, as usual mixing politics with pleasure, while still managing to attend two services on Sunday. On Saturday, he met again with the Committee, but we can only speculate about the substance of these discussions. Then, with the aid of a referral from recipients of two of his letters, he met with Thomas Hutchings, who helped him identify a good location for the OCA tract. Earlier he had met with one of those men, David Rittenhouse, who also had intimate knowledge of that part of the country from his work surveying the western boundary of Pennsylvania. These meetings were followed by a dinner (lunch) with Henry Knox, Secretary of War and President of the Society of the Cincinnati, and a visit with Ebenezer Hazard, Postmaster General and Treasury official, both of whom were OCA investors. He probably probed both for key information on the Ohio Country, since Knox knew about the Indian threat due to his military responsibilities and Hazard about the terrain since he was responsible for mail delivery. So, throughout the day Cutler was using his social skills and contacts to lay the groundwork for a land contract for the OCA.[14]

On Sunday, the Congregational minister spent much of his day attending sermons given by two acquaintances, college presidents Dr. John Ewing of University of Pennsylvania and Dr. John Witherspoon of the College of New Jersey, today's Princeton. But the Lord's Day was not a day of total rest for this busy promoter. In between the two sermons, he enjoyed an elegant lunch at the opulent home of Sir John Temple, the British Consul-General to the United States, dining with Massachusetts Congressman Samuel Holten, a former President of Congress, Dr. Arthur Lee, and Nathan Dane. His busy "day of rest" ended with another meeting with Hazard, this time over supper.[15]

Monday, July 9 brought encouraging intelligence about the West but increasing frustration with Congress. Over the course of three meetings, Hutchins convinced Cutler the area north of the confluence of the Muskingum and Ohio Rivers was "the best part of the whole western country." But two meetings with Carrington's land committee didn't go nearly as well, with Cutler reporting in his journal they "were so wide apart that there appears little prospect of closing a contract." Cutler spent the end of another long day lobbying members of Congress at their tavern on Hanover Square.[16]

On Tuesday the committee made its report to Congress, proposing to give lots 16 and 29 "perpetually" for education and religion and reserving four townships for a university. While the grants were important to the Yankees, the contract offered a price of one dollar an acre, much higher than the OCA was willing to pay, since Connecticut, Massachusetts, and New York were willing to sell frontier land at half that price. Cutler continued his lobbying, while enjoying an exquisite lunch at the home of Col. William Duer, Secretary to the Board of Treasury. Other guests included Sargent, Hazard, and Samuel Osgood, another member of the Board of Treasury. Given the composition of this dinner party, it is likely they discussed Cutler's OCA project and Duer's Scioto Company, recently formed to buy property in Ohio. Over the coming weeks, a relationship developed between these two western projects and their principals that would forever cast a shadow over the otherwise laudable goals of the leaders of the OCA.[17]

Meanwhile, since land negotiations were at an impasse and members of Congress were preoccupied with making final revisions to legislation that became the Northwest Ordinance, Cutler decided it was a good time to visit some of the Convention delegates in Philadelphia. Ironically, one project favored by Cutler and his allies, the establishment of a system of government for the West, was getting in the way of the other, a deal for land. So, just before dusk on Tuesday the Yankee traveler set off for Philadelphia.[18]

Once again Cutler traveled like a man in a hurry, making the ninety-five-mile trip in just two days, arriving at 6:30 p.m. on Thursday, July 12. Over the next two days the lobbyist would use over half the letters of introduction in his possession. Both in group and private conversations he met with twelve of the Founding Fathers, including Benjamin Franklin, Benjamin Rush, Alexander Hamilton, and Roger Sherman, one of the chief architect's of the Great Compromise. He seems to have been operating as a courier for New England's leadership, in addition to his role as the chief negotiator for the Associates. Since both tasks demand secrecy he left little evidence of the content of these discussions. But given the gravity and urgency of the Constitutional Convention's deliberations and the Associates' negotiations we must assume that both occupied much of his time. Still, despite the press of his mission, between Saturday morning and Tuesday evening Cutler managed to tour a hospital, visit two botanical gardens, attend two worship services, see an uncle in New Jersey, and travel fifty-five miles in one day. Needless to say, by the time he arrived back in New York, he was exhausted.[19]

He returned to some very good news, though it was not unexpected. The Northwest Ordinance, the long-awaited plan of government for the West, had easily passed Congress. Of course, Cutler would never have left New York in the first place if he felt the lawmakers needed more encouragement. His journal expressed no concern about its passage and, given the circumstances, he had good reason to be confident. First, drafts of the Ordinance were moving quickly through Congress, which contrasted sharply with the deliberate pace of most legislation. Further, he had letters of introduction for four of the five Congressmen on the committee dealing with the legislation, including Carrington, Dane, Richard Henry Lee of Virginia, and Melancthon Smith of New York, who later became an OCA shareholder. So Cutler's many relationships had placed him in a unique position to influence the Ordinance. Moreover, he had been sent "a copy [of the Ordinance] . . .with leave to make remarks and propose amendments, and which I had taken the liberty to remark upon, and to propose several amendments." Finally, Congress faced unrelenting pressure from unpaid veterans, squatters, Indians, and the failing Seven Ranges project. A workable land deal would begin to address those issues and the Ordinance seemed to be a necessity for the Yankees with whom they were dealing.[20]

So while Cutler had many reasons to expect this outcome, he still must have been overjoyed by the act's final text. Government support for religion and education, the twin pillars of Yankee life, was implicit in Article 3 of the Ordinance's bill of rights:

> Religion, morality, and knowledge, being necessary to good government and the happiness of mankind, schools and the means of education shall forever be encouraged.

This short sentence, axiomatic amongst Americans until the 20th century, was later echoed by the constitutions of many states, which adhered to its exhortation to strengthen government and society through schooling. Its marriage of religion, education, and government must have thrilled Cutler, the Yankee pastor, teacher, and politician. In fact, Cutler was likely its author and may have also written or influenced Articles 1, 2, and 6, which constitute a bill of rights section of the Ordinance. The draft of May 10, presumably advocated by Parsons, had only included provisions for *habeas corpus* and trial by jury, while drafts discussed after Cutler's arrival in July included the new articles. Upon review of the final Ordinance, he observed in his journal that his recommendations had been adopted, though he was only specific about an item on taxation. Not coincidentally, at least eight of the rights delineated in Articles 1 and 2 appear to have been borrowed from the Massachusetts Constitution, which Bay Staters had refused to approve until John Adams added a thirty-article bill of rights in 1780.[21]

Yet while Cutler and his fellow New Englanders had achieved one of their objectives fairly easily, it was too early to celebrate, since the other would prove much harder to secure. Negotiations for the land deal were not going well, as Cutler soon discovered on Wednesday, July 18, the same day he found out about the passage of the Ordinance. While Congress and the committee had discussed the contract twice in his absence, the all-important price remained at $1 per acre. Over the next ten days Cutler pursued an approach of unrelenting lobbying peppered with bold threats.[22]

His personal lobbying efforts included offering financial induce-ments to two key decision-makers and spending a great deal of time with a third. For Colonel Duer he agreed to merge the proposals of the OCA and the Scioto Company into one, which expanded the area to a total of five million acres. The increased size of the new offer appealed to many in Congress. For Arthur St. Clair, the President of Congress and an OCA stockholder, he offered the governorship of the new territory. This appealed to St. Clair for obvious reasons, but it also won over Southern members of the body, whose mistrust of Yankees was lessened by the idea of a Pennsylvanian running the territory. As we have seen, Southern support was needed to pass almost any measure in Congress. But for Samuel Osgood, the Presi-dent of the Board of Treasury, he apparently had nothing to offer. In fact, Osgood was the only person affiliated with the Board that had no present or future monetary connections with the OCA/Scioto group. Nonetheless, Cutler secured his support for the new proposal after two evenings of intense discussions.[23]

Yet Cutler was far from alone in his efforts, as evidenced by statements in his journal that he was employing "every machine in the city" and, in reference to the committee, that the five "trouble-some fellows. . .must be attacked by my friends at their lodgings." Of course, he was not calling for a literal physical assault on the committee members, but his group's tactics did become so desperate that they considered visiting Congressmen in Connecticut, Rhode Island, and Maryland to try to convince them to travel to New York to vote for their plan. Given the degree of Cutler's desperation, it is not surprising that he used threats as an important and effective part of his strategy.[24]

On Friday, July 20 he told Carrington's committee that he was ready to abandon talks, leave town, and buy cheaper tracts from New York, Connecticut, and Massachusetts, who were also willing to accept the highly-depreciated government Certificates at face value. On the following Tuesday he and Sargent delivered to Con-gress an "Ultimatum," a letter that was clearly intended as their final offer, which warned that the Confederation could "lose an opportunity" to raise much-needed revenue and enhance defenses in the West against the Indians and British. Finally, at the end of a long day on Thursday he promised a Congressman that without a deal he "should certainly leave the city the next day." Cutler could make that statement because he believed it, and he proved that he meant it the next morning. After packing his bags for the trip home, he made one final visit to Congress. Like a poker player who wasn't bluffing, the pastor-turned-lobbyist reiterated his intention to leave, added comments intended to intimidate Congressmen about British, Indian, and Spanish designs for the West, and made clear to them that he was serious about buying the cheaper land offered by the states. Putnam's work in Maine on behalf of Massachusetts gave credence to this last threat. At last, having played every card in his hand, Cutler left, while promising he would stay a few more hours to await Congress' decision on his final offer.[25]

Cutler didn't have long to wait. He prepared to leave New York, saying goodbye to some friends, picking up a few letters for Boston, and then dining with his landlord. Finally, at 3:30 p.m. he received the news he had been waiting for. Congress had completely accepted his terms and delegated the authority to finalize the contract to the Board of Treasury. The nominal price was still set at $1.00 per acre, but Cutler received significant allowances for surveying costs, other expenses, and unusable tracts, bringing the net price down to $.67 per acre. Further, Continental Certificates could be tendered in payment at their original par value, even though their current market value was only about one-tenth that amount, effectively reducing the price for Certificate holders to just $.07 per acre. Certainly, this was eminently fair for the veterans, who had waited many years for their bounties, and indeed for all the original holders of this paper, who had seen its value plummet. And while the deal gave speculators the opportunity for huge profits, they also had assumed a frightening level of risk, when one considers that debtors went to prison in that era. Modern critics of these profits, who themselves are shielded from risk by faculty unions and tenure, eagerly point out the potential for gain, but ignore the risk of loss. Still, while the low price was essential to make the deal work, the provisions that helped establish Yankee culture on the frontier were just as important.[26]

The land grants for education (lot 16), religion (lot 29), and a university (two townships), which were tailored to assuage concerns of New Englanders, were apparently not controversial, as they had remained virtually unchanged since the first proposal on July 10. The grant for education followed the pattern of the Land Ordinance of 1785 for the Seven Ranges, but the OCA purchase added lot 29 for "the purposes of religion," restoring the grant that Congress narrowly rejected in 1785. These provisions simply mirrored long-established Yankee practices and, though grants supporting religion would eventually disappear, the others served as a model for many future government agreements. For example, within a year, when former New Jersey Congressman John Cleves Symmes contracted to buy one million acres in an area that today includes Cincinnati, Ohio, the government insisted on grants similar to those in the OCA deal. So, while the financial and cultural terms of this agreement delighted those New Englanders who migrated to the West, its features also seemed to appeal to the nation as a whole.[27]

So, with the signing of this contract the government hoped to finally begin to resolve its problems with veterans, Indians, British, squatters, and the debt. Pioneers got a chance for a new start in the Northwest Territory and the veterans among them received their long-overdue pay, which would end their protests. But further, as Cutler stated, "men strongly attached to the federal government, and composed of young, robust, and hardy laborers" strengthened the frontier against the Indians, British, and squatters, who represented threats that the tiny American army could never thwart without the help of a militia. Moreover, in two ways the deal constituted the government's first effective use of western land, its only asset. First, the sale price per acre exceeded the proceeds received by the states for their property, even though the Ohio Country was more remote, unknown, and dangerous. Second, it called for one large sale, which shifted the operational burden of smaller sales to that one buyer (OCA), and assured large payments to the Treasury, which would allow it to more quickly reduce the national debt. This last feature eliminated several problems that plagued the Seven Ranges project.[28]

The success of the OCA scheme, which relied on large investors, contrasted with the failure of the Seven Ranges plan, which attempted to sell to small, individual settlers. This demonstrated the triumph of the Yankee vision of capitalism and concentrated settlement over the idealistic Southern (and Jeffersonian) dream of a region filled with yeomen farmers. New Englanders knew from their experience in Connecticut that a few investors could quickly sell large tracts and efficiently absorb processing and recording costs. This method proved its worth again, as the OCA paid the United States $500,000 at closing and soon sold almost ten times the acreage of the struggling Seven Ranges. Cutler and his powerful friends accomplished in three months what had eluded Washington, Jefferson, Hamilton, and others for four years. The breathtaking speed of their success, which drew the map for America's westward march, can be largely attributed to Cutler's unique set of abilities and relationships, which he used with unrelenting determination. He appealed to key decision-makers by offering them the carrot of patronage and financial gain, while threatening them with the stick of unresolved problems. Then, during the last week of negotiations he escalated the pressure each day by threatening to cut off talks, until at last he gave a final ultimatum. Still, he and his Associates could not have succeeded without the intense pressure placed on Congress by the Indians, the squatters, and the failure of the Seven Ranges plan.[29]

Unfortunately, despite the magnitude of their accomplishment, their affiliation with their silent partner, Duer, would forever diminish it in the eyes of some. There is little question that the Scioto Company, Duer, and some of his associates engaged in unethical and fraudulent activities. Interested in speculation rather than settlement, the Scioto Company failed in 1792 and Duer went to debtor's prison. Except for a brief period in 1797, he spent the rest of his life in jail, where he died in 1799. He and his associates had squandered their good credit to speculate in government bonds, which led to Wall Street's first crash, the Panic of 1792. Their land speculations left investors without their money and pioneers without their homesteads. Still, though Cutler's final offer to Congress included an option for five million acres for the unnamed Scioto Company, it appears from subsequent events that all parties considered this option separate and distinct from the OCA contract. For example, even though Cutler and Sargent both received shares in Scioto for their cooperation in the lobbying effort, it does not appear that they participated in any meaningful way in its operation or management. As a result, neither Cutler, the OCA, nor any of its principals were ever sued over the Scioto failure, either by its ruined investors, its cheated settlers, or by Duer, whose case still stands as a spectacular example of the personal downside to 18th-century land speculation. Fortunately, Scioto's failure would be more than offset by OCA's success, and wagon wheels would start rolling west even before the end of 1787.[30]

On December 3 the first pioneers, including Cutler's son, Jervis, set out for the Ohio Country from their church in today's Hamilton, Massachusetts. Some walked while others rode in a large covered wagon, fittingly called the *Mayflower*, in a scene memorialized today by a roadside plaque near the church, which still stands. Just eight months later, Cutler made the 751-mile journey to the new settlement, called Marietta, to see it firsthand. Soon after his arrival he delivered a remarkable sermon at the new settlement that proclaimed its evangelical mission, Christianity's importance to society and government, and consequently, Marietta's need for religious and moral instruction.[31]

The Massachusetts minister took the theme of his sermon from Mal. 1:11: "My name will be great among the nations, from the rising to the setting of the sun. In every place incense and pure offerings will be brought to my name, because my name will be great among the nations." Cutler chose this verse because he saw Marietta as part of the fulfillment of Malachi's prophecy. As an evangelical, he felt compelled to follow the Messiah's Great Commission, which exhorted His followers to "go and make disciples of all nations (Matt. 28)." Supported by references to Bible prophecy and Christ's Second Coming, Cutler explained that the expansion of Christianity to the West was simply the latest chapter of the mission that began in Jerusalem, spread throughout the Roman Empire and Europe, and then crossed the Atlantic to America. And just as Malachi had predicted that Christianity would spread "from the rising to the setting of the sun," Cutler trusted that "in like manner, divine truth, useful knowledge, and improvements appear to proceed in the same direction, until the bright day of science, virtue, pure religion, and free government shall pervade this western hemisphere."[32]

Religion was "necessary to good government," in the words of Article 3 of the Ordinance, and it was clear to all at the time that the religion the document referenced was Christianity. According to Cutler, it fosters righteousness, the following of God's will in our lives, as "it exalts human nature, and makes us just what we ought to be in every condition and relation of life. . . .It regulates the passions and animates us to the most virtuous and noble conduct." But while moral people make good citizens, the opposite is also true. In a region that seemed to offer material abundance, "dissipation, luxury, and vice are the almost inseparable companions of ease and plenty." The minister warns his congregation to "be on guard against every thing that is base, vicious, or dishonorable, and endeavor to cultivate all the virtues of a religious and social life."[33]

Yet, since Cutler feels that Christianity is so important to political and social life, he carefully explains to his listeners that the Constitution, ratified just two months earlier, protects their religious liberty. Since the Bill of Rights was not ratified until 1792, he must have assumed passage of the first amendment, or, like so many others at the time, felt that this "inalienable right" need not be committed to writing. In any event, he makes a strong defense for "full toleration," even for those with whom he has religious differences, explaining that "no one kind of religion, or sect of religion, is established as the national religion, nor made, by national laws, the test of truth [punctuation is Cutler's]." Still, he had shown by his insistence on the land grant for religion that he felt government support does not damage religious liberty, so long as it is not limited to any one sect, and in the new territory it was not. Cutler added that Christianity did not need a privileged position in society because "truth can never be in real hazard, where there is a sufficiency of light and knowledge, and full liberty to vindicate it."[34]

Still, Cutler warns that "these desirable effects [of Christianity] can not [sic] be obtained without religious instruction," telling the settlers they should be grateful the community has set aside a fund, lots 16 and 29, to lighten their personal financial burden. The part-time teacher urges the "early attention to the instruction of youth [so] that the rising generation may be taught to remember their Creator, and walk in the paths of virtue and righteousness." The people can only overcome "ignorance" through "religion and learning," which Cutler hopes will "meet with encouragement, and that they will be extended to the remotest parts of the American Empire." Religious instruction is to be anchored in the Bible, "flowing uncorrupted from its sacred sources, rational, moral, and divine." The frontier settlement would struggle mightily to meet Cutler's challenge.[35]

Religion, morality, knowledge, government, and education were seamlessly mixed in this sermon, which was the norm in an era when New England divines spoke and published Election Day sermons that joined rather than separated church and state. Cutler saw Christians as the instrument of God's Providence, shining the warm rays of wisdom down on this new land through religion and education. While many people at the time shared his sentiments, their numbers would grow even larger as a new spirit of religious fervor began to sweep the nation in succeeding decades. Happiness and good government would surely result. And while those fires of religious enthusiasm would soon flash over the West, influencing education as they burned, it would be several generations before the hopes of Cutler and his fellow Calvinists were fully realized.

Manasseh Cutler would never migrate to Marietta. Perhaps an improving economy and solicitous parishioners convinced him to stay home. Or perhaps Manasseh wanted to avoid the physical danger and financial risk of the frontier. Nonetheless, many of his friends and several of his children moved there and another historical marker, this one in Marietta, stands witness to the fact that the new nation finally kept its commitment to its veterans. Posted at the entrance to Mound Cemetery is a Daughters of the American Revolution plaque, inscribed with the names of twenty-five veterans of the Revolution who lie buried nearby. The names *Parsons*, *Putnam*, *Tupper*, *Varnum*, *Whipple*, and twenty others provide material evidence that they had at last received their pay. But while the country's commitments to its army had been fulfilled, its hopes for the teaching of the young would not be realized for many decades. Yet those hopes would be frustrated by a lack of leadership and resources, not from any lack of ideas.

Chapter 4

Lofty Hopes — The Christian Philosophy Behind the First Schools

*I*n schools of education across America our future principals and superintendents learn that Thomas Jefferson, Benjamin Franklin, Benjamin Rush, and others followed a philosophy rooted in the Enlightenment in order to craft our nation's first plans for the public school. Tomorrow's educational leaders also discover that the Founders rejected society's traditional reliance on Faith in favor of a progressive trust in Reason. But even though the Revolutionary Era respected these men like few others, the secular ideology of Jefferson and Franklin placed them far outside the mainstream while the erratic turns of Rush's thinking made him impossible to follow. Not surprisingly, their own generation largely ignored their plans, leading each to abandon school reform for other causes.[1]

Rather than Enlightenment thought, a system of beliefs inspired by the Reformation contributed the leaders and strategies that would eventually produce free, universal education. Its advocates, who were often clergy or devout laymen, saw no inherent conflict between Faith and Reason. Their philosophy, grounded in the authority of the Bible, became so accepted during the Second Great Awakening that its ideas would sweep aside the unorthodox concepts of Jefferson, Franklin, and Rush.[2]

But while beliefs from the Enlightenment set Jefferson and Franklin apart from most school advocates, a concept from classical times created some unity. Intellectuals across the philosophical spectrum agreed that citizens must be educated in "virtue" if their novel experiment in government was to succeed. The people needed to place the common good before personal advantage if they were to rule effectively without the iron hand of a king. But self-government would fail if "vice," which involved putting one's own interests first, were allowed to prevail. Vice could express itself as greed, ostentation, sloth, or frivolous entertainment. These ideas about public good and evil sprang from republicanism, a theory of government developed from the study of the classical civilizations of Greece and Rome. Adopted during the English Civil War and the Glorious Revolution of 1689, republicanism allowed believers and secularists to set aside their religious differences and make common cause. During the American Revolution, the two groups drew even closer, as secular propagandists like Thomas Paine borrowed Biblical imagery, while Calvinist preachers employed republican language to fight their shared battle. The founding generation feared that without virtuous citizens America would surrender to vice, and like other republics in history rot from within until it was destroyed. Yet they shared the hope that if the people could be educated, or as Benjamin Rush put it, "turned into republican machines," the new nation would not merely survive but prosper. Therefore, it was essential that republican principles, embodied in important features of government like the separation of and balance of powers between the three branches of government, be taught to the next generation. Unfortunately, in the aftermath of Shay's Rebellion, it seemed as if vice and ignorance were gaining the upper hand.[3]

Yet while the need for learning was urgent, if it was going to succeed in a nation where most were Christian, it must accommodate religion. Virtually all the leaders in the revolutionary generation, despite their personal convictions, saw religion and morality as vital supports for republican government. Washington eloquently summarized their beliefs in his Farewell Address to the nation in 1796. After describing religion and morality as "great pillars of human happiness" and the "firmest props of the duties of men and citizens," he challenged the patriotism of those who would try to undermine either. Further emphasizing their interdependence, he warned that we should not assume that "morality can be maintained without religion." After acknowledging the positive benefits of the intellectual aspects of education, he returned to the twin pillars, cautioning that we should not presume "that national morality can prevail in exclusion of religious principle. It is substantially true that virtue or morality is a necessary spring of popular government." Finally, he concluded that the nation must "promote, then, as an object of primary importance, institutions for the general diffusion of knowledge." The driving force behind these propositions was the fear that vice would take over, as it had for a time during Shay's Rebellion, unless society placed restraints on itself. While secularists like Jefferson, Rousseau, and Paine felt that humanity would naturally lean towards virtue in the proper environment, Calvinists, to the contrary, were convinced that we would always drift into vice because of our sinful nature. The latter's view won out, both in the conservative design of the new Constitution and in the planning for the first schools.[4]

To understand where the seeds of Calvinism's love for learning were first sowed, one must travel back to the fertile soil of the Reformation. When Martin Luther posted his Ninety-Five Theses to the door of the Castle Church in Wittenberg in 1517, he unleashed powerful forces that would soon upend the religious and social structures of his age. Overnight, sinners could personally gain salvation through a simple act of faith, no longer needing the intercession of a priest or even the Catholic Church. Once "saved," believers became members of the "priesthood of believers," personally responsible for their own spiritual growth and no longer dependent solely on the Church. They were now to understand God and His will for us through *sola scriptura*—by scripture alone—instead of accepting the Church's timeworn traditions and its official interpretations of the Bible. This promised a profound transfer of power from the church to the laity, but before that could happen, Luther had to somehow radically transform their culture. Two formidable obstacles stood in his way: most people were illiterate and Bibles were printed in Greek and Latin, which could be read only by the clergy and a few elites. As a result, he and his followers began to push for universal literacy and vernacular Bibles. This in turn began what historian David Paul Nord has called the "culture of literacy" among many Protestants. For over three hundred years, this legacy of the Reformation would be the primary force behind the rise of literacy and the waves of evangelical literature that washed over the western world. But first, much hard work lay ahead.[5]

Luther argued in the 1520s that the church, the state, and the family all had to share the responsibility for education. After he and his followers visited many German parishes in 1527 and 1528 they were shocked by the peasants' doctrinal ignorance and their pastors' shoddy instruction. Deciding that these problems could only be corrected with systematic teaching, in 1529 he created the catechism, a book in question-and-answer format that instructed Christians on key points of doctrine. While Luther had much to say about education in general, his focus remained on its religious aspects. Instead, a close friend would devote his life implementing Luther's ideas on schooling throughout the Lutheran states of Germany. Philipp Melancthon was a brilliant scholar, theologian, and colleague of Luther's at the University of Wittenberg. His achievements over four decades were so lasting that he is remembered today as Germany's Teacher. After working on the parish surveys with Luther, he wrote *Instruction for Inspectors* in 1528, perhaps the first attempt anywhere to institute standards for instruction and curriculum. Then in 1559 he called for a three-tiered system of schooling in the *School Code of Wurttemberg*, which inspired other similar laws. At the college level, Melancthon taught and wrote on theology, the classics, philosophy, physics, and history during a distinguished career. His involvement with German universities led to their redesign, which left them among the most respected in the world by the time of his death.[6]

But it would take a French expatriate in Switzerland to advance the German plan for schools a step further and to spread it throughout Protestant Europe. The church, the state, and the school were often indistinguishable in the austere Geneva of John Calvin. Because that city was a theocracy, the Bible also served as a legal authority, in addition to being a source of spiritual wisdom. Since it provided such an important guide for matters both worldly and heavenly, Calvin and other ministers taught from it on a daily basis verse-by-verse, in a practice known today as expository preaching. But if the laity were to do their part and engage in similar study, they would need Bibles, other religious materials, and the skills to use them. To meet the demand for literature, a robust printing industry quickly developed, turning out Bibles, commentaries, catechisms, and polemics. To address the need for comprehension, Geneva established a network that included primary schools teaching Greek, Latin, and dialectics and secondary schools, which offered those same subjects, as well as Hebrew, theology, rhetoric, physics, and mathematics. Then in 1569, the city topped off its system when it opened a college to train ministers. Calvin hoped the institution, which in time developed into the University of Geneva, would attract some of the many foreign exiles then living in his city, who would then spread his teaching throughout Europe.[7]

A Scottish émigré would soon prove the wisdom of Calvin's program, with far-reaching consequences for America and education. While John Knox never benefited from the University of Geneva, which opened a decade after he left Geneva, he absorbed many lessons about religion and government during the five years he spent ministering to the city's numerous Scottish and English expatriates in the 1550s. When Knox returned home in 1560, he helped Protestants gain power and quickly implemented many of the practices he had learned from Calvin. First, he fostered the establishment of the Church of Scotland, which would provide much of the inspiration for Presbyterianism. Second, in order to nurture the Church, his *First Book of Discipline* included a national plan of education, which proposed a comprehensive, four-tiered system, starting with elementary schools and capped by an advanced university. Schooling was to be compulsory and affordable, with the Church paying for the children of the poor. While Parliament rejected this plan because of objections to its funding, its ideals would finally become law eighty years later, with implications for reform far beyond the borders of Scotland.[8]

In 1696 Parliament passed an Act for Setting Schools, which mandated a school in every parish and set pay levels for every teacher. This legislation reflected the Scottish conviction that universal education had value for the state, which wanted citizens who were educated, and the Church, which sought members who could read the Bible and understand doctrine. The law built on practices that had been growing since Knox's time: continual improvement, close supervision, and tax support. Since the Church had a close relationship with the state, it was responsible for school inspections and teacher qualifications. The Act worked so well that by the early 18th century every parish had a school, most people paid little tuition, and poor children paid nothing. As a result, in less than a hundred years Scotland would have the highest literacy rate in the world.[9]

Scotland also focused on improving her universities during these years. After undergoing a series of reforms between 1690 and 1730, universities at Glasgow, Edinburgh, Aberdeen, and St. Andrews were considered among the best in the world. These initiatives were closely coordinated with an inexpensive and extensive network of secondary schools, which taught subjects like Latin that were prerequisites for college admission. Similar to the lower levels of learning, opportunities in higher education had been expanding for some time, at least since the middle of the 17th century, and they enjoyed the support of both church and state. Scottish universities were accessible irrespective of religion or social class, distinguishing them from their British counterparts, which limited admission to members of the Church of England and the upper class. Even townspeople could take advantage of them by auditing classes of interest. By the 1740s Scots could study divinity, medicine, and law without traveling abroad. Such broad-based access to education would prove crucial to a pervasive environment of innovation and the impressive accomplishments that would result.[10]

With so many literate people and advanced universities, Scotland enjoyed a vibrant intellectual and cultural life in the 18th century. While England and parts of Western Europe witnessed similar developments, only in this tiny country did it impact such a broad spectrum of people, including much of the middle class and some of the poor, primarily in the lowlands. Widespread literacy translated into big business for publishing, papermaking, and writing.

Middle-class tradesmen like bakers and blacksmiths and lower-class farmers, like the poet Robert Burns, typically owned several books and regularly borrowed from public libraries, which were operating in most towns by 1750. While many of the books they read dealt with religious topics, which was of vital interest to the Calvinists and their university-trained ministers, about half concerned secular topics. And Scots read widely from foreign publications, sparked by their frequent trips abroad for war, adventure, and education. This rich literary environment spawned many voluntary associations promoting science, agriculture, medicine, and music. In turn, this culture inspired material improvements and philosophical innovations that pulled Scotland out of its economic malaise and helped push the western world into the modern age. In the physical world, Scotland was responsible for great advances in industry, transportation, and medicine, including steam power, steamboats, locomotives, paved roads, and practical medical training. In the intellectual sphere, the origins of psychology, sociology, economics, and political science can all be traced to a new system of ideas developed in Scotland. Similarly, the roots of the ideology of America's first schools came from three university professors who drafted the outlines of that system of thought, which later came to be known as Scottish Common Sense Realism.[11]

Rev. Francis Hutcheson, professor of moral philosophy at the University of Glasgow from 1729 to 1746, is best known for the concept of "disinterested benevolence." In his view God created humanity with an inner moral sense that moves us to act with charity towards others without regard to our own physical needs, though we are nonetheless rewarded when we see the positive good that flows from our charity. While this proposition met with opposition from many scholars, it was warmly received by the clergy. And while it originated from Hutcheson's theistic perspective, his concept of benevolence was fully compatible with the secular "virtue" that sprang from classical republican thinking. Consequently, it became an important factor in the alliance between believers and skeptics that developed during the Revolutionary and the Early National periods. In fact, Hutcheson's writings were so influential in colonial colleges that one biographer concluded they had as much impact on the intellectuals of the Revolution as the ideas of John Locke. Hutcheson's insights provided the philosophical foundation for what historians have called the Benevolent Empire, a feverish outburst of reform that accompanied the Second Great Awakening and helped launch America's first schools.[12]

Yet another professor at Glasgow would have an even more profound impact on American thought. Rev. Thomas Reid developed many of the essentials of Common Sense while a professor at the University of Aberdeen in the 1740s and 1750s. He demonstrated some of its key principles when he published *Inquiry into the Human Mind*, on the principles of Common Sense in 1764, the same year he was appointed to succeed Adam Smith on the Glasgow faculty. Reid set out to attack the ideas of Locke, Berkeley, and Hume, and by doing so to defend traditional concepts of religion and morality. He argued that we shouldn't use Reason exclusively to understand the world through deduction. It troubled him that the approach of his opponents could lead to a denial of both the physical world and God. Instead, he believed that we should use our five senses to observe the world and explain it through induction, as Bacon and Newton had done. The everyday experiences of sight, sound, touch, smell, and taste would develop our "common sense," revealing "self-evident" truths. Conversely, propositions that run counter to these daily experiences must be false. Still, Reason had its place in Reid's system; first, to help determine what is self-evident from our senses, and second, to draw conclusions from our initial observations. But one feature of this system stands out.[13]

Common Sense allowed for the coexistence of Reason and Faith, an idea that conflicted with other contemporary philosophies. This was clearly seen when Reid applied his system to theological inquiry. On one of its most fundamental questions, he asserted that the existence of God was proven by the intricate order of the cosmos, the physical similarities of living things, the Bible's testimony about miracles, and human intuitions concerning supernatural forces. Like the Apostle Paul, Reid believed that we are predisposed to belief rather than skepticism. His implicit trust in research, which deals with our observations of the world and its people, would have broad implications for colleges, both in Scotland and in America. Like earlier Calvinists, Reid believed that God revealed truth not only in the Bible, but also through creation. But unlike the scriptures, we read the book of nature with all our senses, not just our eyes. The professor applied this principle in his teaching and in his research. So, soon after arriving at Aberdeen he began to replace the scholastic curriculum, which used deduction to analyze authoritative texts, with a humanist plan that employed induction to study natural history (the observation of plants and animals) and natural philosophy (physics and chemistry), as well as mathematics and moral philosophy. And as a scientist, Reid discussed and corresponded with scholars at prestigious societies on topics as diverse as agriculture, astronomy, economics, geometry, and education. While universities in Scotland and America appeared to mimic Aberdeen, history does not reveal whether this was a response to Reid's plans or to the pervasive influence of Common Sense thought.[14]

On the other hand, given his profound influence on that system of thought, first established in *Inquiry* and later strengthened by two influential essays in the 1780s, there is little doubt Reid's thoughts on morality influenced America's attitudes towards reform, including education, and revivals during the Awakening. In a departure from the traditional Calvinist doctrine of pre-destination, he held that all men had free will and just like Adam and Eve could choose between good and evil, righteousness and sin. In fact, we had intuition, a conscience that allowed us to distinguish between the two. Evil then was not God's fault, but rather flowed from our own bad choices. Since we know from experience that people have a propensity to sin, especially those who are not saved, a just society must create institutions, like schools, to influence its citizens in a positive way. In an interesting parallel to later commonly-held sentiments in America, Reid taught that nations should encourage religion, virtue, and education. In fact, his teaching on free will opened the way for aggressive revivals, like the ones that would sweep America and Great Britain in the 18th and 19th centuries. This precept gave people an active role in the most important decision they could ever make, whether to accept or reject salvation, instead of being passive objects of God's will. Though no evidence exists that Reid ever led revivals, he built two institutions that resolved to nurture good and joined two causes determined to fight evil. In his early years in Aberdeen he helped found its infirmary and later provided funds and administration for another one in Glasgow, two institutions that today are counted among Scotland's largest teaching hospitals, each with more than 1,000 beds. He also was active in penal improvements and antislavery and once sent a petition on the latter to the House of Commons.[15]

Reid's interest in humanitarian aid contrasted with his famous predecessor at Glasgow, Adam Smith, who had shown more interest in economics than reform. While Smith is best remembered for his discussion of laissez-faire policies in *The Wealth of Nations*, that magnum opus also presented his thoughts on education. Contrary to popular belief, while he advocated limited government in most areas, he championed its involvement in public works and institutions that were important for society but too unprofitable to attract private funding. While he criticized government support for colleges, which he found yielded poor results, he favored it for the education of the poor, which he believed promoted order in society. And Smith, though certainly not an orthodox believer himself and possibly even an atheist, endorsed the positive benefits of religious teaching for others. He praised the instruction offered in reformed and evangelical schools and favored compulsory church attendance for the poor. Like his fellow Glasgow professors, Smith had great influence on the founding generation.[16]

Common Sense, as formulated by Hutcheson, Reid, Smith, and others, heavily influenced the thinking of many of America's Founders and was crucial for her society and culture up to the Civil War. Evidence for its reach can be found in the statement "We hold these truths to be *self-evident*" [emphasis provided] and in the title of Paine's *Common Sense*. Jefferson, Madison, Franklin, Rush, and John Marshall, the longest-serving Chief Justice, were all influenced by Scottish teachers or Common Sense writings. Historian Mark Noll has labeled its expression in America the Evangelical Enlightenment, while noting its significance in the Awakening's camp meetings, voluntary associations, and college curricula. Taught in schools, colleges, and churches across the country, this philosophy was so pervasive that most Americans tried to conform to its ideals.

However, the Americans who were most under its spell were the Presbyterian and Congregational ministers who started and operated our first colleges.[17]

Rev. John Witherspoon brought a solid commitment to Common Sense to the College of New Jersey, today's Princeton University, when he became its sixth President in 1768. The recipient of masters and divinity degrees from Edinburgh, Witherspoon installed an approach that mimicked Hutcheson's and a curriculum that copied Aberdeen's. During his tenure Princeton educated students who held key positions in government, education, and the church. In government, its graduates included James Madison, Aaron Burr, six members of the Continental Congress, nine cabinet officers, twenty-one senators, thirty-nine congressmen, twelve governors, three Supreme Court justices, and thirty-three state and federal judges. Nine graduates attended the Constitutional Convention, including two who would draft the New Jersey and Virginia plans. In education, Princeton counted thirteen of its alumni as college presidents. And in the church, during Witherspoon's first seven years alone he trained 30% of all college students who eventually became ministers in British America. So, given his influence his teachings provide a unique window into the ideology of his generation.[18]

Witherspoon, never an innovator, adopted the ideas of others in a philosophy that represented an amalgam of Calvinism and republicanism. Since human beings had an evil nature, they naturally struggled for power over each other; therefore the best system of government needed a series of checks and balances to frustrate that temptation. Madison, of course, expressed this in the Federalist Papers and helped develop it into the separation of powers concept of the US Constitution. Still, citizens needed to operate their new government, even if its powers were to be limited, so they needed virtue and knowledge, qualities they could only acquire through exposure to religion and education. While Witherspoon opposed the establishment of a state church and defended rights of conscience, he nevertheless argued for close cooperation between church and state. And though he held firmly to his own beliefs, he welcomed students of other faiths to Princeton and encouraged the study of opposing views, even those of the atheist Hume. Witherspoon practiced what he preached, both in politics and in religion. In politics he took an active role as a signer of the Declaration of Independence, delegate to the Continental Congress, member of his state legislature, and member of his state's convention that ratified the US Constitution. In religion he defended conservative positions from liberal attacks in Scotland, continued that work when he came to Princeton, and late in life helped unite America's Presbyterians under one organization. And, though his last two decades at Princeton were marked by relative stagnation, his hand-picked successor would inject new ideas and new growth, in the process reviving the institution, but not without provoking fierce opposition.[19]

Rev. Samuel Stanhope Smith succeeded Witherspoon, his father-in-law and mentor, as President in 1795. Like his predecessor, he would use his post to insinuate Common Sense into American society and culture. Among the students who absorbed Smith's teaching were the future presidents of Centre College, the Universities of Pennsylvania, North Carolina, and Nashville, and New York, Rutgers, and Transylvania Universities, which were all vital institutions in the growing nation. For example, Transylvania, while unremarkable today, was unquestionably the most influential university in the South at the time. Princeton graduates also helped establish academies in the South and West that were derisively called "log colleges" because of their shabby appearance. They ranged in sophistication from little more than advanced grammar schools to respected institutions of higher learning. The demand for these institutions was created by the spiritual needs of the 200,000 Scotch-Irish who emigrated from Northern Ireland to North America in the 18th century. Presbyterians required an educated clergy, but the costs and inconvenience of travel to European universities made this local option much more attractive. The colleges were modeled after academies in Ulster, which had been created to alleviate similar problems caused by travel to Scotland. Princeton could trace its own founding to the key leaders of the first log college in Pennsylvania, including Gilbert and William Tennent. These institutions were destined to play an important role in the drive for free public schooling.[20]

Smith was a more creative thinker than Witherspoon, though he too tried to mold Princeton according to the Scottish ideal of a university. Like his former teacher he also leaned on Hutcheson's ideas, marrying Calvinism to republicanism and Faith to Reason. But unlike Witherspoon, he was also heavily influenced by Reid, whose works were not widely read in America until the 1780s. Smith's first address to the college in 1795 emphasizes the familiar themes of religion, morality, and learning that Washington would repeat in his farewell to the nation one year later. According to Smith, piety and morality would result from faith-based education, and those qualities, in turn, would guarantee a virtuous citizenry and a healthy society. Needless to say, the clergy must provide input on the design and conduct of education, especially at the college level. Smith had long been opposed to the separation of church and state, having warned Jefferson in 1778 that it would be a mistake to exclude the church and its ministers from his proposal for public schools in Virginia. He and his fellow Federalists felt their concerns were validated by the anticlericalism, chaos, and violence of the French Revolution, which they saw as the result one should expect from an unfettered secular democracy. These and other ideas would play out during Smith's seventeen years as Princeton's president and the more controversial ones would cause him to lose sleep and eventually his job.[21]

His ideas concerning education, science, and reform revealed his desire to innovate, in contrast to Witherspoon's defense of tradition. In education he advocated schooling for the masses, with an emphasis on moral content. Inspired by Reid, Smith envisioned a two-tier system: first, all children should receive basic moral and civic instruction to make sure they understood the laws of God and the state and second, more gifted students needed higher education to prepare them for leadership. Neither level was controversial; the first echoed the Common Sense belief that education could shape personality and behavior, producing a nation of virtuous citizens, and the second promised to alleviate a desperate shortage of clergy. In science Smith endorsed Reid's view that the study of the natural world was a reliable way to learn about the Creator. So under his leadership Princeton hired the nation's first undergraduate science instructor, raised a great deal of money for lab equipment, and offered a unique curriculum that combined science with the humanities. In reform Smith built on Hutcheson and Reid in his opposition to slavery, his advocacy of education for the enslaved, and his defense of the economic rights of freedmen. Many of his students took to heart his messages about Christian benevolence and civil rights. For example, Theodore Frelinghuysen, Whig candidate for Vice President in 1844, fought for temperance and missions and vigorously opposed both slavery and Indian removal. Indeed, many of Smith's scholars would leave their mark on American society.[22]

Still, Smith's progressive ideas generated great opposition. Peers attacked him for what they saw as his liberal stands on theology, science, and curriculum. Students rebelled against his strict rules for campus life, which may have caused a catastrophic fire in 1802 and which did lead to the suspension of most undergraduates in 1807. Others opposed his abolitionism while still others disliked his education plans, since they instead subscribed to the British notion that widespread schooling was ill advised. Such criticism lasted throughout his tenure, strained his health, and eventually led to his resignation in 1812.[23]

Meanwhile, just 110 miles to the northeast, a pious, hardworking genius would lead another iconic university to embrace universal education and many other reforms. In fact, its students' commitments to those ideals would prove even more important for the nation. Rev. Timothy Dwight was elected President of Yale in 1795, the same year that Smith replaced Witherspoon at Princeton, and like his counterpart he inherited a rebellious student body. Many were captivated by the revolutionary and atheist ideas of Rousseau, Voltaire, and Paine, yet Dwight's steadfast attacks on such thought would bear fruit through revival at Yale and reform in America. And where Princeton entered a period of decline upon Smith's departure in 1812, Yale would strengthen after Dwight's death in 1817, becoming a center of training for many of the key evangelical leaders of the 19th century, including those at the very heart of the school movement.[24]

Dwight's ideology, grounded in the Calvinism of Edwards, his grandfather, and the realism of Reid and Hutcheson expressed itself in the defense of conservative positions, whether the subject was politics, religion, or education. For him the Bible was the final authority on all matters pertaining to earth or heaven. In politics he was a strong Federalist who detested the Jeffersonians, at least in part because he distrusted democracy, which was a centerpiece of their program. He also backed state support for the church, and the denial of public office to non-Christians, two positions that were the norm in the Revolutionary Era, but which were gradually abolished by the first two decades of the next century. In religion Dwight, like other evangelicals, held that all people had the free will to choose between salvation and damnation, a position that drove his interest in revivals and missions. He vigorously opposed Voltaire, Hume, and Paine and every form of skepticism, including atheism and deism, which he viewed as certain pathways to hell. This added further to his dislike for the Jeffersonians, since they often favored skepticism. Further, following Hutcheson on disinterested benevolence, he enthusiastically supported social reform. Dwight put these ideas into action, founding the Missionary Society of Connecticut and the American Board of Commissioners for Foreign Missions, as well as actively fighting slavery. Given his personal involvement, it's not surprising that he saw religion's effect on society as positive. This was especially true in education, where he felt the church could do a better job than the state, a conclusion Adam Smith had reached some years earlier in his observations of Scotland. In fact, like many in his era, Dwight felt that learning without religion was dangerous.[25]

Post-millennialism, a concept found in Chapter 20 of the Book of Revelations, supplied much of the urgency behind Dwight's push for reform. He and Calvinists like John Cotton, Jonathan Edwards, and Manasseh Cutler believed that their efforts to better mankind would usher in a thousand-year period of peace and joy in an American "New Jerusalem," to be followed by Christ's Second Coming, the end of this world, and the beginning of the next. This belief underscored the urgency of the Great Commission—Christ's order to preach to "all nations"—because if reforms were advancing the hour of the Final Judgment, they were also reducing the time sinners had to save themselves.[26]

But when Dwight arrived on campus in 1795 he was much more concerned about the state of men's souls within its walls than those beyond its boundaries. Given the level of skepticism, he immediately began to attack it with logic and reason, using many of Reid's arguments. A secret organization, The Moral Society, was formed on campus in 1797 to promote belief and counter skepticism. Within a few years disbelief evaporated as Yale became caught up in the revivals of the Awakening. Dwight's relentless teaching and preaching about the need for a personal relationship with Christ helped ignite revivals in 1802, 1808, 1813, and 1815. As a consequence of this outburst of piety, attendance at the campus church increased dramatically, and the number of candidates for the ministry soared, from only 5% of the student body in 1792 to 31% in 1805, a trend that would have important consequences for the Benevolent Empire.[27]

Dwight's best teaching opportunities came during the debates he conducted with seniors two times each week. Using reason and the Bible, he and the students debated theological and moral questions such as dueling, prisons, capital punishment, and war. While we know he denounced slavery, prostitution, intemperance, and the theater, we don't know if these were also topics of the debates. The sessions were part of a thorough restructuring of Yale during Dwight's years, which included improvements in the faculty, modernized guidelines for student living, increased emphasis on science, and plans for professional colleges. The last two innovations would prove important for American higher education, as they paved the way for the teaching of physical sciences like chemistry and geology to undergraduates and the creation of professional schools for the education of ministers, doctors, and lawyers. Not the least of Dwight's achievements was the intellectual and spiritual formation of hundreds of students who would have a profound effect on American religion and reform in the decades to come.[28]

The spiritual development of young men at Yale would continue under Rev. Nathaniel William Taylor, but the effects of his work would ultimately reach far beyond the student body. Ordained in 1812, Taylor served as the pastor of the First Church of Christ in New Haven until 1822, when he was appointed the first Dwight Professor of Didactic Theology at the new Yale Divinity School. Princeton, Harvard, and Andover had also recently opened schools to train ministers because the old system was not working. Like Mannaseh Cutler, after a four-year undergraduate program, prospective ministers served an apprenticeship in the home of a pastor, usually an alumnus of a sponsoring college. Students of these "schools of the prophets" left with a license to preach and sometimes the hand of the pastor's daughter in marriage, but pastors were struggling to find time to teach at the same time that interest in the ministry was surging. The passions of the Awakening were increasing the supply of young men attracted to the ministry and the accelerating migration that Cutler had noticed was also creating demand for missionaries to the West. Between 1790 and 1820 an estimated 800,000 New Englanders had moved into western New York, Ohio, Indiana, Illinois, and Michigan. So it was hoped the new divinity school would meet these challenges while also relieving other anxieties of the Congregationalists who controlled Yale, besieged as they were by problems at home and in the West. In Connecticut they had just lost their privileged status as the established state church in 1818 and in the West they continued to lose ground to the Baptists and Methodists, who were adding ministers more quickly due to their lower educational standards and the anti-intellectual attitudes that prevailed there. Yale's program proved to be a big success, especially on the frontier, as one of every four of its graduates before the Civil War settled west of the Hudson River.[29]

Taylor and two other faculty members soon developed what became known as New Haven Theology (NHT), starting with the traditional theology of Calvin and Edwards, but like other followers of Common Sense they placed reason on the same level of authority as revelation. NHT emphasized free will, rejecting orthodox views of predestination and man's innate depravity. NHT held that God had placed human beings in a world where they were free to make good or bad moral choices, including the most important choice, whether to accept or reject Christ and his offer of redemption. This had profound implications for revivals and missions, because if everyone had a free choice about salvation, then Calvinist ministers needed to be more aggressive about spreading the gospel message, something the Baptists and Methodists were already doing quite successfully in the West. This tenet of NHT drew criticism from conservatives because it appeared to diminish God's role in salvation and it would eventually lead to a split in the Presbyterians in the late 1830s. On the other hand, NHT backed reforms similar to those of earlier Calvinists, like Dwight, with one critical difference in emphasis.[30]

Since NHT elevated the individual's role in salvation, followers focused on reaching the "lost" through home missions in the West and foreign missions to exotic places like China. Yale faculty and students illustrated this commitment through the central role they played in founding three groups, the Connecticut Sunday School Union (CSSU), the United Band of Foreign Missionaries, and the Society of Inquiry Regarding Missions, all of which made education a key part of their agenda. First, the Sunday schools, though religion remained their primary purpose, also provided much secular intellectual training and set out to make sure even the children of the poor received basic instruction. In similar fashion, the two missions groups saw schooling as an important tool in their quest to obey the Great Commission. The Congregationalists at Yale and to a lesser extent the Presbyterians at Princeton led the way in this work, supported by their Plan of Union in 1801, in which they had agreed to coordinate their work in the West. They were not alone, as efforts were also underway at Amherst, Brown, Dartmouth, and Williams. Inspired by these groups, colleges sent Protestant missionaries to Ceylon (today's Sri Lanka), China, the Near East, and the Sandwich Islands (today's Hawaii), and into America's Old Northwest, to Ohio, Indiana, Illinois, and Michigan. Many of the missionaries in the fast-growing West would leave a significant imprint on its society and culture, including the development of its first schools.[31]

It was through these apostles that Common Sense, encompassing a spectrum of ideas but driven mostly by New Haven Theology, would come to dominate American thought and influence the nation's development through mid-century. Its acceptance resulted from its harmony with evangelical religion. First, the philosophy accommodated and encouraged the spiritual enthusiasm and social activism of the Awakening. But perhaps even more important, Common Sense enthusiasts seeded its beliefs throughout the rising leadership of the young republic through its colleges, where its pedagogy and textbooks crowded out all other philosophies. No college was more influential than Yale, whose graduates and curriculum shaped the many new institutions that were founded before the Civil War. And nowhere was the influence of the philosophy more evident than in the actions of the leaders that Yale and those other colleges produced.[32]

Leadership would prove critical in creating free schools for all children in the first half of the 19th century. Several generations of activists, legislators, governors, and administrators made it happen everywhere but the South and, not surprisingly, most were college-educated. Their religious, cultural, and educational backgrounds often explained their deep interest in schooling. Concerning religion and culture, many were ministers or pious laymen and a disproportionate number were Calvinists, either Congregationalists or Presbyterians. And most had either been raised as Congregationalists in New England or as Presbyterians in the Mid-Atlantic states or Virginia. Regarding education, the majority who attended college graduated from Calvinist colleges in the East, like Yale and Dartmouth, or Calvinist-influenced institutions in the West like Miami (Ohio), Indiana, and Jefferson College (Pennsylvania). Though these Western institutions were often non-denominational, they operated under Calvinist and Common Sense principles, since they were led and staffed by men who had received their training at Calvinist colleges. Their education, as well as their religious and cultural heritage, is a vital part of this story, for it will become clear that the ideals and practices of the first schools owed a great deal to the influence of Calvin, Reid, Witherspoon, Dwight and the other reformed thinkers.[33]

Part II

A False Start, 1819-1835

Ephraim Cutler

Caleb Atwater

Joseph Duncan

Old Governor's Mansion

Chapter 5

Yankee Leadership — The First Group of Zealots

*F*our Calvinists took the lead during the first phase of America's attempts to provide education for all children. All four had been influenced by Common Sense, while three were Yankees, a people who exhibited very distinctive cultural traits. Most of the activists who would later follow these leaders shared their ideology and ethnicity. So, just as it was important to examine Common Sense thought in order to understand the philosophical foundations of the movement, it is necessary to study Puritan traditions in order to appreciate the unmistakable Yankee cultural influences on the first schools.

In the 17th century New England literally became "new" England almost overnight. Between 1629 and 1640, 21,000 Puritans, seeking freedom from the religious persecution imposed by the King of England, Charles I, and carried out by the Archbishop of Canterbury, William Laud, immigrated to the newly-established colonies of Massachusetts Bay, Plymouth, Connecticut, and New Haven. While economic depression and disease drove some to emigrate, it is a telling fact that the outflow halted abruptly in 1640 as prospects for the dissenters improved during the English Civil War. New England would not experience a comparable migration until the Irish Diaspora began in the 1830's. Sixty percent of the migrants to Massachusetts Bay, as well as many of the pioneers in its neighboring colonies, came from East Anglia and many of the settlers who left from other parts of England had roots there. So not surprisingly, New England's culture looked a lot like East Anglia's, most notably with respect to religion. Puritanism was far stronger in East Anglia than any other part of England and it had insinuated itself into almost every aspect of personal, family, and community life. Its firm commitment to norms decreed in the King James Bible led to remarkable similarities among far flung communities, not only in marriage, work, and government, but even in some of life's more mundane details. For example, the standard size for a barrel of beer was determined from a passage in the Old Testament. In this respect life in New England was not unlike that of Luther's Germany, Calvin's Geneva, or Knox's Scotland.[1]

Of course, it was the Puritans' theological beliefs that set them apart from other Christians and that have made such an important impact on American thinking, even to this day. At the Sermon on the Mount Christ told his followers, "You are the light of the world. A city on a hill cannot be hidden (Matt. 5:14)." Puritans understood this imagery to mean that their lives were to be exemplary, thereby attracting others to the faith. This verse became so ubiquitous that East Anglians had turned it into a cliché, so it then was quite natural for Gov. John Winthrop to invoke it in his famous sermon to Massachusetts Bay colonizers in 1630. The city on a hill metaphor would echo down through the centuries and help give rise to American Exceptionalism, the controversial idea that the United States has a unique, and perhaps even a providential role in world history. When this concept was combined with the postmillennialist desire to bring on the Second Coming, it produced an impatient people who tended to be very committed to their cause. In their spiritual economy earthly actions literally had eternal consequences.[2]

Their views on childhood and discipline would have an important impact on America's first schools. Tainted by original sin, children were predisposed to evil, and their willfulness had to be checked. But while they were closely monitored for those tendencies in the home, they also received plenty of love and affection there. Contrary to our popular conceptions about the Puritans, parents rarely used physical discipline. In fact, older children were often "sent out" or "put out" to relatives or other families because parents feared that their love might lead to neglect of the child's discipline. Nonetheless, parents retained an unusual level of control over their children lives, even extending to such crucial decisions as the choice of a mate later in life. This concept also applied in the classroom so that the teacher or tutor, acting in the place of the parents, could demand absolute obedience, though some children rebelled against this system.[3]

Community was also very important to the Puritans, who in some ways saw themselves as the spiritual descendants of the Jewish nations of antiquity. They were party to a covenant with God, and individual transgressions against that contract, even if committed by a non-believer, could soon bring judgment down on everyone. As a consequence, they placed great reliance on government to promote group unity and order. For example, all residents, even single persons, were required to live in families, which were regularly inspected by town officials. Paradoxically, even as Puritans employed such blatant coercion, they also nurtured voluntary cooperation with a tradition of representative democracy and in some matters the direct democracy of town meetings. They encouraged the community's confidence in government by reducing arbitrary legal decisions and by recording fundamental laws in written town charters, a practice that paralleled their habit of seeking spiritual guidance from a sacred text. Policies like these help explain the willingness of the school founders to sacrifice local autonomy for the interests of the larger community and to favor formal legislation over informal practices.[4]

Intellectual engagement was another hallmark of adult Puritan life, as it had been for Luther, Calvin, and Knox, and it produced very high rates of literacy. For generations East Anglians had employed skills in logic and rhetoric, acquired at the university, to battle the King and the Church of England through the press and the legislature, while across the Atlantic New Englanders used those same weapons to defend the rights of their fragile colonies. And as in other aspects of their culture, religion and theology drove this interest in the life of the mind. Like Luther, they were committed to deep reflection on the Bible's application to their lives, so they built institutions that fostered the research, teaching, and communication of spiritual ideas. And similar to Luther, they were especially concerned with the training of the clergy, so they sent many of their young men for advanced study: in East Anglia to Cambridge, in Massachusetts to Harvard.[5]

But like Luther, Calvin, and Knox, the Puritans emphasized the instruction of youth so that they could read and comprehend the Bible. They hoped this would lead children to first accept salvation and then develop a Christian moral character. While families held the primary responsibility for this, Puritans also established schools, which used a narrow curriculum that included the memorization of prayers, scriptures, and catechism questions. Except for the poor, parents had to pay tuition, though the local community and Christian philanthropists, including businessmen, usually provided some additional funding. While several schools had been started in the 1630s and 1640s in New England, the lack of educational opportunity for many children led the Puritans to turn to government for a solution. By 1650 Massachusetts and Connecticut had passed laws mandating parental involvement in the home and community commitment through the school. Finally, a scant fifty years after the Pilgrims had first landed at Plymouth, every colony in New England except for Rhode Island had passed similar legislation. Unfortunately, as later generations of school reformers would discover, the existence of a law hardly guarantees its execution. Clearly, education fared much better in New England than in any other region of British North America, but even in Massachusetts and Connecticut, those pioneers in education, there were many towns that did not follow these first laws. In fact, progress was so slow that Yankee towns would not fully embrace community-wide learning until well into the 18th century.[6]

Meanwhile, the spirit of Puritanism remained alive, though it alternated between periods of enthusiasm and indifference. After weakening in the late-17th and early-18th centuries it was rejuvenated during the Great Awakening of the 1730s and 1740s, only to fall into decline again during the Revolutionary Era. But even when confronted by the challenges of Unitarianism and skepticism during the Revolution, Puritan ideals refused to die. Like the effect of a fresh breeze on a dying fire, the winds of revivalism would soon breathe new life into their culture, with important implications for the entire nation. And nowhere would they be felt more than in the Old Northwest.[7]

The trend of westward migration that had so disturbed Manasseh Cutler in 1783 was accelerating during the first decades of the 19th century. Like migrants everywhere Yankees hoped to settle in a familiar climate, so they moved west along lines of latitude and settled in the northern part of the region rather than in southern Ohio, Indiana, and Illinois, with some important exceptions. Keeping true to their culture, entire communities relocated west, as had the family and friends of Cutler in 1788. They moved for political, economic, religious, and cultural reasons. First, the Old Northwest seemed to hold the future of the country, so they hoped that their presence there would grow their political influence. Further, like most other migrants at the time, they were attracted by the economic appeal of cheap land. But by far their most compelling reasons were religious and cultural, a point that is underscored by the fact that they often took a minister with them. These faithful descendants of the Puritans felt they were called to serve as a city on a hill, winning the lost to Christ, leavening the culture with Christianity, and preparing the foundation for the millennial New Jerusalem.[8]

By all accounts, their efforts were very successful. Though they represented just a fraction of the population of the Old Northwest, they provided a disproportionate share of the leadership that would transform the region into a locus of political, economic, and cultural power by mid-century. Their church insinuated itself into the workings of the town and the school, thereby fostering unity and promoting a sense of responsibility for community needs. This in turn strengthened the transplanted Yankees in their many battles for temperance, abolition, women's rights, and, of most significance for this story, education. The timing of their migration could hardly have been better, for political power was surging in the West even as it was declining in New England, which provided them with a national stage for their ambitious program of reform.[9]

At the same time that Yankees were determined to find homes for themselves in the physical world, evangelicals were resolved to claim souls for Jesus in the spiritual. In what was destined to become the most powerful religious movement since the Reformation, the Second Great Awakening began in the 1790s in New England. Though its onset is often associated with the Cane Ridge camp meeting in 1801, it actually began in Connecticut and included Timothy Dwight's early efforts to stamp out skepticism at Yale. By the time it had reached its peak at mid-century the nation's clergymen had tripled, its church membership had doubled, and an estimated 40% of Americans held evangelical beliefs. The implications of this movement for education were enormous. The primary goals of the Second Great Awakening were similar to its 18th-century predecessor: an act of faith that led to a sinner's salvation, which resulted in his desire to live according to Christian principles. Evangelists and their disciples hoped to achieve these objectives through public preaching and private prayer, supported by the Bible. In addition to seeking individual renewal, they also worked feverishly for the improvement of society. This secondary objective was driven by their concern for the community's compliance with God's law, the protection that would produce, and their belief that evangelism and reform would hasten Christ's return. Mass reform efforts, if infused with a Christian message, appeared to be an excellent way to accomplish both goals.[10]

While Calvinists in New England may have started the Awakening, they soon realized that they were lagging far behind two other evangelical sects. The Methodists, though they had been discredited by their association with the British, grew quickly after the War under the guidance of John Wesley and Francis Asbury. Asbury would work tirelessly over forty years in the Methodist cause, traveling over 300,000 miles and crossing the Appalachians sixty times while visiting ten states, and all of it by horseback! Eagerly following Asbury's example, Methodist preachers became known for the long "circuits" that they traveled to take the gospel into the backcountry. From just fifty congregations and ten thousand members in the Revolutionary Era they had become the largest denomination in the country by the Civil War with 20,000 churches and over one million members. The Baptists also displayed much faster growth than the Congregationalists and Presbyterians during the same time period.[11]

Though the Congregationalists and Presbyterians would never catch up with the Methodists and Baptists, they had taken a key step near the beginning of the Awakening to try to become more competitive. In 1801 they created the Plan of Union, an agreement that the two denominations initiated in Connecticut, which soon spread to every state in New England except Rhode Island. Essentially, the two sects combined their efforts by accepting ministers and congregants from each denomination as co-religionists. Since their competitors on the frontier outnumbered them, this arrangement made them more powerful and efficient because it combined their resources. Then, in the 1820s New Haven Theology began spreading through both denominations. This development made them more appealing to the pioneers, since it softened pre-destination and depravity, two doctrines that were often potential stumbling blocks for potential converts.[12]

So just as the Awakening was unfolding in the West, these innovations allowed the Yankees to use many of the same methods as the Methodists and Baptists, the most successful of which was the camp meeting. These spectacles drew thousands of sinners and believers alike from great distances, usually to a large forest clearing, where several preachers conducted wildly emotional services that could last for days. Meetings were ecumenical, as they included most Protestant sects, and democratic, since they welcomed male and female, white and black, rich and poor. Asbury, who was an enthusiastic promoter of the events, claimed that between three and four million people—more than one-third of the nation's population—attended them in 1811. By 1820 one thousand such meetings were being held annually. Revivals also broke out in urban areas, though they came a little later, occurred less frequently, and elicited less emotion than camp meetings. It is estimated that these spiritual assemblies reached at least one-quarter of the US population, testifying to their unqualified success.[13]

But as evangelicals surged toward their first goal, the salvation and renewal of the individual, they were accelerating their quest for the second, the societal reform of the nation. These efforts evolved out of early steps to evangelize the Indians, such as Jonathon Edwards' work in Stockbridge, Massachusetts in 1750. While missionary outreach was organized by denomination, later entities that focused on other needs were nondenominational, which permitted people from diverse theological backgrounds to unite behind a common cause. Those associations, which collectively became known as the Benevolent Empire, were built on the philanthropic traditions and ideas of Hutcheson, Edwards, Dwight, and Taylor. The largest included the American Board of Commissioners for Foreign Missions (1810), American Education Society (1815), American Bible Society (1816), American Sunday School Union (1824), American Tract Society (1825), American Home Missionary Society (1826), and American Society for Promotion of Temperance (1826). They would become so successful that they would transform all of American culture and society, though their impact would be especially felt in the West. They also became a model of social cooperation for later secular institutions, since they brought together leaders and members from diverse backgrounds and because they scheduled their meetings to maximize communication and synergy.[14]

The Benevolent Empire generated an explosion of faith-based publishing that was at least partly responsible for the emergence of the nation's first mass media. Certainly, new transportation networks and improved print technology helped book and periodical publication increase five-fold from 1825 to 1850, but much of the surge was due to its Christian content. Literary forms included Bibles, doctrinal tracts, and educational materials, aggressively distributed by the American Bible Society (ABS), the American Tract Society (ATS), and the American Sunday School Union (ASSU). By 1830 the ABS was printing 300,000 bibles a year and was probably the largest publisher in the nation. By 1850 the ATS had visited a half-million families, sold a half-million books, and given away 35,000,000 pages of books and tracts. In addition, every sect owned a publishing house and every major trade publisher had a close relationship with a denomination. And of course, textbook publishing, famous for the ubiquitous and iconic *McGuffey Readers*, was heavily influenced by evangelicals. All of this represented a massive and unprecedented effort to influence the American mind.[15]

Evangelicals also strove to influence the nation's thinking through its leaders. Building on their long-standing commitment to higher education, Congregationalists and Presbyterians began to open colleges in the West. They were so successful that by mid-century they were operating thirty-nine colleges, including Lafayette in Pennsylvania, Western Reserve in Ohio, Beloit in Wisconsin, and Grinnell in Iowa. The Methodists and Baptists, perhaps driven by a spirit of competition, each started fifteen colleges in the same time period. In total, Protestants were operating 88 of the nation's 113 colleges by 1848. Though they were controlled by the denominations, their character was nonsectarian, which attracted students from across the spectrum of Protestantism and helped to unify their students behind shared ideals. Scottish Common Sense Realism underlay most of the curriculum, which guaranteed that the values of the Reformation, not the Enlightenment, would be taught to several generations of American elites.[16]

Many of those leaders were destined to become pastors to the growing numbers of evangelicals. This greatly multiplied the influence of the evangelical sects, since the sermon was such a powerful tool of communication in this era. Historian Mark Noll has shown that Americans in 1840 were six times more likely to hear a sermon than to read a newspaper or letter. As a result, observers such as de Toqueville have noted the ubiquity of Christianity. In fact, a few historians have even argued that evangelicals created a de facto established church, which would represent an ironic turn of events since the last official state religions disappeared in the early part of this period. So, the inescapable effect of the revivals, the associations, the publications, the colleges, and the sermons was to make Christianity the key historical factor in this era of American history.[17]

The Second Great Awakening was so critical in the movement to create public schools because it united so many diverse people behind causes that were driven by similar motivations. At times it united Yankee Calvinists, well-educated elites of the middle and upper classes, with Methodists and Baptists, poorly-educated populists of the lower classes. So, just as evangelicals joined together on other causes, they did likewise for education. Indeed, the argument for the public school lay in its original name, the common school, for it was hoped that the entire rising generation would learn together, absorbing community norms about religion, morality, and civic responsibility. Unfortunately, the powerful forces of unity inspired by the Awakening would not be felt within the movement until the 1830s. So, at the onset of reform in the early 1820s, the most important factor proved to be the determination of a few lonely leaders and, at least in Ohio, that heavy responsibility fell to three sons of New England.[18]

Ohio

The three men responsible for Ohio's first significant public school law had much in common. Born in Massachusetts, they were all descendants of Puritans who settled in New England prior to 1650. Two had been raised under the "putting out" system. Two were Presbyterians, one was a minister, and the other a minister's son who was an active layman. Two graduated from Congregational colleges, taught briefly, then practiced law, and finally devoted a great deal of their lives publishing. But perhaps the most significant characteristic that they shared was their zealotry for education.

The first of the three to immigrate to Ohio, Ephraim Cutler, was sent by his father, Manasseh, to live with his grandfather, Hezekiah, and grandmother, Susanna, on their Connecticut farm when he was three. The little boy was likely placed with them for two reasons: to build his character under the putting out system and to comfort his grandparents over the loss of their son and Ephraim's namesake, who had died in that tragic fall from a horse four years earlier. A bright boy, before his seventh birthday he had memorized the Congregational catechism and had read most of the Bible to Susanna, who he would later describe as "a most excellent woman, strict in her government, but always kind." She died that year, but it is likely that he continued his studies under the direction of the pious Hezekiah. Later, the economic turmoil caused by the Revolution forced him to run the farm for his sickly grandfather, preventing him from attending college, but he followed the advice of a local pastor to study on his own. The love for learning that this developed would later find an outlet in his work for public education.[19]

Ephraim's work ethic and intelligence served him well in 1794 when he, like so many of his neighbors, followed his brother Jervis to

Ohio because of New England's challenges and the Northwest Territory's promise. He quickly established himself as one of its leading citizens, as he received appointments as captain of the militia, justice of the peace, and judge of the Court of Common Pleas. His attainment of these posts probably reflected in part his father's influence, but it also recognized his accomplishments in Connecticut, where he had served in the militia as an ensign, in the justice system as a constable, and in several other community positions. In those days, a military or law enforcement background was very advantageous if you hoped to enter politics one day, which appears to have been part of his well-laid plan. Judge Cutler's time came in September 1801 when he was elected to the last territorial legislature. His career then took a historic turn in December 1802 when he was elected as a delegate to the convention that wrote the first Ohio Constitution. He made important contributions to that document's provisions for religion, education, and antislavery, which had all been core issues for his father. Certainly, his central role at the convention qualifies him as a Founding Father of the Buckeye State.[20]

Section Three of Article VIII, the Bill of Rights, included a declaration that links religion and morality to public education, which paraphrased his father Manasseh's contribution to the Northwest Ordinance. Meanwhile, Section Twenty Six affirmed that the new state would continue its financial support for religion: "the Legislature. . .shall secure to each and every denomination of religious societies. . .according to their number of adherents of the profits arising from the land granted by Congress, for the support of religion." So just as lot 16 in each township was set aside to support schools, lot 29 would continue to aid religion, as it had in the Ohio Company and Symmes purchases. It must have pleased Ephraim, who had felt the effects of inadequate income in a minister's family, since Ohio's ministers would not have to rely solely on their congregations.[21]

Section Three faced no challenge, but Section Two, which outlawed slavery, had many opponents and, if the account of Cutler's admiring granddaughter is to be believed, that included President Jefferson. His party, the Republicans, controlled twenty-six of the thirty-five seats at the convention, while Cutler's party, the Federalists, held only seven. He fought a difficult battle to defend Section

Two, both in committee and before the full Convention. The family tells a story that he was so sick that he had to be carried to the final debate in a bed. Somehow, he made it to the hall and convinced one man to switch his vote, which decided the issue. He later observed, "Thus an overruling Providence, by His wisdom, makes use of the weak often to defeat the purposes of the wise and great of this world, and to His name be the glory and praise."[22]

While slavery was not an ongoing concern of Cutler's, religion and education attracted his attention throughout his life. Given that Yankee parents were deeply involved in their adult children's lives, Manasseh probably gave him guidance on these issues until his death in 1823. In any event, Ephraim was clearly a man of deep faith, which led him to serve as an elder in his local church, to teach in a Sunday school, and in his early seventies to sit as a delegate at the Presbyterian General Assembly. The denomination struggled with controversy during his tenure, eventually dissolving the Plan of Union with the Congregationalists, a development that he deeply regretted.[23]

Cutler's involvement with public education began in 1800 when he was appointed by the territorial legislature as one of seven commissioners entrusted with managing lot 16 and 29 monies for the support of schools and religion. In 1801 he set up one of the first schools in Washington County in his home and nine years later, while living in nearby Athens, Ohio, he started another. Over the years Cutler hired two brothers and a cousin as teachers at these schools. And, in a gesture that reflected his interest in self-study, he helped found the first library in the West. Meanwhile, Section Three's education mandate was followed by sixteen years of inaction, but he never despaired. Beginning in 1819 six years of hard, discouraging work would lead to Ohio's first general laws on education, which was his greatest contribution to the movement. Had Ephraim's father been alive he would have been very proud that his son was helping to make his dream a reality.[24]

Caleb Atwater, the second of Ohio's school founders to migrate to Ohio, possessed similar qualities. Regrettably, we know little of his childhood except that he was born in North Adams, Massachusetts to a descendant of one of the Puritan founders of New Haven,

Connecticut. After his mother died when he was five he was sent out to be raised in the home of a neighbor. As a young adult, religion, education, and economic deprivation developed into important influences on his life. After graduation from Williams College in 1804, Atwater moved to New York City, where he ran a private school for young women while studying theology. He soon was ordained as a Presbyterian minister, but several crises would set his life on a very different path. First, his wife died only one year into their marriage and soon thereafter his own health began to suffer. He then abandoned the ministry, studied the law, and gained admission to the New York bar, but when his new practice struggled he left for Ohio.[25]

Settling in Circleville in 1815, Atwater started another law practice, but it ended in 1821 when he was elected to the Ohio House on a platform supporting education reform and internal improvements. Over the next two decades he devoted himself to the intense pursuit of publishing, politics, education, history, and archeology. He spent such large amounts of time and money on these passions that he was frequently struggling financially. In fact, his life in Ohio can be seen as one long negotiation between his need for economic survival, his concern for others, and his reckless self-indulgence. Biographers reviewing Atwater's letters and other writings have described him as "aggressive" and "eccentric" and these qualities certainly hurt him in both politics and publishing. In politics, he could be intemperate with his opponents, at times leveling unsubstantiated charges that damaged his reputation. His party affiliations were so unstable that he lurched from ardent support for the populist Democrats in the 1820s to staunch defense of the elitist Whigs by the 1840s. It is little wonder then that his frequent attempts to get government jobs were almost always unsuccessful. In publishing, these character flaws also limited his success. Critics charged that his writing was inaccurate and, perhaps as a consequence, his works never produced much income.[26]

Although money was always a problem for Atwater it never seemed to keep him from spending it on things dear to his heart. First, during the drive for state school support in the 1820s he spent a lot of his own funds sending out promotional pamphlets and letters, a practice that would be repeated by many later reformers. Similarly, since the Indian burial mounds that inspired Circleville's name fascinated him, he would spend large sums of money throughout his life acquiring native artifacts. Finally, his interests moved him to write and publish three books: *The Writings of Caleb Atwater* (1833), which discussed Indian artifacts and a trip to a Wisconsin reservation, *A History of the State of Ohio, Natural and Civil* (1838), Ohio's first history, and *An Essay on Education* (1841), which expounds on school philosophy, curriculum, and pedagogy. The last work provides us with a rare insight into the thinking of one of the founding zealots.[27]

Atwater begins *An Essay* by laying out his theory of education, which reflects his Presbyterian background and Common Sense training. First, since humans have three dimensions—physical, mental, and moral—education must develop each. And because children are dependent on God, their parents, and their friends, they must be taught their religious, familial, and social duties. But since "man. . .is a fallen being. . .to a state of moral degradation, beneath even the vilest animal of this lower creation" moral instruction, grounded in God's Word, the Bible, must take precedence over physical and "mental" or intellectual training. In fact, like many of the crusaders, Atwater worries that "the greatest and most prominent defect in our system is the universal preference of mental over moral excellence." So for Atwater then, the ultimate goal is not preparation of the student for this world but for the next. To that end, the emerging common school is important but so too is the Sunday sermon and the Sunday school.[28]

Atwater goes on to critique other elements of education at length. First, he opposes rote memorization and pushes for vocal music, two fairly progressive ideas that for the most part were not adopted during his long life. Further, he criticizes the quality of textbooks in some detail, while extolling the sufficiency of the Bible. While it is not possible to say whether he would have been happy with later changes in other texts, the Bible would remain a classroom staple. And in a belief that dovetails with his concern for moral education, he holds that the personal character of the teacher is an important qualification, a position that was almost universal among leaders of his era. Finally, he ridicules widespread misogynist attitudes that denigrated the learning abilities of girls, and recommends that their instruction be identical to that of boys, something that would be realized, at least in elementary schools, if not in higher levels of education.[29]

But his many failures in law, politics, and publishing had turned him bitter and fearful by the late 1830s. For example, in the introduction to *A History* he complains that "great efforts have been made, are making, and will be made to pull from beneath it, all the main pillars, on which our temple of liberty rests," in a reference to concerns about freedom of speech and the press. By the mid-1840s he was content to completely withdraw to private life, surrounded by his books and his artifacts. He died in 1867, impoverished and forgotten. The failures that marked so much of his life render his achievements during the first phase of school reform that much more remarkable.[30]

While Atwater was the last of the zealots to die, the last to be born was Nathan Guilford, which availed him of better schooling options than his fellow Ohio reformers. He was born three years after the end of the Revolution and its economic and political turmoil had stabilized by the early 1790s. As a result, he was able to attend the district school in the fall and winter, seasons when he was not needed on the family farm in Worcester County, Massachusetts. His typical Yankee education continued under Dwight at Yale from 1808 to 1812. Though his own religious beliefs would stray far from the Puritan ideals of his community school and a Congregational college in the midst of revival, he gained valuable insights into the thinking of his more orthodox fellow students and faculty, which helped make his later work that much more effective.[31]

Following graduation in 1812 Guilford would plunge into education, law, publishing, and politics, experiences that would shape his life over the next four decades. This career path was typical for young professional men like himself and Atwater. First, he ran a school for a short time, but soon began studying the law under an attorney and passed the bar exam. In 1814 he moved to Kentucky, where he continued to teach while running law offices in brief succession in three different cities. In Georgetown he practiced law with Amos Kendall, an association that seems to have had a great influence on later career decisions. Kendall was destined to become a newspaper publisher, US Postmaster, and a very influential supporter of the Jackson and Van Buren administrations. When Kendall withdrew from the practice to devote more time to his publishing and political interests in 1816, Guilford moved to Cincinnati and opened a new law office. Interestingly, Guilford's life soon took an identical turn to Kendall's, as he reduced his legal work when he entered publishing in 1818 and politics in 1821.[32]

Guilford used his interests in publishing and politics to advance his commitment to universal schooling. *Solomon Thrifty's Almanac*, published from 1818 to 1825, primarily contained information on weather, soils, crops, and astronomy to inform farmers and scientists, yet it made room on every page for the promotion of public education. This venture initiated a lifetime of publishing that would see the production of at least two popular textbooks, *The Western Spelling Book* (1831) and *The Juvenile Arithmetic* (1836), and a Whig newspaper, the *Cincinnati Daily Atlas* (1843-1847). Like his publishing work, Guilford's political involvement regularly focused on education. An early biographer aptly labeled him as a "zealous advocate" for reform, and that description was borne out by his immersion in local and state school issues for over four decades. Like his fellow zealots, his most important contribution to the movement was his role in passing Ohio's historic legislation in the 1820s, but he would continue to be engaged in those issues until the year of his death.[33]

It is surprising that Guilford was able to navigate the political world as easily as he did for so many years, given his religious background. His Unitarian and deist beliefs made him at best an outsider and at worst a heretic to the evangelicals who dominated the reform movement. Perhaps his identity as a Yankee, his exposure to Calvinists through his education, and his commitment to republicanism created a bond with the religiously conservative Presbyterians with whom he collaborated. Despite this, his unorthodox religious convictions would eventually cost him an important leadership post.[34]

In one sense the fierce advocacy that Guilford and other zealots had for free schools was also unorthodox, since it was rarely the primary issue for most of their contemporaries. So, since successful politicians forge coalitions while moral crusaders cling to principle, the reformers in Ohio, as elsewhere, often tacked uncomfortably between compromise and intransigence. In 1822 Guilford chose intransigence and his gambit proved quite effective. As a member of a committee charged with creating a state school system, Guilford objected to the majority report because it failed to provide for sufficient taxes. So, at his own expense he distributed "A Letter on Free Education," essentially his own minority report, which passionately argued for a tax on property values. Just as Atwater's *An Essay* provides insight into the philosophy and planning for early schools, Guilford's "A Letter" helps us understand their justification.[35]

Appealing to every Ohioan's sense of community, he argues that "public intelligence and public morals ought to be the peculiar care of every Republic, and as every man is interested. . .in the political safety, good morals, good order, intelligence, and social happiness of the community of which he is a member, he ought to contribute freely to their promotion and support." Then he sets his sights squarely on "the Legislature [which]. . .has an unquestioned right to compel every individual, by a tax, to bear his proportionable [sic] share of the expense." And since the land grants were proving inadequate he argues, "it becomes the duty of the Legislature to. . .make such provision that every child of the Republic, whether rich or poor, should have an opportunity of receiving a common, decent education." For the three decades to come Guilford would do his best to turn that hope into a reality for Ohio's children.[36]

Illinois

Only Illinois would make legislative progress comparable to that of Ohio in the 1820s. This is quite surprising since migration patterns left the Prairie State with few Yankees, who loved schools, and many Appalachians, who cherished autonomy, limited government, and low taxes. As a consequence, the cause of education there found little support among its people and few advocates among its leaders. In fact, Illinois was the only state in the Old Northwest that failed to mention education in its first constitution.[37]

But Illinois did have Joseph Duncan, who was the main champion of his state's progressive law of 1825. Duncan was similar to Guilford in two ways: he was neither college-educated nor descended from Puritans; but he was dissimilar in that he was a devout, lifelong Calvinist. He also differed from all three Ohio zealots in another way; he never risked his health or wealth for the cause, though he was certainly devoted to it through much of his life. We know little of Duncan's childhood but his family offers some solid clues about his adult interests. His father, also named Joseph, was a major in the Continental Army who had migrated with his wife from Virginia to the Bluegrass Region of Kentucky (interestingly enough, to Paris, not far from Cane Ridge). While his own educational attainment is unknown, it is clear from his brothers' that schooling and Calvinism were accorded a high degree of respect in the Duncan home. Three of the boys graduated from colleges run by Calvinists: James and Thomas from Transylvania in Lexington and Matthew from Yale, while John attended Rush Medical College.[38]

But seventeen-year-old Joseph went off to war instead, enlisting as a private in 1812. While veterans in this era sometimes embellished accounts of heroism to enhance their political resumes, by any measure he exhibited great courage while surviving two harrowing experiences. In the first, while carrying Army dispatches by himself through dangerous country, he narrowly escaped capture by Indians. In the second, he was part of a force of 150 Americans that defended Fort Stephenson (located in present-day Fremont, Ohio) against 3,000 British and Indian troops that were supported by cannons and gunboats. They survived a forty-hour bombardment and a sustained attack on the fort, winning a battle that was a turning point in the War. Superiors promoted Duncan three times, elevating him from private to 1st lieutenant, and two decades later Congress would present him with a ceremonial sword for his bravery at Fort Stephenson.[39]

Like many of the young veterans of the War, Duncan liked what he saw of Illinois and moved there in 1818, quickly buying land in various parts of the new and rapidly-growing state. His military experience and reputation helped him earn a commission as a major general in the Illinois militia in 1823 and he would later serve it as a brigadier general during the Black Hawk War in 1831-1832, though he would see no action. Duncan's military service helped launch a very successful political career, which saw him serve as justice of the peace from 1821 to 1823, state senator from 1824 to 1826, US congressman from 1826 to 1834, and governor from 1834 to 1838. He won some big victories along the way, including his defeat in 1826 of Daniel Pope Cook, a respected member of a powerful political dynasty. Duncan's election as governor in 1834 came by a huge 22% margin of victory over his nearest rival.[40]

But Duncan's biggest political success would prove to be the 1825 school bill, which was surprisingly strong legislation given the tepid support for education in Illinois at the time. He would not experience a victory like that again for his state's children, though whenever possible he tried to use his power to further the cause. For example, after his return to state government in 1834 he pushed the legislature once again to support education, but he could make no headway in a hostile economic environment. But while Duncan's dedication to the cause is clear from his public record, his personal motives are not nearly as obvious as the Ohio zealots. In fact, of the four leaders in the movement's first phase he had the least religious zeal, since his life left no trace of radical action produced by religious conviction. According to his daughter, he spoke little about his spiritual beliefs, yet for most of his adult life he was a Presbyterian and he was active in the community life of Jacksonville, a key outpost of Yankee influence and a center for Calvinist religion and reform. Significantly, he served for fourteen years as a trustee at Illinois College and became a good friend of Rev. Edward Beecher, the college's president and son of the famous evangelical leader, Rev. Lyman Beecher.[41]

Perhaps the best indication of Duncan's sentiments can be found in his farewell message to the legislature in 1838, which was a testament to his core political and moral philosophies. First, addressing three current issues, he warns about political patronage, advocates for internal improvements, and argues for a strong militia. Then, he pleads with lawmakers to provide assistance to schools and colleges because "they are the corner-stones [sic] of our free government. Education is the foundation of every enjoyment of man in this world and of blessings in the world to come." Finally, he concludes his list of priorities with an impassioned plea for legislation to eliminate the "degrading and most alarming vice" of intemperance. So his speech highlights two of the main issues for the reformers, education and temperance. Like a true zealot Duncan concludes by crediting "divine Providence" for the state's good fortune and by advising the legislators to "invoke the blessings of God, who holds the destiny of the world in His almighty hand, and who has said that nothing shall prosper that does not acknowledge Him as its author." While crusaders like Duncan explicitly recognized the divine author of history, they first had to overcome earthly circumstances that seemed to be conspiring against their clear vision of a brighter tomorrow. Fortunately for them, in the early 1820s a window of opportunity finally opened and they were quick to capitalize on it.[42]

Chapter 6

Two Steps Forward, One Step Back — Ohio and Illinois

*T*he black smoke crawled lazily up the tall chimney and escaped slowly over a nearby ridge, leaving behind the charred remains of the legacy that had been stolen from Kentucky's children. The haze could be traced back to a small stack of blackened parchment in the still-warm, oversized fireplace of the Governor's mansion in Frankfort. A few unburned fragments remained; one revealing in elegant script *Commonwealth of Kentucky*, another exposing in neat handwriting *$100,000* above a pre-printed line. The fire had resulted from an act of the Kentucky legislature, more specifically, Chapter 264, Section 4, of the Kentucky Acts for 1845, which read:

> That it shall be the duty of the board of education and commissioners of the sinking fund, to surrender to the governor of the state bonds held by them respectively; and it shall be the duty of the governor, upon the receipt of said bonds, to cause the same to be cancelled and destroyed, by burning, in the presence of the second auditor and treasurer.[1]

Those officials obligingly stood by as $917,550 that had been set aside for the instruction of many generations was reduced to ashes in a few short moments. While it is true that the same statute that authorized the cancellation also stated that Kentucky had a "sacred and inviolate" obligation to the Board of Education for the amount of principal plus interest, the fact remained that an enforceable debt had been replaced by a moral claim. Sadly, this action was just one of many instances in which learning had been sacrificed for other purposes. For years the state had used school monies to fund internal improvements such as road construction and river navigation as well as to pay down debt. Unfortunately, many other states sank even lower than the Bluegrass State and drained their own funds through outright negligence and fraud. Fletcher Swift, an early historian of lot 16 monies, complained that twelve states, stretching from Massachusetts to Missouri, had "carelessly diverted, squandered, wasted, and embezzled so shamelessly" at least $28,000,000 ($716,000,000 in today's dollars) from permanent endowment funds, in what amounted to a massive betrayal of the people's trust. Two other historians have concurred with Swift's devastating assessment. In fact, long before the bond burning it had become clear that the plans of Manasseh Cutler and others for lot 16 were failing.[2]

The primary reason for the failure of the land grant funds was a lack of commitment from the pioneers. They simply lacked the will to use the resources that the Founders had envisioned and that lawmakers had provided. As would happen many other times during the long struggle for universal education, most citizens simply found other needs more pressing. An additional, related factor was the absence of centralized oversight that resulted from the principle of localism. This belief was a central feature of the laissez-faire philosophy of the Republican Party of Jefferson and Madison and the Democrat Party of Jackson, who both advocated limiting government and empowering individuals. Adherents to localism succeeded in retaining power over land grants at the district, township, or county level, which created serious conflicts of interest and thusly made them more vulnerable to negligence, waste, and fraud. There is little question that localism, when applied to school finance, failed spectacularly in Ohio, Indiana, and Illinois, the first three states that were formed from the Northwest Territory. Commenting on the Buckeye State's handling of lot 16 monies, Rev. A.D. Mayo, a chronicler of 19th century American education, found "there is no more melancholy chapter in American history than the record of the amazing waste of this great national gift to the people of Ohio." Of the $28,000,000 in total losses, $335,000 was incurred by Indiana and $613,000 by Illinois. While Ohio's losses have not been estimated, they were probably greater than those two states, since both set minimum offering prices per acre, while Ohio did not.[3]

While the leaders of reform in these states in the 1820s faced serious shortages of funding, they also confronted two other obstacles and each was also related to the land. These were not new, for they had also stood in the path of the first generation of educational planners back in the 1780s. The crusaders would make some progress on these issues at first, but their hope eventually turned to discouragement. First, Indians still possessed vast areas of the Old Northwest that were coveted by Easterners. Without property available for settlement few communities would be created and there would be little need for schools. Tragically for the Indians, they were also considered a threat to national security, so America decided upon a policy of removal, which began on a large scale after three decisive victories over the Indians and their British allies. The Battle of Fallen Timbers (1794) and William Henry Harrison's victories at the Battle of Tippecanoe (1811) and the Battle of the Thames (1813) led to treaties that opened up vast sections of Ohio and Indiana for white settlement.[4]

Second, white settlers wanted to buy property cheaply, but like the squatters of the 1780s they had limited ability to pay. So Congress slashed prices, expanded credit, and sold smaller parcels. And, hoping to facilitate this business, the government opened many new offices in the Old Northwest. While these measures boosted the land business, their impact on education was mixed. They encouraged more overall sales, which opened up more townships to settlement and thereby produced more funds, but lower unit prices produced lower land values and consequently reduced lease income from lot 16 within each township. Further, why should a pioneer rent land at all if he could simply move west and purchase it even more cheaply or, better still, squat on it at no cost? As a result, Congress' measures initially produced only modest increases in legal settlement.[5]

No one who settled on the frontier in those early years could have imagined the heights to which the real estate business would soar as a consequence of the War of 1812. Veterans had been promised land bounties by Congress and, like Washington's officers at Newburgh, they began demanding payment even before the War had ended. These young men, hoping to establish homesteads and start families, pressed for the land's rapid survey and transfer. They had dreamed of its potential during their service and were concerned that squatters might beat them to it. The veterans soon got their wish as transactions throughout the region became so hectic that they inspired the now-familiar idiom "land-office business." In Ohio alone between 1812 and 1821 the government sold 3,750,000 acres, more than any other state.[6]

Settlers rushed in, filling up much of Ohio except for its Northwest, then spilling over into Indiana and Illinois. Migration peaked in Ohio by 1820, then surged westward to crest next over Indiana and Illinois. The mad scramble pushed the population of the Old Northwest from 51,006 in 1800 to 792,719 by 1820, a fifteen-fold increase, with pioneers accounting for four-fifths of the growth. While this population boom sparked hopes for increased school attendance, it was spread over such a large area that virtually all Westerners still lived on isolated farms far removed from the nearest schoolhouse. This remained a problem for the rest of the nation as well, since 92.8% of all Americans lived outside cities, despite the increasing urbanization of the East.[7]

In the 1820s the leasing of lot 16 was still yielding minimal amounts of money, so states began to sell the plots and place their proceeds in a permanent fund. While the first such fund had been established by Connecticut in 1795 to hold the payment for its transfer of the Western Reserve, most states waited decades before establishing one. In addition to the proceeds from lot 16, monies also came from the sale of other properties, including federal tracts, which typically carried the stipulation that from 3-10% of the principal be used for learning. Unfortunately, permanent funds failed to adequately protect these resources; to the contrary, their dismal record provides still more damning evidence of a lack of commitment to the cause. First, most of these accounts failed to be truly permanent since many states did as Kentucky had done and reduced their status from a legal obligation of the state to a moral claim on the legislature, which they then invariably spent on other projects. Second, local conflicts of interest that had led to abuses when the property was being leased continued under the new policy.[8]

In the 1830s low prices produced a huge spike in sales, aided by the Pre-emption Acts of 1830, 1832, and 1834, which allowed squatters to buy up to 160 acres at bargain rates. The income to the federal treasury was so great, in fact, that it produced a surplus of over $37,000,000. In 1837 Congress directed that $28,000,000 of it be distributed to the states. Almost two-thirds of them directed at least a portion of their windfall into education and many of those intended to preserve it in a fund. Once again, the states abandoned their initial commitment and treated these funds much as they had handled land grants. Most of this money never found its way into the schools; instead, it was soon diverted to towns, counties, or states for investment in banks, canals, or railroads or to service debt or balance budgets strained by those same ill-conceived investments.[9]

Ohio's experience illustrates all these points, which is surprising given the enthusiasm with which the state had originally embraced the concept of land grants. Like the land grants of the late 1780s, the federal legislation that provided for statehood had offered lot 16 in the Congressional lands that lay within Ohio's borders. Then, at the Constitutional Convention Ephraim Cutler and others had expanded that grant to include tracts in the US Military District, the Virginia Military District, the Western Reserve, and any territory that would be acquired from the Indians. But during Ohio's first decade it became obvious that revenues from leasing this land would be negligible and all too often blatant conflicts of interest were to blame. Even though property values steadily appreciated, revenue at times was only one-tenth what it should have been because local officials or legislators granted lessees terms that were far too generous. In fact, these practices drove lease income so low that from 1815 to 1829 lot 16 payments to the schools had to be halted entirely. The subsequent sale of these plots and the establishment of a permanent fund in 1827 failed to remedy the problem. Localism led to such abuse that a state official would later report, "school land has been taken at six dollars per acre worth at the time fifty dollars. School lands have been sold at less than one dollar and in some cases at less than fifty cents [per acre]." Unfortunately, the records of Indiana and Illinois with respect to their land grants were just as dismal.[10]

For the states east of the Mississippi a severe economic downturn in 1837 wrote the closing chapter on the importance of land sales to the economy, and by extension, to the school movement. The massive transfer of territory from Indian and government possession into private hands was now virtually complete. Yet the end of the sales boom had little immediate impact on the reformers, who had realized two decades earlier that real estate would never solve their funding problem. At that time they had learned a second sobering lesson: that wild swings in the economy could have dramatic repercussions for school reform. For just as the rush for real estate in the 1830s had led to an economic reversal, the dash for property in the 1810s contributed to a decline that is known as the Panic of 1819. As was typical in those days, specie was scarce, so many banks, including many that had just recently opened, issued notes whose value was questionable since it was backed by few hard currency reserves. This sharp increase in the supply of money, mixed with the public's lust for property, raised land and crop prices to unsustainable levels.[11]

This paper paradise began its inevitable collapse with the end of the Napoleonic Wars in Europe. The return of millions of veterans to their farms led to a surge in agricultural production, which caused crop prices to plunge throughout the western world. This produced a cascade of effects: banks called in loans and foreclosed on delinquent farmers, who lacked the specie to make payments. Most people blamed this disaster on the banks and they took out their anger on the industry's political friends, including former Federalists, like Ephraim Cutler, who were also public education's biggest champions. This put a temporary roadblock in the path of the movement because these conservative politicians, who distrusted the masses, were also sailing against a rising tide of democracy and populism. As a result, since they failed to enjoy the support of a majority of the people they would have to rely on persistence and cunning if they were to prevail. Later reformers would find themselves in a similar position and would need to employ equally impressive political skills if they were to advance the cause.[12]

The sporadic successes that the leaders enjoyed outlined a drama that would repeat itself during each of three distinct phases of school improvement over the next forty years. In each stage a handful of activists—zealots, if you will—overcame obstacles and exploited temporary weaknesses in their opponents to secure a soaring victory. But apparent success was all too soon followed by a partial setback, preparing the scene for the next stage, to be acted out by the next generation of crusaders. Throughout this long struggle, conflict would develop along ethnic and religious fault lines, with Yankees and Calvinists showing their support and other cultures and faiths registering their opposition. Yet the object of this fight, at its core, was not so much about ethnicity and theology as it was over funding and control. And, while curriculum—the subjects included—and pedagogy—the methods used to teach them—were debated and altered over the years, modifications to those areas were modest in comparison to the seismic changes occurring in finance and administration. Indeed, the main thrust of the movement was to shift those latter functions from private into public hands.[13]

While progress came in fits and starts and at different times in different places, historians have identified a common pattern of reform. At first, private and parochial schools received a partial subsidy from the state without much oversight. Next, legislatures authorized residents of counties, townships, or districts to organize schools and levy taxes at their discretion. Later, lawmakers offered state money on the condition that those local entities impose a minimum level of taxation. At that stage some centralized supervision was required, but it tended to be sporadic and ineffective. Finally, a statewide property tax was assessed, tuition payments were eliminated, making instruction universally free, and statewide supervision became mandatory.[14]

But in the West prior to 1820 progress was impossible due to low population density, limited economic resources, and a lukewarm commitment to the cause. Interestingly, historian of education Edward Stevens, Jr. has identified four obstacles that impeded literacy in the past and each seemed to also apply to schooling in the

West: low population concentrations, insufficient community funds, inadequate personal wealth, and cultural opposition. First, while Indian removal and migration were beginning to overcome the first problem, density remained a major issue. Second, the Yankees, an unpopular minority, were in too weak of a position to impose their culture on others, and, as we will see, another group vigorously opposed them. Finally, both collectively and individually, Westerners were left with few resources for education after meeting the demands of the frontier and laboring under the crushing impact of the Panic.[15]

As a result, schooling was only for a select few, who surely had a right to question how they could have been so "privileged." One-room buildings, hardly the quaint little red schoolhouses of legend, were often located on undesirable land, perhaps near a dusty road, a fetid swamp, or a noisy sawmill. They were hot in the summer and frigid in the winter, with uncomfortable seating for the students. Since most were privately operated, parents paid a subscription fee, while for those that were community sponsored, parents were charged with a "rate bill," a daily fee that allowed the student to attend beyond those days that were funded by the local government. Due to limited funding most schools were open only two or three months of the year, during summer and winter sessions that were scheduled so as to not interfere with the need for young hands on the farm. Since attendance was voluntary and costly some children received no formal instruction at all, while others received just a few weeks each year. Children as young as three could attend school, but they were there more to receive day care than an education. Students at about age ten attended only in winter, when their services were not needed on the farm. Teachers typically served for only two to three years, when the young men moved on to a profession and the young women to homemaking. While drunk, cruel, or ignorant instructors were not the norm, neither were they the isolated exception. Pedagogy consisted of recitation from textbooks that were infused with moral lessons and classroom management depended on strict and, at times, physical discipline.[16]

Still, we should not assume that children were illiterate despite their limited exposure to quality formal schooling. In fact, Americans as a whole had one of the highest rates of literacy in the world. This was due in part to the nation's evangelical parents, who responded to the call to spread the knowledge of the Bible by teaching their children to read. Yet even though literacy was widespread, reading opportunities were limited since books were expensive and lighting after sunset was poor. Nonetheless, America had the highest newspaper circulation in the world in 1810 and if Americans could not afford their own subscription, they could at least read papers posted in the local tavern or general store. In addition to newspapers and the family Bible, Americans also read many religious tracts, sermons, textbooks, and almanacs. Still, despite the impressive level of literacy that was achieved through home schooling, a couple states in the growing West would soon recognize the value of a system of community education.[17]

Ohio

In the late 1810s education in Ohio had a few bright spots, notably Cincinnati, Marietta, and the Western Reserve, but it remained beyond the reach of most children due the four obstacles described by Stevens. But that was about to change and, as would often be the case during this long struggle, a moral question provided one catalyst and an economic slump delivered another. The moral issue, the Missouri Crisis of 1819-1821, was energizing Ohio's voters, whose turnout reached as high as 90% of those eligible, while at the same time the Panic of 1819 was devastating Ohio, especially Cincinnati. The electorate, reacting to dismal economic conditions, at first took out their anger on the friends of the banks, including school advocates. But the Panic lasted so long that the people were ready to discard their desire for limited government, at least for the time being, in favor of a more activist approach that promised to heal their sick economy.[18]

This shift in the outlook of the masses played right into the hands of the business elites, who welcomed a larger role for government. All the businessmen had economic goals, but the many Yankees included in their number also hoped to create a city on a hill that resembled their homeland, in politics, education, and religion.

Politically, the older generation had been members of the Federalist Party (while it existed) and the younger generation, though they had never been Federalists, gave evidence from their writings that they had appropriated much of its philosophy. Educationally, leaders like Caleb Atwater and Nathan Guilford were graduates of Calvinist colleges and were steeped in the traditions of their homeland. Finally, in their religious affiliations they were typically Presbyterian or Congregationalist, like Atwater and Ephraim Cutler, notwithstanding the occasional Unitarian, like Guilford. In Ohio, as in the rest of the North, it would be men like these who provided the leadership corps for the movement.[19]

Their educational and religious characteristics gave the Yankees distinct advantages over their more-numerous opposition, in what promised to be a new era of hope that emerged near the end of the Panic. First, their level of education, which was much more advanced than their adversaries, provided the debating and rhetorical skills so helpful for political success. Second, their sense of mission, which was derived from their assurance of eternal salvation, gave them the will to labor on through adversity. Third, their connections with the Baptists and Methodists, often built upon their mutual commitment to evangelicalism, multiplied their influence exponentially since those denominations were much larger than the Congregationalists and Presbyterians. But while the New Englanders hoped to provide the political leadership for all evangelicals, important cultural and theological differences would complicate their efforts.[20]

The former Federalists and their younger allies would form the opposition to Jackson in the 1820s and 1830s, first as the National Republicans (not to be confused with the Republican Party of Jefferson and Madison), and later as the Whigs. They saw government as a legitimate tool for building the economic, moral, and intellectual infrastructure for the new nation. Free schools were an important part of a much broader agenda that also included advocating for antislavery, temperance, and the rights of Indians. While these elites believed that they were best suited to guide the nation, they had learned to adopt more populist positions at times in order to win at the polls.[21]

On the other hand, the Republicans, the political and intellectual descendents of Jefferson and Madison, distrusted government and its centralized control. They would later build on that philosophy under Jackson, when they became known as Democrats. They also feared corporations, especially banks, which depended on the state for their charters. While many of them agreed with some aspects of the reformers' program, including free education, they disliked the loss of local control and the taxes needed to create statewide systems. In place of government, they placed their trust in the common man; the farmer, the mechanic, the artisan. Many Baptists and Methodists were solid Republicans (later to become Democrats) and opposed Yankee political initiatives.[22]

The political efforts that would lead to Ohio's first meaningful school reforms began even before the Panic had hit full stride and, oddly enough, they had nothing to do with education. In January 1819 Gov. Ethan Allen Brown, a native of Darien, Connecticut, had urged Ohio to start building a canal system. Like others in the Old Northwest he wanted his state to follow the example of New York State, which had begun construction of the Erie Canal two years earlier, at the urging of Gov. DeWitt Clinton. The severity of the downturn that started later that year delayed Ohio's plans for the canals, but not for long. Several prominent Cincinnatians, among them Judge Jacob Burnet and Dr. Daniel Drake, urged Brown to resume his fight. While Cincinnati had been hit early and hard by the Panic, it was also recovering more quickly than many rural areas and these boosters hoped canals would accelerate the Queen City's economy. Powered by the introduction of steamboats on the Ohio River, Cincinnati had experienced explosive growth before the Panic and was fast becoming the largest distribution center in the West. Cincinnatians, as well as other Ohioans, wanted to continue that momentum by building canals that linked markets in the South with those in the East via the Ohio River, the Great Lakes, and the Erie Canal.[23]

Many of those who supported canals also hoped to create a system of state-supported schools and they began that effort later in 1819. Cutler, elected to the Ohio House that year after a long absence from office, sponsored a bill to divide townships into districts and levy a tax on the value of property (*ad valorem*). His bill easily passed the

House but died in the Senate. In 1821 Cutler tried once again and this time the legislature passed Ohio's most extensive education law to date, permitting townships to set up districts, construct buildings, and levy taxes. But Cutler, Atwater, and Guilford were still deeply disappointed since these provisions were made optional rather than mandatory.[24]

Later that year, due to the people's anger over the Panic, Cutler lost his seat in the House, but Atwater was elected to that body for the first time and he immediately began a crusade for schools and canals. Both faced an uphill battle; the first struggled against localism, the second with opposition to public debt, and both with the people's distaste for taxes. While some legislators supported both movements, many backed one but not the other, so these two factions formed a coalition. In a textbook case of logrolling, each group agreed to support the other's project so that its own goal would be achieved. The plan showed promise because representatives whose constituents lived close to proposed canal routes but who may not otherwise have been willing to support education were willing to do so in exchange for the votes of school enthusiasts who would not have been inclined to support canals, since no routes would come close to their district.[25]

The coalition pushed through two companion bills in January 1822, authorizing Governor Trimble to establish two planning committees: one for schools and one for canals. Atwater, Cutler, and Guilford were all appointed to the seven-member school committee in May and over the next two years each followed his own unique approach to advocate for a statewide system. Atwater waged an active letter writing campaign and, despite shaky finances, published at his own expense several pamphlets that he distributed statewide. Guilford boycotted committee meetings and chose instead to publish and distribute a minority report across Ohio. Meanwhile, Cutler focused on his fellow legislators, working day and night to change their minds. Still, school reform had made little headway and, unfortunately, the canal project had also run aground.[26]

But in 1824 the crusades were helped immensely by two unrelated issues: slavery in the territories and pay for the legislature. The Missouri Compromise was proving more divisive for the Republicans than the reformers and voters were becoming outraged at state representatives, mostly Republicans, who had just voted themselves a raise during hard times. In state elections in October these two factors, when added to interest in canals and schools, produced a turnout 50% higher than the Presidential elections just one month earlier and resulted in a decisive victory for coalition candidates. So, as would often be the case during the long struggle for education, other causes had elicited more passion from voters and inadvertently swung the outcome in favor of the movement.[27]

With the opposition now swept from the legislature, canal proponents moved swiftly to achieve their goal. On February 4, 1825 they passed a bill with the overwhelming margins of 58-13 in the House and 34-2 in the Senate. Five months later, on July 4 Gov. Clinton presided over a gala groundbreaking for Ohio's canals and within just two years the system opened, prompting a surge in the state's economy. In fact, Ohio would lead the entire Old Northwest into a new era of economic growth that historians Andrew Cayton and Peter Onuf have described as "little short of astounding."[28]

On the day after passage of the canal bill, with the help of its backers and Atwater, Cutler, and Guilford, who were all now sitting in the Senate, a school law passed easily, 46-24 in the House and 28-8 in the Senate. It provided for a system of instruction funded with a ½-mill property tax (0.05% of the value), managed through counties, townships, and districts, and supervised through a network of county auditors, school clerks, and teacher examiners. It penalized noncompliance by withholding state funding for five years. When the bill passed, Cutler is reported to have emotionally cited a verse from the book of Luke to Atwater and Guilford: "Lord, now lettest thou thy servant depart in peace, according to thy word, for mine eyes have seen thy salvation."[29]

Four years later Cincinnatians celebrated a new city charter that faithfully carried out the mandates of the 1825 law. Guilford, who had spearheaded the drive for the charter, organized and led a large parade that included many civic leaders and a large number of children. The parade ended at the First Presbyterian Church, where its powerful minister, Rev. Joshua Wilson, asked for God's blessing on their cause. The Queen City at last seemed well on its way to achieving the goals of the zealots.[30]

By 1834 Cincinnati would have almost 5,000 children enrolled, with over half of them in public schools, but most of Ohio would ignore its example. The 1825 law, which had shown so much promise, resulted in few new schools. The prevailing belief in localism combined with the absence of state mandates meant that the legislation could be ignored with impunity and it was. The few schools that resulted were of poor quality and operated for no more than a few months each year. So, only disappointment seemed to follow Cutler's pious prayer and Cincinnati's colorful parade. This pattern of significant advance followed by partial retreat would be duplicated in many other states over the first and second phases of reform. Ohio's zealots of the 1820s had done all they could. It would now be up to the next generation to advance education further down the field.[31]

Appalachian Resistance

One of the reasons that Ohio's Yankees failed to achieve their goals was the fierce resistance they faced from another ethnic group that had also emigrated from the British Isles, the people we know today as Appalachians. Politically-incorrect detractors label them as violent, stubborn, suspicious, and disrespectful of authority, while their defenders describe them as brave, tenacious, independent, and champions of the masses. Their unique patterns of speech, dress, family, work, building, and social behavior are found wherever they have settled. Even in today's America, the imprint of their culture can be seen in NASCAR, heard in country music, and felt in the log cabin.[32]

Most Appalachians were descended from a people who had lived for centuries along the border between England and Scotland. Faced with the hardships that plagued Scotland near the turn of the 18th century, some of them sought a better life in Northern Ireland, while others stayed behind. Eventually, people from both countries immigrated to America. Both became known as Scotch-Irish, a misnomer, since the first group did not stay long enough in Ulster to absorb native Irish culture, and the second came directly from the border area. In addition, still other Appalachians emigrated from Wales, France, and Germany, though due to their smaller number they tended to take on many aspects of the Scotch-Irish culture that permeated their adopted homeland.[33]

Their culture had been indelibly marked by the seven-hundred-year struggle for control of the border between England and Scotland. A state of almost constant warfare, which was marked by unspeakable atrocities and shifting borders, led the Scotch-Irish to remain ever vigilant and prepared for the worst. Historian David Hackett Fischer has demonstrated that this long, sad experience taught them to mistrust government, since warring kingdoms were at the root of their problems, and to fear outsiders, who might be spying for an enemy or stealing for themselves. Fischer showed that the border people tended to cling to their large extended family, the clan, since it was often their only refuge from disaster. Once peace finally came to the borderlands in the 18th century, these fierce fighters, no longer needed for warfare, were soon forced off their land by absentee landlords, whose injustices only reinforced their views about outsiders. At first the Scotch-Irish tried lawful resistance, but when that failed against their wealthier and better-educated opponents, they often turned to mob action and civil disobedience. Such responses to powerful outsiders would continue when they came to America.[34]

Perhaps as a result of Scotch-Irish isolation in the rugged highlands in Scotland, Appalachia, and later the American Midwest, they have managed to preserve many aspects of their culture down through the centuries. In the American Midwest several of their traits and experiences would present significant roadblocks to reform. Perhaps most germane to our story, the Scotch-Irish held fast to localism, which set up a conflict with the Yankees—that very embodiment of the wealthy and educated outsider—who placed their faith in centralized government. And though the Scotch-Irish never formed mobs to fight education as they had to resist land grabs, they often ignored state legislation.[35]

Several other traits of the Scotch-Irish would have a direct bearing on universal schooling in America. First, their ancestors had no tradition of community education. Those on the English side of the border thought it was of little benefit to the lower classes; those on the Scottish side were unaffected by Scottish Realism and its emphasis on learning because it failed to reach their homeland in the Southern Uplands until the end of the 18th century, after most of them had emigrated. Further, related to their lack of schooling and their mistrust of the intellectual, they favored folk preachers, usually Baptists, Methodists, and backcountry Presbyterians, who led emotional revivals that resembled camp meetings. On the other hand, they were repelled by more highly-educated, well-dressed ministers, typically Congregationalists and eastern Presbyterians, whose reasoned sermons reminded them of the often indifferent Anglican clergy that their ancestors had been forced to support. As a result they were underrepresented in the congregations of the latter two denominations, which were the biggest advocates for the movement. Next, due to their distaste for authority, Scotch-Irish parents bristled at the strict teaching style favored by the Yankees. Trying to raise children who exhibited a strong will, independence, pride, and courage, they recoiled at discipline enforced with a hickory stick and lessons taught by rote memorization.[36]

Finally, the Scotch-Irish tendency to relocate spread their culture to many different places, which made them an important factor in the school reform story of many states. Their ancestors had been conditioned for centuries to prepare for the sudden loss of their homestead due to a plundering enemy or a greedy landowner. So when they faced analogous situations in America they knew just what to do. If they were attacked by Indians they were ready to fight or to flee; if, as was often the case, they were squatting on someone else's land and were discovered, they were prepared to abandon it; and if they were apprised of better land in the West, they could quickly relocate, leaving little of value behind. A quarter million of them had emigrated from Ulster, Scotland, and England during the 18th century and by the 1790 census they were dominating the western parts of Maryland, Virginia, North Carolina, South Carolina, and Georgia; southwestern Pennsylvania; and what would soon become the states of Kentucky and Tennessee. This heavily-forested, mountainous region provided water for their homesteads, food for their souls, and isolation for their culture.[37]

But that was just a foretaste of what Appalachians would accomplish in the first half of the 19th century. They were key participants in the great scramble for land that so transformed the West that respected historians, such as Nathan Philbrick and Jack Larkin, have described it as "phenomenal" and "astonishing." This restless people, who had moved so often in the Old World, were now repeating that pattern in the New and it would have profound effects on the drive for schools.[38]

Thanks to geographer John Hudson we have a fairly clear picture of their destinations. Essentially, the further south a pioneer was born, the further south was his new home, and vice versa. Appalachians from the Carolinas and Virginia settled first in the Nashville basin of Tennessee and the Bluegrass country of Kentucky, and then many of them moved on to populate the southern portions of Ohio, Indiana, and Illinois, and the entire state of Missouri. Still further to the north, Appalachians from southeastern and southwestern Pennsylvania and nearby parts of Maryland and Virginia established new homesteads in southern Ohio and Indiana and then later moved into northern Indiana and central Illinois. The last was the largest and most important of the migrant groups.[39]

Of course, while these pathways trace the journey taken by large numbers of migrants, some famous Americans left trails that, though they were unique, still fit into the overall pattern. For example, Daniel Boone, descended from Quakers rather than the Scotch-Irish, was born in Pennsylvania, moved with his family to North Carolina, and after marrying and starting his own family, moved to the Bluegrass and then on to eastern Missouri. Abraham Lincoln, descended from English Puritans who had migrated to Virginia, was born on a farm near Louisville, moved with his family to southern Indiana, and finally, as a young adult, on to Sangamon County in west central Illinois. Many zealots followed a similar pattern. For example, Joseph Duncan, descended from Scotch-Irish Presbyterians who had migrated from Virginia to the Bluegrass, was born there and also made his first adult home in Sangamon County. These notable Americans, as well as those not so well known, were drawn by the allure of cheap land with a good title.

As a result of Appalachian cultural practices, they were certain to clash with the Yankee promoters of free education in those states where both groups had significant populations. Once again, Hudson's study permits us to see with some precision where that occurred. Similar to the Appalachians, Yankees traveled along lines of latitude, so the further north a Yankee was born, the further north was his new homestead. As a result, they predominated in areas between 41°-43° North: Michigan, Wisconsin, northern Illinois, and in Ohio, the Western Reserve in the northeast and, thanks to Manasseh Cutler, the small Yankee enclave of Marietta in the southeast. However, they largely bypassed Indiana, at first because of the barrier created by the Black Swamp and, near mid-century, as a result of the relative ease of travel to Chicago via the Great Lakes.[40]

The sharply different outlooks and customs of the two groups regarding family, community, work, farming, wealth, and government spawned a deep level of mistrust. Appalachians, for their part, had been streaming into the Ohio Valley since the 1770s and felt besieged by the opinionated newcomers from the East, who projected an air of superiority with their proper language and fancy clothes. One of the biggest sources of discord was Christianity, which was very important to both groups. Yankees attempted to impose a strict moral code on their community using erudite sermons and tightly-controlled services. Appalachians, resenting this approach as a challenge to their independence, preferred plain-spoken preaching and a more informal worship style.[41]

Illinois

Few such culture wars occurred in early Illinois due to the almost complete dominance of the Prairie State by Appalachians. In fact, at the dawn of statehood in 1818 only 3% of its citizens were natives of New England. So the population was not predisposed towards community education and, even if it had been, there were few Yankees present to advocate for it. Consequently, these challenging demographics made the state's achievement in the mid-1820s all the more remarkable.[42]

As one might expect, the state's politics reflected the cultural orientation of its citizens. Politicians, who were virtually all Jeffersonian Republicans, copied their first laws from Virginia and Kentucky. In the 1820s they supported Andrew Jackson and their political philosophies were so uniform that they could be differentiated only by their degree of support for the popular Tennessean. His ardent backers were called "whole hog" while his moderate followers were labeled "milk and cider" men. Factions formed over individual issues or evolved from positive or negative reactions to local leaders. The most significant aspect of its politics was that everyone favored localism, preferring the power of family, clan, and local authorities to that of state and federal governments.[43]

There was little indication that the people of Illinois valued education during its early years. For example, it was the only state in the Old Northwest to fail to mention schools in its first constitution. An indirect indicator of its lack of concern lay in its unusually strong support for slavery and indenture. This was so because during an era that some have called the Age of Reform the most vigorous opponents of slavery also tended to be the most outspoken advocates for universal education. So, in state after state the stronger the forces of antislavery the better the prospects for the schools, and vice versa. Yet it was clear from the beginning of the Prairie State that proslavery sentiment was predominant. Article VI of the Constitution of 1818 allowed indenture, which was a thinly-disguised form of slavery. Indenture would be practiced for two more decades and, just six years into statehood, slavery's proponents would even attempt to amend the constitution to legalize the vile practice. So it comes as no surprise then that Illinois, with so many supporters of slavery, contained few backers of community schooling.[44]

While reform suffered due to these hostile cultural attitudes, it was also handicapped by a lack of people. Despite the land rush that benefited Illinois in the years after the War of 1812, the Prairie State still counted only 55,211 residents in 1820, giving it a population that was about one-third the size of Indiana's and one-tenth that of Ohio's. Fewer than four thousand people voted in the Presidential election of 1824. Even by 1830 less than two people per square mile lived in large parts of central Illinois and all of northern Illinois, which were still largely controlled by Indian tribes. As a result, even organizing one-room schoolhouses on the frontier proved to be a challenging task.[45]

Consequently, most learning occurred in the home, while just a few private, tuition-based institutions existed. Featuring Christian themes and books, they were typically sponsored by churches and run by Presbyterian ministers. Churches also offered Sunday schools, which were open to children regardless of their faith. They offered both morning and afternoon sessions and taught reading, writing, and arithmetic in addition to Bible and tract study and hymn singing. In some areas they were the forerunner of weekday schools. This hybrid system of home- and church-based education was quite acceptable to the southern-oriented people and politicians of Illinois.[46]

Given this environment, it is quite surprising then that Joseph Duncan pushed his progressive plan to create the state's first system of free public schools. Elected to the Illinois Senate in 1823, he introduced a bill the following year that proposed to educate all white children between the ages of five and twenty-one. With the support of Edward Coles, governor and newspaper publisher, he was instrumental in passing a landmark law on January 15, 1825. In addition to mandating universal free schooling for whites, this bill created a comprehensive system of supervision. Counties were required to set up districts if petitioned by at least fifteen families. Each district was then to elect officials, including trustees, who were to operate schools for a minimum of three months each year. In addition, trustees were to hire and examine teachers, lease property, and report annually to the county commissioners, who would in turn forward reports to the Secretary of State. The bill also established two new funding sources for education. First, the state was required to distribute to the counties 2% of its revenues, which was fairly insignificant considering the small size of its budget. Further, local voters could levy a tax of as much as 0.5% (five mills) on the value of property. In short, this was very comprehensive legislation for its time, rivaled only by Ohio's provisions.[47]

Unfortunately, Illinois would quickly revert to form, at first by simply ignoring the act, which some disparagingly called the

Yankee Law. In fact, noncompliance was so complete that the state could make no expenditures on schools in 1825 and 1826. Cultural biases were producing multiple concerns: the poor feared their children would leave the farm once they got an education; the childless protested paying taxes to help someone else's child; and the restless worried that they would move again before their children could use the local school. Still others believed that tuition-based schools were superior to public ones. It wasn't long before these attitudes began producing active resistance. When Duncan was elected to the US Congress in 1826, his attention shifted from state to national issues, and the next year the Illinois legislature began dismantling the 1825 law. First, they allowed individuals to opt out of the five-mill property tax, removing an important financial support. Then, in 1829 the legislature repealed its allocation of 2% of state revenues to the schools and its requirement for three months of schooling. Finally, in 1835 they dealt two fatal blows to the movement when they borrowed the entire balance of the permanent fund for internal improvements and repealed the guarantee of free schooling for the poor. In retrospect, while a few school proponents had experienced one short-lived victory, the cultural environment had proven much too toxic for it to stand. In the future it would take a larger group of leaders, this time from New England, to turn the promise of universal education into a reality.[48]

Indiana

Unlike its neighbors to the east and west, Indiana would not make any meaningful progress during the first phase of the crusade. While the state and its citizens had little money, an even greater problem was a shortage of will and leadership. As in Illinois, migration had brought in many pioneers from Kentucky, Virginia, Tennessee, and North Carolina. Their culture soon came to dominate Indiana, shaping its outlook on family, religion, politics, government, and education. As a result, Hoosiers had low levels of literacy, owned few books, and operated few libraries in comparison to other states. These conditions would persist for decades, creating a difficult environment for reform. Low population density also made the formation of schools difficult, although defeat in the War of 1812 induced several tribes to sign treaties, leading to a surge in sales and settlement. For example, in 1817 the Vincennes land office led the nation in sales. Still, treaties would not open up the northern third of the state for settlement until the late 1820s and 1830s, so that part of the state continued to have few inhabitants.[49]

Educational practices were like those in Illinois. Most learning occurred in the home, as it did for Abraham Lincoln. Some children were taught in private schools, which were often conducted by the pastor of a local church. Sunday schools helped fill the void left by the absence of community schools. In fact, by 1829 5,600 students were being taught by 741 teachers in over 100 locations. Ministers and their wives, especially the Presbyterians, were particularly active in this, as well as in other areas of education.[50]

The constitution and early legislation of Indiana illustrate a strange paradox. In direct contrast to Illinois, where the legislature quickly mandated a statewide system even though their constitution failed to mention the subject, Indiana lawmakers failed to act even though their constitution required it. Article IX, Section 1, in a paraphrase of the Northwest Ordinance, extols the importance of "knowledge and learning" for the maintenance of a free government and notes that it should encourage "humanity, honesty, industry, and morality." Section 2 seemingly contains a strong directive: "It shall be the duty of the General Assembly, *as soon as circumstances will permit*, to provide by law for a general system of education, ascending in a regular gradation from township schools to a State University, wherein tuition shall be gratis, and equally open to all [emphasis added]." The strength of this statement is surprising, since of the forty-three delegates to the Constitutional Convention, twenty-seven alone were from Kentucky and thirty-four overall were from the South, places not known for their support of community schools. Unfortunately, the ambiguous phrase "as soon as circumstances will permit" gave politicians a loophole that they would consistently employ over the coming decades. In addition to that unfortunate provision of Indiana's constitution, the Congressional act that enabled it to apply for statehood granted Lot 16 to the townships instead of the state. This strengthened localism, weakened centralization, and undercut later efforts to control and supervise education at the state level.[51]

Politicians began their artful evasion of the Constitution's "mandate" almost at once. In his first address to the legislature, Gov. Jonathan Jennings called for the implementation of Section 2, without providing any guidance on how that should be done. Accordingly, the legislature passed a law in 1816 that *permitted* rather than *required* the formation of schools and that failed to provide for any state supervision. Like Jennings in 1816, Governors Ray in 1825 and Noble in 1831 delivered soaring speeches supporting the value of schools, but Indiana's legislatures never produced the money or mandates to bring to life "a general system of education." In all, they passed seven general laws from 1824 to 1836, permitting various educational activities, but never requiring any of them. In 1832 the power of localism grew even stronger, as responsibility devolved from townships to districts and then in 1836 to parents, incredibly, who were empowered to hire their own teacher if district trustees failed to provide one. Not surprisingly, few schools resulted from these toothless statutes. In fact, it would be another decade before a determined leader from New England would shame Indiana into finally implementing the lofty ideals that it had publicly enshrined in its first Constitution.[52]

South, Middle States, and New England

In the South, like Indiana, the crusade foundered due to a lack of commitment to the value of public education and, if anything, even weaker support. The lowland planters who controlled state politics held views similar to those of English country gentlemen: instruction was the responsibility of the family and the church, though the community should assist in the schooling of the poor. Since Appalachians in the upland South were also skeptical about the role of government, the region had fewer schools than the North and most of them were private and sub-standard. And of course, given prevailing racist attitudes, the children of the slaves were always denied access to an education.[53]

In the Middle States of New York and Pennsylvania, it was not the resistance of any one culture to the idea of schooling, but rather the diverse ethnic and religious composition of the region that created problems. Those differences made it difficult to find common ground on how to teach religion, which was a central mission for education. Dutch and English Protestant pioneers had to coexist with Irish Catholics and Calvinist Yankees in New York, while English Quakers, German Mennonites, French Huguenots, and Scotch-Irish Presbyterians mixed uneasily in Pennsylvania. Both states lacked the religious unity that the Puritan tradition had bequeathed to New England or that the Second Great Awakening had forged in the West. In diverse communities, each group sponsored their own private school; in places where one group predominated, it used its political power to start public schools that nurtured its particular culture and religion. In either case the result for education was division, not unity, and that hurt both states.[54]

New York had no tradition of public support until a wave of Yankee migration after the Revolution sparked a flood of activity. In 1795 the legislature appropriated two thousand pounds a year for five years to be apportioned among any towns that established schools and raised at least half the amount of the state grant from local taxpayers. But when that law expired it was not renewed. In 1805 lawmakers set up a permanent fund, but neglected to direct how distributions should be spent. Finally, in 1812 New York passed a comprehensive law with responsibilities for the district, the town, and the state, including creation of the first state superintendent in the nation. Unfortunately, none of these reforms would be sustained. For example, the position of superintendent was eliminated in 1821 and would not be reinstated until 1854. So despite the early promise shown by the Empire State, it would be among the laggards in the North, largely because of disruptive struggles between its majority Protestants and minority Catholics.[55]

Pennsylvania had long followed the practice of funding only the education of the poor and leaving the rest to the church. Then in 1834 and 1835 the legislature, following an impassioned speech by New England native Thaddeus Stevens, created a statewide system, which included an offer of fifty cents from the state for every dollar raised locally. Despite the fact that the legislation was voluntary for each of the 987 districts that it chartered, it came under sharp attack. Quakers and German-speaking Lutherans and Mennonites jealously clung to their parochial schools, which they hoped would help preserve their religion, culture, and language. While opponents were unable to overturn the law, hundreds of districts refused to take advantage of it. Acceptance of the state's offer would grow, but the Keystone State, like New York, would trail most other states in the North on the road to universal schooling.[56]

Finally, in an ironic turn of events, New England, whose sons played such a vital role in the New York, Pennsylvania, and Ohio movements, would itself regress. For example, while Massachusetts had codified its colonial practices in 1789 and built on them in 1800, by the 1820s it had become clear that community-supported schooling was growing weaker even as private education was expanding. While a few lonely zealots protested this trend, they would have to wait a decade before witnessing real reform.[57]

So, at the end of the first phase of the crusade a few simple truths were becoming abundantly clear to the zealots. On the positive side, surges in migration indicated that low densities would not remain a problem for long, while on the negative, lagging revenues signaled that lot 16 could never fund their dreams. Moreover, cultural attitudes and economic swings could cut both ways, helping at some places and times and hurting at others. While advocates had made some progress in Ohio and Illinois, their joy had soon turned to despair as opponents reversed some of their gains. During the second phase of reform new leadership would take them closer to their dream and, once again, Yankees would be at the forefront.

Part III

Professional Leadership Faces Resistance, 1836-1842

Rev. Samuel Lewis

Horace Mann

Henry Barnard

Rev. Calvin Stowe

Chapter 7

Circuit Riders for Public Schools —
The Second Group of Zealots

*7*he leadership corps expanded dramatically during the second phase of the movement, a period that saw growing professionalism among the crusaders and emerging support from the people. But by the era's end only three reformers had tasted success and they would have to put up a ferocious fight to try to retain their modest gains. The lives of the three bore many similarities: all were descended from Puritans, raised by Calvinists, and trained as lawyers. But perhaps even more striking was their willingness to sacrifice both health and wealth in the service of reform. They suffered from physical and mental maladies throughout their adult lives and endured the premature deaths of several loved ones, all of which cast a pall over their public successes.

While all three zealots recorded comparable achievements during these years, historians, at least during most of the 20th century, have chosen to highlight the ideas and actions of one leader, to downplay those of a second, and to virtually ignore those of the third. Ironically, that last man, Samuel Lewis of Ohio, most closely resembled the majority of his fellow reformers and was lauded by them for his many contributions to their cause. But historians have instead recognized Horace Mann of Massachusetts as the Father of the Public Schools, while seemingly scrutinizing his every word and deed. Yet Mann shared fewer characteristics with his cohorts than did Lewis and, though his accomplishments were certainly impressive, they were no more remarkable than those of Lewis and several other education pioneers. In a further irony, Mann's good friend, Henry Barnard of Connecticut, helped build the myth of Mann's dominance of the movement, in the process diminishing history's appraisal of his own remarkable record.[1]

These distortions of the past blur our understanding of the leadership of the common school movement. Certainly, the three share many traits and beliefs with the rest of the reformers, including the value of hard work, sacrifice, piety, and morality, and as we will see they demonstrated these both in their crusade and in the schools they began. But one key difference between them has not previously been fully appreciated. Lewis and Barnard, both evangelicals, held a very pessimistic view of humanity while Mann, a Unitarian, possessed a more progressive outlook. The evangelicals' view won out and that victory would have important consequences for the nation's first classrooms.

Samuel Lewis—Ohio

Fortunately, we can piece together a fairly reliable picture of the evangelical reformer, Samuel Lewis, through his own observations and those of his son, his contemporaries, and early historians. While no one person can represent the broad group of reformers of the 1830s, Lewis' life gives us a better window than most into the leadership of the movement. In addition to his heritage, his cultural background, his career path, and his zealotry, he was also, like so many of the crusaders, an evangelical minister and an abolitionist. Among his many accomplishments he served as the first superintendent of Ohio's common schools and a founder of Cincinnati's first public school. He was also a key figure in two antislavery political parties that repealed his state's racist Black Laws and established its first schools for blacks.[2]

Lewis seemed destined for his life's missions. His father, Capt. Samuel Lewis, was a descendant of Rev. John Robinson, the beloved leader of the Puritans in England and the Netherlands, so his Calvinist roots ran deep. Because his father was often at sea, young Samuel spent much of his childhood with his maternal grandparents in Scituate, Massachusetts, a town that sits twenty-five miles southeast of Boston on the Atlantic coast. Two influences from his Yankee childhood would remain with him throughout his life. The first, the importance of his faith, was instilled through unrelenting instruction from his grandparents, his aunt, and his father. The second, the value of hard work, was acquired through long hours of labor on the family farm. These pervasive New England characteristics were observed in many of the zealots, though they could be expressed in very different ways. Both would become core principles of the nation's first schools.[3]

While New Englanders in theory were committed to community education, in practice many relied upon home or private schooling. Lewis spent less than one year in school, after which he was tutored at home by his aunt and grandparents and for a short time at the residence of Rev. Erastus Otis, a Methodist minister. He later recognized the shortcomings of this arrangement, complaining that "could I have had these advantages [formal schooling], with how much more usefulness could I now serve my country and my God. I feel the defect of early education and discipline so much that I often blush and mourn over myself, and nothing but a sense of duty can keep me in a field where half my strength is lost for the want of these very advantages." Regrets such as these fueled his mission to provide for others the instruction that he had been denied.[4]

One reason for Lewis' lack of formal schooling was that he took on a man's job at an early age, as did so many other New England youths. At age 11 Lewis began serving as a cabin boy on his father's ships, which sailed along the coast as far north as Maine and as far south as the West Indies. One day while working off Cape Cod within sight of his hometown, Falmouth, the young boy had an experience that influenced him for the rest of his life. Left alone to tend one of his father's ships at anchor, he carelessly leaned over the rail while drawing water, lost his balance, and plunged into the water below. Soon he found himself struggling for life; without a rope his efforts to climb on board failed, without a shipmate nearby his cries for help went unanswered, and without the ability to swim to the distant shore his hopes were fading fast. His children recalled that Lewis recounted, "in a few moments, I gave up, and strove to resign myself to die. All the deeds of my short life came across my mind; I tried to pray, and to lie quiet in the hands of my heavenly Father. Soon my mind began to revert to my father's family, and, beyond all others upon earth, to my mother. I thought of her grief and distress when my body should be swept ashore, or all search for it abandoned. I thought of the agony of suspense that would torture her mind, till it was certain that I no longer lived." The image of his mother and the sight of his hometown encouraged him to pray to God and soon the exhausted boy was able to redouble his efforts to climb back aboard. Somehow he was able to make it back on deck, but he related "as I turned and looked down upon the water, where I had so lately awaited death, I was horrified at the sight of a monstrous shark, lashing the waves in disappointment as he turned away from the vessel. I fell upon my knees in a moment, and returned thanks to God, who had so wonderfully spared me from the death far more dreadful than the one I had before expected."[5]

No matter what skeptics might think of such a melodramatic story, which was told so many years after its events had unfolded, it makes clear that Lewis' faith was important to him at a young age. In fact, he had recently joined the Methodist Church, an unusual action for a young person living in mostly Congregationalist New England. While we can only speculate about whether his conversion resulted from a talk with his Methodist tutor or a revival at a camp meeting, his religious commitments would, like those of the other reformers, inspire a life of self-sacrifice, which he would repeatedly show in his dealings with his family, his friends, and Ohio's school-children.[6]

In 1813 his life took an important turn when his family, reeling from losses in Captain Lewis' business, decided to move to Butler County in Southwestern Ohio. Like so many others had done, Samuel and the other Lewis men walked beside their wagon as far as Pittsburgh and then sailed down the Ohio for the last leg of their trip. Once there the teenager worked incessantly, either on his family's farm, on other farms, or in carpentry or surveying. Yet instead of keeping his pay, he turned most of it over to his parents, who were struggling to support their nine children. In addition to his faith, dedication to work and devotion to family would become the hallmarks of his life.[7]

In 1819 at the age of 20 he moved to Cincinnati to study the law, despite his limited funds and inferior schooling. Undaunted, he prepared for the bar exam with a single-mindedness that would mark his later efforts for education and antislavery. His routine was brutal: by day, he worked for the Clerk of Common Pleas and the Ohio Supreme Court; by night, he studied under Judge Jacob Burnet, often ending his day well past midnight. Since he was still sending part of his pay home, he was left at times to live on stale bread and water. Yet Lewis persevered and was admitted to the bar on April 2, 1822. In his first case, he convinced the court to reverse an earlier decision, something rarely done in those days. Word of this and other victories spread, and he quickly built a booming practice. By 1824 he was accumulating savings for the first time in his life, so he spent $3,500, a substantial sum in those days, to buy a 165-acre farm for his parents. Once again, he was showing that he placed work and family above other things. His business continued to expand over the next decade, making him independently wealthy, but money failed to satisfy and overwork, including lots of travel to Columbus, left him exhausted. In 1834, suffering from a shattered constitution, he retired at the age of 35.[8]

Lewis' brief but successful legal career provides a window through which we can see the major influences on this life. In addition to the importance of work and family, his psychological and physical challenges, his Christian worldview, and his commitment to an improved society were all in evidence during those years, as they would be during his time in the education and abolitionist movements. The first element, his psychological profile, was hardly ideal for someone who needed to work with others to achieve the goal of a reformed society. As an introvert, he was introspective, shy, sensitive, and generally uncertain of himself. These handicaps were never more evident than when he neared the end of his legal studies. Despite Lewis' exhaustive preparation, Judge Burnet had to press him to take the bar exam, which involved answering questions before the Ohio Supreme Court. His son, William G.W. Lewis, relates that "he went literally with fear and trembling" and was speechless at the first question. After a long pause he finally found the nerve to respond and went on to pass the exam. His life was filled with similar anecdotes, illustrating that he was able to summon the inner strength needed to meet most challenges that came his way.[9]

His predisposition to shyness at times went to an extreme, producing in him what psychologists today call social anxiety. As he described in one of his letters "my disposition to avoid company is growing on me, and I avoid even meeting any old acquaintance. . . . When I am talking with an old acquaintance, and any one of his friends comes up, I instinctively step aside to avoid an introduction. This manner has always marked me more or less, but I now find it growing upon me, and though I choose thus to avoid company, and enjoy myself best alone or at home, I begin to fear too much indulgence in this habit." Social anxieties are often found in people with an obsessive-compulsive personality type, and while we can never know if Lewis' case fits that diagnosis, it is interesting that his love for work seems to have been a compulsion. More than once he pushed himself into a downward spiral of depression.[10]

The first episode came during the third year of his demanding legal practice. In 1824 in a letter to his aunt he confessed that he spent much of his time alone, crying. Later in that same letter, he indicated that poor self-esteem was contributing to his gloomy mood; in response to a complement from his aunt, he protested, "were you acquainted with me, you would find things to censure, perhaps condemn." He had at least five periods of depression that were bad enough to force him to temporarily withdraw from public life: in 1834 from the law, in 1839 from education, and in 1847, 1849, and 1851 from politics. The lasting effects of an injury suffered delivering the US mail during his adolescence, the deaths of three of his children, and the attacks of his political foes all contributed to his struggles. Still, time after time, Lewis was able to break free from his self-imposed prison to rejoin the fight against injustice.[11]

Lewis' resilience in the face of so many obstacles raises two questions: first, how did this reclusive man generate the energy to break out of his gloomy moods, and second, where did he find the confidence needed to engage in the very public field of politics? His son, William Lewis, observed concerning his father's fight against slavery, "there remains one motive to be noticed that operated upon the mind of Mr. Lewis, as well as thousands of others. . . . It was his Christian principle that made him an abolitionist, and if all such political motives as we have mentioned above had been wanting, still the moral one would have been sufficient." So, while Lewis' courage may have had other sources, Christianity was a key influence, as it was for many of the other crusaders. Certainly, the early spiritual instruction that Lewis received from his family and Reverend Otis laid the foundation for his faith, which in turn inspired his passion for evangelicalism and reform. A couple of anecdotes from his early years in Ohio bear this out; in the first, after hearing an appeal from a circuit rider for help in spreading the Gospel, he contributed all his money to the cause, and in the second, while working among carpenters who often had far too many drinks, he never took the first.[12]

Lewis' beliefs infused every corner of his adult life: his duty as a minister, his role as a father, his service as a crusader, and his work as a lawyer. It was in that last area that he revealed the lengths to which he would go to speak out against behavior that he believed was sinful. Early in his legal career he heard rumors that an attorney for one of his clients was struggling with drinking and gambling. Another ambitious young barrister might well have chosen to ignore these failings in a colleague, especially someone he hardly knew, but not Lewis. Instead, he wrote to the lawyer in blunt language, questioning him about the extent of his vices. And while it was clear from the communication that Lewis worried about the effect the lawyer's habits could have on his client's legal representation, he also cared for the man's own spiritual health. Lewis took such actions because he believed the law was his calling, just as he would later view his work on education and abolition, and he saw himself as a reformer of the profession and a defender of the oppressed. Early on, while studying for the bar examination, he had written to his grandfather that "it will be recollected, to the shame of many, that virtue and morality have at this time but few advocates at the bar. . . . If I can attain. . .to vindicate the injured poor, and protect those who have no friends or fortune on which to lean, when the oppressor would take unjustly the bread from their mouths, I shall be content. And when I shall receive the truly-enviable appellation of *'my deliverer'* from a poor man or woman, I shall be well repaid for this my exertion [emphasis is Lewis']." Indeed, on one occasion he was the only lawyer that would defend an accused murderer and, in a defense that demanded a great deal of fortitude and skill, he saved the man's life.[13]

Lewis also acted out of concern and courage while serving as a Methodist minister. In 1824 he joined Wesley Chapel, soon became a key member, and later was licensed to preach, despite his lack of formal training. While he was never called to a congregation on a full-time basis, he frequently substituted for pastors at other churches, a practice that he continued until just a few months before his death. At one funeral for a young woman, he brought many to faith in Christ as a result of an emotional sermon. But Lewis' concern for his fellow man's souls was matched by his courage to challenge their consciences. Even though he knew that if he avoided controversy he was more likely to be asked to return, he pointedly attacked slavery at two different churches. Sermons like these, in addition to his numerous letters to newspapers on slavery and civil rights, made his stance on these issues very clear. As a result, some pastors chose not to engage him. As he had done in his practice of the law, he never sacrificed the truth for expediency.[14]

Teaching the truth, as Lewis saw it, was also at the forefront of his relationships with his family, which included six children. When he was home, he prayed with them; when he was away on one of his frequent trips, he wrote them letters that offered advice on Christian living. Sounding much like his Puritan ancestors, he warned them to avoid indulging in the things that money could buy, including excessive "pleasure" and fine dress. He urged them to "think again how many poor women would with that same amount of money purchase the means of feeding a family of children." In addition to admonishing them about sinful behavior, Lewis showered them with a great deal of spiritual encouragement. In an 1836 letter he urged his children to strengthen their relationship with Christ. In 1845, after telling his daughters to "always think of the comfort of others before your own," he reminded them of their many blessings and advised them to show "gratitude to your heavenly Father." He then urged them to "read your Bibles" and "do not forget *to pray, to pray, to pray often* [emphasis is Lewis']."[15]

While Lewis was never reluctant to tell others how to live their lives, he was just as likely to show them by his example. This was evident throughout his years as an antislavery crusader, and is aptly illustrated by an incident from 1843. At the time the fight against slavery was often unpopular and dangerous in Southwestern Ohio, which bordered a slave state and profited from trade with the South. Twice in the last seven years angry mobs had destroyed abolitionist presses with the acquiescence of many of the area's most prominent citizens. In this tense environment Lewis had invited antislavery activists to a meeting at a Presbyterian church in Cleves, Ohio. Members of the family of the late president, William Henry Harrison, and many others, including youths wielding clubs and guns and fortified with alcohol, rallied to try to halt the meeting. Though friends warned Lewis of a dangerous confrontation, he ignored their pleas.[16]

Lewis related to his son that as he and his fellow reformers approached the church they were met by the crowd, which was led by J. Scott Harrison, a Congressman and son of the late president. Harrison told the reformers that few locals favored abolition and "if they attempted to hold a meeting there. . .they could not be responsible for the consequences." Lewis addressed the mob, explaining that he was there "to advocate no principles, but those of the Gospel of Christ, and the American declaration of rights." He warned "they alone would be held responsible by God. . .for any violence which might occur." Finally, he "asked them whether it had come to this, that American citizens could no longer peaceably assemble and present their views to each other, without being. . . threatened with violence, and for no other reason than that they were a minority."[17]

The pastor of the church, Reverend Blanchard, then offered a novel solution. Those in favor of the meeting would stand on the right and those opposed would stand to the left, in a scene evocative of the Bible's account of God's separation of the sheep from the goats on Judgment Day. When this human ballot was tallied it clearly favored the antislavery side. Seeing that he had lost, Harrison left, but many of his angry supporters stayed behind, in an attempt to further disrupt the meeting. In defiance of the shouting rabble, the activists loudly sang the hymn *How Firm a Foundation*, which Lewis followed with a public prayer. The departure of the mob's spokesman, the sound of the pious song, the sentiment of the fervent prayer, and perhaps even the waning effects of alcohol drained the last drop of the mob's courage and they began to drift away.[18]

While Lewis, like many of his fellow crusaders, was dedicated to solving many of society's problems, it was abolition that consumed most of the last thirteen years of his life. Time-and-again he accepted the nomination of small third parties in contests that he had no chance of winning. For the Liberty Party he ran for the state senate in 1842, US Congress in 1843, and governor in 1846; for the Free Soil Party he ran for US Congress in 1848, governor in 1851, and governor once again in 1853. It took zealots like Lewis, who were willing to exhaust personal assets, to risk professional careers, and to even face physical danger, to build the foundations that were essential for the next phase of the fight against slavery. While he failed to win any of his campaigns, respectable vote totals in 1848 and 1853 showed that during his two decades of self-sacrifice and service the aging crusader had earned the admiration of many, both inside and outside of reform circles. In the 1848 contest he received more votes in his district than did ex-President Martin Van Buren, the Free Soil candidate for president, and in the 1853 election he received almost 50% more votes than the average candidate of his party. Through all these years he was able to overcome his physical and mental suffering.[19]

Like his commitment to end slavery, Lewis' passion for education was seemingly without limit. It began in 1819 when he and a few other young people operated three Sunday schools for 250 poor children who would have otherwise received no instruction. In a letter to his aunt he lamented the fact that "the lands appropriated by Congress do not yet yield a sufficient revenue to support them [community schools]; and. . .the state Legislature has never yet taken the subject into consideration." It is likely that this discovery helped inspire his later demands for publicly-funded schooling.[20]

Soon after the passage of Ohio's education bill in 1825, Lewis persuaded a wealthy farmer, client, and friend, William Woodward, to create an endowment to fund Cincinnati's first free high school. Woodward at first included the money as a bequest in his will but then in 1826 the persistent Lewis prevailed upon him to give it immediately. Shortly thereafter, Lewis was able to convince Thomas Hughes, whose farm adjoined Woodward's, to endow another high school. Both institutions, which were named after their benefactors, remain important elements of today's Cincinnati Public School system. Lewis served as President of the Board of Trustees of the Woodward fund for the rest of his life and received several public commendations for his work there.[21]

In the 1830s Lewis filled a key leadership role as one of the organizers of the Western Literary Institute and College of Teachers, a Cincinnati-based, multi-state organization that proved extremely effective in organizing the emerging common school movement. As we shall see, its members would have a far-reaching impact on reform for decades to come. In fact, Lewis and other members of the Institute successfully lobbied Ohio's legislature to pass a landmark law in the late 1830s, leading to his appointment as the state's first Superintendent of Common Schools in March 1837. He accepted the twin tasks of determining the effectiveness of the schools as well as investigating the use (and misuse) of education funds. Ohio's laws had been widely ignored up to that point and the economic pressures created by the Panic that began that year were already emboldening those resistant to reform and opposed to school taxes. To make matters worse, Lewis faced these challenges with very little administrative support from the state.[22]

Nevertheless, Lewis decided, predictably, that he must visit as much of the state as possible in 1837. He soon embarked on a grueling journey by horseback, in a trip that was evocative of his fellow Methodist circuit riders, traveling 1,500 miles, visiting three hundred schools and forty county seats, and struggling with his physical and mental problems. He complained, "I arrived here to-day almost worn down; have rode on an average twenty-six miles a day, this week. I generally spend three or four hours a day in conversation, answering questions, giving explanations, and making suggestions."

He worried that "the task before me is so great, that. . . . I shall hardly be able to get through." He bemoaned the fact that, "I work hard, day and night, and find it a kind of up-hill business. If men would only do something, even in opposition, it would be better than it is. Almost every man agrees with me; thousands listen and applaud; and even candid men of sense declare they never heard this subject treated with so much interest, then leave it to go alone, or get on unaided by their efforts. Still I am not discouraged, . . .hoping at least for the final triumph of sound principles and practice."[23]

By December, after just nine months at his new post, Lewis was already confiding to his parents that he was sick from overwork. Still, in 1838 he traveled the state again, visiting sixty-five counties in addition to editing six issues of the *Ohio Common School Director* and performing other duties. His traveling companion during that summer was Rev. William Holmes McGuffey, who was soon to become famous for his ubiquitous *Readers*. Finally, in December 1839 the stress had become too much for him. When it seemed certain that a Democrat-controlled legislature would reverse the reforms for which he had worked so hard, he resigned, offering the apology that he had simply tried to apply "the true spirit of Christian philanthropy." Depressed and embittered, he abandoned statewide education efforts forever, though he remained active in improving the local schools of Cincinnati. For example, in the early 1850s, even as his health failed, he worked to merge his city's schools into a single district that had the mission of teaching all children, including blacks and girls, and constructing new buildings.[24]

It was quite fitting then that ground was broken for the new Woodward High School on July 28, 1854, the day that Lewis went to meet his Maker. At its dedication in 1856, his portrait was hung in the assembly hall, next to that of the school's namesake, William Woodward. Soon after his death, the Union Board of High Schools memorialized his work with the following resolution:

> Resolved, That the death of our President has not merely deprived this Board of one of its foremost and most valued members, but has taken away from the great cause of free education, an advocate and ornament who was second to none in its role of distinguished

names, and that we thus record these sentiments in the hope that such an example may not die, but live to incite others to *go and do likewise* [emphasis is the Board's].[25]

While Lewis' plans to establish a system of free schools were thwarted in the 1830s, he lived to see many of them implemented in the 1850s. In just three years he and his fellow zealots had drafted the blueprints for the state's system, which would earn him the acclaim from a few observers as the Founding Father of Ohio's schools. Still, despite his impressive accomplishments, most modern historians have ignored him.[26]

Horace Mann — Massachusetts

Meanwhile, educators, historians, and biographers have studied Horace Mann extensively for over 150 years, leaving us with a rich understanding of the Massachusetts crusader. Interestingly, he and Lewis had many life experiences that paralleled each other. Both he and Lewis were descended from first-generation Puritans and were born within three years and sixty miles of each other. They each underwent life-changing religious experiences in 1810, began legal apprenticeships in 1819, and started successful legal careers within a year of each other, Lewis in 1822 and Mann in 1823. They became the first chief education officers of their respective states in 1837, exhausted themselves through overwork that same year, and battled hostile Democrat majorities that tried to abolish their positions in 1840.[27]

Yet the similarities between the two included not just the eerie synchronization of their lives, but also their personality traits, health struggles, and cherished causes. Both were hypersensitive to criticism, yet were so committed to their core beliefs that they felt obligated to confront others, even total strangers. The stress caused by these incidents, the grief generated from the death of family, and the burden produced by overwork damaged their physical and mental health, which led at times to debilitating depression. Despite these problems, they fought for decades for temperance, education, and the rights of slaves and free blacks. Still, as we will see, it was not just their similarities, but also their differences, especially those related to their spiritual commitments, that allow us to better understand the corps of leaders who created America's first public schools.

While Mann's endeavors as the Secretary to the Board of Education in Massachusetts have made him famous, the rest of his public service, though it has largely been forgotten, was also impressive. Prior to his work on schooling he sat for eleven years in the Massachusetts legislature, which, at his urging, established the first state-operated mental hospitals in the country. Then, after he completed his work for the Board he served for five years in the US Congress, primarily fighting to end slavery. Yet his public accomplishments, while admirable, were hardly unusual for a reformer.[28]

In so many ways it is easy to see that the inspiration for Mann's public service came from his private life. His childhood in Franklin, Massachusetts was very typical for a New Englander, including zealots like Samuel Lewis and Ephraim Cutler. Beginning at age seven Mann worked long, boring days on the farm and, starting at age thirteen when his father died, his duties grew even more demanding. Since his struggling family needed his help on their farm, he was never able to attend school more than ten weeks a year. Perhaps this was a blessing, since his district school, as described by historian Frederick Binder, had a curriculum that was "narrow," pedagogy that was "stultifying," and teachers who were "cruel" and "stupid." In winter the building let in drafts, rain, and snow and was heated by a solitary fireplace that caused those seated nearby to sweat but left those sitting at a distance to shiver.[29]

Sundays brought anxious hours in church listening to the preaching of Congregational minister Nathaniel Emmons, who described humankind as being divided between the saved and the damned. This led Mann in his private moments to agonize over the thought that he or his family members might be condemned to hell. Then, when Mann was fourteen Emmons delivered a sermon following the tragic death of Mann's brother, Stephen, which caused him to question his beliefs. In violation of community norms and the pastor's injunctions, Stephen had skipped both services on the previous Sunday, most likely to fish or swim, and had drowned. Emmons used Stephen's tragedy as an opportunity to preach about the eternal penalty for dying without conversion, implying that the boy had not been saved. From that day on Mann became obsessed with the vision of his beloved brother in hell, but instead of accepting the justice system of orthodox Congregationalism and its terrifying God, he questioned it and later adopted the more optimistic Unitarianism with its more loving God. Still, though Mann would never revert to the Calvinist faith of his youth, in many ways its influence never left him.[30]

Mann signaled his break with Calvinism but also his continuing faith in God when he chose to attend Brown University, in Providence, Rhode Island. While it was just thirty miles from his home, it was also not under the control of an orthodox clergy, like Yale, nor did it possess a heretical faculty, like Harvard. The curriculum stressed memorization, recitation, and polemics. The last skill was not only developed through the writing of bi-weekly essays, but also through debates at the United Brothers Society, a social and literary club. Both experiences would later prove invaluable to Mann's legal, political, and reform activities. His essays praised Franklin, Washington, and the United States, while they condemned Europe and the Pope, whom he called "the vice regent of hell." Interestingly, these compositions from the man historians have crowned as the leader of education reform made no mention of Jefferson, even though those same scholars have claimed that the ideas of our third President were critical for the movement. Mann's valedictory address in 1819 deserves special attention since its title, "The Gradual Advancement of the Human Species in Dignity and Happiness," shows how far he had moved from the doctrine of the depravity of man to the notion of progress. This concept would prove to be an important influence on his educational philosophy.[31]

But while Mann had abandoned the Calvinists' religion, his years after graduation showed that he readily embraced their philosophy, Scottish Common Sense Realism. After a brief legal apprenticeship, he enrolled at the law school of Judge Tapping Reeve in Litchfield, Connecticut, the first such institution in the United States and the alma mater of many prominent politicians and jurists. Common Sense had a strong advocate at the law school in the person of one of his instructors, James Gould, who had graduated from Yale at a time when it was a spawning ground for that ideology. This exposure likely only increased the hold of Common Sense on his thinking, since he had already been introduced to it at Brown while studying William Paley's popular *Principles of Moral and Political Philosophy*. An indication of his fascination with this system of thought was that in his spare time he studied the works of Thomas Brown, one of its leading proponents. One can see the influence that Common Sense had on Mann from an important public speech he made in 1826. With President John Quincy Adams in the audience, Mann sharply criticized the French Revolution, in a clear rebuke to the Revolutionary Enlightenment and the skepticism that it had encouraged.[32]

Still, while Mann's education inspired him to contemplate a lofty matter like philosophy, his poverty forced him to take on the mundane task of earning a living. So soon after he was admitted to the bar in 1823 he began the practice of law and, despite a great deal of competition, he prospered from the start. While some of Mann's success in this and other endeavors can be attributed to his intelligence, most of it can be traced to the impressive work ethic that he had acquired back on the farm in his hometown. Years later, as he reflected on his work for the State Board of Education, he recalled: "I labored in this cause an average of not less than fifteen hours a day; from the beginning to the end of this period I never took a single day for recreation, and months and months passed without my drawing a single evening to call on a friend." Unfortunately, like Lewis (and many other leaders, for that matter), Mann could work so hard that it damaged his health. This compulsion eventually would have fatal consequences for both men.[33]

In addition to his work ethic, Mann's Calvinist upbringing also nurtured a predilection for critical scrutiny, not just of others, but also of himself. As a result, he formed a personality that was both sensitive and serious. His sense of justice made him unafraid to challenge people over reform issues, but unlike Lewis, who always acted in a polite and peaceful way, Mann could be abrasive and intemperate toward those with whom he disagreed. Those tendencies were obvious during several disputes that erupted during his tenure as the Board's Secretary. In fact, biographer Jonathan Messerli, referring to perceptions that Mann's ancestors were intolerant and that Unitarians had no fixed creed, has described him as "a Puritan without a theology."[34]

The death of Mann's wife in 1832 almost left him "a Puritan without faith." After searching for meaning in her death and finding none, he began to question the very existence of God. How could a loving God let his beloved Charlotte die? Fighting depression, insomnia, and exhaustion, he alternately fretted about a world without God or, perhaps influenced by Emmons' sermon on the fate of his brother, a heaven without Charlotte. After two torturous years, a noted Unitarian minister, William Ellery Channing, through personal counseling and a sermon on the afterlife, helped him to begin to resolve his doubts in God's favor and to slowly emerge from his depression.[35]

Spirituality was obviously important to Mann, as it was for the other zealots, who, as we know, were mostly Calvinists. Yet even though his Unitarian faith set him apart from them, with the exception of several highly publicized disputes, he and they managed to forge a tenuous working relationship. Both groups agreed on the idea of progress, though they came to that position using very different reasoning. Calvinists (and most other Protestants), based on their interpretation of the Bible, believed that with God's help a race that was basically sinful could continually improve and thereby hasten Christ's return, the onset of the Millennium, and the beginning of everlasting life. Unitarians, relying upon Enlightenment ideals (like those captured in Mann's valedictory speech), held that with enough research and education a race that was inherently good could greatly improve its lot in this world. Still, even though the two groups shared many common beliefs, when Unitarians found themselves in positions of authority, they tended to generate a great deal of suspicion from Calvinists and other Protestants. That was true for Mann as well as the other Unitarian leaders within the movement.[36]

Like so many other reformers, Mann worked for progress against many of humanity's problems, including poverty, disease, hunger, and prisoner abuse. But while he had a variety of concerns, the issues that consumed most of his time were education for the child, freedom for the slave, and compassion for the insane. In 1829 Mann took a leadership role on this issue in the Massachusetts House, where he first commissioned a survey of the treatment of the mentally ill and then successfully urged passage of a bill to construct a "Lunatic Hospital." Mann subsequently headed the commission that built the hospital, helped pass a bill that directed its operation and secured its funding, and then aided in the selection of its first superintendent. As we will see, six years later when his state established its system of common schools he would repeat this tested formula for success: first identify the problem, next pass legislation to correct it, and then personally follow through to make sure the law is administered properly.[37]

Unfortunately, though the formula worked effectively to protect the insane and to educate the children it would not lead to a similar path to success in his crusade for the enslaved. But Mann had no way to know that in 1848 when, after twelve years as Board Secretary, he ran for and won John Quincy Adams' seat in the US House of Representatives. The long hours and the bitter fights at the Board had made him weary and sick, but they had not diminished his appetite for reform. He was ready to jump into another cause, the antislavery fight, at a very critical point for the movement. But this battle was different than those he had fought in Massachusetts because it took place on a national stage, where the main actors were not united by the common culture of one state, but instead were separated by the regional differences of the country. And since he was just one of 230 members in the House, he lacked the ability to direct the political process, as he had done as a member of the leadership in the Bay State. As a result, Mann felt it was better to compromise on antislavery principles so as to make some headway rather than to remain steadfast and gain nothing. Predictably, his middle way drew fire from both extremes: pragmatists like Daniel Webster and purists like Charles Sumner and Joshua Giddings. He lost the Whig nomination for his seat in 1850, yet he still won a close election under the banner of the Free Soil party. But when he lost his campaign for governor in 1853, again as the Free Soil candidate, he left politics for good.[38]

Still, Mann is not remembered today for helping create the first state mental hospital or for working to end slavery. His fame, recorded in countless modern textbooks, has resulted from his twelve-year term as Secretary to the Massachusetts Board of Education. Unlike Samuel Lewis, who began working on education as a young man, Mann did not discover the struggle until middle age, when he entered it in a tentative and unenlightened way in 1837. During his previous ten years in the legislature, even though he had been involved with several other reforms, he had ignored every opportunity to work on education and had failed to work with groups such as the American Institute of Instruction, an organization based in New England that had a function similar to that of the Western Literary Institute.[39]

That all changed with the passage of the School Law of 1837. As Senate President, Mann had worked closely with James G. Carter, Chair of the House Committee on Education, to push this historic law through the legislature. In a shock to many, the position of Secretary to the State Board of Education was offered to him, instead of Carter, who had been the acknowledged leader of the movement since the 1820s. No one was more surprised than Mann himself, who doubted his ability to handle the job, given his ignorance about school theory and practice and his unfamiliarity with conditions around the state. But the Board wanted him for his superior political and rhetorical skills, not his knowledge of education. After vacillating for two months, he finally made his fateful decision right before the Board planned to name their secretary. Like so many other zealots, he closed his robust law practice and abandoned his promising political career to enter, in the words of Messerli, "the holy and patriotic crusade." Friends were puzzled by his actions, which clearly subordinated his personal wealth and prestige to the future of the children of Massachusetts.[40]

Mann immediately set about correcting the serious deficiencies that had given rise to his indecision. First, like a true son of the Enlightenment, he began to develop a philosophy of education. For the former Brown valedictorian this meant studying the writings of philosophers, including Common Sense thinkers Thomas Brown and Victor Cousin. He also pored over newspapers, which often contained articles on schooling, and William Russell's *American Journal of Education*. And, in an attempt to both learn and build contacts, he attended his first meeting of the American Institute.[41]

Second, in order to learn firsthand about local conditions and to promote education, he visited scores of towns and schools in his first year, traveling over 500 miles and in the process wearing out a saddle and a pair of riding pants. While he saw many encouraging signs, he also discovered many disheartening problems, which he would bluntly lay before the Board in his First Annual Report. Some opponents challenged him directly while others tacitly agreed with him but then ignored his recommendations once he had left town. The responses to Mann's entreaties paralleled those that Lewis had described to his family and they had a similar effect. By January 1838 Mann was physically and mentally exhausted. After a brief period of recuperation he returned to work, but the cycle of burnout, rest, and renewal would be repeated during the first few years of his crusade. In fact, his resilience, in conjunction with a political climate that favored his party, allowed him to remain in his post when Lewis could not.[42]

Mann revealed the source of his strength just two months before his death when he proclaimed his guiding principle to the newest graduates of Antioch: "Be ashamed to die until you have won some victory for humanity." And when his life had come to a close he had indeed recorded many victories for his fellow man: for the nation, its first state mental hospitals and normal schools, and for his state, the foundations of a system of government schools. But regarding education, Mann came late to the fight and his accomplishments, while laudable, were no more remarkable than Lewis, Barnard, and several others. And while he exhibited many of the traits of the zealots, his Unitarian beliefs and the optimism that they generated make him an imperfect exemplar of the leaders of the movement. Still, while Mann was not the singular leader that historians have virtually beatified as Father of the Public School, most saints would indeed be proud of the victories that he won for his fellow man.[43]

Henry Barnard—Connecticut

While we know a great deal about Mann's thinking, we are left mostly to speculate about the motives that drove Henry Barnard, the great Connecticut zealot, who is described by his biographer,

Edith MacMullen, "as a benign and shadowy figure." This is quite odd, since he survived Mann by forty-one years and exceeded his service to the movement by thirty-two years. As a result, he wrote far more than Mann and more than any other crusader of that era, yet those writings that survive, though they have been studied fairly extensively by historians, are very guarded about his thoughts. Fortunately, while Barnard's writings force us to speculate about his mind, the public record is clear about his many accomplishments. He was the first chief education officer for two states, the chief executive for two colleges, the first Commissioner of Education for the nation, and the editor for the most important school journal of the 19th century. And through extensive travel and publishing he developed a communications network unrivaled by any of his contemporaries.[44]

Further, we also have a clear sketch of the community that helped shape Barnard. MacMullen has described Hartford, Connecticut, where he spent his youth, as "a Puritan town where the Bible, Webster's spelling book, and the conservative Connecticut Courant were the bastions of local culture." Indeed, Calvinist theology and Federalist politics went largely unchallenged in what was then a small town. So little Henry, like so many other Yankee children, was encouraged to read the Bible and to work hard. Much of that work revolved around his education, which was quite good by the standards of the day. He attended a "dame school," a district school, an academy, and, after receiving tutoring from his pastor, Rev. Abel Flint, the prestigious Hartford Grammar School.[45]

His schooling had prepared him well for Yale, which he considered the highlight of his education. In the late 1820s Common Sense philosophy was exerting a strong influence there, especially in theology and science. In the former, Nathaniel Taylor was advocating New Haven Theology, while in the latter, Benjamin Silliman was arguing that there was no conflict between faith and science. Exposure to Common Sense must have left its mark because several years later he was still reading works written by its proponents. But Barnard acknowledged that the "school, college, or professors" did not shape his intellect nearly as much as the "books, libraries, and debate." Like Mann he joined a social and literary club, in his case the Linonian Society, which offered students the opportunity to socialize, read, debate, and even to produce plays.[46]

In addition to feeding his intellect and expanding his social network Barnard was also strengthening his faith at Yale. While he delivered many speeches at the Linonian and in classes, the only one that survives, "A Dissertation on The Services rendered by Christianity to poetry," testifies to the depth of his spiritual convictions. In an oration that argues in florid language for the superiority of Christianity over the classics, he describes "the utility and moral beauty of the Christian religion, its superiority over every other in its power to invigorate the understanding and purify the affections. . .it appeals to every feeling which can improve and dignify the human ear." Still, while historians Merle Curti and Vincent Lannie both observed that Christianity seemed to motivate his reform efforts, he left us with scant evidence of this in his other writings.[47]

After graduation from Yale and a failed attempt at teaching Barnard began to study the law and in 1835 he was admitted to the bar, though he never practiced it. He soon made an extended tour of Europe, and though he studied several issues there, education failed to attract his attention. In 1837 at age twenty-six Connecticut voters elected him to the legislature and once again, while he worked on a variety of causes, he ignored the condition of the schools. But that was all about to change.[48]

Beginning in 1838 Barnard embarked on a thirty-two year career in educational politics and administration when the State Board of Education offered him the position of Secretary to the Board, which he had just helped create. Even though he knew the schools were in bad shape, he agonized over whether or not to accept the job. This established a pattern of indecision that lasted for most of his life. He finally accepted the post and then, like Lewis and Mann before him, set out on a fact-finding trip, which took him to over two hundred schools in that first year alone. He would repeat those travels every year, in addition to his many other duties, until 1842 when a hostile legislature controlled by the Democrats abolished his position. Their rejection left a despondent Barnard sick and confined to his bed, but he would not stay idle for long.[49]

The next year Rhode Island engaged Barnard to study the condition of education within its borders. In 1843 the state offered him the job of Education Agent and in 1845 the post of Commissioner of Public Schools. He clearly accomplished a great deal there, organizing 1,100 meetings, delivering 1,500 speeches, disseminating 16,000 pamphlets, and distributing 1,200 books. Yet, in what became another life-long pattern, he neglected his duties for long periods of time, either to take the education gospel to other states or simply because he failed to give the job his complete attention. Extensive time outside the region was nothing new for him, since in the two years before he had taken the job as Agent, he had toured every state, visited sixty municipalities, and spoken before eleven legislatures. By 1848 complaints were mounting as Barnard was spending less time at his office in Providence and more at his home in Hartford. Finally, in 1849 he resigned under pressure, following more of his complaints of exhaustion and illness. His problems may have been partially psychosomatic, as his friends suspected, since this episode, like several others, had occurred while he was under attack from political opponents.[50]

Barnard for once showed little reluctance when he accepted an offer to become Connecticut's first Superintendent of Common Schools in 1849, but the rest of his conduct over the next six years plowed familiar ground. While he initially succeeded in creating the state's normal schools, lackluster administration, health complaints, extensive travel, and neglect of duty marked the rest of his tenure. His health concerns possessed a degree of legitimacy after 1852 when he sustained injuries in a wagon accident. Following a trip to Europe he resigned in 1855, since he was no longer willing to confine his work to just one state when he felt he could help the entire nation.[51]

During his many trips Barnard so impressed education officials that many of them offered him their top administrative post. In fact, the boards of Indiana University and the University of Michigan both seriously considered him for their presidencies and he could have had the Indiana job if he had wanted it. In 1858, after much deliberation, he accepted the position of Chancellor at the University of Wisconsin, but he accomplished little, in part because, predictably, he spent most of his time back home in Hartford. After once again complaining of health problems, he resigned in 1860, leaving many Wisconsin crusaders bitterly disappointed. In mid-decade he served for just one year as the chief administrator at St. John's College in Annapolis with strikingly similar results.[52]

Barnard abruptly resigned from St. John's in March 1867 to accept the nomination as the first Commissioner of the US Department of Education, an institution for which he had been lobbying for over a decade. This was a historic moment for the history of education in America, but the beginning of three unhappy years for Barnard. Once again, poor administration, long absences, and political opposition would mark his tenure, which ended with his dismissal by President Grant in 1870.[53]

While his firing marked the end of his career in public administration, he had already begun a slow withdrawal from it as early as 1855. In that year Barnard launched plans for a venture in educational publishing, which became one of the distractions that hampered his work as an administrator. In 1856 with the help of a fellow reformer he produced the first volume of the *American Journal of Education*. Over the next twenty-five years he would publish a total of thirty-two volumes, ranging in size from 622 to 941 pages. The *Journal's* circulation suffered due to its lack of focus, its concentration on administration over instruction, and Barnard's poor administrative and marketing skills. It never made a profit yet his obsession to keep it alive kept him on the verge of bankruptcy for most of his life. Still, despite the *Journal's* shortcomings it influenced many school leaders of Barnard's generation, especially those in the East, and supplied educational historians with a great deal of helpful material for many decades to come. In fact, in an ironic twist its numerous references to Mann may have burnished Barnard's close friend's reputation and inadvertently diminished his own.[54]

Barnard's willingness to risk his wealth and health for his faith-inspired cause marks him as a zealot, and indeed that is how he described himself, going so far as to compare himself to Peter the Hermit, a leading figure of the first Crusade. This reveals that he saw his work for the schools more as a religious mission than as a civic project. So if we then think of Bernard as a missionary of sorts, we can say that through his countless speeches and innumerable publications he evangelized for his cause for a longer time and to greater effect than any of his contemporaries. In fact, while many of them, including Lewis and Mann, strayed from the crusade for years at a time, Barnard devoted himself to it for almost his entire adult life.[55]

Clearly, Lewis, Mann, and Barnard experienced the most success of any of the reformers during the second phase of their struggle. But one needs to take care not to deduce from their achievements that these men dominated the movement. The cadre of zealots expanded so rapidly during the 1830s that, even though none of the others tasted success like these three, it is best to think of them as types rather than as preeminent leaders. For those purposes, Barnard is not the best example simply due to the lack of details about his personal life. And Mann, despite the fact he is upheld by so many as the Father of the Public Schools, also falls short as the best exemplar for the movement, due to his Unitarianism and its influence on his thinking. Only Lewis, the evangelical, gives us a reliable picture of the selfless crusaders who toiled during this phase of reform.

Like the other reformers, including Barnard, Lewis and Mann left no doubt that they were willing to sacrifice their physical and mental health during their single-minded quest for justice. Indeed, these two men, in addition to the many other strange parallels of their lives, would share one final experience that highlighted their zealotry. In 1853 during Lewis' final unsuccessful campaign, despite failing health he traveled the state and in the process weakened himself even further. But unlike his previous setbacks, this time he failed to rally and died the following year. In similar fashion Mann's last project, also begun in 1853, would contribute to his demise. Even though he fought for six years to launch Antioch, his work ended in failure, resulting in the bankruptcy and sale of the college. A physically exhausted and mentally discouraged Mann died in 1859. Had a compulsive work ethic and total dedication to a cause finally killed them both? Fortunately, the sacrifices made by Lewis, Mann, and Barnard were not in vain. For in the late 1830s it was their leadership, in the face of daunting obstacles, which brought the second phase of school reform to Ohio, Massachusetts, and Connecticut.[56]

Chapter 8

The Perfect Moment — Ohio, Massachusetts, and Connecticut

*O*nly Ohio, Massachusetts, and Connecticut managed real reform during the movement's second phase in the late 1830s. Ohio and Connecticut, under the direction of Samuel Lewis and Henry Barnard, implemented historic education laws, but opponents would soon reverse some of their gains. On the other hand, Massachusetts, under Horace Mann's direction, was able to pass and successfully defend its new legislation from attack, but even the Bay State would find its progress stalled over the next decade. Results in these states resembled the two steps forward, one step back pattern that had unfolded in Ohio and Illinois in the 1820s. And as in the first phase, economic distress and its political impact would affect the timing of the crusade in these three states. The rest of the states failed to advance because, in contrast to the three successful ones, they could not overcome two major obstacles. First, the Midwest, South, and Border regions contained large numbers of people who opposed public instruction for cultural reasons. And second, every region suffered from the economic privations of the Panic of 1837, which made the funding of schooling exceedingly difficult.

In telling this story, the same historians who favored Mann and neglected Lewis focused on the movement in Massachusetts and Connecticut while ignoring it in Ohio, presenting a picture that is mostly Eastern, urban, and secular, rather than Western, rural, and religious. And yet, as this story unfolds we will see that Ohio and its evangelical zealot represent the cause far more accurately than do Massachusetts and its rationalist leader. Meanwhile, Connecticut's crusade, with its "benign and shadowy" reformer, Barnard, remains to this day difficult to categorize and compare to other states. Fortunately, economic historians have left us with a much better understanding of the events surrounding the Panic of 1837, which had such a profound effect on reform. They tell us that in the early 1830s the economy began to rise and fall erratically as a result of a dispute between Andrew Jackson and the Bank of the United States (BUS) over peoples' access to loans. When credit was plentiful business boomed and prices soared, but when it was scarce the economy slowed and prices plunged. Jackson felt that too much paper money was recklessly fueling a land boom in the West, while supporters of the BUS believed that credit was necessary to fund a healthy economy. In the spring of 1836 the Texas Revolution began to interrupt the flow of Mexican silver into the world economy and then in the summer Jackson ordered banks to accept "specie" (gold or silver) rather than paper money for federal land, forcing banks to call in many loans. This action brought on another slump, which spiraled into the Panic by May of 1837.[1]

The decline came on quickly and its consequences rivaled anything seen during the Great Depression. Banks foreclosed on farms and other businesses when debtors could not pay off their loans in specie. Many banks then failed because they lacked hard money to repay loans from other banks. Over the next year prices dropped 22% across the board and even more in the agricultural sector. While a brief recovery interrupted the decline, prices from 1837 to 1844 dropped an astounding 83%. The Panic was especially damaging for debtors and those involved in the market economy. Industrial unemployment hit 30%, which forced many people in the cities onto relief. This prompted a very engaged electorate, as it had in 1819, to ask who or what was to blame.[2]

The Whig party had a simple answer for them; Jackson and the Democrats had brought on the Panic by demanding the use of hard money. In response, the Democrats charged that the banks had caused it by circulating too much paper money. Sharp differences over this and other issues, usually dealing with the proper role of government, created loyal bases of support for both parties. Whigs, who were often merchants or farmers dependent upon distant markets, also wanted the government to fund canals, turnpikes, and railroads, which would lower their transportation costs. Democrats, who were typically urban workers or farmers isolated from markets, wanted the government to limit spending and taxes. While their fiercest clashes involved economics, disagreements spilled over into moral and social issues, including education. Whigs urged the government to sponsor community schools that would develop good Christians and citizens while Democrats wanted no part of this and other reforms, since they cherished the rights and autonomy of the individual.[3]

The Whigs won most of those battles in the late 1830s for two reasons. First, the Democrats had been on the defensive, especially in the West, even before the Panic began. Jackson's opposition to banking and internal improvements had proved unpopular because many residents thought those policies would hurt their region's growth. As a result, Old Hickory's Vice President, Martin Van Buren, received far fewer votes in the Presidential election of 1836 than Jackson had just four years before. In fact, he won only because the Whigs split their vote among three candidates. Second, since the Democrats had held power in Washington for nine years, they found it difficult to shift blame. So, Whigs swept most elections in the late 1830s and since they were the primary advocates for public education, they ushered in the second phase of school reform in Ohio, Massachusetts, and Connecticut.[4]

Ohio

During this part of the story the Buckeye State would be the first to taste success, as well as the first to suffer defeat. Two aspects of its experience closely resembled that of other states, including those that made progress and those that did not: Whigs and Calvinists led the movement and an unpredictable economy greatly affected the timing of its advances as well as its setbacks. The zealots began their work in earnest in January 1836, when some members of the Western Literary Institute met in Columbus to form a state society that began to press the legislature to address the educational needs of the Ohio's children. Since the Whigs held only one-third of the legislature, the group made no progress at first, but they were about to benefit from a volatile shift in voter preferences, one of several that occurred during the period.[5]

Power swung abruptly to the Whigs in the fall of 1836. In addition to blaming the national Democrat Party for the faltering economy, they attacked the state party for two unpopular positions: their desire to ban small bank notes, which they had passed into law, and their plan to curtail charters for banks and other corporations. Whig candidate Joseph Vance defeated Democrat Governor Robert Lucas in October, as Whig seats in the state legislature soared from 33% to 49%. Vance won with a platform that advocated re-charter of the BUS, completion of internal improvement projects, and application of Ohio's share of the federal surplus to education. The party's gains encouraged them to move on their agenda in early 1837. In January, Rep. W.B. Van Hook, who had attended the Institute's state convention a year earlier, reported legislation out of his House committee that proposed establishing a Superintendent of Common Schools. In February, the bill cleared the House by a narrow margin, 35-34; then on March 22 it cleared the Senate on a voice vote. The historic proposal would soon become law.[6]

Yet the bill would never have survived except for some clever logrolling. Just like its predecessor in 1825, Ohio's School Law of 1837 passed with the votes of internal improvement supporters, who had agreed to back it in exchange for help they had just received from the reformers. Less than three weeks before its enactment, on March 4 education advocates had helped pass the Ohio Loan Law. Ironically, the "Plunder Law," as it was called by its critics, handicapped the cause for many years in two ways. First, it authorized a large increase in state debt to help finance the private construction of canals and railroads. While the statute greatly expanded the state's transportation network, it came at a terrible cost. Most of the canal companies and many of the railroads failed, which left the state struggling under a huge debt load. Second, it designated Ohio's share of the federal surplus, $2,007,260, for the school fund, but at the same time it permitted counties, the state, and the Canal Fund to borrow unlimited amounts from it for any purpose. In a short time all the monies had been borrowed, replaced by notes promising to pay the fund interest at 5% per annum. In effect, the fund's health had been compromised because assets of unquestioned value had been exchanged for the liabilities of weak creditors. So, both provisions served to limit the state's ability to properly fund schools at a critical point in their development.[7]

Lewis became Ohio's first Superintendent on April 1, thus preceding Mann by three months and Barnard by a year. While his duties would not be codified until 1838, they resembled those of chief education officials in many other states: (1) to assess current conditions, (2) to investigate school funds, and (3) to make recommendations to the legislature. After completing his exhausting inspection tour of the state, he presented his grim findings at a public meeting in Columbus in December. Lewis' First Annual Report detailed many problems, including inattentive supervisors, unqualified teachers, crowded classrooms, and inequitable funding that favored the rich. Further, many of the middle and upper classes were sending their children to private and religious schools, which fostered the impression that they were better than those sponsored by the community. The new superintendent offered many suggestions that were not implemented, including teachers' institutes, high schools, evening schools, normal schools, libraries, and a state university. But he made other recommendations that would soon bear fruit, including new township, county, and state taxes that were to be distributed in proportion to the number of children in each district, which would eliminate inequities between rich and poor. He warned that state monies should only be allocated to communities that taxed themselves, which he hoped would encourage their commitment to education. Finally, after reporting that lot 16 lands had sold far below their market value, he urged controls to protect against their misuse.[8]

Lewis had good reason to expect that the legislature would be receptive to his ideas, since the deepening Panic had helped increase Whig seats to 56% of the House in October 1837. Urged on by

Gov. Vance, on March 7, 1838 the new majority passed a law that embraced much of the Superintendent's vision. The act established a hierarchical system of supervision and reporting, which led from the school to the township (Township Clerk), to the county (County Auditor), and finally to the state (Superintendent). It spelled out the Township Clerk's duties in detail, including a requirement that he place a tax levy on the ballot for any budget shortfall. The bill also strengthened Lewis' position in several ways: it listed his duties, increased his salary from $500 to $1,200 per year, lengthened the Superintendent's term to three years, and authorized publication of the *Ohio Common School Director Journal*. The legislature also approved two tax levies, a two-mill county tax and a five-mill state tax, and it created a $200,000 fund to protect lot 16 lands. But as bright as the future seemed at the moment, the winds of the economy were about to shift dramatically once again, emboldening the Democrats and casting a shadow over much of the crusaders' work.[9]

Weather, improbably enough, had a lot to do with the abrupt change in the political climate. Bad weather produced a poor harvest in England in 1838, which, following the laws of supply and demand, led to higher crop prices, first in England and then in America. This, in turn, expanded credit, which began to revive the economy in September, thereby boosting prospects for the Democrats, whose political fortunes were still tied to the economy. In October Vance lost his bid for reelection and the Whigs surrendered control of the House, winning only 47% of its seats. At the start of the next session Democrats tried to eliminate Lewis' position and to lower the state tax. While those efforts failed, by 1839 they had succeeded in lowering the county tax, reducing the power of Township Clerks and school directors, and eliminating the *Journal*. And in a further insult to the overworked Lewis, they rejected his request for a clerk.[10]

The economic recovery continued into the fall of 1839, leading to disastrous results for the Whigs in the October elections, which left them controlling only 32% of the seats in the legislature while a Democrat continued to occupy the Governor's mansion. The Democrats had swept the election while pledging to restore anti-banking legislation that the Whigs had repealed in March 1838, the same month that party had enacted the landmark education law. The

Democrats fulfilled their promise on banking in March 1840, and at the same time abolished the position of Superintendent. But Lewis, despondent and exhausted after the shattering losses of the previous year had already resigned effective December 1, 1839.[11]

Even though, in an ironic turn of events, the climatic and political weather vanes soon changed direction again, it was too late to help Lewis and his friends. Good weather produced an abundant harvest in England in 1839, which led to low crop prices and a shortage of specie in that nation's banks, which once again tightened credit, both at home and abroad. When banks in America followed suit, the economy resumed its decline in November 1839, just one month after the Whigs' electoral debacle. As conditions worsened throughout 1840, people increasingly focused on politics. With a Democrat (Van Buren) in the White House, they made his party pay a terrible price in the fall. The Whigs elected Thomas Corwin as Governor and captured 71% of House seats in October, more than doubling their seats from a year earlier. Unfortunately, both the people and the state were so strapped for funds that no one, not even the Whigs, dared advocate increased spending or higher taxes for any purpose, let alone for a new program like government schools.[12]

Despite this setback, in three short years Lewis and his fellow zealots had made dramatic progress. The numbers of schools in operation and children in class increased 68% and 69%, respectively. Spending from private and public sources soared, which helped administrators extend learning for the average student to over four months. Whigs had used shrewd political dealing during a period of economic volatility to advance their movement by two steps. But in the end their political opponents, assisted by a change in that same economy, had pushed it back one. As a result, the cause of free education in Ohio would have to wait another decade before taking its next and final step.[13]

Other Midwestern States

None of the other states in the Old Northwest would experience the success of Ohio because their crusaders could not overcome either the cultural attitudes of their citizens or the financial problems of their economies. In Indiana, while population density had increased since the 1820s, cultural opposition to the cause still predominated and that sentiment was reflected in the state legislature. The Whigs who controlled the state's government in the 1830s were mostly Appalachians who lacked the Yankee commitment to learning. Further, like their fellow party members in other states, they were capitalists who pushed for internal improvements that they hoped would lower their transportation costs. As a result, in the late 1830s Indiana launched grandiose canal schemes that would cripple the state's finances, prevent the passage of meaningful education laws, and hinder its ability to fund schools for many years. The movement in the Hoosier State would have to wait until the final phase of reform when a determined minister from New England would awaken the state from its slumber.[14]

Illinois was remarkably similar to Indiana during these years. Appalachians opposed any attempts to transfer control of education to the state and Yankees remained few in number. And despite large-scale migration into central and northern Illinois after the conclusion of the Black Hawk War, population densities were still low in many areas. Like Indiana and Ohio, the Prairie State began huge canal and railroad projects that by 1840 had brought financial distress similar to its neighbors. Still, while the state failed to enact any legislation during the 1830s like its law of 1825, it planted a seed that would bear fruit during the cause's final phase. Ironically, one of those internal improvement projects, which initially hindered its ability to fund schools, would eventually bring two things that it desperately needed: rapid growth and education-loving Yankees.[15]

Finally, Michigan, though it had a very favorable cultural makeup, was so sparsely populated during the 1830s that the crusade made little progress there. Its northern location was both a blessing and a curse. While its latitude attracted New Englanders the cold climate and poor soil retarded its growth. As a result, while Michigan passed some of the most progressive laws in the nation during the second phase, its isolation meant that few children benefited from them.[16]

Massachusetts

Meanwhile, back east the Bay State embarked on the reform trail just three months after Ohio. Its experience matched that of other states in two ways: first, the economy had a great affect on the movement's political power, and second, Whigs led the cause while Democrats opposed it. But two aspects of the Massachusetts crusade made it quite unique, beginning with its politics. First, the Whigs dominated almost every election, so they seldom had to make deals or create coalitions to pass legislation, nor would they see it overturned, as did their fellow party members in Ohio and elsewhere. Second, Unitarians formed a larger part of the leadership than in any other state, which reflected the fact that the sect was much more plentiful in Boston than elsewhere. As a result, their beliefs were challenged less in eastern Massachusetts than anywhere else in the country. So, because of the Commonwealth's unique qualities, other states, such as Ohio, give us a much more accurate picture of the national movement.

But the exceptional nature of Massachusetts has failed to deter generations of educational historians from examining many aspects of its crusade while ignoring all but the most basic facts in other states. In one sense their error is understandable in light of the long-standing commitment that New Englanders had made to learning. As we have seen, they were heirs to the Puritan tradition of support that stretched back to the 1640s and before that to Europe. In 1789 the Bay State, having just become part of the United States, enacted a statute that codified many of the practices that had become accepted over the years, including requirements for minimum school terms, curriculum standards, grammar schools, teacher qualifications, and local supervision. But despite its promise, over the next four decades education in the Commonwealth atrophied as the result of widespread apathy. Ironically, the three Yankees in Ohio were advancing the project at the same time that their fellow New Englanders back home were losing ground.[17]

Still, one heroic Bostonian, James Gordon Carter, took on the task of revitalizing the system during some of its darkest years. Starting in 1821, Carter wrote many newspaper articles, which were widely read in New England, later published in book form, and then circulated throughout America and Europe. Carter lamented the decline of community education, called for the creation of teachers colleges, and pointed out the inequities caused by the academies. He warned that without significant improvements the schools might not even exist in twenty years. Carter lobbied the Massachusetts legislature tirelessly and in 1826-7 it passed laws that strengthened local supervision and reporting, guaranteed that each child had a textbook, and created America's first public high schools. But Carter also witnessed two stinging defeats: in 1827 legislators rejected his plan to start normal schools and in 1837 they repealed a provision that had required districts to raise taxes and file reports as a condition for receiving state money.[18]

The 1837 session yielded three additional defeats. Carter, who had fought for education for sixteen years, was leading reform efforts in the House while Mann, who had just recently become interested in the cause, directed matters in the Senate. They sought: (1) the deposit of their state's share of the federal surplus into its school fund, (2) a requirement that districts could only access that fund if they levied taxes equivalent to at least $3 per student, and (3) authorization for the state's first normal schools. But to their dismay, the legislature allocated just half the surplus to the fund and it rejected the other two proposals outright. Matters looked bleak indeed for the movement.[19]

Still, in the midst of these defeats Carter and Mann managed a victory that, while seemingly insignificant and disappointing at the time, has since become a staple of educational history textbooks. The popular Whig governor, Edward Everett, in his annual address in January had asked the legislature, which was packed with his fellow party members, to create a Board of Education. Advocates wanted the Board to be headed by a superintendent, as it was in Ohio, but after their first attempt failed, they adjusted it just enough to narrowly carry the legislature. The law now provided for a Board headed by a Secretary with powers that one historian has described as "mild and inoffensive." The Board was comprised of eight members, including the Governor and Lieutenant Governor ex-officio, and a Secretary with an annual salary of $1,000. The Board had no power beyond collecting and summarizing reports from the schools and making an annual report to the legislature, which included recommendations. Once Mann reluctantly accepted his unexpected appointment as Board Secretary on July 1, he faced a host of problems, all of which were rooted in public apathy: inadequate funding, inattentive supervision, unsatisfactory textbooks, unprepared teachers, and not surprisingly, poor attendance. He observed all these deficiencies and more during his long tour of the state, which he articulated to the Board in the first of twelve Annual Reports. But he also communicated in other ways, including speaking at county meetings and teacher institutes and publishing the bi-weekly *Common School Journal*. Though he had little power other than the "bully pulpit," he would use his formidable writing and speaking skills to bring incremental improvements to Massachusetts education over the next eleven years.[20]

The first such advance involved the development of teachers. The concept of special colleges to train instructors, called normal schools, had originated in Prussia. Several intellectuals had visited the German kingdom and written reports that praised its creation of such schools, including Victor Cousin, a French philosopher, and Calvin Stowe, an Ohio educator, in 1835 and 1838, respectively. In 1835 the Rev. Charles Brooks, a Massachusetts minister, had traveled to Prussia and had been so impressed by its educational system that for the next three years he lectured throughout his state on its virtues, including its use of normal schools. His promotion seems to have had its effect because in 1838, at the urging of Carter, Mann, Brooks, and Everett, the legislature authorized the first teachers colleges in the country, just one year after it had rejected the idea and eleven years after Carter had first introduced it. When legislators enacted five other school laws that year, the future suddenly looked bright for the cause, but lawmakers also passed a statute that came close to destroying everything they had built.[21]

Carter, Mann, and many other Whigs were, like Samuel Lewis, strong proponents of temperance and they pushed through the "15-gallon law," which prohibited the sale of alcohol in quantities under fifteen gallons. The practical effect of the legislation was to outlaw the sale of drinks sold by the glass in grog shops or bars. This enraged Irish-Catholic immigrants, who were growing in number, and boosted their party of choice, the Democrats. Unfortunately for the Whigs, this controversy coincided with the short-lived economic recovery, which helped their opponents, as it had in Ohio and most other states. As a result, in November 1839 after a heated campaign the Democrats won a sweeping victory, leading to their control of both houses of the legislature for the first time in the state's history and occupancy of the governor's mansion for the first time since 1825. This outcome was unthinkable, given the previous dominance of the Whigs. For example, the Democrat candidate for governor, Marcus Morton, had run for that post every year since 1828 and this was his first win. And just two years earlier, in November 1837, his party had captured only 13% of the seats in the legislature.[22]

While the Democrats had seized control due to the 15-gallon law and the economy, leading activists, like Orestes Brownson and Governor Morton, made clear that they also opposed Mann and the Board. Mann's plans to standardize textbooks, curriculum, and pedagogy violated the principle of local control that Democrats held so dear and the dominance of the Board by Whigs and Unitarians created an atmosphere of mistrust, based on political and religious differences. The Democrats took action on March 7, 1840, when a House committee approved abolishing the Board, eliminating Mann's position, and closing the normal schools. Mann quickly prepared a response and by March 11 its key points were circulating as a minority report. Apparently it was quite effective, because on March 18 the Board's defenders easily defeated the measure, 245-182. While Whigs overwhelmingly defended the Board, one-fifth of them favored its elimination; and while Democrats mostly opposed the Board, one-third of them voted to defend it. So, there were many exceptions to the parties' core positions on the schools.[23]

Before the Board's opponents could launch another assault the economic winds shifted once again and the threat to the crusade dissipated almost as quickly as it had appeared. In fact, soon after the last vote of the 1839 election was counted the Panic regained its hold on commerce and before long the Whigs were once again blaming the faltering economy on the banking and monetary policies of the Democrats. So in November 1840, aided by William Henry

Harrison's populist campaign, they defeated Morton and took 70% of the seats in the legislature. While the Democrats would never again seriously threaten education in the 1840s, they had neverthe-less been encouraged by their victory and the Whigs had been chas-tened. The political environment had now become less favorable for the reformers and it would prove to be one of three factors that prevented further meaningful legislation in Massachusetts during Mann's tenure there.[24]

Mann's intemperate nature provided a second explanation for the halt in lawmaking after 1840. Perhaps it was his Calvinist upbringing that made him so self-righteous, but whatever the source, he found it easy to label his critics in the most offensive ways. He once admonished Board opponents as "political madmen" and he was hardly gracious after his victory in 1840, when he called his opponents "bigots and Vandals [that] had been signally defeated in their wicked attempts to destroy the Board of Education." With such comments, it is easy to see how he generated fierce opposition.[25]

The third obstacle was a series of disruptive battles between the Board and religious conservatives in 1838, 1844, and 1846 over the appropriate role of religion in the schools. While most evangelicals supported the Board in these disputes, a significant number of them opposed it because they believed that Unitarians (and Universalists) were heretics and therefore could not to be trusted to supervise the schools. In Mann's case their fears were probably unfounded since he insisted upon the teaching of religion and morality, including the use of the Bible. His critics feared the power of the Unitarians, who, in addition to dominating the Board, controlled Harvard and many other institutions in greater Boston. But influential as members of that sect were in the city, they were always fairly insignificant and powerless elsewhere in the state. As a result, these religious contro-versies would arise throughout Mann's career and sap his strength.[26]

By 1848 the disputes over religion and the lack of legislation had taken their toll on Mann, leading him to resign from the Board and run for Congress. Despite his modest powers as Secretary he had used his platform to prod Massachusetts to make significant improvements in its educational system. He rarely innovated, but instead took other's ideas, sold them to the citizenry, and then implemented them. Progress was slow, but during his tenure he helped grow the school year by a month and increase appropriations and teacher salaries by 100% and 50%, respectively. In addition, the state spent $2,000,000 to build many new elementary schools, fifty high schools, and three normal schools. And, in a significant development, he had changed the perceptions of most parents, who were beginning to favor public schools over private ones. Still, the steady advances Massachusetts experienced over his twelve years were modest in comparison to the explosive growth that Ohio had seen in just three years under Lewis. In the end, apathy, economics, religion, and Mann's personality had placed a stumbling block in the way of reform in the Bay State. It would take a lot of hard work by another generation of dedicated zealots before the Commonwealth secured its final victory.[27]

Connecticut

To the south, the cause came to the Land of Steady Habits just one year after it arrived in Massachusetts. The movements resembled each other as well as those in many other states in two ways: the Whigs dominated their leadership and the economy affected their progress. Yet two other elements made Connecticut's crusade unlike the Bay State's but similar to that of most other states. First, since Calvinists dominated its leadership, religious tensions, such as those that Boston's Unitarians had generated, were not a factor. And second, while the movement took a couple tentative steps forward, some of its progress would be reversed within a few short years.[28]

Certainly, Connecticut's history of support for learning, which was a legacy from its Puritan heritage, proved a great asset to its leaders. Organizations dedicated to the movement had formed as early as 1799 and by the 1820s large numbers of activists were gathering in conventions to discuss ways to advance their cause. But Connecticut's heritage, as it had in Massachusetts, also created a liability because the apathy that it bred in the people often negatively impacted the funds spent on education. For example, many residents believed that its school fund, which had been set up in 1795 with the proceeds from the sale of the Western Reserve lands, relieved their duty to raise other monies. And when the state received its share of the US surplus in 1836 the money was either mismanaged by local officials or redirected for other purposes. As a result, observers reported decrepit buildings, crowded classrooms, unskilled teachers, nonstandard textbooks, and abbreviated sessions. As Barnard would later tell it, "our district schools had sunk into a deplorable condition of inefficiency, and no longer deserved the name of common in its best sense." As a result, he opined, "there was not one educated family in a hundred that relied on the district school for the instruction of their children."[29]

By 1838 the reformers could no longer tolerate such conditions. Barnard, who had not previously shown an interest in the crusade, developed a comprehensive plan for Connecticut that envisioned a statewide system of primary, intermediate, and high schools, an elected board, a full-time superintendent, and a state tax. Further, he hoped that costs for parents could be kept low. In June legislators, led by the Whigs, took a small step when they enacted a statute that authorized an appointed Board with a Secretary who was to be paid $3 per day plus expenses. Barnard reluctantly accepted the position, even though it lacked the power implied by Lewis' title (Superintendent), and fell far short of paying the fulltime salaries enjoyed by Lewis and Mann. The Secretary's duties were limited: to collect semi-annual reports from school "visitors" (supervisors), to make an annual report on conditions to the Board, and to present recommendations.[30]

Bernard's activities over the next four years looked remarkably like those of Lewis and Mann. In the first year alone he visited two hundred schools and gave sixty lectures, in an exhausting effort to investigate conditions, develop recommendations, and promote solutions. His methods, which by now should sound familiar, included private discussions, public conventions, teacher institutes, official reports, letters, and publication of the *Connecticut Common School Journal*. Reformers united behind Barnard's calls for a system of graded schools, consolidated districts, teacher associations, better teacher pay and training, normal schools, and paid supervisors. District taxes would pay for these improvements and make it possible to waive rate bills for parents of the poor. At the grass roots level, his efforts led to teacher exams in forty towns, school associations in fifty towns, and a few teachers' organizations. On the other hand, at the political level, despite his party's control of the legislature, he could neither elevate his position to that of superintendent, something others had been attempting since 1827, or eliminate rate bills. And he made little progress towards his goals of limiting local power and creating statewide standards. Finally, in 1841 he received approval of consolidated districts, "grammar" schools (like high schools), teacher examinations, pay for supervisors, and waiver of rate bills for the poor, but even these advances would prove to be short-lived.[31]

In 1842 the economy brought about a change in the political balance of power and this time it hurt the Whig Party. In Connecticut, as in Massachusetts and Ohio, the party had risen to power in 1837-1838 by successfully blaming the economic slide on Democrat banking policies. But during the lull in the Panic in 1839, unlike the other two states, Connecticut's Whigs had not lost control of government. Then, as the economy worsened once more in 1840 and 1841 the party's power grew, as a result of its promise to fix the economy. But when the Panic persisted into 1842 a restive and disappointed electorate turned to the Democrats in such numbers that it produced one of the largest reversals in state electoral history. Amazingly, the Whigs' share of seats in the House dropped from 67% in 1841 to just 32% in 1842.[32]

Democrat Gov. Chauncey Cleveland soon signaled his intention to take advantage of his party's huge majority. In his inaugural address he charged that the concept for the Board had been copied from Prussia, an aristocratic nation that was a poor model for democratic America, and that it generated unnecessary expenses. He then proposed repealing recent school legislation, including the 1841 law, and eliminating the Board and its Secretary. While Cleveland did not mention Barnard's poor administration and lack of focus, they were likely a consideration for the legislature. A joint committee approved a bill that accomplished the Governor's goals and it quickly passed both houses by a 2:1 margin. Unlike Ohio, Connecticut made no provision to shift the Board's responsibilities to the

Secretary of State, so education reform had received a true death-blow.[33]

Nonetheless, one should not minimize Connecticut's accomplishments under Barnard, especially when compared to those of most other states, which had shown little or no appetite for the movement through the early 1840s. After all, it had briefly placed into law a comprehensive plan for public education that included paid supervision, professional teaching, and improved school buildings. Still, in comparison to the gains made by Ohio, its progress must be considered modest at best. In fact, both in terms of the scope of its laws and the condition of its schools, Connecticut lagged behind Ohio by a couple decades. The relationship of each state to its founding provides the key to understanding this disparity. Connecticut was beginning its third century and had become comfortable with its approach to education; Ohio, on the other hand, had not yet emerged from its pioneer era and was still creating new institutions, like schools, to help its citizens cope with life on the frontier. As a result, a fog of apathy handicapped reformers in Connecticut while a spirit of innovation lifted them in Ohio. Connecticut's crusaders shared this problem with their associates in the Bay State, in addition to the difficulties brought about by the economy and the personal flaws of their leaders.[34]

Education Philosophies of Lewis, Mann, and Barnard

Yet despite their personal weaknesses, Lewis, Mann, and Barnard were the only state leaders to experience even modest success during the second phase of reform. That should provide reason enough for us to study their philosophies of education. Still, we need to be careful not to see them as national leaders, as generations of historians have done for Mann, and, to a lesser extent, for Barnard. For one thing, Mann and Barnard did not even become active in the movement until 1837 and 1838, respectively, yet by that time the crusade was already thriving throughout New England and the Midwest. And while the official reports, journals, and letters of the three were widely distributed, so were the writings of many other advocates who were just as active at the time. So, it is better instead to think the three as types, as examples of a much larger cohort of zealots who collaborated in many ways with one another on behalf of their cause.[35]

Any examination of the philosophies of the three presents a challenge. Lewis had a brief career in education reform, did not publish much, and has rarely been studied by historians. On the other hand, Mann served in the movement for twelve years, wrote a great deal, and has been studied by scholars for over 150 years. Yet Mann was more interested in implementing the ideas of others than in developing his own. Finally Barnard, though he published a massive amount of material that was produced by others, disclosed little of his own thinking, including his philosophy on schooling. Still, when we analyze their extant writings—problematic as they may be—and also consider their many actions and policy recommendations, we can deduce their main ideas.[36]

The three leaders agreed upon a three-fold mission for the new schools: liberal arts, civics, and moral education for the rising generation. Mann took an approach, as described by historian Lawrence Cremin, which came "remarkably close to the evangelical conceptions of the day—a common piety rooted in Scripture, a common civility revolving around the history and the documents of a Christian Republic, and a common intellectual culture conveyed via reading, writing, spelling, arithmetic, English grammar, geography, singing, and some health education." Similarly, Lewis wrote that the schools should teach the "sound principles of Christian morality," "the sound principles of our government," and reading, writing, arithmetic, and other subjects. Meanwhile, Barnard demonstrated his agreement with the other two through his actions, rather than through his writing. Given their shared religious and cultural backgrounds, it is not surprising that the three men had developed similar philosophies.[37]

Of the three purposes, liberal arts education is the most familiar to us today, since it constitutes most of the curriculum in our 21st century schools. Lewis felt that the abilities "to read, and write, and cipher" were essential for "the future fathers and mothers of Ohio. . .to discharge the high and important responsibility of hereditary rulers of a mighty nation." Mann held that these skills would improve general prosperity, which was likely a reflection of New England's need for people who could read, write, and do math in its many growing businesses. So while Lewis envisioned the benefit of liberal arts education to government, Mann saw its value to the economy.[38]

But the three reformers felt that civic education was even more important because they believed the very survival of their form of government depended upon it. Like the Founding Fathers, they had studied the classic civilizations of Greece and Rome and found that those republics had failed because they had too few citizens who were willing to put their country's interests ahead of their own. The three leaders believed that with proper instruction the rising generation could be taught to love their country and that they would then respond by leading lives of public virtue. For example, Lewis remarked in his first report to the legislature that "the sound principles of our government are to be taught—that lesson which Washington gave, namely, that 'next to our God, we owe our highest duty to our country'." In order to accomplish that, he explained, "habits of self-government, economy and industry must be enforced." In a new nation, with so many people separated by religion, geography, and now, due to the recent surge in immigration, culture and language, civic education was the glue that would hold them together.[39]

Yet the three men believed that moral education was the most important purpose of all. In fact, both Mann and Barnard feared that the practical skills of reading, writing, and arithmetic, which were so necessary for success in the new market economy, could be used for ill because the schools were not giving enough attention to moral training. For example, Mann questioned in his Ninth Report whether the schools were nurturing "the higher faculties in the nature of childhood—its conscience, its benevolence, a reverence for whatever is true and sacred." He worried that they instead were "only developing. . .the lower instincts and selfish tendencies of the race—the desires which prompt men to seek, and the powers which enable them to secure, sensual ends. . . . . .irrespective of the well-being of others. . . . Are they so educated, that, when they grow up, they will make better philanthropists and Christians, or only grander savages?" Moral education had to be stressed above everything else because, as Lewis stated in his first report, "It can not be too deeply impressed on all minds, that we are a Christian, as well as a republican people; and the utmost care should be taken to inculcate sound principles of Christian morality. . . . On this should every teacher take his stand, and make it a paramount work, to train up the rising generation in those elevated moral principles of the Bible; and here should be taught all the social and relative duties, with proper inducements to correct action." In other words, moral training produced young citizens who would help create and preserve a just society.[40]

Mann used similar language in arguing for the value of moral instruction. He began by referencing a passage from the scriptures (Prov. 22:6) that was as familiar then as it is now to evangelicals, "Train up a child in the way he should go, and when he is old he *will not* depart from it." He then belabored the point, "The Scripture does not say that he *probably* will not depart from it; or that in nine cases out of ten he will not depart from it; but it asserts, positively and unconditionally, that he WILL NOT depart from it [emphasis is Mann's]." Mann explained that God intended for humanity to act in moral ways, that He had made available the wisdom needed to do so, and if we failed to acquire or pass on those ways to others, we were to blame.[41]

Mann, like Barnard and Lewis, was convinced that morality should be taught through the precepts of the Christian religion. Throughout his years as Secretary, Mann showed unstinting support for the teaching of religion, including the reading of the Bible. It was his commitment to a nonsectarian approach to such instruction that had led to his many conflicts with religious conservatives, not any objection to its use in the schools. In fact, he reserved some of his sharpest rhetoric for this subject, calling "hostility to religion in our schools, as the greatest crime which I could commit against man or against God." In typical fashion he called those who thought morality could be achieved without teaching religion "ignorant" and even "insane." Lewis and Barnard were equally committed to the practice, but since their personal beliefs and policy prescriptions on the subject were so solidly orthodox they experienced little controversy.[42]

Yet while the crusaders agreed on most aspects of educational philosophy, they differed on the best approach to discipline and their conflicting worldviews tell us why. Mann adopted the Unitarian and Enlightenment position that humankind was inherently good and that with proper learning it could improve even more. As a result, he readily accepted the humanist belief that the relationship between teacher and student resembled that of parent and child and therefore the classroom environment should be based on a system of love and reward, not fear and punishment. The concept had originated in the writings of Rousseau, the French philosopher; it had captivated Johann Pestalozzi, a Swiss educator; and it had then influenced Prussia's practices, which were admired by so many Americans. Mann's adoption of the idea brought him into conflict with many evangelicals, who held the opposing view that humanity was sinful and untrustworthy. Consequently, they felt that children were in need of close supervision and correction, including physical and psychological punishment, if necessary. Since they dominated the leadership of the movement, almost all 19th-century classrooms adopted strict discipline and use of "the rod." It would be more than a century before Mann's alternate philosophy of discipline would completely replace the wooden "board" of education in the schools. But with the exception of discipline, Lewis, Mann, Barnard, and indeed most of the leadership during the movement's second phase agreed upon its core purposes. Their unity would persist into the third and final phase of the cause and would bring significant benefits to America's children.[43]

South, Border, and Middle States

Zealots in the other regions of the country were also unified, but unfortunately they could not overcome the negative attitudes and obstacles that they confronted. In the South the situation had changed little since earlier in the century. Learning remained a private matter, though communities sometimes made provisions for the children of the poor. In 1837 Georgia passed a weak statute, but repealed it in 1840, the same year that laws in Ohio and Massachusetts had been attacked. In 1839 North Carolina enacted legislation permitting counties to create their own systems, but it did not require them to do so. And, some activists in Virginia pushed hard for common schools, but they accomplished little, a common result for Southern reformers before the Civil War.[44]

Conditions were little different in what later became known as the Border States, where attitudes similar to the South prevailed. Kentucky had demonstrated an indifference towards education well before its governor burned school bonds in 1845. The Commonwealth passed a statute in 1838 that provided for a state superintendent, county and district supervisors, and professional teachers, but local voters had to approve the taxes needed to fund the system and when they balked it never materialized. In fact, few counties filed the reports required by the legislation and not one new school resulted from it. Similarly, Missouri enacted a law in 1839 that included some of the same features as Kentucky's, including a state superintendent. At first its provisions were ignored and then in 1841 the position was eliminated.[45]

The Middle States made little progress in these years due to their ethnic and religious diversity, which was increasing due to the arrival of large numbers of Catholics from Ireland and Germany. Since the movement's chief purpose was to promote moral and religious education, it made the creation of a single system that could accommodate both Catholics and Protestants very challenging. Pennsylvania's laws of 1834 and 1835 were eventually accepted by most districts, resulting in improved opportunities for its children, but the state's gains still fell far short of those made in Ohio, Massachusetts, and Connecticut. Meanwhile, New York made no progress toward free public education during these years. Both the Empire State and Pennsylvania could not create statewide systems in part because they failed to find a way to assimilate Catholic immigrants into their schools and communities.[46]

So, as the second phase of the movement drew to a close, Whig reformers in Ohio, Massachusetts, and Connecticut had taken a few, tentative steps toward free schooling for all children. Along the way they learned the bitter lesson that their enthusiasm, though enabling them to overcome cultural opposition at times, was no match for powerful economic and political forces, which dictated the timing of their successes and failures. Meanwhile, fellow activists throughout the rest of the nation had made even less progress, but crusaders everywhere were unified behind a common set of goals, plans, and hopes, which were reflected in the philosophies of Lewis, Mann, and Barnard. The movement was frustrated by its failure to give all children access to moral, civic, and liberal arts education, but it was determined to succeed. A key component of that would be the dramatic expansion of its leadership corps, beginning in the 1830s.

Part IV

Broadening the Base Brings Success, 1843-1865

Rev. Lyman Beecher

Rev. William Holmes McGuffey

Rev. Caleb Mills

Rev. John Pierce

Chapter 9

Greenhouse of the Public Schools —
The Western Literary Society

An abundance of leadership marked the third and final phase of the school crusade, just as its scarcity had distinguished the first two periods. This was the key to its success because even though more people were warming to the idea of public education, it had never been a social movement that percolated up from the masses, but rather a top-down crusade that depended on a limited number of dedicated advocates. One organization in particular, which was situated at the heart of evangelical power in the West, attracted and developed members who directed the reform program in many states in the 1840s and 1850s. Though the individual accomplishments of many of these men were impressive, three of them would make contributions that were vital to the cause: one helped establish a network of reformers, one provided textbooks infused with the crusade's philosophies, and another recommended a plan to put those ideas into action.

Rev. Lyman Beecher

No one exemplifies antebellum era reformers better than Lyman Beecher, whose Yankee upbringing resembled the childhood of so many zealots. Like them, he was descended from Puritans who had immigrated to Connecticut in 1638. When his mother died soon after his birth, his father sent him to be raised by his aunt and uncle on their farm in Guilford. His days were mostly filled with back-breaking labor interrupted by some occasional hunting and fishing, but parts of those years were spent in a small, primitive school-house, where he learned to hate the icy cold of winter and to fear the everlasting flames of hell. So, at age sixteen he leapt at the chance to escape to New Haven to prepare for admission to Yale, which accepted him two years later.[1]

Beecher's first two years in New Haven were unremarkable, but in 1795 Rev. Timothy Dwight arrived and began his busy regimen of preaching, teaching, and revivals, which quickly transformed the campus atmosphere from skepticism to belief. But the new president would also have several profound, direct impacts on Beecher, who would cry upon hearing of Dwight's death in 1817. First, his preaching led young Beecher to dedicate his life to Christ in 1796 and to join the Yale Moral Society the following year, inspiring his lifelong interests in revival and reform. Second, Dwight and Yale gave Beecher his strong belief in post-millennialism, which amplified his passion for the other two interests, since he could literally bring on the Second Coming with, as he put it, "the promotion of revivals of religion, and the hastening forward of the glad day when the whole world shall be converted unto Christ." Finally, Dwight spread conspiracy theories to his students, suggesting, for example, that Jefferson was supported by a secret, secular society, the Illuminati of Bavaria. Beecher also developed very close ties to Rev. Nathaniel William Taylor, whose New Haven Theology encouraged revivals and missions, thereby helping Congregationalists and Presbyterians to compete more aggressively with Baptists and Methodists in the battleground of the West.[2]

Beecher began a career in the ministry in 1810 in Litchfield, Connecticut, a town that was home to many wealthy, cultured citizens, including the founder of the nation's first law school, Judge Tapping Reeve, who had recruited Beecher after reading one of his sermons. For the next sixteen years he devoted himself to revivals and reforms, especially temperance, and his hard work and social connections over time made him the best-known minister in New

England. In 1826 Beecher moved to Boston to set up an influential new church on Hanover Street. Conservative Congregationalists there had recruited him to fight the Unitarians, who had begun to dominate the religious, cultural, economic, and educational life of the city after years of control by the orthodox descendents of the Puritans. The Unitarians rejected the traditional doctrines of trinity, hell, and salvation, which made them dangerous heretics in the eyes of the Calvinists, so they had formed their own denomination in 1825. Six years after Beecher had been hired to lead the conservatives in a vigorous counterattack it was widely agreed that he had gotten the better of his opponents.[3]

Despite this success, however, Beecher was forced to consider another move after fire gutted the Hanover Street Church in January 1830. In October he accepted an offer to become the first President of Lane Seminary in Cincinnati, but he lingered in Boston for two more years because of many pleas to reconsider from his congregation and friends, including Reverend Taylor. Beecher certainly had many reasons to migrate; some that were pushing him away from Boston and some that were drawing him towards Cincinnati. On the negative side, Beecher's biographer Vincent Harding has suggested that, in addition to the fire, his preaching was producing few converts, his theology was generating attacks from both liberals and conservatives, and his health problems, as well as those of his wife, a daughter, and a son, were weighing heavily on his mind. On the positive side, two factors were pulling him to the West. First, he was very concerned with Catholic activity there. It is unlikely that this was his primary reason for leaving, since Boston, the largest port of entry for Irish Catholics, had presented no shortage of opportunities for a fight. But second, and far more important than any other reason for his move, Beecher was convinced that the West would play a pivotal role in the salvation of souls and the Second Coming of Christ. Both these goals were clearly influenced by his time at Yale under the tutelage of Dwight and Taylor. Tellingly, the last comments he made to his Boston congregation were filled with hope, proving that he was more attracted by the challenges of the West than he was driven by his problems in the East.[4]

As he described in his book, *Plea for the West*, his vision came from Isaiah 66, which predicted the spread of Christianity throughout the world. He was convinced that the United States would lead the way into the millennium. When he spoke of the coming "moral and political emancipation of the world," it was clear that he felt his new home must reflect evangelical and Whig norms rather than the religious and political beliefs of others. He feared that Democrats, who he called "demagogues," would manipulate the growing numbers of ignorant voters, whose unchecked self-interest would destroy the nation, in a manner similar to the decline of the Roman republic. For Beecher and the zealots, the solution lay in the political and religious instruction of every child, "the education of the head and the heart of the nation," in conformity with their beliefs. Beecher planned to achieve his goals by planting and growing two institutions, the church and the school, with the help of a third, the seminary. The latter's role was to produce young ministers, who in turn were to start churches that would form the backbone of a new network of schools, colleges, and still more seminaries. This was not a new idea, but rather a call to accelerate earlier efforts in the West that had grown out of traditions that first developed in New England. For over two hundred years college-trained clergy in that region had played a key role in education, encompassing private learning, community schooling, and religious training.[5]

This push for more ministers, churches, and schools was an important part of the Benevolent Empire, which was reaching the peak of its influence during the 1830s, as the Second Great Awakening swept across the nation. Clergymen and devout laymen, like the leaders of the movement in its two earlier phases, hoped that education would help eradicate ignorance, drunkenness, slavery, and a host of other sins. Since they shared those same goals with the other voluntary associations that comprised the Empire, they collaborated with them in many ways; in fact, they often were part of one or more of the other organizations. Beecher, for example, was involved in many of them and was personally dedicated to its struggles against slavery and intemperance. In fact, Beecher's planned move to Cincinnati was part of a large, coordinated campaign of the Benevolent Empire, known as the "Valley Campaign." As one of the

Empire's leaders, he had proposed that the American Bible Society, the American Tract Society, and the American Sunday School Union coordinate a plan to win the Ohio and Mississippi valleys for God. The campaign involved flooding these regions with religious literature, mostly Bibles and tracts, and sending evangelicals to explain their message. Since Beecher had urged others to emigrate, he could hardly ignore his own advice, which he finally did in 1832.[6]

While Beecher never directly involved himself in education for any extended period of time, either at the state or national levels, he had an important impact on its overall success in two ways. First, his coordination and management of several of the Empire's key organizations strengthened the school movement, since it drew a portion of its strength from the others. Second, he exerted a significant influence upon several people who made important contributions to the cause, including his son-in-law, Rev. Calvin Stowe, and his good friend, Rev. William Holmes McGuffey.[7]

Western Literary Institute

But Beecher's top achievement was helping to start an organization that was destined to become the most important school reform group in the country. In 1834 he joined with Samuel Lewis and seven others to incorporate the Western Literary Institute and College of Professional Teachers. While the organization had already held three annual meetings, the incorporation greatly improved its effectiveness. At its gatherings delegates discussed papers dealing with many facets of education, ranging from finance to physics. They must have been quite popular, since participation soared from just twenty-one delegates from five states in 1833 to seventy-four delegates from fourteen states by 1837. Delegates in that year represented most of the states west of the Appalachians, ranging from Pennsylvania west to Missouri and from Michigan south to Louisiana. The Institute would convene every year until 1841 and in addition to the delegates many teachers and other reformers attended its meetings, which once drew a crowd of 2,000. Calvinism was a strong influence among the delegates, who were often either Presbyterian or Congregational ministers or Baptist and Methodist ministers who had been trained in Calvinist schools or raised in Calvinist homes in New England. With so many ministers in attendance, proceedings at times resembled revivals.[8]

The Institute would play a vital role in the expansion of the movement's leadership corps, which was critical if the crusade was to succeed. The small number of advocates had handicapped the cause during its first phase and, though the organization helped expand their numbers dramatically during the second, except for Lewis, Mann, and Barnard, they would be frustrated by the economic and political effects of the Panic of 1837. Still, by the time the environment for reform improved near mid-century, the hundreds of leaders spawned by the Institute and the Benevolent Empire would carry the movement to victory. The organization had two stated purposes: (1) to promote public schools, and (2) to professionalize teaching through training, standards, evaluation, and pay increases. It set about accomplishing those objectives by collecting, discussing, and distributing information and ideas about education. Its primary tools were the annual meeting and its published proceedings, the *Annual Register*, which commenced with the Third Annual Meeting in 1833 and was distributed to school leaders and government officials throughout the country. For example, in 1835 copies were sent to twenty-four colleges and many seminaries in the West, along with an invitation to the next annual meeting. In 1836 three sets were mailed to the governors and "officers" of every state legislature in the West. By distributing the *Annual Register* so diligently, the Institute was able to spread its message throughout the Valley during a critical time for the cause.[9]

In addition to the *Annual Register*, the organization, its officers, and its committees sent out many other communications and reports to elected officials and other leaders in the Valley. For example, in 1835 and 1837 committees sent letters and reports that urged officials to enact laws conforming to the Institute's vision. In addition, its Secretary frequently corresponded with movement advocates from Massachusetts, New York, and Pennsylvania, college professors from many states, and national political figures such as John C. Calhoun and Henry Clay. The organization directed its correspondence and reports at decision-makers in the states as a result of a policy that it had adopted in 1835. In an era when the federal government's interest in schooling was minimal and local governments' actions were often uninspired, the states presented the most promising target for reform. So the Institute required members in each state to create an auxiliary that had two tasks: first, to form a teachers association, and second, to hold a convention in the state capital during a legislative session. These meetings, which typically included both lawmakers and governors, proved to be very effective venues for lobbying state government. In addition, the auxiliaries often published periodicals and sponsored lecture tours. By 1840 such groups were operating in eighteen states and two territories.[10]

The Institute's ideas and actions, not surprisingly, reflected its two stated purposes, which leap passionately from the pages of the *Annual Register*, beginning with the 1833 meeting. For example, an anonymous speaker stresses that schools must be launched immediately so that they can begin to remove "the shackles of vice, superstitions, and ignorance." Another declares that "As Teachers, Fellow Citizens, and as men, and as Christians, we have become thoroughly convinced. . .that unless an effective system of Popular Education be established in these Western States, we are on the very eve of losing all that moral and rational freedom which our civil and political institutions give us a right to expect." Finally, the *Annual Register* ends with the plea: "but we supplicate you, Fellow Citizens, we implore you, we most earnestly beg of you, *do, do* something more than you have done. . .that every youth in this free country shall be able at least to read. . .that he is also instructed in the history of his country, and in the knowledge of its laws. . .how shall he either observe or do them, while he remains ignorant of them [emphasis is the speaker's]?"[11]

In 1834 the Institute indeed took action to "*do* something more" to promote education. In addition to incorporating itself, it also appointed Samuel Lewis, the Methodist reformer, Albert Picket, the group's President, and Elijah Slack, the President of Cincinnati College, to a committee charged with researching the question "What is the best mode of establishing and forming common schools in the west?" Picket, author of textbooks and publisher of an education journal, had opened the meeting by reminding the audience "we are aiming to bring into practical operation the best systems of instruction. And what may we not hope to accomplish by our exertions!" Hoping to stir them to action, he declared "There is power in Union—There is power in Knowledge—There is power in Christianity. Let us combine these elements of power and direct their augmented energies to the diffusion of knowledge throughout our land." So the Institute's speakers seemed to overflow with good will towards humanity.[12]

But that same year the Institute, through its Executive Committee, also revealed a sinister motive that lay beneath its sense of urgency: "The Valley, filling up at the rate of 150,000 to 200,000 a year, most importantly exhorts this body to energetic and persevering action. The most disastrous consequences would result from the ignorance and misrule of a foreign immigration, if the guardians of education, and the teachers of science and morals do not act in concert. . ." So like Lyman Beecher, they felt compelled to establish schools that favored evangelical Protestantism over foreign Catholicism. Still, nativism was just one of several motivations for their movement, which would benefit greatly from several other actions taken by the Institute.[13]

In 1835 the organization, continuing its activist approach, appointed Lewis and Stowe to a committee to lobby "the western states" for the cause of common schools and they in turn sent a letter to state governments in the Valley urging them to enact new laws. Then in 1837 Alexander Campbell gave his "Report on Creating State Departments of Public Instruction" at the Institute's annual meeting. In response, it sent each Governor in the West and a thousand of its supporters a report that outlined a model state system that included a department of education headed by a full-time superintendent.[14]

In addition to promoting schools, the *Annual Register* also revealed the delegates' commitment to the Institute's other purpose, the creation of a professional corps of teachers. Starting with the Third Annual Meeting in 1833, the Institute prescribed a rigorous curriculum including "double-entry bookkeeping, criminal law, Jewish, Grecian and Roman antiquities, Moral Science, [and] Land surveying." It planned to test and certify instructors on these subjects, as well as French, Spanish, German, Greek, and Latin, which included familiarity with Virgil, Cicero, and Horace. Since they were setting such high standards for teachers they recognized that their pay had to be increased. An unnamed speaker complained that society required "a man to have spent two or three years apprenticeship to his trade, before you will intrust [entrust] him to finish a piece of mechanical work; your Smiths and Carpenters must be persons of science and creditable execution in their respective crafts, or you will not employ them, even if they should offer to do their work at an extremely low price. . .Why then, should the business of Teaching form an exception to this general rule of valuation? Here you would seem to act in opposition to your own principles; you do not seek for a *good* teacher, but a *cheap* one [italics in Register]." Teacher pay would remain an ongoing concern.[15]

Finally the delegates, like their fellow reformers, were committed to a system that imparted moral principles through reading and reflection on the Protestant Bible. Though this was not one of the Institute's stated objectives, it was strongly implied at every annual meeting. In 1834 Thomas Grimke, whose sisters, Sarah and Angelina, were famous for their abolitionist efforts, "urged the importance of the introduction of the Bible into schools of every grade." After Grimke's proposal received the support of many others, including the respected Cincinnati physician Doctor Drake, the assembly "Resolved unanimously, that the Bible be recommended as a *regular textbook* in every institution of education, in the west [emphasis provided]." While this may seem like an unusual practice to us, the Bible at the time was considered not only an essential aid to religion and morality, but also, according to historian George Marsden, "widely revered as an authority on all subjects, including history and the sciences."[16]

The prominent place that the Institute gave to moral instruction is evident from the statements of its President, Albert Picket. In 1834 he emphasized, "Firmness, moral firmness, is, therefore, a marked requisition in the character of the teacher. . ." For Picket ". . .There is no safety but in God and the People: one God and the Whole People. And hence. . .we must know God—the relation in which we stand to Him, and to one another: and the acquisition of this knowledge is Education. . .Education, a gentle, a Christianizing, a rational Education." Then in 1836 he proclaimed "Education, in its true sense, is the instrument appointed by the Supreme Being to mould the moral, intellectual and physical powers into system, strength and beauty. . . ." Finally, in 1837 he warned, "It is a mistake to suppose that the moral culture of the mind is of no consequence to its intellectual. . .In moral we include religious education. All who acknowledge the authority of the Gospel must know that religious principles and religious affections constitute an *essential part, if not all* of moral excellence. The principles of action which Christianity inculcates, give stability and refinement to human nature, and it cannot be denied, that they should hold in every parent's mind, a high place in the education of his children. We believe in no moral codes founded on mere human reason." He ended by reminding the audience "There is but *one true God, and one true Bible*: and if happiness here and hereafter is worth obtaining, let that *Bible be the guide of life*; let its words be stuck deep in children's hearts [emphasis is Picket's]."[17]

Delegates echoed Picket's sentiments. For example, the *Annual Register* for 1837 recorded speeches entitled "The Importance of Moral Education Keeping Pace with the Progress of the Mechanical Arts" and "The Moral Dignity of the Office of the Professional Teacher." In "The Moral Influence of Rewards, In a System of Education, Founded Upon the doctrine of the Word of God" Rev. S. W. Lynd quoted Washington's endorsement of religion in his Farewell Address and declared, "The religion of the Bible is the great safeguard of our political institutions." Through the efforts of the Institute it became official public policy in Ohio to use the Bible to teach religion and morality. The Ohio Teachers Association would work to keep this policy in place for the next half century and many other states in the Valley would follow suit. This practice, especially because it usually meant using the KJV, led to many bitter disputes with Catholics.[18]

The Institute, its auxiliaries, and its attendees, including such notables as Beecher, Lewis, McGuffey, and Stowe, would have such a large impact on the cause that it would be difficult to overstate their contributions. In fact, the first public systems of Ohio, Indiana,

Illinois, Michigan, and Kentucky were all directly attributable to the activities of the organization and its members. Those reformers also started many colleges, and, in the process of advocating for all levels of education, they published numerous journals and made many speeches. In fact, the achievements of twenty-one Institute attendees from just those five states were significant enough that they merited profiles in the *Dictionary of American Biography*, a collection of historically-significant Americans.[19]

Despite the vital role that the Institute and its members played in reform in the middle third of the 19th century, historians have often focused instead on the role of the American Institute of Instruction (AII). While the Institute (1831-1845) had a far shorter life than the AII (1830-1918), it impacted a much larger portion of the country than the AII, which limited its activity mostly to New England during the antebellum era. Further, as in the case of Mann, the AII was not nearly as significant to the crusaders in New England as the Institute was to the advocates in the Valley. Indeed, the public record reveals the central role that Institute members played in the movement in the Old Northwest and Kentucky. In Ohio, Lewis, Stowe, McGuffey, and other attendees were key participants in the wave of education improvements that swept across the state in the late 1830s. In 1840 Picket pushed for graded schools and Bible reading to the Cincinnati School Board. And in the 1850s Delegate H. H. Barney, following in Lewis' footsteps, would become the state's second superintendent.[20]

In Indiana, three delegates stand out in the battle for free schools. Andrew Wylie, a Presbyterian minister and the first President of Indiana University (known at the time as Indiana Seminary), was very active in conventions that called for common schools in the 1830s. John Irwin Morrison, a graduate of Miami University and a faculty member at Indiana, chaired the committee that drafted the education section of Indiana's 1851 constitution. William McKee Dunn, a graduate of Indiana and a faculty member at Hanover and a founder of Wabash, both Presbyterian colleges, helped write education provisions while serving on Morrison's committee. Unfortunately, while these delegates made impressive attempts at reform, their efforts would face stiff resistance.[21]

In Illinois, four delegates, who were all ministers and faculty members at Illinois College in Jacksonville, led that state's crusade. The Congregational institution had been founded in 1829 by a group of seven graduates of Yale (known as the Yale Band), including three of the four delegates, who had pledged to go west as missionaries and to use education as a key tool for spreading Calvinism. Edward Beecher, son of Lyman, left a prestigious church on Boston Common to assume the first presidency at the college, which consisted of one small building on the edge of a dusty frontier town in central Illinois. The college's faculty and graduates soon became a powerful force for the cause in the state. In the 1830s Truman Post and Jonathan Baldwin Turner, who had not been an Institute delegate, worked with Governor Joseph Duncan, an Illinois College trustee, to pass legislation. In the 1840s and 1850s Turner continued to be a very important figure in the reform movement. And, perhaps most important of all, Newton Bateman, a graduate of the college and a student at Lane Seminary, would become the dominant figure in his state's fledgling education system from the 1850s through the 1870s.[22]

In Michigan, one delegate was so prominent that he is recognized as its Father of Public Schools. Rev. John D. Pierce, a graduate of Princeton Theological Seminary, went to Michigan as a missionary, with a charge similar to that of the Yale Band. He would go on to shape the education provisions in the first (1836) and second (1850) Constitutions for his state. As Michigan's first Superintendent of Public Instruction, he had the primary responsibility for implementing a comprehensive system.[23]

Finally, in Kentucky two delegates towered over the movement, one during the second phase, and the other during the last phase. The first leader, Rev. Benjamin O. Peers, was an Episcopalian priest who had been raised as a Presbyterian. He was, successively, a student, a professor, and acting President of Transylvania College, which was a locus of power for reform in Kentucky. In the 1830s Peers worked very closely with the governor to pass landmark common school legislation, which showed great promise but came to an end in that fire in the governor's mansion. The second leader, Rev. Robert J. Breckenridge, was a Presbyterian minister and member of a prominent Kentucky family. In 1848 he would be appointed Superintendent of Public Instruction and after working closely with the Commonwealth's second constitutional convention he was elected Superintendent after the new constitution was approved in 1851. Their biographers have described both men as the Father of Public Education in Kentucky.[24]

These advocates, who did so much for the movement, were also intimately involved with a complementary crusade that created many new colleges during this time period. Several delegates who had built the common school systems of Indiana, Illinois, and Michigan also founded colleges and served on their faculties. Indeed, they and other crusaders helped triple the number of colleges during the Second Great Awakening and, like the common schools, the new institutions reflected their religious commitments. By 1848 85% of the nation's colleges were either associated with or strongly influenced by a Christian denomination, one-half were affiliated with an evangelical sect, and one-third with a Calvinist denomination. As one might expect then, the Valley's colleges were well represented at Institute meetings. Nineteen university presidents participated in at least one, including the first presidents of Indiana University, Wabash, Hanover, and Illinois Colleges, and the presidents of the University of Cincinnati (3), Transylvania University (4), Centre College, the University of Georgia, the University of Nashville, and the University of Tennessee, which was known at the time as East Tennessee College. Among many individual accomplishments, John Pierce helped organize the University of Michigan. Rev. Theron Baldwin, a minister and one of the founders of Illinois College, helped start and develop several colleges for the Congregationalists in the West. And Jonathon Baldwin Turner, the reformer and Illinois College professor, successfully lobbied for the creation of the University of Illinois, as well as the Morrill Act, which created the nation's system of land grant colleges. Of course, all of this was in line with Lyman Beecher's vision for the Valley Campaign, which had included the planting of Calvinist colleges. Since those institutions produced many ministers, there were more hands for the Lord's work, but there were also more well-educated, motivated advocates for the cause of schooling. In an era when only a few men earned a college degree, this gave the zealots a huge advantage in advancing their agenda.[25]

The delegates and their fellow crusaders knew that the promotion of their plans to a large number of leaders would be crucial to their success. Picket had understood this as early as 1818, when he began publishing the *Academician*, the first journal that dealt exclusively with educational topics. As a result, delegates published scores of such works, both with public and private funds. Following a practice that was common in Prussia, many of them were underwritten by state legislatures, such as the *Ohio Common School Director*, edited by Lewis, the *Michigan Journal of Education*, edited by Pierce, and the *Illinois Journal of Education*. Others were financed by state teachers associations or subsidized out of an advocate's personal funds, in the same way that Barnard had financed his journal. Ministers were the most consistent contributors to these periodicals, so they naturally tended to dwell on moral and religious instruction rather than the secular aspects of teacher training, but they mostly promoted the schools.[26]

The delegates and other reformers also realized the power of the spoken word and this led them to become active in the lyceum movement. Lyceums, which got their name from the temple in Athens where Aristotle had done most of his teaching, began in Great Britain and were first promoted in America in William Russell's *American Journal of Education* in 1826. They grew quickly and by 1831 were operating in over nine hundred towns. While lyceums were more popular in New England than the Midwest, Ohio had more than either Massachusetts or New York, probably due to its many school-loving Yankee settlers. While lectures covered a broad range of topics, the most popular ones lined up perfectly with the Institute's purposes: the promotion of free public education and teacher training. Lyceum members paid an annual subscription fee to attend weekly lectures, which is similar to today's adult education. Since ministers gave more of these talks than members of any other occupation, they often resembled evangelical sermons.[27]

Rev. William Holmes McGuffey

While the Institute helped develop scores of these zealots, two in particular stand out because their contributions affected the entire country, not just their home state. The first of the two, Rev. William Holmes McGuffey, gave insight into his views on the "Duties of Teachers and Parents" to attendees at the Fifth Annual Meeting in 1835. He began with the obligations of the teachers to the schools. First, they were to spread "a love of learning and an adherence to sound morals and true religion." Second, they must be competent. Third, they were to shape the students' character through Christian moral instruction, since "the christian religion is the religion of our country. . . . On its doctrines are founded the peculiarities of our free institutions. From its sanctions are derived the obligations to veracity imposed in the administrations of justice. . . . It can not be eradicated, or even opposed, without imminent hazard of all that is beautiful, lovely, and valuable in the arts, in science, and in society." Fourth, they must subordinate their authority to parents, who had the ultimate responsibility for their children. Next, McGuffey outlined the four obligations that parents had to the schools. They were to maintain adequate buildings, provide suitable books and supplies, prepare their children for instruction, and take responsibility for their learning. In emphasizing the last point he admonished parents that "We must *ourselves* be the prominent and persevering teachers of our children, during the whole period, in which their characters are forming. . . . We must not leave it to hired help [emphasis is McGuffey's]."[28]

Although that was certainly sound advice, McGuffey's contribution to the crusade would come not from the words that he spoke but from the ones he would write; the common schools needed textbooks and he was uniquely qualified to supply them. His heritage, childhood, and education all placed him within the cultural and religious mainstream, providing him with insight into the sensibilities of those who would buy his books. He was born into a Scotch-Irish family in Western Pennsylvania and was raised as a Presbyterian in Ohio's Western Reserve, where he absorbed its Calvinist and evangelical norms. At a young age McGuffey had memorized entire books of the Bible and other literature, which earned him the reputation as a child prodigy. In addition to some limited opportunities for learning at home and in local schools, he lived and studied under three Presbyterian ministers. That included Indiana's Andrew Wylie, when he served as the President of Washington College, one of several Presbyterian log colleges in the West. Both before and during his years at Washington McGuffey taught school, which provided him with a valuable perspective for his career as a textbook author.[29]

After graduation from Washington College in 1826 he began his life-long career in higher education. His first position was as a professor of ancient languages at Miami University in Oxford, which is thirty miles northwest of Cincinnati. In 1829 he was ordained and, while he was never called to serve his own congregation, he preached frequently on college campuses and in neighboring churches for the rest of his life. In 1832 he persuaded Miami's president to appoint him to its chair in moral philosophy, a prestigious subject that was taught by the president at most colleges. But McGuffey's ambition made him unpopular with his colleagues in Oxford, including the president, and in 1836 he was forced to resign. Over the next seven years he held the post of president at Cincinnati College (1836-1839) and Ohio University in Athens (1839-1843), but unfortunately his years at the former institution were marked by his poor administration and his time at the latter by his conflicts with students and townspeople. Perhaps as a result of the economic impact of the Panic of 1837, his tenure at both colleges ended with their closure, but these were still very important years for McGuffey and his legacy.[30]

It was during McGuffey's time in Southwest Ohio that he built friendships with the Beecher family, which gave him the opportunity to produce his history-making contributions to American education. In 1836 Connecticut native Winthrop Smith of Cincinnati publisher Truman and Smith asked one of Lyman's daughters—historians disagree on whether it was Catherine or Harriet—to compile a series of four graded readers. When the offer was refused, McGuffey's good friend, Calvin Stowe (Harriet's husband), referred him to Smith and the two soon agreed to a contract. By 1857 McGuffey had written five *McGuffey's Eclectic Readers* and his brother Alexander had written another. The textbooks were an immediate success, with sales reaching 7 million by 1850 and 47 million by 1870. Unfortunately for McGuffey, his agreement with Truman and Smith limited his total royalties to just $1,000, making it one of the worst deals in the history of publishing! Though the *Readers* would continue to bear his name, he had no involvement with the series after he wrote the sixth in 1857. A transition to new editors, who would make substantial revisions in subsequent years, had little effect on sales, which reached 107 million by 1890, and ultimately, an astounding 122 million by 1920. The *Readers* dominated textbook sales in the South and Midwest.[31]

Historians gush with praise for the impact the *Readers* had on American culture and society. For example, Richard Mosier calls them "the most famous and influential textbook[s]" in American history. In the classroom, the books had been officially adopted by thirty-seven states by 1890; in the home, they had been purchased and read by more Americans in the 19th century than any book other than the Bible. In fact, they were so commonplace that original copies can still be easily acquired. Still, in addition to the impressive number of copies sold, several other factors magnified even further the impact of the *Readers* on American society. First, several students typically used the same copy of the texts. During the first half of the century, students were responsible for bringing their own textbooks to class. So, once a girl finished her *Reader*, she would pass it on to her younger brother, and so on until the book had worked its way through the family. When the last child left school, it would often be sold to a neighbor. And of course, once school systems began to provide texts to students in the second half of the century, children in many successive classes used the same *Reader*. Finally, many others, who were taught by their parents at home, also used the series.[32]

Second, pedagogy at the time depended heavily on the use of textbooks. Especially in the first half of the century, teaching was a poorly paid occupation, so as a consequence it became a stepping-stone for young men before entering a profession or for young women before becoming a homemaker. So teachers, who had little training and experience, were either unable or unwilling to prepare their own lesson plans. Instead, they had students read the text-books, memorize passages, and then recite them before the class. So in essence, textbooks became the de-facto curriculum.[33]

Third, people's reading choices were so limited, for a couple reasons, that the *Readers* and the Bible may have been the only literature available to adults in many homes. First, books in this era were very expensive. Second, even if affordability was not a factor for a family, an entire category of books, novels, were considered by many evangelicals to be sinful, so they refused to buy them. As a consequence, the *Readers* were often the only secular books that many people read as an adult.[34]

Finally, the most important reason for the cultural impact of the series was that its moral message resonated so well with evangelicals, who comprised such a large portion of the nation's students, teachers, administrators, and parents. McGuffey, for example, served on faculties at Miami, Cincinnati, and Ohio that were dominated by his fellow Presbyterians, which served to reinforce his religious convictions. He subscribed to the principle that "religion, morality, and knowledge" were all essential components of a child's education. As a result, the *Readers* contained more moral and religious content than their competition, which in large measure explains their success. And while later editions, which received no input from McGuffey, contained less material that was explicitly religious, they had just as much moral content as earlier ones.[35]

A closer look at the series reveals the prevalence of this message: sins are a slippery slope, with minor transgressions leading to more serious ones; heaven and hell wait in the next life, but bad deeds are never rewarded in this one; and finally, knowing God is central to understanding the natural world. Half the lessons deal with moral concepts, including salvation, righteousness, honesty, piety, and kindness. Lessons from the Bible, which are a major emphasis for McGuffey, support many of these same themes, though they studiously avoid sectarian controversies that might divide Protestants. Titles from the *First Reader* (1841 edition) include "Virtue in Humble Life," "Ingratitude to Our Supreme Benefactor," "Highly Culpable," "On Filial Piety," "Praise Due to God for His Wonderful Works," "Care and Generosity," "Immortality," "Heaven," and

"Socrates and Lamprocles—Disrespect to Parents, Is in No Case Allowable." Stories in the *Third Reader* (1837 edition) include "The Bible," "More About the Bible," "Sermon on the Mount," "The Goodness of God," "Touch not-Taste not-Handle not," and "Character of Jesus Christ." Other lessons from various *Readers* celebrate such Benevolent Empire reforms as abstinence from alcohol, keeping the Sabbath, and charity towards the Indians.[36]

A second theme that persists throughout the series is a conservative political message. This is not surprising when one recalls that Scottish Common Sense Realism dominated the nation's colleges, including McGuffey's alma mater. As a consequence, selections included famous Federalists and Whigs such as Alexander Hamilton, Daniel Webster, and John Marshall, while they excluded leading Democrats like Thomas Jefferson and Andrew Jackson. Moreover, the Democrat Party's commitment to a more secular society made the writings of its leaders unacceptable to McGuffey and the Whigs, who saw a central role for the Christian religion and its followers in all aspects of society, including government. Deists like Thomas Paine were even more objectionable.[37]

A final theme that is found throughout the series is a conservative economic lesson that celebrates laissez-faire capitalism, property rights, and the pursuit of wealth. If you treat people honestly, work hard, and love God, He will reward you in this world, but once you acquire riches, you have a responsibility to be benevolent towards the poor. These sentiments, of course, follow directly from the Common Sense ideas of Adam Smith and Samuel Hutchison. Many industrialists, like Henry Ford, who studied from the *Readers* at home, and John D. Rockefeller, who likely used them at school, would become noted exemplars of this ideology. As a result, McGuffey and his *Readers* had a profound influence on 19th- and 20th-century economics and philanthropy.[38]

Rev. Calvin Stowe

Like McGuffey, Rev. Calvin Stowe would make a vital contribution to the movement through his writing. And similar to his friend, his heritage, childhood, education, and profession would place him in a unique position to advance the cause, not just in his home state of Ohio but also throughout the Valley. Stowe was the prototypical Yankee in several ways. He was descended from Puritans who immigrated to Massachusetts in the 1630s. His father died when he was six, leaving the family with little money, so at twelve young Calvin was apprenticed to a papermaker. Despite his poverty, he used the earnings from his apprenticeship to pay for a typical Yankee education, which included instruction at a district school and two academies. Some advanced Calvinist training followed at Bowdoin College, where he was valedictorian of the class of 1824 and was awarded a masters degree in 1827. After two years of editing and writing, Stowe became professor of Greek at Dartmouth College, where he served for two years. His new profession would allow him to have a big impact on the movement, just as it had for McGuffey, and like his friend the Beecher family would be the key.[39]

In 1833 Stowe moved to Cincinnati to accept the Chair in Biblical Literature at Lane Seminary, which was led by Lyman Beecher. In 1834 Stowe's wife died and in 1836, following a pattern that was commonplace in his native New England, he married Harriet, the daughter of Lane's President. (His new wife, of course, was destined to become the author of the influential novel *Uncle Tom's Cabin*.) His move to Cincinnati, his position at Lane, and his marriage to Beecher's daughter all served to place him at the epicenter of evangelical power in the Valley in the mid-1830s. He, like Beecher, was one of the founders of the Institute and served as a delegate from Ohio.[40]

In 1836 Stowe, who had already planned to travel to Europe to buy books for Lane, was commissioned by the Institute and the state legislature to study the Prussian educational system, which was considered to be one of the most advanced in the world. Upon his return Truman and Smith published his report, *The Prussian System of Public Instruction, and Its Applicability to the United States*. Stowe praised schooling in the German kingdom, calling it superior to Ohio's approach and inspiring him to propose a similar system for the Buckeye State. In 1837 Stowe presented his findings to the legislature in his *Report on Elementary Education in Europe*, which so impressed lawmakers that they distributed 10,000 copies, including one to every district in the state. Subsequently, the legislatures of Massachusetts, Michigan, North Carolina, Pennsylvania, and Virginia reprinted the *Report* and circulated it throughout their states, as well.[41]

In *Prussian System* Stowe began by praising the foundation of the system, which was based on the educational philosophy of the Reformation and constructed under the watchful eye of Frederic William III, the Calvinist King. Stowe admired its commitment to compulsory education, a practice that would not become widespread in the United States for at least fifty years. He remarked — mistakenly — that the Puritans also required all children to attend school. He went on to commend the system for its broad curriculum and its emphasis on teacher training, which was apparent to him from the many effective instructors that he observed in the classroom. He saw both as weaknesses in Ohio.[42]

Stowe reserved special praise for the emphasis the Prussians placed on "religious instruction, as a means of forming the moral character of children, according to the positive truths of Christianity." Every school session began and ended with scripture reading, singing, and prayer and while such training was required for all children, the system was extremely sensitive to the needs of its diverse population of Protestants, Catholics, and Jews. For example, clergymen from each of the three faiths regularly inspected classrooms; districts tried to reflect their religious composition when making appointments to their boards. And while "the bible is the basis of religious instruction in all the schools," which had to please Calvinists, "the protestant children are taught from the protestant translation, and the catholic children from the catholic translation, and the Jewish children from the Old Testament, if the parents require it." Though this policy seemed quite tolerant, Prussia went even further by permitting parents to opt out, so long as they or a clergyman of their choice taught the child, who was then to be tested for his or her knowledge. Had America adopted such enlightened policies it is likely that its schools would have experienced much less religious controversy. Further, while the children's salvation was the first goal of their spiritual training, Stowe opined that the schools would receive a secondary benefit because "without religion — and, indeed, without the religion of the bible—there can be no efficient school discipline." Clearly, he saw many lessons for America in the Prussian approach to religious instruction.[43]

But Stowe's most important insights for the movement came from his analysis of the secular aspects of the Prussian system, which inspired his design of a similar scheme for Ohio. First, he envisioned a "Secretary of Public Instruction," who would oversee a multi-level arrangement, including elementary schools in every district, high schools in every township, college preparatory schools in every county, normal schools in every Congressional district, and a state university. A central board would assist his statewide supervision while a local education inspector would help in every county. With the exception of the normal schools and the university, Ohio and many other states would establish systems similar to this one during the third and final phase of reform.[44]

Historians agree that knowledge of the workings of Prussia's system had great influence on the crusade in America. And while a number of zealots visited the kingdom and wrote and talked about their experiences, none had an impact equal to Stowe's. In 1835 Victor Cousin published an influential report and that same year Charles Brooks began speaking throughout Massachusetts about his trip to Prussia. In 1836 Stowe published his *Prussian System*, while he presented his *Report* to the Institute and legislature in 1837 and distributed it in 1838. While Cousin's and Brooks' recommendations were spread mostly across New England, Stowe's were sent across the nation, thereby exposing more of the advocates to his message during a time when they were formulating their ideas. Mann's 1843 report, though it was also sent throughout the nation, was distributed seven years after Stowe's, long after most of the movement's leaders had already agreed upon a basic framework for reform.[45]

So by the early 1840s, the movement was blessed with an expanded corps of crusaders who, like those in earlier periods, consisted primarily of ministers, Calvinists, New Englanders, and political conservatives. Given the composition of its leadership, it comes as no surprise that it emphasized the moral and religious aspects of education. Armed with organization from the Institute, textbooks from McGuffey, and plans from Stowe, it was prepared to begin another attempt at free schooling for all children. Yet before it could make any meaningful progress, it would first need to deal with the negative effects from the economy and, once those abated, it would then have to navigate treacherous crosscurrents brought about by temperance, antislavery, and nativism. Once again, it seemed that the movement was at the mercy of forces more powerful than itself.

Chapter 10

Topping Out Ceremonies — The End of the Beginning in the North

$\mathscr{B}$y the mid-1840s the gloomy conditions of the Panic of 1837 were receding at last, thereby brightening the outlook for reformers. At the same time, the nation experienced social trends, like improved literacy and longer school sessions, which indicated that the public was warming to the ideas of the zealots, despite their failure to pass much legislation during the movement's second phase. Meanwhile, ethnic and cultural factors remained critical for any progress: in the North Yankees fought with Appalachians, while in the South the scarcity of New Englanders left the cause with few advocates. Then too, massive migration affected it in several ways, both positively and negatively. Finally, and perhaps most signifi-cantly, activists in the North had to contend with the volatile impact of the antislavery, temperance, and nativist social crusades, while those in the South had to deal with the curse of slavery.[1]

The South

While that evil practice was not the only factor that affected education reform in the South, its significance becomes clear when one examines the region's most powerful white ethnic group. Slave owners, who dominated politics wherever there were plantations, inherited cultural beliefs from their English ancestors and in many ways resembled the landed gentry of their homeland. Everyone had their natural station in life; on the plantation some were destined to be slaves, some to be overseers, and some to be owners, so any learning other than for the children of the elite was wasteful and unwise. Except as preparation for a trade or occupation, the owners opposed schooling for poor whites, since they might try to rise above their station. And they were adamantly against schooling for slaves, even rudimentary instruction in literacy, because they feared it would lead them to dream of a better life and to seek freedom. Further, the elites had no economic incentive to support community schools. They could afford to pay for private tutors and academies for their own children, why then should they pay to teach the children of others? Lastly, since Northern antislavery advocates were the biggest promoters of the cause, the Southerners were suspicious of its purposes.[2]

A white ethnic group with less power than the slave owners, the Scotch-Irish, fought the movement for a different reason than the planters, but their convictions were just as deeply embedded in their culture. For centuries they had mistrusted centralized government and defended local autonomy, so they instinctively fought efforts to delegate authority for school supervision and taxation to the state or county. Though they lacked political power at the state level, they held considerable influence in the backwoods areas of the South, especially the Appalachians. But not all the Scotch-Irish were opposed to reform. A small but determined group of them had been trained in Calvinist colleges in the West and as a result they tended to be enthusiastic advocates. Still, on balance most members of the two main white cultural groups in the South opposed the cause, while school-loving New Englanders, who argued its case so effectively in the North, were not present in large enough numbers to make a difference.

Other factors also worked against public education in the South. First, migration affected the region's eastern and western sections, though in very different ways. Appendix I shows that from 1820 to 1860 significant westward movement held population growth in its states along the Atlantic seaboard to 174%, the lowest rate in the country, while its states to the west expanded at a 425% rate, which was only surpassed by the astounding 1,093% surge in the Midwest and Far West. As a result, in the states along the seaboard densities remained so low that it was difficult to organize schools, except in the few cities in the region. On the other hand, the states to the west, though they enjoyed increasing populations, faced an entirely different set of problems. Like the pioneers in the Midwest, settlers in those states had to acquire Indian territory, navigate a volatile land market, and otherwise build a new society out of a frontier wilderness. Unfortunately, under those tough conditions schools were often considered a luxury.[3]

So while attitudes towards public education were generally negative across the region, states seemed to embrace or reject it largely to the extent that slavery thrived within their borders. According to the 1850 US Census, North Carolina and Tennessee, which had relatively few plantations, achieved attendance rates of 32% and 27%, while results in the rest of the states, which were all more committed to slavery, ranged from 18% to 9% (Appendix II). Louisiana (18%) seems at first to be an anomaly, but while it was home to many plantations it also contained the largest city in the South, New Orleans, whose population density made the formation of schools more feasible. Virginia (14%) also had a higher rate than other states with large slave populations, but it had many education activists in its western areas (today's West Virginia). Meanwhile, attendance in Texas, Arkansas, Alabama, Georgia, Mississippi, South Carolina, and Florida ranged between 13% and 9%. For the South as a whole, just one child in six attended in 1850, which marked the region as the worst in the nation.[4]

Predictably, poor teaching, administration, and supervision plagued Southern public education. In rural areas, where most people lived, schools were called "Old Field" because they were located on a plot of overworked land. Typically, communities or churches provided the building, hired a teacher, and charged parents tuition. In several cases state funds provided assistance for the children of the poor. In the 1840s and 1850s a few states took some tentative steps towards universal schooling, but reforms in the South trailed the North by decades. And even those minor advances would be erased by the Civil War. Consequently, children in these states would have to wait until the Reconstruction Era before free schooling would become a reality.[5]

The Border States

Slavery also affected education in the Border States, though to a lesser degree than in the South. These states acquired their name because they formed a "border" between the eleven states that succeeded from the Union in 1860-1 and the free states to the north. The Border States, which held fewer plantation owners than the South, were ambivalent about slavery, a practice they tolerated but for which they refused to fight.

Culture and migration were also important factors for the movement in the two largest of these states, Kentucky and Missouri. The Scotch-Irish chose to settle in large numbers there: in Kentucky in the Bluegrass region, as we have seen, and in Missouri in the part of the state south of the Missouri River that was known as Little Dixie because of their large numbers there. Many of them opposed the crusade, but in Kentucky Peers, Breckinridge, and many other evangelical ministers were dedicated to the cause. So, since some zealots were outspoken while slave owners were relatively quiet, those two states showed a better commitment to the cause than did most of the South. In fact, due to their similar cultural backgrounds and political landscapes, they resembled the two Southern states that had the best educational systems, North Carolina and Tennessee. Still, due to ongoing opposition their schools would fall far short of those in the North.[6]

The movement fared no better in the other Border States. Delaware and Maryland made even less legislative progress than Kentucky and Missouri during the second and third phases. Barely one child in five (22%) attended school in 1850 in the Border States (Appendix II), which exceeded the average for the South by 5%, but fell far short of every Northern state. And what was even more unfortunate, the Civil War hurt education in these states so badly that lasting systems would have to wait until its conclusion.[7]

The North

In the North, education was not hurt by slavery, since the region contained no slave owners and only a few defenders of the evil practice, but like the South it faced the powerful, changing forces of ethnicity and migration. Ethnicity proved to be of vital importance in the Midwest and New England due to the strong Yankee commitment to the cause in both those regions and because of the many Scotch-Irish who fought on opposite sides of the issue in the Midwest. Migration occurred on such a massive scale in the Midwest between 1820 and 1860 that it affected the movement in the region in three ways. First, as Geographer John Hudson has shown, Yankee and Scotch-Irish settlers preferred different areas of the Midwest. Second, the sheer size of the exodus, which was the largest in American history, had a profound effect on the North. New England, because of its slow, internal rate of increase, remained committed to its traditions, while the Midwest, due to its explosive, ten-fold rate of growth, had no choice but to continually re-invent every aspect of society, including education (Appendix I). Third, the migration came like a wave that spread slowly from east to west and, because of the ease of travel through the Ohio River valley, it first filled up the southern portions of Ohio, Indiana, and Illinois and then the northern parts of those states, before finally moving on to Michigan and Wisconsin. As this human tide arrived in each state, it increased population density, making school organization easier, but at the same time it created the challenge of building a stable society in the midst of chaotic conditions.[8]

A third factor, social reform, had a great impact on the North's politics, but unlike ethnicity and migration it had little affect on the South's. During the crusade's final phase concerns over several emotional issues began to overtake worries about the economy. While its wild swings during the Panic of 1837 had at times helped the Whigs advance the cause in states like Ohio, Massachusetts, and Connecticut, its fluctuations had hurt them in most other places. But by the mid-1840s the economy was improving and political attention was shifting to social issues, like antislavery. Indeed, for the next fifteen years zealots in the North would have to navigate the political crosscurrents created by three turbulent movements: temperance, antislavery, and nativism. Advocates were often as active in these other reforms as in their crusade for education. Ironically, their passion for those other issues often complicated their work for schools; most of the time it helped the cause, but at times it stood in the way.[9]

Temperance

Horace Mann's support for the 15-gallon law certainly hurt his work for the State School Board; in fact, it nearly cost him his position as its Secretary. He and his fellow Whigs were part of a nationwide movement that tried to respond to the misery brought about by widespread alcohol abuse. In the decades after the War of 1812 alcohol consumption had soared for several reasons. First, for the producer it was quite profitable. Farmers had access to all the ingredients they needed to make whiskey, beer, and wine. Westerners could distill whiskey from corn, which often sold at low prices, then sell it locally or in the East at a large markup. Second, for the consumer it was cheap, convenient, and, at least if used in moderation, healthier than other beverages. Finally, alcohol could make any occasion a whole lot more fun. As a result, the nation was literally drowning in booze. People drank everywhere; at public social functions, at militia musters, and at work, but mostly they drank at home. Historian Bruce Dorsey calculated that Americans in 1830 drank at four times today's rate of consumption. Such levels of drinking created huge problems for individuals, families, and society, which soon attracted the attention of the reformers.[10]

In 1826 evangelical ministers and lay people began what would become the American Temperance Union (ATU), one of the many arms of the Benevolent Empire. The ATU grew so rapidly that by 1835 it had 8,000 local chapters, which included 1.5 million members, or one of every five free adults. Their crusade, in addition to the work of others, would cause alcohol consumption to drop by one-half from 1830 to 1840 and by another third by 1850. Public drunkenness became socially unacceptable. Almost all this progress resulted from the voluntary responses by alcoholics to personal appeals from the activists, not from legislation, which did not appear in earnest until the 1850s.[11]

Despite the success of the direct approach, Bay State reformers had decided to legislate sobriety with their 15-Gallon Law. Its repeal in 1840 sent a chilling message to activists around the country, who put statewide laws on hold until the 1850s. While the movement's one-on-one approach had not been controversial, its legislative efforts sparked heated political battles and forced each party to take sides. Whigs, who were often backed by evangelicals, pushed for temperance and prohibition laws. Democrats, who were frequently supported by whiskey-drinking Irish Catholics and beer-and-wine drinking Germans, insisted on the right to imbibe. Since these same groups typically chose opposite sides on school legislation, the presence of a temperance measure on the ballot could have a big effect on education, as it had in Massachusetts in 1840.[12]

In 1851 the passage of many local statutes, the growing acceptance of temperance, and the fear of surging Irish-Catholic immigration emboldened activists to try once again to pass a statewide law. Maine enacted legislation that year that prohibited the manufacture of liquor for general use, permitted its sale for medicinal or industrial purposes only, and provided for its search and seizure. Over the next four years, fifteen states and territories followed suit by enacting what became known as "Maine Laws," while another four tried and failed. These campaigns were very divisive, tended to weaken the parties, and had a big effect on the fate of education legislation, which was being introduced in many of these states at the same time. As a result, temperance would have an important impact on school reform during the critical years of its final phase.[13]

Antislavery

Another cause that complicated the crusade for education was antislavery. While slavery had troubled the nation in its first four decades, it wasn't until the 1830s that it began to produce major cracks in the bedrock of national unity. In the first half of that decade Nat Turner led a bloody revolt, Virginia's legislature failed to work out a compromise over slavery, and Great Britain finally decided to abolish the practice. As a result, its supporters in the South became increasingly defensive and began to censor antislavery literature, while its defenders in the North rioted against free blacks, threatened abolitionists with violence, and destroyed their printing presses. These developments brought about a strong counter-reaction from abolitionists, who flooded Congress with petitions for abolition in the District of Columbia and for their right to send literature into the South. Like the other branches of the Benevolent Empire, they soon developed a large association to further their agenda. In 1832 they formed the American Antislavery Society and within six years it had over a thousand chapters, including 274 in New York and 213 in Ohio. But while their numbers were growing exponentially, they remained unpopular. In addition to exposing themselves to physical danger, as Lewis had at the antislavery meeting, they also risked their political futures and their livelihood. Even in the North, where most people felt slavery was wrong, they nonetheless felt strongly that others should not try to impose their will on the South.[14]

By the mid-1840s antislavery had become the most important cause in the North. But just as rising interest in temperance had complicated the task of school advocates, so did the growth of anti-slavery sentiment. First, many of the zealots left the Whig Party for the Liberty Party, which created a political rift between propo-nents of education. At first, this development seemed to hurt the cause because it damaged the party that was a reliable sponsor of its legislation, but in several states it ended up helping the move-ment. Second, the issue weakened the three major evangelical sects, which provided much of the movement's ideological support. After years of bitter debate the Methodists (1844), Baptists (1845), and Presbyterians (1857) each split into northern and southern churches. Finally, the rise of antislavery created a leadership drain for the school movement just as it was starting to gain traction with the public. As we have seen, both Samuel Lewis and Horace Mann abandoned the common school movement to work on antislavery. Fortunately, Institute members and others were joining the crusade at the same time.

In 1848 antislavery took a further step with the formation of the Free Soil Party, which opposed the expansion of slavery into the

Western territories. From that point on, opponents of slavery, who remained strong advocates for schools, showed increasing power and often provided the deciding votes on many issues in legislative bodies across the land. The passage of the Kansas-Nebraska Act in 1854 damaged the Democrats badly, marked the beginning of the end for the Whigs, and gave birth to the Republicans, a new antislavery party that would have important implications for education. [15]

Nativism

A third social movement, nativism, had a vital role to play in the drive to provide free schools for all children. A wave of Irish Catholic immigration in the late 1840s gave rise to an ugly outpouring of hate. This development occurred at the same time that differences over temperance and antislavery were weakening the two major parties, which struggled to maintain a middle way between the extremes. Further, the Whig Party, which included many of those who were intolerant of Catholics, worried that the Irish propensity to vote Democrat would give that party the balance of power. Into this unsettled environment stepped the Know Nothings, who were quite unambiguous in their hatred for all things Catholic. As a result, it was easy for the new group to attract many Whigs and even some Democrats, who were worried about growing foreign influence. [16]

The success of the Know Nothings was swift and shocking because they usually made their plans in secret, often ran as write-in candidates, and always hid their identity. In fact, they had acquired their name because members were to say they "know nothing" if asked about their association with the group. In the Congressional elections of 1854, which were held in the wake of the Kansas-Nebraska Act, Know Nothings and their allies wrested control of the House from the Democrats, who saw their share of seats plummet from a dominant majority of 67% to a powerless minority of 35%. Previously, such dramatic swings in power had resulted only from severe changes in the economy. Know Nothings posted similar results in state and local elections all across the country in 1854 and 1855, and while their lasting impact at the federal level would be negligible, their effect on state efforts for education would be profound and lasting.[17]

The emotional reactions to Catholic immigration, Maine Laws, and the Kansas-Nebraska Act created a "perfect storm" in 1854. In the political chaos that ensued, nativism, temperance, and antislavery operated like powerful magnets that pulled advocates away from their old party affiliations. Proponents of these three causes formed temporary alliances, which either gave them control over state legislatures or provided them with enough leverage to bargain with the two main parties on their issues, including education. Like their predecessors in the earlier phases of the movement, Northern school reformers in the decade before the Civil War proved to be shrewd political opportunists and their skills would benefit America's children for many years to come.[18]

Ohio

Economic weakness and political turmoil in the Buckeye State in the early 1840s had eliminated Samuel Lewis' position and damaged the state's movement, but it experienced a powerful renewal during the second half of the decade. Temperance, antislavery, and nativism each proved to be important factors and, as in most states in the North, evangelicals would lead the way. Further, many of these zealots were Yankees, like the Cutlers, Atwater, and Guilford, who had migrated from New England.[19]

Samuel Galloway was not a Yankee, but like other Scotch-Irish who were educated in Calvinist institutions, the devout man shared many of their traits and beliefs. He was a life-long Presbyterian, a graduate of Miami University, a student at Princeton Theological Seminary, and later a professor at Miami and Hanover. In 1844 he was elected Secretary of State in the Whig sweep of that year, which also made him the *ex-officio* State Superintendent of Common Schools. For the next six years, he conducted a frenetic schedule of speaking, writing, and organizing that produced significant improvements in education funding, supervision, and training. In many ways he helped lay the foundation for the ultimate success of the movement in the mid-1850s. As one might expect, his educational philosophy flowed directly from his Calvinist and evangelical beliefs, which presumed that humans had been tainted by The Fall. Of course, his linkage of education to religion and morality represented mainstream thinking at the time; Whig Governors Corwin and Ford expressed similar sentiments in their annual messages to the General Assembly in 1841 and 1849, respectively.[20]

The Whigs followed their 1844 sweep with more victories in the next two elections. They took advantage of their power in 1847 when they passed the "Akron Law," following a series of speeches by Henry Barnard and some intense lobbying by Congregational minister J. Jennings. This act, which was patterned after similar statutes already in place for Cincinnati, Columbus, and Cleveland, granted twenty-five counties in or near the Western Reserve the ability to establish free school districts, select supervisors, and levy taxes. The Yankee background of the inhabitants of this region was an important factor in the law's passage. Then, in 1848 it was extended to every county in the state. In addition to legislative action, Ohio's reformers also focused on teacher training, which they hoped to accomplish through "teachers institutes," which were conferences that could last anywhere from two days to two weeks. The state convened its first institute at Sandusky in 1845, the same year that Massachusetts and Michigan conducted their first institutes and just two years after New York held the nation's first. The number of counties conducting such meetings grew to eight in 1846 and, after the state made them mandatory for all counties, to thirteen in 1847. Galloway promoted them in his annual reports and Asa D. Lord, a Presbyterian minister and president of a private normal school in the Reserve, argued for them in his *Ohio School Journal*. Both men also helped create the Ohio State Teachers Association (OSTA). Lord praised it in his *Journal* for "elevating the profession of teaching and. . .promoting the interests of schools," while Galloway was elected OSTA's first president in 1847. OSTA would prove to be a powerful advocate to the legislature and the public for better schools and teachers.[21]

While Ohio's educational revival of the late 1840s could not have happened without the leadership provided by Galloway and others, schools were also gaining growing acceptance among the people at large. Between 1846 and 1850 the number of teachers and schools nearly tripled, while the investment in buildings more than doubled. It is clear that this explosive growth resulted from funding and operational improvements that were carried out voluntarily at the local level, since no statewide mandates were in place at the time, though that would soon change.[22]

In an odd twist of fate, the beginning of the end for the Whigs also marked the end of the beginning for the school movement. In 1848 the Free Soil Party emerged like a butterfly out of the remains of the Liberty Party and in the process it attracted many disenchanted Whigs. For the next five years the third party elected enough of its members to the Ohio Legislature that neither of the two major parties could achieve a majority, which forced them to negotiate for the support of the Free Soilers. They in turn used their leverage not only to advance their main cause, antislavery, but also to pass important laws dealing with education and the civil rights of free blacks. This last initiative provides insight into the extent of their power, since they were able to convince the Democrats to vote to eliminate the Black Codes, which restricted the civil rights of Ohio's 20,000 free blacks. This was remarkable, since just three years earlier many Democrats had proposed an act that would have expelled all free blacks from the state![23]

In 1850 the legislature, under pressure from the Free Soilers, enacted a very strong law that created a State Board of Instruction and a State Superintendent. However, the statute was never implemented because the state's system of governance was in flux. A year earlier Free Soilers had cooperated with Democrats to call a convention to rewrite the Ohio Constitution. Voters subsequently approved a convention and elected delegates. While education was not among the main goals of the convention, activists inserted two strong provisions into Article VI of the Constitution, which was approved by citizens in 1851. Section 1 mandated that lot 16 (schools) and lot 29 (religion) lands "shall forever be preserved inviolate and undiminished." Section 2 charged the General Assembly with the responsibility for establishing "a thorough and efficient system of common schools throughout the State." So school reformers had finally gained the constitutional support and the political power with which they could build a system of common schools across the state. It is fitting that Manasseh Cutler's grandson, William Cutler, first through his leadership in the House in the 1840s and later as a delegate to the convention, had helped bring the hopes and dreams of his grandfather Manasseh so close to fruition.[24]

The reformers' long wait finally came to an end on March 14, 1853 when Ohio passed a landmark law that abolished rate bills and established a two-mill state tax for schools and another levy for libraries. Township boards of education were charged with running the schools, which diminished the power of local districts and thereby made Ohio's schools more uniform. Not surprisingly, the legislation was enacted at the urging of Gov. Reuben Wood, a Northern Democrat who was opposed to slavery, a native of Vermont, and the son of a clergyman. The act reestablished the position of State Commissioner, thirteen years after its elimination, and Rev. Hiram H. Barney, who had been an active member of the Institute, was its first appointee. In reviewing the statute the new Commissioner cited Samuel Lewis' 1839 recommendations as its inspiration. Like Lewis and so many others Barney advocated both "moral and mental" education to "enable them [children] rightly to comprehend their duties and relations to God, to the State, and to their fellow-men."[25]

Yet the zealots had little time to celebrate because the new law, like those of 1825 and 1838, faced intense opposition. Their adversaries were motivated not just by education but also by the controversies that developed out of the temperance, antislavery, and nativist crusades. The disputes energized both school opponents, who fought the other three causes, and the reformers, who supported them. Democrats, who were able to seize the upper hand, pushed to abolish the Superintendent's position, limit the township's taxing authority, and eliminate the library levy, as well as to advance other anti-school measures. They fought the law because they objected to its expansion of centralized power at the expense of local control, they feared that the common schools would indoctrinate Catholic children in Protestant beliefs, and they simply did not like the Whigs and Free Soilers, who were their traditional adversaries on so many issues.[26]

Finally, in 1854 the turmoil created by the Kansas-Nebraska Act, Catholic immigration, and the Maine Law weakened both major parties. Stepping into the power vacuum that this created, Galloway led a fusion party of former Free Soilers, Whigs, anti-slavery Democrats, and Know Nothings to a sweeping victory in the fall of that year. Though opponents of education would succeed in suspending the library tax in 1856, they failed to overturn any other part of the reform agenda, which was successfully defended by yet another third party, the Republicans, in 1855 and 1856. So after nearly four decades of struggle, Ohio had finally succeeded in fulfilling Manasseh Cutler's dream when it became one of the first states in the nation to provide free schooling for all of its children. This was only fitting, since it had been the first state in the West to embrace the educational vision of the Founders and the Northwest Ordinance with its first constitution.[27]

Indiana

School reform in Indiana in the latter half of the 1840s benefited from an improving economy and, as it had in Ohio, from the effects of migration. Indiana's finances were finally on a sound footing: the Panic was over, the debt crisis had been addressed, the need for investment in infrastructure was declining, and agricultural production—mostly corn and hogs—was surging. The numbers of new settlers in the Hoosier State had peaked in the prior decade, creating many areas that for the first time were dense enough to support a school. But migration was a mixed blessing because, while its sheer size helped the cause, its cultural composition hurt, due to the large number of Appalachians. Southern Indiana, which held four-fifths of the state's population in the 1840s and much of its political power, was one of the primary destinations for the group. Their dominance is evident from the birthplaces of the state's Congressmen in that decade: while many had been born in Kentucky, only two hailed from New England. Predictably then the Democrats, who abhorred centralized government, controlled the state's politics at mid-century, while the Whigs struggled to enact their ambitious agenda. The latter party pursued more moderate legislation than their counterparts in other Midwestern states, perhaps because they had to co-exist with so many Democrats. In fact, in politics Indiana had all the appearances of a Border State, which had negative consequences for the Hoosier school movement.[28]

But even when Yankees were outnumbered, as they were in Indiana, they were a determined lot and Caleb B. Mills was no exception. Mills had developed his outlook on life during his typical New Hampshire upbringing. Calvinist ministers were completely in control of his education, beginning with a local school, followed by an academy, and then at Dartmouth College, where he was required to participate in daily prayer, theological studies, and Sunday worship. In 1826, during a revival that shut down the college for a week, Mills accepted Christ and decided to become a minister. To prepare himself for his life's work, after graduation he entered the Calvinist seminary at Andover and, though he interrupted his study for two years of missionary work, he graduated in 1833. He was soon ordained a Presbyterian minister and, though it was always secondary to his other work, he would serve as a pastor and preacher for the rest of his life. Upon graduation from Andover Mills accepted an offer through the American Home Missionary Society (AHMS) to serve in Crawfordsville, Indiana on the first faculty of what would later become Wabash College. While he would spend almost a half-century at Wabash, his contributions as a college professor would pale in comparison to his work for schools. From 1837 through 1839 Reverend Mills joined many others in the crusade. Unfortunately, similar to many other states, economic and political setbacks stymied legislative action in the Hoosier State. And while the cause continued to hold his attention in the early 1840s the environment remained hostile to the movement.[29]

Finally, by 1846 the economy and population density had improved to the point that reform seemed much more feasible. That year, Mills composed and delivered to every legislator an anonymous "Address" from "One of the People" on the first day of their new session. This would be the first of six such letters that he wrote, five of them to lawmakers and one to delegates to a constitutional convention. They received so much attention that popular newspapers reprinted two of them and the state distributed 5,000 copies of the last one in 1852. In fact, their influence was so great that many historians have called Mills the Father of Public Education for Indiana.[30]

In Mills' first four Addresses he attempted to embarrass the legislature into action by pointing out that Indiana had higher rates of illiteracy than every state in the Midwest and several in the South. He blamed this on uninspired communities, unprepared teachers, and inadequate textbooks, which, as he sarcastically reminded them, were conditions that developed while the state government had "raised $0" for education. Activists rallied around his calls for action but legislators responded with caution; first, by placing a nonbinding referendum on the 1848 ballot and second, by enacting a law in early 1849 that left its adoption up to the voters of each county later that year. Both measures passed, but Mills' analysis revealed a troubling pattern for the zealots. Many of those politically powerful Southern counties, which had the highest rates of illiteracy and the largest concentrations of Appalachians and Democrats, rejected the statute. As a result, children in one-third of Indiana's counties were still not guaranteed access to free schooling. With Mills' prodding that was about to change, if only for a few years.[31]

The emergence of Indiana's Free Soil Party in 1849 gave the crusaders leverage in the legislature, just as it had in Ohio, because the Democrats needed their votes. When the Democrats won the elections later that year, they called a Constitutional Convention to address several issues that were important to them, which opened up a new opportunity for the activists. After Mills gave his Fifth Address, John I. Morrison, a Calvinist and Institute member, pushed a strong plank on education through his committee, which a coalition of Free Soilers, Whigs, and Northern Democrats approved on the convention floor. Significantly, the section on schools no longer gave the legislature the latitude to implement it "as soon as circumstances will permit." The constitution was presented to the voters, who ratified it by a large majority, and it took effect on November 1, 1851. Mills, Gov. Joseph A. Wright, a Democrat and a devout Methodist, and Daniel Read, a native of Marietta and a descendant of Massachusetts Puritans, all urged the first legislature under the constitution to obey its directive on common schools. After months of political maneuvering, the state enacted a comprehensive 147-section law on June 2, 1852. While much of it codified existing law, it also prohibited rate bills, rejected the district system, created a State Superintendent of Public Instruction, and authorized new taxes, including a township tax. While the crusaders had not gotten everything they wanted in the statute, at the time it represented two steps forward for their cause.[32]

Unfortunately, for the rest of the decade the law faced opposition from the Democrats in the Southern portion of Indiana, who used their control over state politics to fight for a return to low taxes and local control. In 1854 their hand was strengthened by two separate rulings on the law from the Indiana Supreme Court, which was dominated by Democrats. The Court ruled the township tax unconstitutional and found that the law's transfer of lot 16 funds from townships to the state violated the original federal land grant. Yankee superintendents, including Mills (1854-1856) and William Larrabee, a Maine native and Methodist minister (1852-1854, 1856-1859), fought back but they were clearly on the defensive. The Supreme Court decisions would stand for fifteen years, which caused Indiana's schools to take two steps back. So Indiana, primarily due to the influence of its many Appalachian settlers, would lag every other state in the Midwest in the development of its schools. And because there were so few Yankees, social reform, which was such an important factor in the movement in other Northern states, was not nearly as significant in Indiana. As a consequence, Hoosier children would have to wait until the 1880s to enjoy a completely tuition-free education.[33]

Illinois

The story of Illinois school reform clearly illustrates the importance of the Yankees, who in just one decade transformed the state from one that was coolly indifferent to education to one that warmly embraced it. This dramatic change began when supporters of internal improvements, including Governor Thomas Ford, managed to transform the Michigan and Illinois Canal from a financial disaster into a resounding success. The Prairie State's canal, its rapidly expanding railroad system, and its relatively cheap land attracted almost three-quarter of a million migrants in the 1840s and 1850s. While most of them came from Indiana and Ohio, many also came from New England. The Yankee settlers quickly began to shift political power away from the Appalachians in the southern part of the state toward the north, where it has remained to this day. This had a huge impact on the third phase of the movement, as did the inspired leadership of Ninian Wirt Edwards and Newton Bateman.[34]

Beyond his public accomplishments we know little about Edwards, but fortunately we know much more about Bateman, whose family had roots in Scotland and England. Along with so many others, his family migrated to the Illinois frontier in 1833. Despite a lack of money, he was able to enter Illinois College in 1839, where he was influenced by several instructors who had attended the Institute, including Edward Beecher. Upon graduation in 1843 he enrolled at Lyman Beecher's Lane Theological Seminary, where he planned to study for the ministry, but illness forced him to leave within a year. The Calvinist faculty at both institutions urged their students to rally for certain social causes, including resistance to slavery, opposition to intemperance, and support for public education, extending from common schools to colleges. Bateman seems to have learned his lessons well. During the beginning of his career he served as a teacher, principal, and county superintendent; later, he established the state's first free high school, helped found its first normal school, and worked to create the United States Bureau of Education. Finally, at the end of his career he served as President at another Calvinist institution, Knox College, from 1874 to 1892. Still, he is best known in Illinois for the fourteen years he served as State Superintendent (1859-1863, 1865-1875), when he did the hard work of nurturing the reforms that had taken root in the 1850s.[35]

The advances that Bateman helped bring about would not have been possible without that startling shift of power in the mid-1840s when New Englanders arrived in the North, attracted by canals, railroads, and cheap land. Up to that time, Appalachians had dominated the state's politics in its most populated section, the South. In fact, through 1846 every governor was from that part of the state and none of them had the Yankee roots that zealots typically possessed. But from 1846 through 1860, three Yankees would serve as

Governor and, while two were Democrats and only one came from Northern Illinois, they all reflected the changing culture of the state, which was increasingly dedicated to reform. Of course, since many of the settlers were Calvinists, they were convinced that education's first task was to teach religion and morality.[36]

By the late 1840s the zealots were holding conventions, publishing journals, and lobbying legislators, but they were making little progress. Finally, when party ties began weakening in 1853 over antislavery and temperance, the crusaders saw their chance. In December they formed the Illinois State Teachers Association, which appointed Bateman as its first agent and lobbyist. They quickly achieved their first goal in February 1854, when a special session of the legislature created the state's first Superintendent of Public Instruction. Edwards was appointed to the post in March and was charged with recommending legislation to create a statewide system of free public schools. His task was made much easier that year when the antislavery, temperance, and nativism issues created, according to state historians, "mass confusion" and "political chaos." Like other states, a fusion movement quickly developed that attracted Northern Democrats, Whigs, and Free Soilers. In November they swept the elections and school advocates within their ranks stepped up the pressure for reform. The zealots' long struggle finally ended on February 15, 1855 with the passage of a law that established a statewide system of free schools. Among other provisions it provided for a state tax on real property, a township tax that was required to get state aid, a six-month school year, and a comprehensive scheme of supervision that included an elected state superintendent, county superintendents, and township boards of education. In the first year alone under the new law state spending increased ten-fold.[37]

But the crusaders' success came at a price, for they were forced to make two concessions to the bill's skeptics from Southern Illinois. First, despite Edwards' call for power to be transferred to the townships, the statute kept it with the districts, which appealed to those in the southern part of the state who favored local control. Second, two-thirds of the state tax was distributed according to the number of school-age children, but one-third was allocated according to the number of townships in a county, which essentially spread those funds by area, irrespective of population density. This provision tended to favor areas that were less densely populated and areas that had lower property values, so it tended to help much of Southern Illinois, while it hurt many areas in the North. While these provisions helped gain passage of the bill, its final vote count still reflected more backing from northern counties than southern ones. The opposition quickly gathered its strength and tried to repeal the law in 1857, but pro-education forces in the North, including the new Republican Party, proved to be too strong. Instead, Republican Gov. William Bissell led a successful drive that same year to open a normal school, which was the first public university in the state. By the onset of the Civil War, as a result of vastly improved funding and Bateman's superior leadership, the state's system would show great improvement. So, thanks to an influx of Yankees, Illinois, which had shown little interest in the cause before the 1850s, had joined Ohio in guaranteeing that all of its children, even the poor, would receive a sound education.[38]

Michigan

Unlike Illinois, Michigan never faced much opposition to reform, since so many of its early settlers were Yankees who had either migrated directly from the region or were descendants of New Englanders who had first settled in Western New York or Ohio. This becomes clear when you look at the origins of many of its leaders during its pioneer years. For example, Lewis Cass, the state's first Territorial Governor, was born in New Hampshire; Isaac Crary, its first Congressional Representative, was born in Connecticut; and William Woodbridge, its first Territorial Secretary and second Governor, was born in Connecticut. Cass and Woodbridge both had lived for a while in the Yankee town of Marietta and all three men were descended from early Puritans. As a consequence of its heritage, the state always placed a high value on moral education.[39]

So, unlike Indiana and Illinois, it was not the culture of its people that presented a problem for Michigan's movement, it was their scarcity. Many areas simply did not have a large enough population density to support a school. In 1830 the vast territory—which included Wisconsin until 1836—contained only 31,639 people, which at the time represented just one-fifth the population of Illinois and much smaller fractions of Indiana and Ohio. Thanks to better roads from Ohio, improved steamboat travel on the Great Lakes, and the allure of cheap land, its population grew to 212,267 in 1840 and 397,654 in 1850. But even that impressive rate of growth had left the state with fewer residents than any other Midwestern state a decade earlier. Indeed, as late as 1850 large swaths of Michigan were still rural and unsettled. As a result, despite its many Yankees its reform program trailed those of Ohio and Illinois by fifteen to twenty years.[40]

One of those New Englanders, John D. Pierce, did what he could for over twenty years for the crusade in Michigan. Like so many other reformers, he was descended from Puritans who settled in New England in the 1630s. He grew up in New Hampshire, where he received just two months of schooling a year. Still, he was determined to get a college education, so at age twenty he studied under a Congregational minister in order to gain entry to Brown University, where he fell under the spell of Common Sense Realism before earning a degree in 1822. He studied briefly at Princeton Theological Seminary and was ordained by the Congregationalists in 1825. In 1831 after leading a church in New York, Pierce accepted a call from the AHMS to serve as a missionary in Michigan. Over the next two decades, in addition to his service to the Congregational Church, he would work tirelessly for the education of the youth of Michigan. Among other achievements, he helped draft the schooling provisions of the state's first two constitutions, he aided the formation of the University of Michigan, he represented his state at the Institute in 1837, and, in his most significant accomplishment, he guided the state's schools as its first Superintendent of Public Instruction from 1836 to 1841. James B. Angell, University of Michigan President for thirty-eight years, stated, "Henry Barnard did no more for the schools of Rhode Island, nor Horace Mann for those of Massachusetts, than John D. Pierce did for those of Michigan." His views on the purposes of education were very similar to those of countless other zealots.[41]

Reverend Pierce certainly had an opportunity to shape Michigan's schools as the leader of a tiny group of activists that had directed the crusade from the mid-1830s through the early-1840s. The Michigan movement during the second phase resembled Ohio and Illinois during the first because, with just a few activists, it was trying to construct a system in a state that was struggling to turn an under-populated wilderness into a developed society. Clearly, the cause had several noteworthy accomplishments, including two provisions in Michigan's first constitution. First, for the first time in the United States it created a Superintendent with authority over a system that ranged from the primary to university levels. Second, it gave lot 16 monies to the state, rather than the townships, which weakened local control. With the support of these provisions and a law that implemented them, enrollment increased by 500% from 1837 to 1839. Still, despite Pierce's untiring efforts, including travel "in lumber wagons and stage coaches, through rain, mud, frost, and storm," he and his fellow activists would ultimately fail to reach their goal of tuition-free education for all children. Michigan, like every other state in the Midwest, drastically cut support for the schools in the wake of failed internal improvements projects and the Panic of 1837. Many residents simply ignored the 1837 law while the state removed the school districts' right to tax, and, like its neighboring states, raided its education fund to make debt payments.[42]

But the zealots, refusing to quit, redoubled their efforts during the third phase of reform. In 1850 Pierce and Crary, who had collaborated on the education section of Michigan's first constitution, were elected as delegates to Michigan's second constitutional convention. While there was much debate on the new constitution's provisions on education, they received the overwhelming approval of the delegates in August and of the citizens in November. Among other requirements it ordered the state legislature to eliminate rate bills within five years; so, at long last it appeared that the crusaders had finally reached their goal of a free education for all children. Yet in a development that is hard to explain, the legislature failed to eliminate tuition by 1855; in fact, it waited until 1869 before finally complying with the constitution. The delay is puzzling because Yankees were such a powerful presence in Michigan education. For example, until 1881 every one of the state's superintendents was a native of New England or Western New York. Further, the Republican Party, which controlled the state's politics after 1854, pushed social reforms, which included the creation of common schools. Since most of the opposition to tuition came from rural areas, it is likely that people in those areas felt they lacked enough people to support a school. It was ironic then that Michigan, a state that was comprised mostly of residents who supported the cause, would not fully embrace it until fifteen years after Ohio and Illinois, two states that contained many fierce opponents to reform. So it appears that some obstacles, such as low population, were just too much for even the most ardent of advocates to overcome.[43]

Wisconsin

Wisconsin was like Michigan in that a high percentage of its pioneers were Yankees who tried to shape their new homeland in the image of New England. From Wisconsin's time as part of the Michigan Territory through its first decades of statehood their influence was pervasive. As a consequence, the state made community education a priority and its reform movement looked much like Michigan's. The Badger State was also similar to the Wolverine State in that it was settled later than its neighbors to the south; in fact, since it was further west, its development came even later than Michigan's. Its first wave of migration came at the end of the Black Hawk War when New Englanders and New Yorkers swept into Wisconsin in numbers so large that one state historian called them "almost unbelievable." Still, by 1840 the territory held only 30,945 people, which represented just one-seventh the population of Michigan and even smaller fractions of each of the other states in the region. So densities were too low to support schools in most areas. Ironically, a second wave of pioneers came during the 1840s because of the Panic of 1837, which hurt the rest of the region, but helped the Badger State in two ways. First, other states were struggling with failed internal improvement projects, but Wisconsin, because of its later start, had not made such colossal mistakes. Second, the Panic's desperate economic conditions were driving many Yankees west in search of cheap land. As a result, by 1850 the state's population had leaped almost ten-fold, to 305,391.[44]

The man who tried to capitalize on this increase, Michael Frank, resembled his fellow crusaders in several important ways. For the first thirty-five years of his life he lived in western New York, which had been transformed by the culture of its Yankee pioneers. It is likely that his neighbors helped inspire his interest in temperance, antislavery, and education. The latter cause, rooted in his troubling experiences in New York as a student, teacher, and administrator, became his passion. For most of his life he used his platform as a newspaper publisher—which was a common occupation for reformers—to argue for education and other causes. In fact, the central role that he played in lobbying for schools in Wisconsin's last years as a territory and in drafting its first law as a state have led most historians to recognize him as the Father of Wisconsin's Public Schools. But despite what Frank shared with most of the movement's other leaders, he differed in three key ways. First, he was one of the few who came from German stock. And, though most of them came to Christ at an early age, he delayed making a profession of faith until he was 36, even though he had attended Christian churches for many years. Finally, his support for Ceresco, a settlement of Fourier socialists in Wisconsin, marks him as a critic of capitalism, which was a very unusual position for an activist.[45]

But while Frank's ethnic background, spiritual experiences, and economic convictions set him apart from most reformers, the same cannot be said for many of his Wisconsin collaborators, who were mostly Yankees. Indeed, of six important education leaders in his state, two were born in Connecticut, one each came from Massachusetts and New Hampshire, and one was born from Puritan stock in New York City. And of the Badger State's first three governors, who helped nurture its nascent system, two were born in Connecticut and one in New York. The large number of Yankees in the state had built a strong Congregational Church; in fact, Frank himself had joined that denomination when he finally became a Christian. Their influence would prove invaluable to him.[46]

Frank began his work in earnest in the early 1840s, just as masses of New Englanders were migrating into the Territory, which made the creation of schools feasible for the first time. Frank fought for his cause in two ways: as a legislator he argued with his colleagues about the benefits of legislation and as a publisher he wrote editorials and printed flyers extolling its merits. Activists were cheered by a small victory in 1845 and soon organized large conventions, where they hoped to influence education provisions in Wisconsin's first constitution. While voters rejected their efforts in 1847, they overwhelmingly approved their second attempt in 1848. It required free education for all children, a State Superintendent, a fund to hold lot 16 and other monies, local taxes, and a public university. The legislature quickly charged Frank and two others with the task of writing the state's first school act, with the goal of re-codifying existing law and implementing the new constitution. The resulting bill, which was patterned after New York State's, was enacted in 1849, making Wisconsin one of the few states that had accomplished the goal of free schools for its children. But while the act was commendable in many ways, it contained three weaknesses. First, it left the system under-funded since lot 16 lands had been poorly managed, as they had in most other states. Second, it relied on local control, which left power with many small, independent districts. Finally, it limited the Superintendent to a mostly advisory role. There were many weaknesses in the system. For example, a Superintendent in 1856 observed, "from a personal inspection of the schoolhouses in many parts of the State, I know that they are *mean and murderous things* [emphasis added]." Certainly, his statement likely involved some hyperbole, since many states had schools that were far worse than Wisconsin's.[47]

Still, while the reformers were disappointed with the new system's failings, they must have been thrilled with its emphasis on Christian values. As a consequence, the schools tended to elevate the Reformation's values of religion and morality above the Enlightenment's secular goals. Most of them conducted daily Bible reading and many used denominational texts, even though they could spark controversy from time to time. Of course, the zealots saw ancillary, secular benefits flowing from their emphasis on spiritual formation. They believed, perhaps too optimistically, that schools could literally change the world by eliminating crime and producing responsible citizens.[48]

Wisconsin's overconfidence in the power of education may have flowed from the speed and ease with which it had established a statewide system. That success, in turn, had resulted not only from its Yankee culture but also from its politics, which, like Michigan's, was marked by unity with respect to education. While Northern Democrats, Whigs, Free Soilers, and Republicans (organized in Wisconsin in 1854), may have fought over some issues, they had common beliefs about reform, including education. So because of the state's cultural and political unity, its chapter in this story includes little controversy. We can only speculate, of course, but Michigan, which had so much in common with Wisconsin, might have followed a similar path had it not been for the huge debt it labored under as a result of its failed internal improvements programs.[49]

So Yankee leaders in the Midwest, as they had done in earlier phases of reform, took advantage of the political instability of the 1850s to move their states toward a free education for all children. Ohio, Illinois, and Wisconsin reached that goal by the Civil War, Michigan would follow soon thereafter, while only Indiana would fall short. More than one-half the children (54%) in the region attended school in 1850 (Appendix II), which was more than double the rate achieved in the Border States. Michigan (73%), Ohio (65%), and Wisconsin (58%) had the highest rates, while Indiana (41%) and Illinois (38%) had the lowest. The attendance for Michigan and Wisconsin, which was a reflection of their Yankee heritage, is especially impressive considering their many sparsely-populated frontier areas. On the other hand, the rates for Indiana and Illinois show the strong influence of the Appalachians in the southern sections of those states.

The Middle-Atlantic and New England

Like the Southern, Border, and Midwestern regions, the movements in the Middle-Atlantic and New England reflected the culture and history of their people. States in both areas, with one exception, would fail to achieve the zealots' goals, although for very different reasons. And once again, religion would play an important role.

During the final phase of the cause Middle-Atlantic states continued to struggle as a result of their lack of religious unity. In the Midwest the crusade had been directed by Calvinists who hoped to shape the religion and morals of their states, but in the Middle-Atlantic, which was America's most diverse region, they had much less influence. The area's many denominations—Catholics in particular—had opposing viewpoints about what constituted a proper instruction in religion, so reform struggled. For example, Pennsylvania adopted a very progressive law in 1834, but as late as 1866 it was still not mandatory and twenty-three districts had opted out of its provisions. New York and Pennsylvania would wait until 1854 and 1857, respectively, to create lasting, full-time state superintendents and New York and New Jersey would not eliminate rate bills until 1867 and 1871, respectively. The region's school attendance patterns in 1850 (Appendix II) reflected the difficulties faced by its activists. New York's rate (69%) was the highest but lower than four states in other areas. The Empire State benefited from the large number of Yankees living in its northern and western sections and the large concentration of people living in New York City. Pennsylvania's (52%) and New Jersey's (50%) rates fell below three Midwestern states, even though they had a two-century head start.[50]

The crusade in New England also moved at a slow pace, which was quite ironic given that the region had spawned most of the reformers for the rest of the country. The region's problem was not a lack of religious unity but rather a proclivity for taking its educational heritage for granted, which it had been doing for over fifty years. A renewal came in the mid-1840s as the controversies over Texas, the Mexican-American War, Polk's vetoes, and tariffs strengthened Whig power in the region. As a result, in 1845 and 1846 advocates passed laws creating a superintendent in every state in the region except Massachusetts, which had already installed Horace Mann as Secretary to its Board in 1837. Despite this advance, with the exception of Massachusetts, apathy returned and the rest of the region would not offer its children free schools until the 1860s, when Vermont (1864), Connecticut (1868), and Rhode Island (1868) finally eliminated their rate bills. In spite of this slow improvement in New England's laws, three-fourths of its children attended school in 1850 (Appendix II), which gave it the best attendance in the nation. Clearly, this flowed from the value that the culture placed on education. Rates varied significantly among individual states: Maine (93%), Vermont (92%), New Hampshire (77%), Connecticut (67%), Massachusetts (62%), and Rhode Island (54%). Rhode Island's low rate likely reflected its status as New England's most religiously diverse state. Interestingly, the first four had higher rates than Massachusetts, even though they would not commit to tuition-free education until a decade after the Bay State.[51]

Massachusetts

Massachusetts was the only state in the region to achieve success in the 1850s because at the same time that political instability was damaging the old parties, nativism was giving birth to a new one. In a sad turn of events, this hateful ideology played a key role in insuring that all the state's children would receive a free education. Trouble began in 1853 when a coalition of Democrats and Free Soilers, despite opposition from the Whigs, called a convention to revise the constitution. The coalition, which had elected a majority of the delegates, put a new constitution before the electorate, but they soundly rejected it as well as the politicians who had endorsed it. Coalition members were furious and many mistakenly blamed the Irish, whose numbers had recently surged because of the potato famine. Know Nothings in Massachusetts successfully harnessed this rage when they formed the American Party, which promptly attracted many Free Soilers, Whigs, and others who previously had no interest in politics. It stressed anti-immigrant and anti-Catholic policies much more than fusion parties in other states, although like them it also worked for temperance and antislavery. The group quietly built an extensive network of lodges and required that members vote only for its endorsed candidates.[52]

On November 13, 1854 the American Party channeled all that anger into what historian Michael Holt has called "one of the most sweeping victories ever achieved by an American political party."

Their candidate for governor won with three times the votes of his nearest opponent; they won every statewide office, every state senate seat, and 380 of 390 house seats. Their insistence on secrecy made their victory especially surprising. This election, in addition to similar contests in many other states, marked the beginning of the end for the Whig Party, but it proved to be a blessing in disguise for education.[53]

Encouraged by its remarkable mandate, the new government moved quickly to implement its agenda in 1855. Since the Know Nothings believed in an activist government, they increased state spending by 50%, which required large tax increases. And in order to advance nativism, the very reason for the existence of their party, legislators limited the rights of recent immigrants to vote and to hold office. Moreover, the lawmakers, who were likely influenced by the two-dozen clergy included in their number, passed an especially strong temperance law. Further, they proved their commitment to civil rights for blacks by requiring the integration of the schools.[54]

As often happens when politicians overreach, their program stimulated so much opposition that parts of it were soon overturned, but that would not be the case for its education components. Much of the state's increase in taxes went to the schools, which offered free textbooks to all students and free schooling to all the state's children. Still, the legislation was not entirely benevolent, as it included several provisions that specifically targeted Catholics: it forbade foreign language instruction, required daily Bible-reading from the King James Version, barred use of state money for sectarian purposes, and, for the first time anywhere, required children under fifteen who worked in factories—many of whom were Irish—to attend at least eleven weeks of school each year. So, progress for the children of Massachusetts came at a price for its many Catholics.[55]

Conclusion

So, Ohio, Illinois, Wisconsin, and Massachusetts had guaranteed free schooling for all children by the outbreak of the Civil War and many other Northern states would follow in the 1860s. Yankees and Calvinists clearly played a key role, since reform fared so much better in states where they were a significant presence. Moreover, the temperance, antislavery, and nativist movements proved to be essential factors because they evoked such emotional responses from both sides of the common school debate. But while the crusade in its final phase experienced great success throughout the North, there were significant, persistent differences between the New England, Mid-Atlantic, and Midwest regions. Two separate surveys in 1870 showed that enrollment was expanding at a rapid rate in the North Central region, which is essentially the Midwest, while increasing at a more moderate pace in the North Atlantic region, which encompasses New England and the Mid-Atlantic. Further, this disparity would continue to grow for the rest of the century. Another indication of these regional differences was that enrollment in rural areas, which predominated in the more recently-settled Midwest, exceeded rates in urban areas, which were concentrated in New England and the Mid-Atlantic. These results reflect the fact that, with the exception of Massachusetts, New England and the Mid-Atlantic were largely apathetic and continued to rely too much on land grants for education funding, while the Midwest found significant new sources of money. Sadly, the South fell even further behind all other regions as a consequence of its negative attitudes and the devastating effects of the Civil War.[56]

Unlike the two earlier periods of reform, the last phase would not see a repeat of the discouraging two steps forward, one step back pattern of the 1820s and 1830s. The main reason for this was the emergence of the Republicans in the 1850s and their complete domination of the Democrats over the next three decades. Republicans, who remained strong advocates for education, won every Presidential election from 1860 through 1880. Republicans held the governor's office continuously in Ohio until 1874, in Illinois until 1893, and, except for one term, in Massachusetts until 1883 and in Michigan and Wisconsin until 1891. In all of New England, from 1858 through 1890 Republicans served eighty-three of ninety-seven gubernatorial terms of office. In this environment opponents of the cause, who typically were Democrats, were badly outnumbered.[57]

Yet success for the zealots did not mean that their battles were over, for they would struggle over the next seventy-five years to add many essential features to the common school system, such as the grouping of students by grade, the modern high school, and compulsory education. In that respect they were in a position similar to the builders of a skyscraper, who stop to celebrate the "topping out" of the structure's steel skeleton before going on to raise its walls and finish its interior. So, by the middle of the 19th century, the zealots could see that they were winning the battle to create state systems of public schools for America's children. The only task that remained was to implement their ideas in the nation's newly-acquired territory in the West. Not surprisingly, a familiar cast of characters would lead the way.[58]

Chapter 11

The Mission Expands to the New Frontier — Texas, California, and Oregon

*O*ver a hundred years ago, historian Frederick Jackson Turner famously argued that life on the frontier transformed the views of pioneers, but that was certainly not true concerning their opinions about schools. Indeed, the ethnic and religious heritage that Anglo settlers brought with them to Texas, California, and Oregon continued to direct their attitudes towards learning. Migrants from the Deep South left it to the family and the church, those from the Border States insisted on local rather than state control, while only those from New England fought to establish statewide systems of education. Yankee leadership was the key to the movement's success, but economic, demographic, and political conditions also had to be favorable. And just as had been the case in the East, until a sufficient number of students lived in an area and their parents and the state possessed enough resources to fund schools, initiatives failed. Further, the zealots had to navigate treacherous political crosscurrents created by slavery. As a result, their story mimics that of their counterparts in the South, the Midwest, and New England.[1]

Texas

Education in the Longhorn State suffered the same fate as in the other states that formed the Confederacy. Its Anglo settlers, who came mostly from the Deep South and the Appalachian mountains, showed little interest in the crusade because of their cultures. Further, the pioneers and their government had to focus their time and money on building other aspects of their society first. So while there were several attempts over the years to open community schools, they invariably resulted in only a handful of institutions.[2]

Those failures began when Texas was a part of Mexico. Beginning with her independence in 1821, Mexico enacted legislation that mandated public education but then failed to fund it. The northern state of Coahuila adopted laws encouraging schools, but by 1834 only five existed there. A new school faced two obstacles: first, Mexicans and Anglos lived in such isolation that few areas could support one, and second, due to racism the Catholic priests who ran missions serving the Indians were only interested in providing basic vocational and religious instruction. The first problem began to fade during the 1830s as large numbers of Americans began immigrating to the region. Soon some Anglos were complaining about the lack of schools, but when their pleas went unanswered they fell back on their Southern preference for private and church education. As most Americans know, the Anglos had other, much more serious disputes with the Mexican government, which led to the dramatic Battle of the Alamo and the Revolution of 1836. Unfortunately, the Republic of Texas was no more inclined to start schools than its predecessor. While its constitution called for a "general system of education" and its lawmakers passed laws in 1838, 1839, and 1840, Texans ignored them and continued to cling to their Southern ways. Some children were taught in private or church-sponsored institutions, often by ministers, but most studied at home, if at all.[3]

At the same time the economic hardships of the Panic of 1837 were bringing to Texas even more Americans, who were attracted by its abundant, cheap land. Many of them soon began to argue for its annexation by the United States, for two reasons. First, the immigrants subscribed to the concept that became known as Manifest

Destiny, which asserted that the United States was foreordained to expand to the shores of the Pacific. Second, in a related belief many evangelicals felt compelled by the Great Commission to spread the message of Christianity around the world. These two powerful forces drove the population from just 30,000 in 1836 to 142,000 by 1846. But the politics of slavery prevented the Republic from becoming part of the United States during its nine-year existence. Southern migrants who owned slaves worried that a distant government would interfere with their cotton business, Northern abolitionists feared that the entrance of another slave state into the Union would hurt their cause, and Northern Whigs trembled at the prospect of a state that was likely to be filled with loyal Democrats. Finally, in 1845 President Polk broke the impasse when he proposed the annexation of both Texas and Oregon, the former a slave state, the latter non-slave. Annexation brought Texas its third government in nine years but it failed to brighten prospects for the zealots. The state's Constitution ordered lawmakers to make "suitable provision for. . .public schools" and to "establish free schools throughout the state," but education's advocates and opponents would argue about the meaning of those words for years. In order to comply with another provision that required property taxes to support schools the legislature passed a law that allocated 10% of all tax revenues to a school fund, but like so many initiatives in Texas and elsewhere this was never done.[4]

After languishing for a few years the cause seemed to finally blossom in the mid-1850s, as it did in so many other states. Changes in demography, money, and attitudes all played a part. First, surging migration increased the population to 212,000 in 1850 and to 604,000 by 1860, which facilitated school formation and increased pressure for a statewide system. Further, the state received a windfall—$5,000,000 of US bonds—in return for surrendering its land claims in New Mexico. Moreover, wealthier Texans who supported slavery worried that their children would be exposed to abolitionist propaganda if they sent them off to study in the North. Finally, many crusaders were tiring of the earlier initiatives that had looked promising on paper but had never materialized.[5]

Not surprisingly, a Yankee led the way. Elisha Pease, a descendant of Puritans who immigrated to Salem, Massachusetts, was born in Connecticut, educated in Massachusetts, and settled in Texas in 1835 at the age of 26. For the next four decades he would serve its government in numerous capacities, ranging from helping to write the Republic's Constitution to serving several terms in the Lone Star State's House and Senate. His election as Governor in 1853 opened the way for many improvements. Though he was a Democrat, he held many of the same beliefs as the Northern Whigs and the Republican Party, which he joined after the Civil War. Similar to other advocates he believed that government should help alleviate human suffering, so during his two terms the state started institutions for the deaf, dumb, blind, and insane. And like several other reformers he tied the funding of internal improvements, like railroads, to education.[6]

Pease's work culminated in the School Law of 1854, which: (1) moved $2,000,000 of the US bonds into a permanent fund; (2) required it to pay the tuition of poor children; (3) permitted private schools to be converted to public; and (4) established a comprehensive state system. The last provision established a county board, comprised of the commissioners and the top county executive. The board was to partition the county into districts, which were to be operated by three elected trustees. Certainly this statute represented real progress, but it failed to guarantee a free education for all white children; for example, districts had to provide school buildings in order to access state funds and most parents still had to pay a rate bill to cover the teacher's salary. But like similar laws in many other states, this one would fall short of its objectives. While per student spending by the state soared from $0.62 in 1854 to $1.50 in 1855, absolute funding levels remained quite low. In part this occurred because of widespread cultural opposition. Additionally, since Texans had to devote most of their resources towards building a new society on the frontier, they balked at paying higher taxes. Making matters worse, the new act allowed districts to reimburse parents for children attending private or parochial schools, so there was little money left for common school salaries or buildings. As a result, most children were educated in the home, some in private or church-sponsored institutions, and a handful went back East to study. Still, literacy was widespread, so parents apparently were successfully teaching the basics.[7]

But while reform lagged in Texas it was not for lack of advocates. First, similar to so many other places evangelicals led the way from the start of the Republic up to the Civil War. Presbyterian ministers helped write the provisions dealing with education in the Republic's Constitution. And evangelical ministers, including many Yankees, served as advocates, administrators, and teachers for both public and private schools. Predictably, those institutions reflected their goals: evangelization—bringing "unsaved" children to accept Christ as their Savior—and discipleship—showing those children how to live a Christian life. These schools used the KJV Bible, presented it using Protestant methods, and taught ethics from a Protestant perspective. Second, German pioneers in the Hill Country also fought for the movement, as they had everywhere they settled. Their two main settlements there, New Braunfels (1845) and Fredericksburg (1846), were both populated by Prussians, whose advanced systems of education had been admired and studied by Stowe, Mann, and many other Americans since the early 1830s. Education was very important to these Germans, who typically built schools alongside their churches within a year of their arrival in Texas.[8]

Despite the work of these two groups, they failed because they simply were outnumbered. In 1850 only 5% of Texans had emigrated from the North and just 5% had come from Germany, while a majority (54%) had left the South, including supporters of slavery from the Deep South and opponents of centralized government from Appalachia. While the last two groups had their own cultural reasons for opposing state-controlled schooling, the issue of slavery created another obstacle. Many of them defended it, either because it benefited them directly (15% of the populace owned 75% of the slaves), indirectly, or because they objected to the efforts to control what others did with their "private property." As a result, the vile practice was supported by a large majority of the population. For example, the first bishop of the Catholic Diocese of Galveston-Houston owned slaves and his successor was an advocate for the Confederacy at the onset of the Civil War. On the other hand, the

Northerners and the Germans fought slavery, usually because of their religious beliefs. This led the Southerners to mistrust the crusaders, which damaged cooperation between these groups on other causes, such as education.[9]

The zealots certainly had to have the Southerners' help to effect any political change, since demography dictated that Democrats controlled Texas while Whigs constituted a permanent minority. While this provides a partial explanation for the reformers' weakness, the policies and composition of the national Whig Party made matters even worse. In the 1840s the Party had fought annexation and opposed the Mexican War, which were both very popular in the state, and in the 1850s, despite defections to third parties, it still included many members who opposed slavery. As a result, the Party had even less influence in the state than it might have otherwise.[10]

The reformers received no help from nativism, either. The Know-Nothing Party, though it achieved some success in the mid-1850s, had little lasting influence on Texas politics, since nativists never managed to win over a majority of the state's citizens. At their peak, they gained the support of the iconic Sam Houston, controlled one of every five newspapers, and elected many state legislators and mayors. But slavery divided them, and since they attacked Germans and Mexicans with their propaganda, the powerful Democrat Party, which reached out to those two groups, condemned the Know Nothings. As a result, they never achieved the success that they had in the North.[11]

So, in most respects Texas resembled the rest of the Confederacy. In 1850 only 13% of its children attended school and the crusade's opponents continued to hold the upper hand for the rest of the decade. Then, even though the state received little direct damage from the Civil War, the conflict's impact reduced attendance even further, to only 7% by 1870. But that would soon change since the federal government had just forced the state to adopt a new constitution that guaranteed a system of free schooling.[12]

California

While it may be hard for us to imagine today, in many ways California resembled the Border States of Kentucky and Missouri during its first two decades. Its first Anglo settlers, many of whom were Scotch-Irish, resisted the ideas of centralized supervision and taxation for education. Like the Texans and other pioneers, its residents had to devote most of their resources to building other aspects of society on the frontier. As a result, the movement would languish until the Civil War brought about a tectonic shift in its politics. Throughout the struggle, New Englanders led the way.[13]

Yankees and schools were both scarce in California in its years as a Spanish colony and after 1821 as a Mexican province. The lack of concern for education resulted from traditional notions of race and class. Like their fellow clergy in Texas, the padres who operated the missions for some of the 75,000 Indians who lived in the area saw little reason to give them any instruction beyond basic religious and vocational training. Similar to the English gentry, they feared that educated natives would become dissatisfied with their station in life and disrupt the social order. Several governors planned to open schools for the rest of the children, but they only started a few and those often employed poorly-trained ex-soldiers who used harsh discipline. The wealthy either hired local tutors or sent their children off to Mexico City or the Sandwich Islands (Hawaii). So, very few children attended school in early California and it appears that most children were not being taught at home either, since illiteracy was commonplace.[14]

Education in California, like Texas, also suffered from low population density, but that changed almost overnight with the discovery of gold in 1848. Just 650 Anglos had lived there in 1845, but the Gold Rush raised its total population to 92,597 in 1850 and to an astonishing 264,435 just two years later. While most were attracted by the prospect of instant wealth, some were ministers from New England who were intent on winning souls for Christ. Their number included many Congregationalists and Presbyterians, who would help build San Francisco's first schools. They founded them, taught in them, promoted them, and lobbied for them. They were responsible for many firsts, including the first free school in 1849, the first state law in 1851, and the first city school ordinance. A missionary served as the city's first school superintendent and Yankees filled every seat on the city's school board in 1853. It appeared that the New Englanders were determined to make San Francisco's schools look just like Boston's.[15]

As a result of their influence, the first state Constitution, which was drafted in 1849, had provided for a Superintendent, a fund that controlled monies from lots 16 and 36 (California was the first state to get two sections per township), and a system that provided a minimum of three months of instruction each year. Further, it ordered the legislature to "direct, by all suitable means, the promotion of intellectual, scientific, moral, and agricultural improvements." The system's funding was to come entirely from land grants, even though that approach had failed in every state where it had been tried. Despite the apparent strength of these directives, California's schools experienced little growth in the state's early years. The governor had ignored the subject in his first message to the legislature and the rest of government and most of the state's residents followed his example. By 1851 land grants had not produced any money, so a new state statute encouraged communities to start schools at their own expense. Consequently, seven of the state's twenty-seven counties had just thirteen schools and another seven had none. This widespread noncompliance led the State Superintendent at the time to charge that the education section of the Constitution "has been practically a dead letter."[16]

The movement's preeminent leader in this period was Judge John Marvin, who lacked the heritage of a typical zealot. He was born in Pennsylvania and was educated there in his early years, rather than New England. However, he was exposed to Yankee culture and thought while earning an undergraduate degree at Wesleyan University in Connecticut and a law degree at Harvard, where he studied under legal giants Joseph Story, Simon Greenleaf, and Charles Sumner. Like many of his peers, he taught school to earn part of his college tuition. After graduation from Harvard he served as its librarian for a while and wrote a reference work that became so influential that some historians have called him the Father of Legal Bibliography.[17]

Marvin was elected California's first Superintendent of Public Instruction in 1850, just one year after his arrival. Despite receiving no salary and no budget he drove two bills through a reluctant legislature: a minor one in 1851 and a much more significant one in 1852. The latter secured a $50,000 appropriation for education, created a state board, re-authorized the State Superintendent's position, organized county and district boards, and mandated a three-month school term, teacher examinations, and yearly teacher institutes. To fund this ambitious program, the law included a five-mill state tax and permitted local entities to levy as much as three additional mills. The act looked good on paper but, like those in many other states, it fell victim to a combination of indifference, incompetence, and obstruction. Lawmakers reduced the $50,000 appropriation in each of the next two years. In 1853 Marvin reported, "not a dollar. . .has been distributed. . .for the support of common schools." In 1854 he observed, "education is in a critical state, owing to the defects of existing laws" and he complained of a "legislative sleep." His requests for libraries, uniform textbooks, and full-time county superintendents were all rejected. Interestingly, Marvin reported that California had a 22% attendance rate in 1852, which was the same as Kentucky's, Missouri's, and the average rate for all Border States in the 1850 census.[18]

Marvin paid a big political price for his devotion to the cause in June 1853 when the Democrats failed to re-nominate him for another term. In a final indignity, in 1854 an outraged legislature refused to print his last, lame duck report because of its many pointed criticisms. Reform would make little progress for the rest of the decade. In 1858 one of Marvin's successors, who admitted to "discouragement" and "despair," reported that the state was spending $2,000 per convict, but a mere $9 per student.[19]

This dismal situation can be traced to three factors. First, similar to the situation in Texas, Southerners dominated the electorate. So their preferred party, the Democrats, were able to frustrate the plans of the zealots, who usually aligned themselves with the Whigs and later the Republicans. Slavery was a key issue that divided the two factions and it would become a major factor in the struggle for free common schools in the state.

Second, Mexicans and Indians, since they had rarely been exposed to education, did not support it, which left the outnumbered crusaders with no allies in their fight. Lastly, many Californians lived either in areas of low population density, or in the case of the mining camps, in places with few children. As a result, school formation in the state's early years was often impractical. Certainly, California's population grew 43% from 1852 to 1860, but considering the size of the state its growth did not overcome the problem of low population density. So, in the decade before the Civil War these three obstacles proved too difficult for even the crusaders to overcome.[20]

Though these crusaders failed to create free public schools, the schools that they were able to start, both public and private, had a strong Protestant character and nativism played a large part in that development. Bitter, internal fights over the slavery issue in the mid-1850s weakened the Democrats, which allowed the Know Nothings to sweep city and state elections. They quickly passed legislation that banned all funding for sectarian schools and required reading of the KJV Bible and Protestant moral instruction. The act presumed that Catholic instruction was sectarian, while Protestant teaching was non-denominational and eligible for funding. At the same time, many Protestants joined vigilante groups to control crime and to rein in what they felt was a corrupt government. Sensational but isolated incidents between Catholics and Protestants included a murder, a lynching, a fatal duel, and the burning of a Catholic Church. While these groups did not specifically target Catholics, members of that faith often received "street justice" from the vigilantes.[21]

One of those attracted to the vigilante movement was John Swett, who had recently arrived from New England. He would later confess in his autobiography that he might have enrolled in the 1856 vigilante group had the line not been so long. But his life would be marked much more by devotion to a cause than hatred for any group. His leadership, aided by a radical change that the Civil War would bring to California politics, was critical for the success of the common school crusade in the 1860s. During his remarkable, sixty-year career he served as teacher, principal, city superintendent, state superintendent, textbook author, and education advocate. In recognition of his many accomplishments, historians of every era have referred to him as the Father of California's Public Schools.[22]

Swett was born in New Hampshire and, like so many other reformers, was descended from Puritans who immigrated to New England before 1650. From an early age he absorbed his community's Calvinist values, though his parents were religious liberals who accepted many of the beliefs of the Unitarian Church, which he would later join. He studied for eight years at a district school and three years at an academy and heard many Congregational sermons and lyceum lectures. After graduation he taught for four years and then in 1851 he enrolled in a normal school in New Hampshire. The school was run by William Russell, the influential leader who had launched the *American Journal of Education*, one of the movement's first journals, and the American Institute of Instruction, one of its first organizations. He had influenced many of its key advocates, including James Carter and Horace Mann. Though Swett's stay at the school was brief, he and Russell would correspond with each other over the next fifteen years. Their relationship would prove to be one of several important influences on Swett's educational philosophy. Russell advocated child-centered, humane instructional methods, which Swett would also promote. Other progressive thinkers shaped his worldview, including Ralph Waldo Emerson, John Muir, Johann Pestalozzi, and Herbert Spencer, an important contributor to the ideas that became known as Social Darwinism. So unlike most of the zealots, his ideology was nourished by liberals and humanists rather than orthodox Congregationalists like Dwight or Beecher.[23]

Still, much like Mann, Swett retained the Calvinist moral standards of his youth. For example, during his brief stay in one of California's mining camps, his conduct provided a vivid contrast with that of the prototypical miner. He later boasted that during his time there he "neither used tobacco nor whiskey. . .never played a game of cards" and "lived up to the rigid standard of an old Puritan community." Over the years, he also developed a great deal of respect for the important role his fellow Yankees had played in reform. In fact, late in life he became so convinced that New Englanders had launched the crusade that he traveled home to research and document their role for posterity. So when Swett came west in 1853 to seek his fortune in gold, he brought with him a Puritan's character and a progressive's ideas. Like most other miners, he failed and was forced to find other employment later that same year. With the help of a friend he secured a position as teacher and principal at Rincon School in San Francisco. He would remain there for the next nine years, building a great deal of respect in the field.[24]

In 1862 Swett was given the opportunity to lead statewide reform because of a remarkable transformation of California's politics. By the outbreak of the Civil War the Democrat Party had became hopelessly divided between those loyal to the Union and those who held Southern sympathies. Their infighting weakened the Party, which allowed Leland Stanford, the son of Massachusetts natives and the descendent of 17th-century Puritan settlers, to become the first Republican elected Governor of the state in 1861. The next year, a Congregational minister recruited Swett to run for State Superintendent for the Union Party, which had just been formed by Republicans and Democrats who were opposed to the Confederacy. Swett, who had been a Republican since its first days in the state, easily defeated his two Democrat opponents. The new party swept the elections of 1862, 1863, and 1864, opening the way for meaningful legislation.[25]

Not surprisingly, the new superintendent envisioned a system that resembled the one he had left behind in New England. Schools should stress civic and moral training, which could include Bible reading without comment as long as the community approved the practice. They should be free, open to all, and enforce high standards for curricula, textbooks, and teachers. Among the reforms he sought were uniform textbooks, libraries, a state journal, and teacher training, certification, and organization. Like most other states, California's land grant money had been wasted and in any event was not likely to adequately fund the system's needs, so his most urgent need was for additional tax revenues. In his final report the outgoing superintendent painted a bleak picture of the state's schools, just as Swett was about to take office.[26]

For the next four years Swett, using methods similar to other zealots, relentlessly pushed his agenda with the support of a friendly legislature and two Yankee governors, Stanford in 1863 and Frederick F. Low from 1863 to 1867. Low was born in Maine, educated in common schools, and exposed to the cause while attending Boston-area lyceums. The law of 1863, which borrowed heavily from Newton Bateman's system in Illinois, authorized almost every detail of Swett's vision, but it failed to provide adequate funding. Lawmakers had approved a state levy of only five mills that year, so Swett worked to mobilize Californians through a massive petition drive. As a result, in 1864 the legislature required counties to charge a tax of at least $2 for each child and in 1866 it increased the county tax to $3 and the state tax to eight mills. Districts were also required to raise enough local funds to provide a minimum of three to five months of free education, depending upon their size. These revenues permitted a historic change in 1867, the elimination of the rate bill, and as a result the statewide system that the Constitution had envisioned was finally in place.[27]

The results from just five years of reform were remarkable. From 1862 to 1867 state spending tripled, county taxes doubled, attendance doubled, and several months were added to the average school calendar. In 1865 alone, tax revenue soared by 92% and instruction time increased by an entire month. In addition to the new revenue, the state's growing population, which increased by 47% during the decade, made schools feasible for the first time in many places. So although many private institutions continued to exist, public education was thriving in California's larger towns. Now that the structural and financial improvements that Swett desired were in place and the state was maturing, he seemed on the verge of leading the movement to even greater heights.[28]

Unfortunately, at the peak of his success in 1867 evangelicals attacked Swett over concerns about his Unitarian faith. While the two groups had a history of collaboration on various issues, evangelicals often suspected that Unitarians were not sufficiently orthodox when it came to Christian doctrine, moral instruction, and the proper use of the Bible in the schools. In fact, religious conservatives had tried to drive Unitarians Nathan Guilford and Horace Mann from office, succeeding with the former and failing with the latter. Swett had been attacked in 1862 when he was called an agnostic and an infidel and now he was being criticized for his policies on religious instruction, in particular on the use of the KJV Bible. Swett, from his first years in California had felt that the state, which included many Catholics and Jews, was too diverse to require all students to study from the Protestant Bible. He believed that it could be read without comment at the teacher's discretion, but if anyone objected the lesson must wait until after school. The fall election brought a bitter defeat for Swett and his fellow Republicans, who were driven from office in a Democrat landslide.[29]

Despite this setback, the movement would lose little momentum. By 1870 55% of California's school-age children were attending school, which exceeded every Border State but Missouri (57%). Certainly, the Golden State's rising population helped the cause but its density was still far below most other states. Further, the frontier state at times had needs that took precedence over schools. But the political revolution brought about by the Civil War and the reforms instituted by zealots like Swett insured that it would look a lot less like the South and more like the North in the decades to come.[30]

Oregon

Like California, Oregon also resembled a Border State in the 1840s and 1850s. Scotch-Irish from the east, who constituted a significant segment of its first pioneers, resisted the idea of centralized supervision and taxation. Further, even more so than in California, the demands of building a society in the wilderness were deemed more important than education. And like any area on the frontier it lacked enough people and funds to organize schools. As a result, the reform movement struggled until the Civil War hurt its opponents and brought its friends to power. Nowhere in the country was that corps of crusaders so dominated by evangelical ministers than in the Beaver State.[31]

The zealots not only created Oregon's public schools, but they also pushed for its Anglo settlement and its admission into the United States. Their story began in 1831 when a mysterious visit by four Indians to St. Louis intrigued many evangelicals, inspiring them to send missionaries out West to find and convert their tribe.

Methodist minister Jason Lee and Presbyterian minister Marcus Whitman, both Yankees, founded missions in the region in the mid-1830s, but when their work with the natives faltered, they abruptly changed course, deciding instead to try to attract Anglo settlers, who they would then evangelize and disciple. Two emotional ideas, the secular mandate of Manifest Destiny and the spiritual command of the Great Commission help explain their efforts, which could be extreme. For example, Whitman once made a foolhardy, winter trip over the Rockies to the East to save his mission and promote settlement in Oregon.[32]

But while patriotism and faith inspired the leaders of the Great Migration, raw economics drove its participants: the Panic of 1837 made their life very difficult in the East, severe flooding displaced many from their homes in the upper Mississippi River valley, and Oregon enticed them with 640 acres of free land. Consequently, the Anglo population of the area—all of present day Oregon, Washington, and Idaho and parts of Wyoming and Montana—soared from just 1,500 in 1843, to 6,000 in 1845, and to 13,294 by 1850. As the migrants poured in, Protestant missionaries made the establishment of schools a key aspect of their work, for several reasons. First, the sinful lifestyles of many pioneers challenged their desire for a God-fearing community. While the adults seemed a lost cause, the zealots hoped to save their children through education. Second, Catholics, who had their own schools, threatened to mold society according to Papal norms. So like Lyman Beecher and the evangelicals of the Ohio Valley, they planned to shape the culture through their own institutions. Third, many evangelicals were descended from the Puritans (Lee and Whitman, for example), whose love for learning had been passed down to the current generation. Lastly, low church attendance led to meager donations, which forced ministers to earn income from teaching. As a result, by the early 1840s ministers were operating several schools in the region. In fact, prior to the founding of the Oregon Territory ministers were responsible for most of the area's formal education.[33]

When the missionaries helped to create the Provisional Government in 1843 they tried to establish a statewide educational system through the provisions of its Constitution, which reiterated Cutler's famous statement on "religion, morality, and knowledge." Unfortunately, the zealots failed because of three very familiar problems. First, while Oregon's population was growing rapidly, only a few places had enough children to form a school and enough taxpayers to pay for it. Second, the demands of constructing an entirely new society left little time or money for education. Finally and most importantly, many of the pioneers were Scotch-Irish from the Ohio River valley and others were from the Deep South. Both groups saw little reason to raise taxes for schools that would be controlled by a central government. So, after two attempts at reform failed under the Provisional Government, education remained in private hands. Sadly, none of those obstacles disappeared after Oregon became a US territory in 1848. Worse, the California Gold Rush created a huge exodus, including many ministers who left to serve the miners. But while the Gold Rush initially hurt the Territory, it's effects soon turned positive. In just a few years the disappointed miners returned to reestablish homesteads and a few successful ones brought money back to invest. So the population began to increase once again, but even that failed to help the cause, which still suffered from too little money, too few children, and a lack of advocates throughout the 1850s.[34]

Certainly, the lack of progress was not the fault of Congregational minister George Henry Atkinson. Reverend Atkinson was energetic, knowledgeable, and persuasive, whether he was promoting Oregon to potential settlers or education to its citizens. A powerful speaker, he played an important role in the development of the area's agriculture and in the founding of its schools. For the latter, for over four decades he served as a teacher, principal, and county administrator, and has been called the Father of Oregon's Public Schools as a result of his relentless work. In fact, across the nation only Swett and Barnard toiled longer for the cause. But at the core of all his achievements, whether economic or educational, was his unflagging dedication to Christianity. Atkinson acquired his devotion to that faith, as well as many other traits, while growing up in New England. He was born and educated in Massachusetts and graduated from two colleges run by Congregationalists: Dartmouth in 1843 and Andover Seminary in 1846. He married Nancy

Bates that same year and in 1847 he and his bride undertook the long voyage around Cape Horn to Oregon to establish a mission for the AHMS. A living challenge to Turner's thesis, Atkinson never warmed to western culture; in fact, in almost every way he remained a typical Yankee throughout his long life.[35]

Of course, moralism was one of that people's most distinguishing features and Atkinson, much like Samuel Lewis, was fearless in challenging those who fell short of his exacting standards. For example, as a young college student he wrote his uncle, "Be not angry with me, for this letter. I feel that you are in danger, and that I must clean my skirts of your blood, if you after a few days more, shall be found in Hell." Clearly, for Atkinson the fate of his uncle's soul overcame the fear that his relative might find his letter impertinent. In a similar vein, he regularly condemned drinking, gambling, and dancing, which he saw as tools of the devil, even though "men of the world blame and reprove me for speaking to persons on the subject at the wrong time." Yet according to a biographer, he was usually able to make his points without offending the "sinner."[36]

While Atkinson's moralism reflected his Calvinist background and training, so did his educational philosophy. His charge from the AHMS in 1847 had directed him to open "churches, schools, whatever would benefit humanity—temperance, virtue; the industrial, mental, moral and religious training of the young, and the establishment of society upon sound principles by means of institutions of religion and learning." But since many of Oregon's adults seemed indifferent to the Congressional pastor's message, he concentrated on their children for the next forty years. In 1888, one year before his death, Atkinson shared his thinking in a lengthy address to the National Education Association. He began by chiding earlier speakers for focusing on knowledge and discipline rather than intelligence and morals, as the Puritans had done. Students must be taught to be "law-respecting and law-abiding citizens" lest they become part of the "lawless class," which was the greatest threat to the Republic. Schools must not only teach the Constitution and laws but also the Old and New Testaments. Students must be shown the bright line that separates good from evil and they must be urged to follow the "Great Teacher and Law-giver." In conclusion, he implored, "Why not resolve, and with unfaltering purpose, enforce our resolution to restore God's Book of Human Rights and Laws – the Bible. . .in our public schools. . . . In closing, we venture to hoist the banner of liberty and law over every school house in America. The Bible our textbook!"[37]

Atkinson's commitment to the crusade had begun in 1849, just one year after his arrival in Oregon, when he wrote the education section of Gov. Joseph Lane's Inaugural Address. At Lane's request he then drafted the School Law of 1849, a comprehensive statute that attempted to create a system of common schools for the new territory. To provide financing it levied a state school tax of two mills per $1.00 of property value, allowed local districts to assess an additional tax, and set up a permanent fund for land grants and other revenues. To establish supervision it mandated an elected State Superintendent, county and district committees, and required examinations for teachers. But similar to the response in many other states, few communities utilized Oregon's first law, which faced immediate political attacks. In 1851 the legislature eliminated the position of county superintendent and transferred its duties to the county commissioners. That same year lawmakers halved the state tax and in 1852 they eliminated it completely. Further, they presumed that land grants—lots 16 and 36, the same as California—would provide most of the system's funding, despite their repeated failure in almost every state. Predictably, Oregon would add its own chapter to the sorry history of land grants. Slow surveys and greedy speculators hindered the production of revenue, which limited the size of the permanent fund. As a result, the schools suffered from poor instruction, lacked essential supplies, and tried to survive using rate bills.[38]

Oregon's weak commitment to education convinced Atkinson and other zealots that private institutions were needed to fill the void. The obstacles to the cause, including the attitudes of many Southerners and Appalachians, were just too much to overcome in the 1850s. So, in 1852 Governor Lane, Atkinson, and the AHMS collaborated to open a private normal school for women in Oregon City. At Lane's request, Governor William Slade of Vermont convinced single young females from his state to enroll in the school at the

AHMS's expense. The program paid quick dividends, as many of the school's graduates became teachers in area schools, which were mostly private institutions. The school's founders called it a seminary, which gives us a clear indication that they believed teaching was a calling to a spiritual mission. Indeed, Baptists, Congregationalists, and Methodists operated most of the area's private schools. Ministers were deeply involved with them, both as teachers and as superintendents. As one might expect then, these institutions, whether private or public, reflected widely-held Protestant beliefs. As a result, they stressed Bible-reading, prayers, and textbooks that comported with evangelical norms. For example, Atkinson imposed those very practices on the Clackamus County system in the early 1860s while serving as its superintendent and later on the Multnomah County schools (Portland) during the two terms he served as their leader. One of the evangelicals' motivations was the presence of many Catholics in the area. Much like Lyman Beecher, they worried about the influence that Catholicism could have on Oregon's culture, and they hoped to shape it according to their own ideals.[39]

The number of state schools finally began to grow when lawmakers corrected the setbacks of the early 1850s with a new law in 1854. This statute reinstated the two-mill state tax, permitted a district tax, created elected county superintendents, established rules for districts, and instituted many other improvements. As a result, the number of public institutions increased for the rest of the decade, although they were still outnumbered by private schools. This trend was aided by Oregon's population growth, leading to calls for statehood and culminating in the Constitutional Convention of 1857. Delegates approved and voters ratified a document that promised "a uniform and general system of common schools." The assembly's Committee on Education, which included three Yankees and borrowed from the constitutions of four Northern states, produced two other key provisions. It made the Governor the State Superintendent, which conferred prestige on the position, but also guaranteed that it would be part-time. It also required that lots 16 and 36 be placed in a Permanent Common School Fund and created a Board composed of the Governor, the Secretary of State, and the State Treasurer to administer it.[40]

But despite the Constitution's enlightened plans, the opponents to centralized supervision and education funding remained strong. Some of them argued that Oregon's population was still too widely scattered to form schools, while Appalachians and Southerners objected to the involvement of government in a matter that they considered private. It is clear that the second group had a great deal of power in the state through the late 1850s. For example, many citizens had fought for a constitutional provision, albeit unsuccessfully, that would have permitted slavery. And voters approved another measure by a margin of 8 to 1 that actually barred free blacks from the state! But in 1859 the Southerners' power began a rapid descent when the state's Democrat Party split apart as a result of the bitter national debate over the admission of Kansas. In 1860 former Governor Lane ran for Vice President on the Southern Democrat ticket, which supported slavery in the South and its expansion into the territories. Lane and his running mate garnered 34% of Oregon's vote, only 254 votes behind the Republican Lincoln, who won the state's three electoral votes. If the Democrats had not split their vote between Northern (headed by Stephen Douglas) and Southern factions (headed by John Breckinridge and Lane) they would have won the state in a landslide. But just one year later, when the secession of the Confederate states led to the Civil War, the state's Democrats became completely discredited since most Oregonians, even if they were not outright abolitionists, backed the preservation of the Union. So the main critics of the movement lost all support, which opened the door for the Republicans, who were the primary boosters of education.[41]

In 1862, when Democrat John Whiteaker, a self-educated, proslavery native of Southern Indiana, left the Governor's office he was replaced by Republican Addison C. Gibbs, an educated, antislavery Yankee from New York State. Gibbs was the first non-Democrat elected as Oregon's chief executive and the former normal school student and teacher became a strong advocate for the zealot's cause. At the same time, the state was now well positioned to support the movement since its economy was prospering from a new gold rush and it was insulated from the ravages of the distant war.

As a result, Gibbs pushed the cause in his Inaugural Address and the legislature soon passed an act that made many improvements to the 1854 law. The statute gave a clearer definition of the responsibilities of county superintendents, district boards, and local teachers. Unfortunately, the Governor continued to serve as the part-time State Superintendent and, as in so many states, the law was ignored at times. Then after the war the Democrats regained power, which further delayed reforms, including efforts to increase pay for instructors. At last, LaFayette Grover, a Democrat but also a Calvinist-trained native of Maine, worked for and signed Oregon's historic Law of 1872, which set up a State Board with a full-time Superintendent. The act gave them both extensive responsibilities, including regular reporting to lawmakers and supervision of school officers, districts, teachers, curriculum, and textbooks. And after years of delay, land grant funds finally began to flow to the schools, which would help a great deal in meeting their needs.[42]

So, by 1872 Oregon had shown a solid commitment to the education of its children. Indeed, the US Census taken two years earlier had documented the enormous progress that it had already made at the local level, even before passage of the landmark legislation. While the student attendance data in its census were unreliable, it had far more teachers and schools relative to the total number of its school-age children than California or any Border State. In fact, if its census data can be trusted, it was educating more of its children than all but three states in New England. This is a remarkable outcome, given the struggles of the crusade before the Civil War, but unfortunately we can only speculate about its causes. Certainly, the growth of the population, the expansion of the economy, and the effects of the Civil War all played a part. It is likely that these developments helped the zealots, who had played such an essential role in the settlement of Oregon and in the founding of its government, to finally overcome resistance from the Southerners to bring about the state's remarkable transformation.[43]

Conclusion

The story of the movement in Oregon, California, and Texas was remarkably similar to the narrative that had unfolded in New England, the Midwest, and the South a few decades earlier. That is unsurprising, since the prerequisites for success were the same in every state. First, large-scale education on the frontier was not possible unless certain structural conditions existed. Until enough settlers were concentrated in an area there were too few children to form a school. Related to that, until those same pioneers had financed what they considered to be more fundamental needs in their community, there was too little money to fund the cause. Over time, all three states eventually reached that stage of development, but something else was needed. Success could only come at the time and at the place where advocates became strong enough to overcome their opponents. Since both advocacy and opposition resulted from a people's ingrained cultural beliefs and the three states had unique cultural mixes, they had different results. Texas, which had just a handful of zealots but a large number of adversaries, experienced real reform only when the federal government imposed it during Reconstruction. On the other hand, California and Oregon, which contained an abundance of the reformers, built extensive systems in the 1860s. Further, similar to other successful states, Yankees, evangelicals, ministers, and Republicans dominated their leadership. So in a sense, the three states represented a microcosm of the country as a whole: Texas was the typical Southern state, and California and Oregon resembled Border States before the Civil War and the Midwest or New England once the war had shifted political power to the zealots.

One aspect of the story for the West differed from the East. The temperance, nativist, and antislavery social movements, though they existed in all three states, had little impact on the development of common schools. Temperance and nativism had provoked a great deal of controversy in the states in the East that had large German Catholic and Irish Catholic populations, but those ethnic groups were relatively small in the West. Antislavery was not much of a factor either, because the predominance of Southern sentiment in the three states kept its adherents from acquiring much power.

In conclusion, this story is about faith. It is about faith because the chief advocates for the crusade were Calvinists who saw education as an effective way to reach the rising generation with their message of eternal salvation and their rules for moral living. Indeed, they believed that religious training was even more important for children than the acquisition of intellectual skills and the development of good citizenship. Not surprisingly, these crusaders adhered to a philosophy rooted in Luther's Reformation, rather than Rousseau's Enlightenment. As a result of their pessimistic view of man, they favored teachers who demanded discipline and maintained firm control over the curriculum. In state after state, from Ohio to Oregon, their willingness to sacrifice their comfort, their time, and their treasure truly earned them the title "zealot."

Yet there is also a "story" behind the story. Textbooks and research monographs for more than a hundred years have given us a very different account of the origins of the public schools. Strangely, the Calvinists and their religious motives are relegated to a secondary role in many of these books. Further, the philosophy that inspired the movement is purported to be the Enlightenment rather than the Reformation. In most of these histories the needs of capitalists or the effects of capitalism play a major part. In fact, the contrast between the conclusions of *Founding Zealots* and most of the other accounts is so profound that it demands an explanation. So, in the epilogue we will highlight those differences, we will attempt to explain why they occurred, and we will suggest a reasonable reform that can lead to an improved understanding of our past.

Epilogue

Two Myths Exposed and Explained

S ince 1889 educational historians have described the movement
that started the public schools as essentially urban, eastern, and
secular, despite much evidence that it was primarily rural, western,
and religious. As a result, they lavish a great deal of attention on
Massachusetts, while barely mentioning Ohio and other states in the
West. Further, they dwell on leaders like Horace Mann, who was dedicated to worldly objectives, at the expense of the evangelicals, who
were deeply committed to spiritual goals. The differences between
their accounts and *Founding Zealots* are remarkable.[1]

Indeed, as I worked on this book I found the variances so great
that I felt compelled to discover their cause. While that seemed like
a challenging task, since it included trying to determine the personal beliefs of the other researchers, I nonetheless tried to answer
that question. After all, the undertaking was no different than the
analysis that scholars routinely perform on historical figures in their
own work. After much study, I concluded that the differences could
be explained by the origins of the theories proposed in the other
narratives, the personal ideologies of their authors, recent trends in
historical research, and, regrettably, two apparent biases within the
profession.

The result has been to leave us with two enduring myths.
The first is the widespread notion among the populace, including

many teachers, that Horace Mann was the Father of America's Public Schools. Instead, the historical record shows that his work, while impressive, was no more important to the cause than several reformers in the Midwest and the Far West. Yet soon after Mann's death his notoriety began to grow when his good friend, Henry Barnard, featured his work in the influential *American Journal of Education*. The two served as chief education officers for adjacent states and had grown so close that Mann tried to get Barnard to succeed him when he resigned his post to run for Congress. While recent scholarly articles and monographs have begun to question the extent of Mann's role in the crusade, textbooks used to train teachers overflow with discussions of Mann, while remaining virtually silent on the zealots.[2]

The second myth, which is related to the first, is actually a collection of theories about the origins of the schools. These interpretations all attribute their start to the struggle for power between capitalists and workers in Eastern cities, which were just starting to become industrialized. These ideas took shape under the influence of three powerful factors. First, from the very first accounts, the scholars who wrote them had both an Eastern and an urban perspective. Most were either born in the Northeast or did their graduate work there; in fact, most either studied or taught at just one institution, Columbia University in New York City. Further, since they needed access to primary sources for their research, it was easier for them to visit archives in New York and other cities in the East than to travel to the West. While the work of educational historians is far more diverse today, it still tends to overemphasize the larger cities in the East.[3]

Second, it is clear from many of the historians' accounts that they favored forms of government that relied upon centralized planning, including socialism. In particular, Columbia's faculty included many activist progressives, who felt schools must reform society according to their vision. As a consequence, most academics explained the origins of the movement as a response to industrialization, capitalism, and workers' rights. For some their ideology was implied, while for others it was quite explicit. An example of the former was Columbia Prof. Ellwood Patterson Cubberley, who first published *Public Education in the United States* in 1919. This best seller made him an iconic figure among his colleagues for over three decades. While its progressive views are somewhat subdued, they are still quite evident in the once-popular text.[4]

Others have been much more explicit about their personal ideology, both with their interpretations and their direct statements. For example, Joel Spring, author of the popular textbook *The American School, 1642-2004*, bluntly opines in its first chapter, "a major part of the history of US public schools is the attempt to ensure the domination of a Protestant Anglo-American culture in the United States." Of course, the control of the proletariat by a class of capitalist elites is a staple of Marxian analysis. These ideas are so widespread among historians that respected scholar Nathan Hatch observed in 1995 that many of them have a "neo-Marxist preoccupation with the formation of social classes."[5]

While few scholars are actually self-identified Marxists, almost all of them are aligned with the political left, which tends to accept the fundamental assumptions and theories that Marx had about capitalists and workers. According to two recent surveys, college faculties today contain far more progressives and Democrats than conservatives and Republicans. While this has likely been the case for a long time, the disparities have grown even more over the last twenty-five years. Rothman, Lichter, and Nevitte found the greatest differences in the humanities, the social sciences, and the performing arts. For example, in their study only 7% of the faculty in education and only 4% of those in history claim to be Republicans. That degree of dominance leaves room for even the most radical of ideas to flourish unchallenged. For example, while Marxism is not the most important influence on educational thought, according to a 2009 dissertation by Isaac Gottesman, it made several key contributions to American education and its history from the 1960s through the 1980s. And certainly it helped sustain the theories about the common school that are based upon the struggle between industrialists and workers.[6]

Similar factors also help explain why religious reformers and their motives are largely absent from these accounts. Scholars for a long time have produced secular and materialist explanations of history, while ignoring and at times even disparaging religious actors and perspectives. This was at least in part due to the atheists and agnostics on college campuses, where they were far more prevalent than among the general public. It also resulted from their progressive, socialist, and (for some) Marxist proclivities, which led them to cast religion and its effects on society in a bad light. Ironically, while higher education was born on campuses founded by evangelicals near the start of the 19th century, by the end of the 20th almost all of its institutions, including many that had begun with a religious foundation, were essentially secular.[7]

Two recent surveys reveal the extent of secularism in academia. Tobin and Weinberg found that many more professors identify as secular and progressive on matters of faith than those who say they are religious and conservative. Of course, that makes sense when one considers the political profile of the typical campus, since progressives and Democrats tend to be more secular than conservatives and Republicans. Oddly, according to Rothman, Lichter, and Nevitte, progressive influence even extends to the subjects of religion and theology, where only 5% of faculty identify themselves as political conservatives. Such lack of diversity has led religious historian George Marsden to conclude that colleges have become so secularized that "in place of a Protestant establishment we now have a virtual establishment of nonbelief." According to Marsden, "secular humanism," the rational belief system that John Dewey helped launch in the 1930s, has been widely accepted on the nation's campuses. As a result, he claims that nonreligious viewpoints are valued much more than those with a religious origin. So, as it does in matters of politics, progressive thought dominates academia regarding religion.[8]

This one-sided nature of today's campuses becomes even clearer when one considers the extremes of the religious spectrum. On the one hand, Tobin and Weinberg found that atheists were five times more likely to be encountered in the faculty lounge than on the street; whereas one is much more likely to find religious conservatives, including evangelicals, anywhere but behind a college lectern. These inequities are also illustrated by the manner in which progressives and conservatives, both religious and political, are distributed throughout higher education. Gross and Simmons and Rothman, Lichter, and Nevitte found that most conservatives tend to be concentrated at its least-prestigious institution, the two-year college, while progressives are found in much greater numbers at its pinnacle, the doctoral-granting research university.[9]

The result of all these influences, with a few notable exceptions, has been to virtually ignore the zealots in the origins of the public schools. Educational historians might have avoided this unhappy result had they reached the same conclusion as noted historian Jon Butler, who recently warned that it is unwise to "assess American history before the Civil War without taking religion seriously." Butler went on to observe that many scholars find evangelicalism an important factor in the many moral crusades of those years. One of those, of course, was the common school movement, yet most of its experts have largely sidestepped the religious factor. To borrow an analogy from George Marsden and Joseph Conforti, the story of the birth of public education without religion is "like Moby-Dick without the whale," yet many have made just that error.[10]

Since 1889 at least twenty-eight historians have written extensively about the origins of the schools. Nine ignore the religious factor completely, while ten others use imprecise terms like "Christian" and "Protestant" to describe the movement's ideology. Only nine correctly identify either Calvinism or evangelicalism as central factors. Yet even some of those scholars omit the religious affiliations of individual leaders and most gloss over the spiritual motivations that lay behind their actions. Such oversights are remarkable when one considers the large number of evangelical ministers and laymen that headed the crusade in almost every state. In fact, out of all these accounts only Lawrence Cremin and William Reese correctly identify the zealots and properly credit Scottish Common Sense Realism as their driving philosophy. And only Paul Theobald observes that they maintained a pessimistic, rather than an optimistic view of man.[11]

Instead, most of the historians focused a great deal on just one reformer, Horace Mann, and by making that ill-advised choice they wrote stories that were far more secular than *Founding Zealots*. Mann, in part due to his Unitarian faith, dealt mostly with the material problems of this world, in contrast to the zealots, who devoted themselves more to spiritual matters. Further, his state, Massachusetts, contained many more Unitarians than any other state. Yet Mann and Massachusetts were very unrepresentative of the country at large, which contained far more evangelicals than secular-oriented Unitarians. Nevertheless, eight scholars claimed that Enlightenment ideas, which were most popular in Unitarian Boston and its environs, undergirded the cause though Common Sense Realism prevailed in the colleges that educated almost all of its leaders. Ironically, the researchers devoted a great deal of analysis to Enlightenment thinkers Voltaire, Hume, and Rousseau, who the Realists literally despised. Further compounding their error, they painstakingly explained and analyzed the educational thought of Franklin, Jefferson, and Emerson, men who were clearly neither Calvinist nor Evangelical.[12]

As a result of their preference for socialist theories, most of the historians claimed the movement arose from class warfare between capitalists and workers in the nation's cities. Leaving few doubts as to where their sympathies lay, they either praised the meritorious efforts of workers to use the schools to lift themselves up or they condemned the cynical schemes of capitalists to misuse them in order to oppress the working class. Surprisingly, none of the scholars ever attempted to explain how capitalism could have been such an important factor in an era when America was so profoundly rural. Instead, they proposed three primary explanations for the crusade, all of which are connected in one way or another to class struggle.[13]

While it may seem curious that so many historians over such a long time could settle upon only three interpretations, historian David Hackett Fischer has described the process that allows this to happen. First, a respected researcher proposes a theory and then for the next few decades graduate students publish related studies on a smaller scale, which make only minor changes to the original. Finally, another well-regarded scholar proposes a completely different interpretation and the cycle begins anew. This tendency among historians, in addition to their focus on the urban East and their convictions about the proper functions of government and religion in society, may well have contributed to their fixation with the role of capitalists and workers in the first schools.[14]

The most popular of the three, which has been put forth by at least seventeen scholars, is known as the "labor-education" thesis. Essentially it claims that the workingmen's movement of the late 1820s and the 1830s had a key role in the cause. There are at least three problems with this theory. First, while the labor activists certainly promulgated many plans, beyond some soaring prose they produced few direct results. Second, while they did almost all of their work in the urban areas of the East, schools actually grew faster in rural areas and in the West. Finally, the political phase of what was America's first labor movement lasted only from 1828 to 1832, so it did not even exist during the late-1830s and the mid-1850s, when most school reform occurred.[15]

In 1971 Jay Pawa described how the labor-education thesis was created and how it developed into a myth. His devastating critique showed that it began with an untested theory by leftist historian Richard T. Ely in 1886. Marxist and socialist scholars readily accepted it over the next three decades, perhaps because it aligned perfectly with their political and social sympathies, especially their admiration for the labor movement. Ely's interpretation gained momentum when it was endorsed by several eminent scholars: Arthur M. Schlesinger and Mary Beard in the second decade of the 20th century and then key educational historians at mid-century. This idea, in a slightly modified form, is still discussed at length in five major textbooks used for teacher training. Meanwhile, Pawa's work has largely been ignored, proving that myths can have a very long life.[16]

Almost as many experts have embraced the "social equity" theory. This is a claim that leadership of the crusade, including workingmen and their allies, supported the common school idea in order to elevate the financial condition of the lower classes and by so doing to produce more economic equality. This theory fails for a couple of reasons. First, as we have seen, the workingmen were only active for a very brief period of time, which limited their influence. Second, while a few of the zealots wrote about the good that could come from teaching all social classes in the same schools, that was always a secondary, rather than a primary goal. Their hopes lay in God's delivery of justice in the next life rather than man's ability to produce it in this one.

Finally, six historians attributed the rise of the schools to the "social-control" or "work-discipline" theories. They charged that capitalists saw them as a way to groom passive workers for their factories and reliable debtors for their banks, yet none of the six attempted to show a link between the religiously-motivated leaders of the crusade and the industrialists. While four scholars acknowledged the importance of "Protestants" and "Christians" to the cause, except for Carl Kaestle and Joel Spring they failed to see any religious motives underlying the emergence of public education. This, of course, ignores the religious identity of almost all the movement's leaders and it overlooks the content of their writings, which rarely mentioned a desire to help capitalists. Instead, they revealed a passion to achieve religious goals: salvation for the "lost" and discipleship for the "saved." If we are to accept Aristotle's dictum that the burden of proof should be placed on the critic rather than the writer of a document, then we must reject the notion that the zealots possessed some sort of hidden agenda to advance capitalism.[17]

Recently, three trends in the practice of history have helped to solidify the myths. First, in the 1960s came social history, which was an effort by the discipline to focus on the daily lives of ordinary people, especially the poor and the oppressed, and less on great leaders, leading institutions, and political systems. It soon became popular and when it was applied to the study of the first half of the 19th century, it greatly reduced the attention given to the activities of white males, like the zealots. Soon after that development came cultural history, which was an initiative to examine the issues of gender and race, with a special emphasis on disadvantaged groups, especially women, blacks, and Latinos/a. That too tended to deemphasize the study of white males. At the same time, many scholars became influenced by post-modern intellectuals and literary theorists, which caused them to question the very feasibility of determining objective truth. To make matters worse, historians gradually adopted technical language that was quite opaque to most non-specialists, especially the general reader.[18]

The first two trends had devastating effects on the popularity of academic history: undergraduates rarely chose it as a major and general readers stopped buying books written by its practitioners. Understandably, these movements also had an impact on the study of the origins of the schools. After the mid-1980s the topic seemed to stir little interest among educational historians, since, due to the structure of society during the antebellum era, it dealt with elite white males struggling to achieve political objectives rather than women or blacks resisting oppression. Both trends have served to keep the deeply-flawed accounts of the dawn of public education firmly in place.[19]

A third unfortunate trend is the prevalence of "presentism" among many of today's researchers. Presentism is essentially a logical fallacy (*nunc pro tunc*) in which the historian lets his understanding of the present distort his analysis of the past. At times, it can simply be a natural, unintended error but in many troubling cases in educational history it has resulted from the conscious desire of researchers to use their findings to try to transform modern society. Its practitioners tend to search the past for heroes and villains that support their personal positions on political, economic, social, spiritual, racial, or gender issues. As Pulitzer Prize-winning historian Gordon Wood has said about some of his colleagues, "these unhistorical historians ransack the past" to find "communities to emulate, or they seek out abuses of patriarchal power in the past that we in the present must avoid." During the 1930s, many progressive and socialist educators felt that capitalism would soon be replaced by socialism, so as a consequence they felt a duty to use history to prepare the rising generation for its new reality. But by the end of the decade, socialism had instead given way to liberalism in academia as the brutality and repression of Stalin's Russia became known. Then in the 1960s and 1970s, left wing educational historians once again began to use history as a way to create social change.[20]

While we can identify presentism in many of today's textbooks and in a few recent monographs, we can also find a clue to the intellectual milieu that nourishes this fallacy in the current work of the historians of education. Simply put, the vast majority of them are more interested in recent history than the distant past. For example, the *History of Education Quarterly*, the journal of the History of Education Society, publishes far more scholarly articles on the 20th century than on all earlier centuries. Further, from 2007 through 2011 it published five times as many articles for periods since the Civil War than for periods preceding it. While this does not prove presentism per se, it does demonstrate that the profession has its gaze fixed squarely on the recent past at the expense of earlier periods. A similar pattern for research monographs indicates that today's scholars are not very interested in periods like the era of the common school. So similar to the deleterious effects from their emphasis on social and cultural history, the neglect of earlier time periods has also worked to keep the two myths alive.[21]

All three trends, though they have had serious negative implications for our understanding of the origin of the schools, were rooted in good intentions: social history was initiated to uplift the masses, cultural history to assist disadvantaged groups, and presentism to use scholarship in the service of progress. But a more insidious factor was also at work. According to recent surveys professors are quite prejudiced against evangelicals. Tobin and Weinberg found that 53% of them had negative feelings toward the group, far exceeding the Mormons, who came in at 33%. Yancey asked scholars to rank various political, religious, and social associations according to whether they would help or hurt a job applicant and evangelicals came in third from the bottom, ahead of only NRA members and "fundamentalists." Tobin and Weinberg's work seems to indicate that evangelicals are disliked because of their religious beliefs, their positions on abortion and gay rights, and their support for the Republican Party. This is not surprising given the overwhelmingly progressive political and religious orientation of academia.[22]

Their bias can be quite explicit and frank, as expressed by the respected scholar Richard Rorty in his essay "Universality and Truth": "The fundamentalist parents of our fundamentalist students think that the entire 'American liberal establishment' is engaged in a conspiracy. The parents have a point. Their point is that we liberal teachers no more feel in a symmetrical communication situation when we talk with bigots than do kindergarten teachers talking with their students." Rorty went on to boast, "we are going to go right on trying to discredit you [the parents] in the eyes of your children, trying to strip your fundamentalist religious community of dignity, trying to make your views seem silly rather than discussable. While Rorty admitted that his approach to teaching fundamentalist children made him seem like a Nazi propagandist, he justified his effort because it separated the students from their "frightening, vicious, dangerous parents."[23]

Of course, stereotyping, bias, and discrimination typically occur in far more subtle ways, and as a result they are very difficult to detect. Except for carefully-designed surveys, we can only speculate about stereotyping and bias, since they are states of mind. Then again, we can look at real world metrics to determine if a group's degree of inclusion or achievement lags the general population. But even in those cases, evidence that seems to result from discrimination may actually be caused by other factors. Still, for evangelicals real world employment statistics appear to confirm the bias found by the surveys. Since Yancey discovered that one's evangelical identity often hurts his or her chances for a faculty appointment, it is not surprising that Tobin and Weinberg found that evangelicals, who represent 33% of the population, make up only 11% of college faculty. This may also explain why Gross and Simmons found that only 1% of faculty at elite, doctoral institutions identify themselves "born again."[24]

Several scholars are convinced that the suppression of conservative viewpoints is damaging for evangelicals, higher education, and the public at large. For example, Yancey thinks the bias he found in hiring extends to decisions about tenure, curriculum, research, and publication. Yancey, Marsden, and Bruce Kuklick are especially concerned that it has interfered with a researchers' right to free inquiry, which necessarily limits our knowledge of the world. Not surprisingly, Paul Boyer found widespread neglect of religion in US history textbooks and courses, both in the schools and universities.[25]

As one might expect, the potential for bias has spawned many legal disputes. In fact, several non-profit Christian legal organizations devote a significant amount of their resources defending the rights of conservative Christians in schools and universities. Three of the larger ones are Liberty Counsel (www.lc.org), Alliance Defending

Freedom (www.alliancedefendingfreedom.org), and the American Center for Law and Justice (www.aclj.org). The Foundation for Individual Rights in Education (FIRE) (www.thefire.org), a secular organization, defends the liberty and dignity of students and faculty in higher education. The case files of all four are filled with successes.

While I am admittedly a sample of one, for the twenty years that I have worked on this project I witnessed many instances of bias and discrimination and most involved the three trends. First, I heard numerous examples of political and religious bias from the lectern at public lectures and academic conferences. Speakers would warm up the crowd by making disparaging remarks about George W. Bush or the Republican Party, sometimes with reference to evangelicals. Lecturers obviously sensed that their comments would be welcomed by the audience, which often responded with laughter. As a conservative, I was made to feel uncomfortable and unwelcome more than once.

Second, I sensed that reverse discrimination was affecting the advice that I received on my research, which out of necessity involved white males since only they could participate in politics in antebellum America. In one instance, senior staffers at a major cultural institution in Ohio told me that a project that I proposed was unappealing because it featured no blacks or women. Their implied message was that I should find members of those groups in my research so that I could include them in my narrative. On many other occasions, scholars were more likely to suggest that I investigate the role of blacks and women in the first schools, at times mentioning specific people, rather than to advise me on ways to improve my study of evangelicals. In other words, to borrow from Gordon Wood, I was urged to "ransack the past" to make minorities part of my story.[26]

Third, in several discussions academics questioned me as to how my research could be "useful," which is a sentiment that can easily cause a loss of one's objectivity and lead to the error of presentism. Since most historians of education are dedicated to training future teachers and administrators, it is easy to see how they might succumb to the temptation of performing research because they assume it will help their students.

In conclusion, I believe that the two common school myths exist because of three predominant characteristics of academic history: the religious, economic, and political ideologies of its practitioners, the biases that those beliefs have created, and recent trends in scholarship. While several professors have pointed out the harm done to higher education by these factors, the best and most comprehensive treatise on the subject is *The Outrageous Idea of Christian Scholarship*, written by George Marsden in 1997. After first outlining many of the same problems that I have described, he proposed a solution: the diversity that scholars seek for historically-disadvantaged groups should be expanded to include conservative Christians. Since it is near dogma on today's campuses that diversity by race, gender, and other traits produces superior instruction and research, his proposal has the advantage of building on existing practices. Further, it is the equitable thing to do and it honors the spirit of the free exercise clause of the First Amendment.[27]

Beyond its moral justification, there are ancillary benefits to Marsden's plan. Just as colleges report that their mission is strengthened by the inclusion of minorities on their faculties, the addition of more evangelicals would also enrich campus life. Like blacks, latinos, and women evangelicals would bring their unique interests to teaching, research, publication, and community service. For example, their familiarity with the Bible would enrich the study of American History, since journals, letters, and official documents prior to the 20th century are replete with biblical references. Many investigators of those periods are handicapped by their lack of Bible literacy, just as someone studying foreign immigrants would be limited by his or her inability to read the settlers' native tongues.

Yet Marsden's recommendation doesn't go far enough. The concept of diversity should also include political and economic conservatives, since most of the arguments that support the inclusion of evangelicals also apply to those groups. Certainly, the addition of more evangelical scholars would also add many who are politically conservative, since they are one of the most reliable supporters of the Republican Party, but political conservatives hold a variety of religious beliefs, ranging from atheism to fundamentalism. Consequently, their inclusion in a new, revised definition of diversity is necessary if learning, teaching, and research are to benefit from all major viewpoints.

Research published in *The American Enterprise* in 2002 on the party affiliations of faculty at eighteen universities illustrates the severity of the problem. At institutions ranging from the Ivy League to private colleges, they found departments in the humanities and social sciences with as many as 10, 20, or even 30 members that employed only 1, 2, or 3 staff who were registered with their board of elections as a conservative. Of the 81 departments, 28 had no conservatives. Given these imbalances, it is likely that many students are receiving instruction that reflects skewed political and economic perspectives and that research results are suffering from those same biases, just as teaching and research have been hurt by the dearth of evangelical voices on campus.[28]

Hopefully, academics will soon see the wisdom of including conservatives—both religious and political—in their diversity policies or the fear of litigation may force them to do so. In any event, until that day we are likely to continue to suffer from the flaws of our current system, including the perpetuation of the two myths of the common schools.

Appendices

Appendix I

US Population, 1820 and 1860

Region	State	1820	% of Total	1860	% of Total	% Growth 1820-1860
Mid-Atlantic	New Jersey	277,575	3%	672,035	2%	242%
	New York	1,372,812	14%	3,880,735	12%	283%
	Pennsylvania	1,049,458	11%	2,906,215	9%	277%
	Region	2,701,665	28%	7,460,845	24%	276%
Midwest/						
Far West	California	N/A		379,994	1%	N/A
	Illinois	55,211	1%	1,711,951	5%	3,101%
	Indiana	147,178	2%	1,350,428	4%	918%
	Iowa	N/A		674,913	2%	N/A
	Michigan	8,896	0%	749,113	2%	8,421%
	Missouri	66,586	1%	1,182,012	4%	1,775%
	Minnesota	N/A		172,023	1%	N/A
	Ohio	581,434	6%	2,339,511	7%	402%
	Oregon	N/A		52,465	0%	N/A
	Wisconsin	N/A		775,881	2%	N/A
	Region	859,305	9%	9,388,291	30%	1093%

Region	State	1820	% of Total	1860	% of Total	% Growth 1820-1860
New England	Connecticut	275,248	3%	460,147	1%	167%
	Maine	298,335	3%	628,279	2%	211%
	Massachusetts	523,287	5%	1,231,066	4%	235%
	New Hampshire	244,161	3%	326,073	1%	134%
	Rhode Island	83,059	1%	174,620	1%	210%
	Vermont	235,981	2%	315,098	1%	134%
	Region	1,660,071	17%	3,135,283	10%	189%
South (Atlantic)	Delaware	72,749	1%	112,216	0%	154%
	Florida	N/A		140,424	0%	N/A
	Georgia	340,989	4%	1,057,286	3%	310%
	Maryland	407,350	4%	687,049	2%	169%
	North Carolina	638,829	7%	992,622	3%	155%
	South Carolina	502,741	5%	703,708	2%	140%
	Virginia	1,075,069	11%	1,596,318	5%	148%
	Region	3,037,727	32%	5,289,623	17%	174%
South (Central)	Alabama	127,901	1%	964,201	3%	754%
	Arkansas	14,273	0%	435,450	1%	3,051%
	Kentucky	564,317	6%	1,155,684	4%	205%
	Louisiana	153,407	2%	708,002	2%	462%
	Mississippi	75,448	1%	791,305	3%	1,049%
	Tennessee	422,823	4%	1,109,801	4%	262%
	Texas	N/A		604,215	2%	N/A
	Region	1,358,169	14%	5,768,658	18%	425%
	Other	21,516	0%	400,621	1%	1,862%
United States	Total	9,638,453	100%	31,443,321	100%	326%

Source: US Census Bureau.

Appendix II

Student Attendance by Region and State, 1850

Region	State	Children Ages 5-19	Students	Students % of total
New England	Connecticut	116,676	79,003	67.7%
	Maine	213,211	199,745	93.7%
	Massachusetts	306,562	190,292	62.1%
	New Hamp-shire	104,359	81,237	77.8%
	Rhode Island	45,993	24,881	54.1%
	Vermont	108,647	100,785	92.8%
	Region	895,448	675,943	75.5%
Mid-Atlantic	New Jersey	174,234	88,244	50.6%
	New York	1,053,585	727,156	69.0%
	Pennsylvania	842,766	440,743	52.3%
	Region	2,070,585	1,256,143	60.7%
Midwest/Far West	California	9,610	219	2.3%
	Illinois	337,442	130,411	38.6%
	Indiana	403,914	168,754	41.8%
	Iowa	76,492	30,767	40.2%

Student Attendance by Region and State, 1850

Region	State	Children Ages 5-19	Students	Students % of total
	Michigan	152,025	112,382	73.9%
	Ohio	767,267	502,826	65.5%
	Wisconsin	105,080	61,615	58.6%
	Region	1,851,830	1,006,974	54.4%
Border	Delaware	34,913	11,125	31.9%
	Maryland	212,393	44,923	21.2%
	Kentucky	395,574	86,014	21.7%
	Missouri	273,057	61,592	22.6%
	Region	915,937	203,654	22.2%
South (Central)	Alabama	313,209	37,237	11.9%
	Arkansas	86,855	11,050	12.7%
	Louisiana	170,556	30,843	18.1%
	Mississippi	241,919	26,236	10.8%
	Tennessee	418,125	114,773	27.4%
	Texas	83,206	11,500	13.8%
	Region	1,313,870	231,639	17.6%
South (Atlantic)	Florida	33,226	3,129	9.4%
	Georgia	372,387	43,299	11.6%
	North Carolina	345,438	112,430	32.5%
	South Carolina	258,718	26,025	10.1%
	Virginia	552,667	77,764	14.1%
	Region	1,562,436	262,647	16.8%
	Other	51,583	5,694	11.0%
United States	Total	8,661,689	3,642,694	42.1%

Source: US Census.

Appendix III

Further Information for Individual States

A great deal of information is available on the origins of our first public schools at the state level. This book has been especially designed with section headings and index entries so that the reader can easily find or note its treatment of a particlar state or region. But since this book attempts to tell a story that spans nine decades and more than thirty states, a great deal of the detail on individual states had to be excluded. In order to provide assistance to researchers and to students and others who are interested in further study, I am assembling some of that information at www.foundingzealots.com and I welcome your visits there. I plan to gradually add to it over time.

Notes

Abbreviations Used

BDAE

Biographical Dictionary of American Educators, edited by John F. Ohles. Westport, CN: Greenwood, 1978.

BDG

Biographical Directory of the Governors of the United States, 1789-1978, edited by Robert Sobel and John Raimo. Westport, CN: Meckler Books, 1978.

DAB

Dictionary of American Biography, edited by American Council of Learned Societies. New York: Scribner, 1946.

EAR

Encyclopedia of the American Revolution, edited by Mark Mayo Boatner. 3rd ed. Mechanicsburg, PA: Stackpole, 1994.

WLI

Western Literary Institute. *The Annual Register of the Proceedings of the Western Literary Institute and College of Professional Teachers*. 5 vols. Cincinnati, 1834-1838.

Works of MC

Cutler, William Parker, and Julia Perkins Cutler. *Life, Journals, and Correspondence of Rev. Manasseh Cutler, Ll.D*. 2 vols. Athens: Ohio University, 1987. Reprint, originally published in 1888.

Chapter 1: Obstacles at the Starting Line

[1] *EAR*, s.v. "Continental Army," "Mutiny," "Newburgh Addresses," "Washington, George"; Richard H. Kohn, "The Inside History of the Newburgh Conspiracy: America and the Coup D'etat," *The William and Mary Quarterly* 27, no. 2 (1970): 187-220; — — — —, *Eagle and Sword: The Federalists and the Creation of the Military Establishment in America, 1783-1802* (New York: Free Press, 1975), 31-32; Paul David Nelson, "Horatio Gates at Newburgh, 1783: A Misunderstood Role," *The William and Mary Quarterly* 29, no. 1 (1972): 143-58; C. Edward Skeen, "The Newburgh Conspiracy Reconsidered," *The William and Mary Quarterly* 31, no. 2 (1974): 273-98; Harry M. Ward, *The American Revolution: Nationhood Achieved, 1763-1788* (New York: St. Martin's, 1995), 125, 222-26; Russell Frank Weigley, *History of the United States Army*, enl. ed. (Bloomington: Indiana University, 1984), 77.

[2] Library of Congress, "The Newburgh Conspiracy," *American Memory*, http://www.loc.gov/teachers/classroommaterials/presentationsandactivities/presentations/timeline/amrev/peace/newburgh.html.

[3] Kohn, *Eagle*, 32; Library of Congress, "The Newburgh Conspiracy." The former colonies were governed by "The United States in Congress Assembled" under the Articles of Confederation from March 1781 until the US Constitution was ratified on November 21, 1788.

[4] *EAR*, s.v. "Continental Army"; Kohn, *Eagle*, 33-34; Jack N. Rakove, *The Beginnings of National Politics: An Interpretive History of the Continental Congress*, 1st ed. (New York: Knopf, 1979), 321-22, 34, 38; Ward, *American*, 225-26; Weigley, *History*, 77-78.

[5] Robert A. Becker, "Currency, Taxation, and Finance, 1775-1787," in *A Companion to the American Revolution*, ed. Jack P. Greene and J. R. Pole (Malden, MA: Blackwell, 2000), 390; Rakove, *Beginnings*, 314-17; Ward, *American*, 291-92.

[6] *EAR*, s.v. "Pay, Bounties, and Rations"; *Works of MC*, 1:122.

[7] Peter S. Onuf, *Statehood and Union: A History of the Northwest Ordinance* (Bloomington: Indiana University, 1987), 29-40.

[8] Ellwood Patterson Cubberley, *Public Education in the United States, a Study and Interpretation of American Educational History*, rev. and enl. ed. (Boston: Houghton Mifflin, 1934), 14-20; George M. Marsden, *Religion and American Culture* (San Diego: Harcourt, 1990), 20-30; Paul H. Mattingly, "American School Teachers Before and After the Northwest Ordinance," in *"—Schools and the Means of Education Shall Forever Be Encouraged": A History of Education in the Old Northwest, 1787-1880*, ed. Paul H. Mattingly and Edward W. Stevens, Jr. (Athens: Ohio University, 1987), 46; National Humanities Institute, "Constitution of Massachusetts, 1780," *Who We Are: The Story of America's Constitution*, http://www.nhinet.org/ccs/docs/ma-1780.htm. See "PART THE FIRST"; Peter S. Onuf, "The Founder's Vision: Education in the Development of the Old Northwest," in *"—Schools and the Means of Education Shall Forever Be Encouraged": A History of Education in the Old Northwest, 1787-1880*, ed. Paul H. Mattingly and Edward W. Stevens, Jr. (Athens: Ohio University, 1987), 5; Joel H. Spring, *The American School, 1642-2004*, 6th ed. (Boston: McGraw-Hill, 2005), 11-16.

[9] Becker, "Currency," 389; *EAR*, s.v. "Continental Currency"; George Wells Knight, *History and Management of Land Grants for Education in the Northwest Territory (Ohio, Indiana, Illinois, Michigan, Wisconsin)* (New York: Putnam, 1885), 8; Andro Linklater, *Measuring America: How an Untamed Wilderness Shaped the United States and Fulfilled the Promise of Democracy* (New York: Plume, 2003; reprint, first published in 2002 by Walker), 62; Mary M. Schweitzer, "The Economic and Demographic Consequences of the Revolution," in *A Companion to the American Revolution*, ed. Jack P. Greene and J. R. Pole (Malden, MA: Blackwell, 2000), 559-60; Ward, *American*, 197-202, 17-19. Pickering later served as Secretary of War and Secretary of State.

[10] *EAR*, s.v. "Putnam, Rufus"; Howard Cromwell Taylor, *The Educational Significance of the Early Federal Land Ordinances* (New York: Teachers College, 1922), 19-20. Quotes from *Works of MC*, 1:159-72.

[11] Carl F. Kaestle, "The Development of Common School Systems in the States of the Old Northwest," in *"—Schools and the Means of Education Shall Forever Be Encouraged": A History of Education in the Old Northwest, 1787-1880*, ed. Paul H. Mattingly and Edward W. Stevens, Jr. (Athens: Ohio University, 1987), 33; David B. Tyack, "Forming Schools, Forming States: Education in a Nation of Republics," in *"—Schools and the Means of Education Shall Forever Be Encouraged": A History of Education in the Old Northwest, 1787-1880*, ed. Paul H. Mattingly and Edward Stevens, Jr. (Athens: Ohio University, 1987), 32; Quotes from *Works of MC*, 1:124.

[12] *DAB*; Quote from *Works of MC*, 1: 172-73.

[13] Kohn, *Eagle*, 17-38; Rakove, *Beginnings*, 311-22; Taylor, *Educational*, 17.

[14] *EAR*, s.v. "Morris, Robert"; Rakove, *Beginnings*, 312-17, 39-52; *Works of MC*, 1:174-77;

[15] George W. Knepper, *Ohio and Its People*, 2nd ed. (Kent, OH: Kent State University, 1997), 51-54; *Works of MC*, 1:173.

[16] Knepper, *Ohio*, 51-54.

[17] Henry Steele Commager and Milton Cantor, *Documents of American History*, 10th ed., 2 vols. (Englewood Cliffs, NJ: Prentice Hall, 1988), 1:49; Malcolm J. Rohrbough, *The Trans-Appalachian Frontier: People, Societies, and Institutions, 1775-1850* (New York: Oxford University, 1978), 16-25. Quote from *Works of MC*, 1:174;

[18] Andrew R. L. Cayton, *The Frontier Republic: Ideology and Politics in the Ohio Country, 1780-1825* (Kent: Kent State, 1986), 3,7; Knepper, *Ohio*, 57, 157.

[19] Cayton, *Frontier*, 12; Indiana Historical Bureau, "The Virginia Cession," http://www.in.gov/history/2898.htm; Knepper, *Ohio*, 49-51; Linklater, *Measuring*, 62; Rakove, *Beginnings*, 287. Quote from *Works of MC*, 1:173.

[20] Cayton, *Frontier*, 12; Knight, *History*, 9-11; Library of Congress, "Journals of the Continental Congress, 1774-1789," *American Memory*, http://memory.loc.gov/ammem/amlaw/lwjclink.html. For the Report of Government for the Western Territory, commonly called the Ordinance of 1784, browse to Vol. 26, pp. 275-279.

[21] Knight, *History*, 12; Onuf, *Statehood*, 21, 29-30; Malcolm J. Rohrbough, *The Land Office Business: The Settlement and Administration of American Public Lands, 1789-1837* (New York: Oxford University, 1968), 4.

[22] Commager and Cantor, *Documents*, 1:111-16; Library of Congress, "Journals of the Continental Congress, 1774-1789." Browse to Vol. 28, pp.293-296.

[23] Library of Congress, "Journals of the Continental Congress, 1774-1789." Browse to Vol. 28, pp. 293-296.

[24] *EAR*, s.v. "Populations."

[25] Quote from William Kailer Dunn, *What Happened to Religious Education? The Decline of Religious Teaching in the Public Elementary School, 1776-1861* (Baltimore: Johns Hopkins, 1958), 29n; Mark A. Noll, *A History of Christianity in the United States and Canada* (Grand Rapids, MI: Eerdmans, 1992), 135-36.

[26] Cubberley, *Public*, 92-93; Knight, *History*, 14; Library of Congress, "Journals of the Continental Congress, 1774-1789." Browse to Vol. 28, pp. 375-381; Onuf, *Statehood*, 21. For the next 100 years, the only states not to use this model were Maine and West Virginia, which had both been created out of other states (Massachusetts and West Virginia, respectively) and Texas.

[27] Library of Congress, "Journals of the Continental Congress, 1774-1789." Browse to Vol. 28, pp. 375.

[28] Ibid. Browse to Vol. 28, pp. 375-381.

[29] Knepper, *Ohio*, 52; Linklater, *Measuring*, 75-78.

[30] Knepper, *Ohio*, 50-51.

[31] Linklater, *Measuring*, 63, 79; Rohrbough, *Land Office*, 15-16; Weigley, *History*, 595.

[32] Linklater, *Measuring*, 79.

[33] Onuf, *Statehood*, 30, 41; Rohrbough, *Land Office*, 10.

[34] Onuf, *Statehood*, 29, 36-39, 51-52.

Chapter 2: The First Yankee Leader

[1] *DAB*; *Works of MC*.

[2] *DAB*; Dennis Nicholas Ulrich, "Manasseh Cutler: Early American Scientist" (MA thesis, Miami University, 1974), 108-09. *Works of MC*.

[3] Lee Nathaniel Newcomer, "Manasseh Cutler's Writings: A Note on Editorial Practice," *The Mississippi Valley Historical Review* 47, no. 1 (1960).

[4] Brooks Mather Kelley, *Yale: A History* (New Haven: Yale University, 1974), 66-67; Newcomer, "Cutler's Writings," 94-95, 97, 99, 100; Lee Nathaniel Newcomer, "The Big World of Mannaseh Cutler," *The New-England Galaxy* 4 (1962): 37; Louis W. Potts, "Manasseh Cutler, Lobbyist," *Ohio History* 96 (1987): 103-06; *Works of MC*, 1:208-09, 12, 25, 34. American popular history and culture has left us with a very distorted view of the Puritans, who were much less "Puritanical" than their modern characterizations imply.

[5] *DAB*; Mary Walton Ferris, *Dawes-Gates Ancestral Lines: The American Ancestry of Rufus R. Dawes* (Milwaukee, WI: Cuneo, 1943), 220; Potts, "Lobbyist," 102. *Works of MC*, 2:358, 62;

[6] Ferris, *Dawes-Gates*, 213-14; Newcomer, "World of Mannaseh Cutler," 29-37; Potts, "Lobbyist," 104. The parsonage still stands, as does his church, the First Congregational Church, in Hamilton, Massachusetts. It houses church offices and classrooms used in the church's Sunday School program.

[7] *Works of MC*, 1:1, 4-5.

[8] Roland Herbert Bainton, *Yale and the Ministry: A History of Education for the Christian Ministry at Yale from the Founding in 1701*, 1st ed. (New York: Harper, 1957), xii, 41; E. Brooks Holifield, *Theology in America: Christian Thought from the Age of the Puritans to the Civil War* (New Haven, CT: Yale University, 2003), 3-4, 7, 10-12, 25, 31-32, 66, 94, 103; Noll, *History*, 87-88, 154-56. The scripture is taken from Matt. 28:19-20.

[9] Bainton, *Yale*, 35-43, 46; Ulrich, "Manasseh Cutler," 8-10.

[10] *Works of MC*, 1:16-17.

[11] Ibid., 1:17.

[12] Bainton, *Yale*, 49; Ferris, *Dawes-Gates*, 211-12; *Works of MC*, 1:9-15, 17-29.

[13] Manasseh Cutler, "Manasseh Cutler Sermons," Special Collections, Dawes Memorial Library, Marietta College, Marietta, OH; *Works of MC*, 1:29-35.

[14] Bainton, *Yale*, 19-25; Holifield, *Theology*, 11, 29, 39, 93-94, 102-15; Noll, *History*, 91-97. *Works of MC*, 1:25-26.

[15] Cutler, "Manasseh Cutler Sermons"; Alan Heimert, *Religion and the American Mind, from the Great Awakening to the Revolution* (Cambridge: Harvard University, 1966), 90; Holifield, *Theology*, 104, 15; Noll, *History*, 97.

[16] Bainton, *Yale*, 25-26; Cutler, "Manasseh Cutler Sermons"; Heimert, *Religion*, 82; Noll, *History*, 105-10.

[17] Newcomer, "Cutler's Writings," 98-99; Ulrich, "Manasseh Cutler," 1, 8-11, 108-09.

[18] Newcomer, "Cutler's Writings," 98; Ulrich, "Manasseh Cutler," 84-96.

[19] Ulrich, "Manasseh Cutler," 39-40, 43-54; *Works of MC*, 1:75, 78-79, 84.

[20] Newcomer, "World of Mannaseh Cutler," 32-33; Ulrich, "Manasseh Cutler," 59-65, 83. *Works of MC*, 1:72-73;

[21] *DAB*; Ulrich, "Manasseh Cutler," 66-76.

[22] Newcomer, "World of Mannaseh Cutler," 32-33. *Works of MC*, 1:88-89, 2:364-66.

[23] *Works of MC*, 2:364-67; Newcomer, "World of Mannaseh Cutler," 32-33.

[24] *EAR*, s.v. "Lexington and Concord"; David Hackett Fischer, *Paul Revere's Ride* (New York: Oxford University, 1994), 252, 56-58. Quotes from *Works of MC*, 2:48.

[25] *EAR*, s.v. "Boston Seige"; *Works of MC*, 2:50, 53-55, 59-60.

[26] Heimert, *Religion*, 58; James H. Hutson, *Religion and the Founding of the American Republic* (Washington, DC: Library of Congress, 1998), 37, 40; Mark A. Noll, *America's God: From Jonathan Edwards to Abraham Lincoln* (New York: Oxford University, 2002), 58-59. *Works of MC*, 2:11.

[27] Cutler, "Manasseh Cutler Sermons," #309; Hutson, *Religion*, 40-46, 50-54, 117(n); Noll, *History*, 120; — — — —, *America's God*, 73-85. *Works of MC*, 1:49, 51, 54, 56, 60, 63-64, 73-75, 77, 79, 85, 87, 94.

[28] Hutson, *Religion*, 53-54. Modern day evangelicals hold essentially the same beliefs concerning prayer, government, and this scripture.

[29] Bainton, *Yale*, 66; Heimert, *Religion*, 253-80, 357-8, 66, 87, 406-8, 17-18, 23, 33, 65-66, 70, 73-76, 77; Hutson, *Religion*, 46. Quotes from *Works of MC*, 1:50-55. Cutler served as a chaplain for three weeks during the Battle of Rhode Island. He met several important generals there, including the Marquis de Lafayette, John Hancock, and James Varnum, and experienced war firsthand at the front.

[30] Ferris, *Dawes-Gates*, 220; Newcomer, "Cutler's Writings," 89; Potts, "Lobbyist," 102, 04.

[31] Cutler, "Manasseh Cutler Sermons"; John Mack Faragher, *The Encyclopedia of Colonial and Revolutionary America* (New York: Facts on File, 1990), 85. *Works of MC*, 1:35-36, 38-39, 41, 50, 58, 61-62, 78, 86.

[32] *DAB*; *Works of MC*, 46, 55, 64, 72, 83, 85-7, 90-93.

[33] *Works of MC*, 1:56-59, 75.

Chapter 3: Miracle at New York City

[1] Cayton, *Frontier*, 16-18; Potts, "Lobbyist," 106, 08; Louis W. Potts, "Visions of America, 1787-1788: The Ohio of Reverend Manasseh Cutler," *Ohio History* 111 (2002): 101, 06, 08. Quote from *Works of MC*, 2:239-40.

[2] Cayton, *Frontier*, 16-21; *DAB*; Ohio Company, *The Records of the Original Proceedings of the Ohio Company (1786-1796)*, 2 vols., ed. Archer Butler Hulbert

(Marietta, OH: Marietta Historical Commission, 1917), 1:xxxix, xxxvii-xi; Lois Mathews Rosenberry, *The Expansion of New England* (Boston: Houghton Mifflin, 1909), 126-27.

[3] *EAR*, s.v. "Continental Army."

[4] Ohio Company, *Records*, 1:1-4, 6-12; Rohrbough, *Land Office*, 11.

[5] *DAB*; Cayton, *Frontier*, 12, 20-23; *EAR*, s.v. "Putnam, Rufus," "Shay's Rebellion"; Forrest McDonald, *E Pluribus Unum: The Formation of the American Republic, 1776-1790* (Boston: Houghton Mifflin, 1965), 148-52.

[6] McDonald, *E Pluribus Unum*, 107-08, 79; Ohio Company, *Records*, 1:12; Potts, "Visions of America," 102-03.

[7] R. Freeman Butts, *Public Education in the United States: From Revolution to Reform* (New York: Holt, 1978), 17-18; Jack Ericson Eblen, *The First and Second United States Empires: Governors and Territorial Government, 1784-1912* (Pittsburgh: University of Pittsburgh, 1968), 1, 37; Andro Linklater, *Measuring America: How an Untamed Wilderness Shaped the United States and Fulfilled the Promise of Democracy* (New York: Plume, 2003), 80-82, 143-50; Ohio Company, *Records*, 1:154-56.

[8] *EAR*, s.v. "Society of the Cincinnati"; Ohio Company, *Records*, 1:xl-xlv, 1-5. In May 1783 at Newburgh, officers had formed the Society of the Cincinnati, named after the Roman citizen-soldier, Cincinnatus, who twice abandoned his plow to save Rome. While it was primarily a fraternal and social organization, it facilitated ongoing conversations among the officers that led to continued pressure on Congress. Ninety percent of the Society's charter members had signed the Newburgh petition. Interestingly, many officers were also members of the American Union Lodge of Masons, formed at the War's inception, including Parsons, Putnam, Sargent, and Tupper.

[9] *DAB*; *EAR*, s.v. "Jackson, Henry," "Meigs, Return," "Varnum, James," "Whipple, Abraham"; Ohio Company, *Records*, 1:22.

[10] Ohio Company, *Records*, 2:235-42.

[11] Ibid., l-lv; Potts, "Lobbyist," 109.

[12] Ohio Company, *Records*, 2:235-42; Potts, "Lobbyist," 109-10. Quotes from *Works of MC*, 1:203-21, 23,-26, 28, 30. In his twelve-day trip to New York, he made extended observations of seven women who were young, attractive, or both. On July 5, the last day of his trip, he stopped for breakfast at Mrs. Haviland's beautiful tavern in Rye, New York. While thoroughly complimenting the house and grounds, he found that "the owner is still more extraordinary. She is a widow of fifty, in a rich, gay dress, and affecting the airs of a young girl of sixteen. She has an only daughter, equally tasty in dress, who is. . .really handsome." Their chatty conversation might easily have convinced Manasseh that they were flirting with him. On June 29 in Connecticut he disapprovingly called the tavern-keeper "a churlish clown," but he found that the man's "wife made a much better appearance. She is a good-looking woman, handsomely dressed, and very obliging, and seems to have deserved a better husband and a better house."

[13] Potts, "Lobbyist," 111-12; *Works of MC*, 1:228-30.

[14] Rufus King, *Ohio: First Fruits of the Ordinance of 1787* (Boston: Houghton, Mifflin, 1888), 174; Potts, "Lobbyist," 112. *Works of MC*, 1:230-31.
[15] Potts, "Lobbyist," 112; *Works of MC*, 1:231-36. Cutler's thoughts strayed long enough from politics, religion, and land prices to notice Sir John's wife, the daughter of Gov. Bowdoin of Massachusetts: "Lady Temple is certainly the greatest beauty, notwithstanding her age, I ever saw. To a well-proportioned form, a perfectly fine skin, and completely adjusted features, is added a soft, but majestic air. . . . Her smiles, for she rarely laughs, could not fail of producing the softest sensibility in the fiercest savage. . ."
[16] Potts, "Lobbyist," 112; *Works of MC*, 1:236-38.
[17] Library of Congress, "Journals of the Continental Congress, 1774-1789."; Potts, "Lobbyist," 112-13; Taylor, *Educational*, 36; *Works of MC*, 1:239-42, 304;
[18] Potts, "Lobbyist," 113. *Works of MC*, 1:242.
[19] *DAB*; Potts, "Lobbyist," 113, 15-16. *Works of MC*, 1:229, 52-92.
[20] Andrew R. L. Cayton and Peter S. Onuf, *The Midwest and the Nation: Rethinking the History of an American Region* (Bloomington: Indiana University, 1990), 11; Paul Finkelman, "Slavery and the Northwest Ordinance: A Study in Ambiguity," *Journal of the Early Republic* 6, no. 4 (1986): 349, 52-53; Knight, *History*, 15; Library of Congress, "Journals of the Continental Congress, 1774-1789." Browse to Vol. 32, pp. 213, 222, 225-227, 238-244, 276, 281-283, 292, 306, 310, 327-332; William Frederick Poole, *The Ordinance of 1787, and Dr. Manasseh Cutler as an Agent in Its Formation* (Cambridge, MA, 1876), 31. Quote from *Works of MC*, 1:242.
[21] Commager and Cantor, *Documents*, 1:107, 31; Library of Congress, "Journals of the Continental Congress, 1774-1789." Browse to Vol. 32, pp. 281-283, 313-320, 333-343; Mattingly, "American," 45; Potts, "Lobbyist," 115; Taylor, *Educational*, 34; Tyack, "Forming," 26; *Works of MC*, 1:26, 293.
[22] Library of Congress, "Journals of the Continental Congress, 1774-1789." Browse to Vol. 32, pp. 345-346, 350-351; Potts, "Lobbyist," 117; *Works of MC*, 1:292-93.
[23] Ohio Company, *Records*, 1:lx-lxv, lxx-lxxi; Library of Congress, "Journals of the Continental Congress, 1774-1789." Browse to Vol. 33, pp. 399-401; Potts, "Lobbyist," 117-19. *Works of MC*, 295-300;
[24] *Works of MC*, 1:294, 300-03.
[25] *EAR*, s.v. "Tupper, Benjamin"; Potts, "Lobbyist," 118; Quotes from *Works of MC*, 1:294-5, 99-300, 02-04.
[26] Library of Congress, "Journals of the Continental Congress, 1774-1789." Browse to Vol. 33, pp. 429-430; Potts, "Lobbyist," 121-22. *Works of MC*, 1:304-05.
[27] Knight, *History*, 18; David B. Tyack, Thomas James, and Aaron Benavot, *Law and the Shaping of Public Education, 1785-1954* (Madison: University of Wisconsin, 1987), 32-33. The first proposals had set aside four lots for a university.
[28] Library of Congress, "Journals of the Continental Congress, 1774-1789." Browse to Vol. 32, pp. 238-241. *Works of MC*, 1:304.

29 Knight, *History*, 17-18; Potts, "Visions of America," 104.

30 *EAR*, s.v. "Duer, William"; Ohio Company, *Records*, 1:lxv-xcii.

31 Newcomer, "World of Mannaseh Cutler," 30-31; *Works of MC*, 1:411, 2:39-50.

32 *Works of MC*, 2:439-44.

33 Ibid., 2:444-47.

34 Ibid., 2:444, 48.

35 Ibid., 2:445-49.

Chapter 4: Lofty Hopes

1 Gerald Lee Gutek, *An Historical Introduction to American Education*, 2nd ed. (Prospect Heights, IL: Waveland, 1991), 33-35; Spring, *The American School*, 50-53; Wayne J. Urban and Jennings L. Wagoner, *American Education: A History*, 2nd ed. (Boston: McGraw-Hill, 2000), 61-79. Many other textbooks and monographs also focus on the Enlightenment and its American figures in order to explain the ideas behind the first schools, often at the expense of the Reformation.

2 Daniel Walker Howe, *What Hath God Wrought: The Transformation of America, 1815-1848* (New York: Oxford University, 2007), 449-50; Holifield, *Theology*, 106-08; Hutson, *Religion*, 31-35; Henry Farnham May, *The Enlightenment in America* (New York: Oxford University, 1976), 181-83, 324-34, 61-62; David B. Tyack, "The Kingdom of God and the Common Schools," *Harvard Education Review* 36, no. 4 (1966): 447-48, 50-56.

3 Quote from David Freeman Hawke, *Benjamin Rush: Evolutionary Gadfly* (Indianapolis: Bobbs-Merrill, 1971), 284; Heimert, *Religion*, 357-547; Carl F. Kaestle, *Pillars of the Republic: Common Schools and American Society, 1780-1860*, 1st ed. (New York: Hill and Wang, 1983), 5, 75-99; Forrest McDonald, *Novus Ordo Seclorum: The Intellectual Origins of the Constitution* (Lawrence: University Press of Kansas, 1985), 190-91; Noll, *America's God*, 53-92; Gordon S. Wood, *The Creation of the American Republic, 1776-1787* (Chapel Hill: University of North Carolina Press, 1998), 49-73, 91-124, 393-427.

4 Commager and Cantor, *Documents*, 1:173; Lawrence Arthur Cremin, *American Education: The National Experience, 1783-1876*, 1st ed. (New York: Harper, 1980), 103-04; Dunn, *What Happened?*, 41; Jack P. Greene, *The Reinterpretation of the American Revolution, 1763-1789* (New York: Harper, 1968), 38-45, 69; Hutson, *Religion*, 57-66; May, *Enlightenment*, 253; McDonald, *E Pluribus Unum*, 189; Noll, *America's God*, 203.

5 Lindsay Jones, *Encyclopedia of Religion*, 2nd ed. (Detroit: Macmillan, 2005); David Paul Nord, *Faith in Reading: Religious Publishing and the Birth of Mass Media in America* (New York: Oxford University, 2004), 14-18.

6 Frederick Eby, *Early Protestant Educators* (New York: McGraw-Hill, 1931), 179-80, 213-14; Gerald Lee Gutek, *A History of the Western Educational Experience*, 2nd ed. (Prospect Heights, IL: Waveland, 1995), 142-43; Jones, *Encyclopedia of Religion*.

[7] Eby, *Early*, 234-35; Gutek, *History*, 143-47; Diarmaid MacCulloch, *The Reformation*, 1st ed. (New York: Viking, 2004), 231-40.

[8] Arthur Herman, *How the Scots Invented the Modern World: The True Story of How Western Europe's Poorest Nation Created Our World & Everything in It*, 1st ed. (New York: Crown, 2001), 15-23; Jones, *Encyclopedia of Religion*; Douglas Sloan, *The Scottish Enlightenment and the American College Ideal* (New York: Teachers College, 1971), 15-17.

[9] Herman, *How the Scots*, 22; Sloan, *Scottish*, 17-19. The Scots were also motivated by a severe economic crisis, which was precipitated by a failed settlement in Panama that was plagued by fraud and rampant speculation. They wisely viewed education and innovation as a way out of their crisis.

[10] Roger Emerson, "The Contexts of the Scottish Enlightenment," in *The Cambridge Companion to the Scottish Enlightenment*, ed. Alexander Broadie (Cambridge, UK: Cambridge University, 2003), 18-19; Herman, *How the Scots*, 25-26; Sloan, *Scottish*, 17, 19, 23-32.

[11] Emerson, "Contexts," 17-24; Herman, *How the Scots*, 23-26, 193, 320-36; Daniel Walker Howe, *Making the American Self: Jonathan Edwards to Abraham Lincoln* (Cambridge, Mass.: Harvard University Press, 1997), 52-57.

[12] Alan Charles Kors, *Encyclopedia of the Enlightenment*, 4 vols. (New York: Oxford University Press, 2003); Luigi Turco, "Moral Sense and the Foundations of Morals," in *The Cambridge Companion to the Scottish Enlightenment*, ed. Alexander Broadie (Cambridge, UK: Cambridge University, 2003), 137.

[13] Herman, *How the Scots*, 262-63; H. C. G. Matthew, Brian Howard Harrison, and the British Academy, *Oxford Dictionary of National Biography* (New York: Oxford University Press, 2004); Nicholas Wolterstorff, "Reid on Common Sense," in *The Cambridge Companion to Thomas Reid*, ed. Terence Cuneo and Renâe van Woudenberg (New York: Cambridge University, 2004), 77, 82, 84-86.

[14] Cotton Mather, *The Christian Philosopher*, ed. Winton U. Solberg (Urbana: University of Illinois, 1994; reprint, with introduction and notes by Winton U. Solberg, originally published in 1721), 7, 13, 17, 295, 307; George M. Marsden, *The Evangelical Mind and the New School Presbyterian Experience: A Case Study of Thought and Theology in 19th-Century America* (New Haven: Yale University, 1970), 47-49; M.A. Stewart, "Religion and Rational Theology," in *The Cambridge Companion to the Scottish Enlightenment*, ed. Alexander Broadie (Cambridge, UK: Cambridge University, 2003), 32-33; Dale Tuggy, "Reid's Philosophy of Religion," in *The Cambridge Companion to Thomas Reid*, ed. Terence Cuneo and Renâe van Woudenberg (New York: Cambridge University, 2004), 289-99; Paul Wood, "Science in the Scottish Enlightenment," in *The Cambridge Companion to the Scottish Enlightenment*, ed. Alexander Broadie (Cambridge, UK: Cambridge University, 2003), 104.

[15] Alexander Broadie, "Reid in Context," in *The Cambridge Companion to Thomas Reid*, ed. Terence Cuneo and Renâe van Woudenberg (New York: Cambridge University, 2004), 32-24, 47; Marsden, *Evangelical*, 48-49, 51-52;

Matthew, Harrison, and the British Academy, *Oxford Dictionary of National Biography*; Tuggy, "Reid's," 301-04.

[16] Cremin, *National Experience*, 128-30; Kors, *Encyclopedia of the Enlightenment*.

[17] Samuel Fleischhacker, "The Impact on America: Scottish Philosophy and the American Founding," in *The Cambridge Companion to the Scottish Enlightenment*, ed. Alexander Broadie (Cambridge, UK: Cambridge University, 2003), 317-33; May, *Enlightenment*, xvi-xviii, 337-49; Noll, *America's God*, 93-105.

[18] *DAB*; Bruce Kuklick, *A History of Philosophy in America, 1720-2000* (Oxford: Clarendon, 2001), 47-49; Herman, *How the Scots*, 258, 390; Noll, *America's God*, 105, 24-25; May, *Enlightenment*, 64-65; Sloan, *Scottish*, 103-45.

[19] *DAB*; Herman, *How the Scots*, 244-45; Kuklick, *History*, 47; Noll, *America's God*, 125-27; Sloan, *Scottish*, 140-43.

[20] Cremin, *National Experience*, 27; *DAB*; Noll, *America's God*, 176; Benjamin W. Redekop, "Reid's Influence in Britain, Germany, France and America," in *The Cambridge Companion to Thomas Reid*, ed. Terence Cuneo and Renâe van Woudenberg (New York: Cambridge University, 2004), 328-29; Sloan, *Scottish*, 36-46, 149-53.

[21] Cremin, *National Experience*, 24-27; Noll, *America's God*, 104-05, 12-13; Mark A. Noll, *Princeton and the Republic, 1768-1822: The Search for a Christian Enlightenment in the Era of Samuel Stanhope Smith* (Princeton: Princeton University, 1989), 127-49, 87-91; Sloan, *Scottish*, 154-62, 74-76. Jefferson's ideas of separation of church and state repeatedly doomed his plans for schools in Virginia, since they were so far removed from the thinking of mainstream Virginians.

[22] *DAB*; Noll, *Princeton*, 9, 187-91, 201; Sloan, *Scottish*, 154, 60-61, 70-71, 75-78, 83.

[23] Cremin, *National Experience*, 26-27; *DAB*.

[24] Bainton, *Yale*, 72-73; *DAB*; John R. Fitzmier, *New England's Moral Legislator: Timothy Dwight, 1752-1817* (Bloomington: Indiana University, 1998), 3; Kelley, *Yale*, 117-18. Dwight read the Bible at four, learned Latin at six, entered Yale at thirteen, and graduated with highest honors at seventeen.

[25] Bainton, *Yale*, 73-74; *DAB*; Fitzmier, *Timothy Dwight*, 4, 7, 17, 41-44, 63-64, 82-85, 158, 62-70; Ralph Henry Gabriel, *Religion and Learning at Yale: The Church of Christ in the College and University, 1757-1957* (New Haven: Yale University, 1958), 54-62, 78, 81.

[26] Fitzmier, *Timothy Dwight*, 18, 98, 181; Holifield, *Theology*, 48-49, 123; Hutson, *Religion*, 47; Noll, *Princeton*, 80, 93-96; ————, History, 118; Potts, "Lobbyist," 105; William J. Reese, *America's Public Schools: From the Common School to No Child Left Behind*, rev. ed. (Baltimore: Johns Hopkins University, 2011), 13.

[27] Bainton, *Yale*, 76-77; Gabriel, *Religion*, 65-69, 71-72, 75; Kelley, *Yale*, 122, 23.

[28] Bainton, *Yale*, 77; *DAB*; Fitzmier, *Timothy Dwight*, 3, 56-57; Gabriel, *Religion*, 56, 135-37, 77.

[29] Bainton, *Yale*, 49, 79, 80; *DAB*; Marsden, *Evangelical*, 9-10; Tetsuo Scott Miyakawa, *Protestants and Pioneers: Individualism and Conformity on the American Frontier* (Chicago: University of Chicago, 1964), 85-91.

[30] Bainton, *Yale*, 96-100; *DAB*; Gabriel, *Religion*, 132-37; Marsden, *Evangelical*, 46-52.

[31] Bainton, *Yale*, 127-41; Gabriel, *Religion*, 141-44; May, *Enlightenment*, 321; Miyakawa, *Protestants*, 99-105.

[32] Daniel Aaron, *Cincinnati, Queen City of the West, 1819-1838* (Columbus: Ohio State University, 1992), 224-26; Cremin, *National Experience*, 27; Gabriel, *Religion*, 102-09; Daniel Walker Howe, "Church, State, and Education in the Young American Republic," *Journal of the Early Republic* 22, no. 1 (2002): 14-15; Howe, *What Hath God Wrought*, 455-69; Kelley, *Yale*, 162-64; Kuklick, *History*, 38-41; May, *Enlightenment*, 64-65; Noll, *History*, 154-57, 66-69; Sloan, *Scottish*, 237-47.

[33] Thomas W. Hagedorn, "The Strange History of the Origins of the Public School: What Happened to the Ministers?," unpublished paper presented at the *Christianity and American History Conference* (Lynchburg, VA, 2007); Howe, *Making*, 12; — — — —, "Church," 12-13, 23-24; Lloyd P. Jorgenson, *The Founding of Public Education in Wisconsin* (Madison: State Historical Society of Wisconsin, 1956), 117-32; B. Edward McClellan, *Moral Education in America: Schools and the Shaping of Character from Colonial Times to the Present* (New York: Teachers College, 1999), 15-30; Noll, *Princeton*, 145-47; Redekop, "Reid's Influence," 323-27; Reese, *America's Public Schools*, 13, 17-19, 33-35.

Chapter 5: Yankee Leadership

[1] David Hackett Fischer, *Albion's Seed: Four British Folkways in America* (New York: Oxford University, 1989), 13-17, 31-38, 46-47, 57-62; Samuel Eliot Morison, *The Puritan Pronaos: Studies in the Intellectual Life of New England in the 17th Century* (New York: New York University, 1936), 3-5; Wallace Notestein, *The English People on the Eve of Colonization, 1603-1630*, 1st ed. (New York: Harper, 1954), 261-62.

[2] Cremin, *National Experience*, 57, 73; Fischer, *Albion's*, 18-20, 46-47; Howe, *What Hath God Wrought*, 285-9, 450, 69; Marsden, *Religion*, 60; Russel Blaine Nye, *The Cultural Life of the New Nation, 1776-1830*, 1st ed. (New York: Harper, 1960), 50-51; Alan Simpson, *Puritanism in Old and New England* (Chicago: University of Chicago, 1955), 20, 23, 76, 78. The city on a hill metaphor has been invoked by many Republican politicians, including several times by President Ronald Reagan.

[3] Fischer, *Albion's*, 98-102; Edmund Sears Morgan, *The Puritan Family: Religion & Domestic Relations in 17th-Century New England* (Westport, CN: Greenwood, 1980), 65-79, 103.

[4] Fischer, *Albion's*, 72-73, 189, 96-201; Morgan, *Puritan*, 6-10. The number of antecedents of modern American practices that can be found in the mundane details of daily Puritan life is striking.

[5] Fischer, *Albion's*, 39, 49, 133-34; Morison, *Puritan*, 13-17, 81; Notestein, *English People*, 62-63, 131-34; Simpson, *Puritanism*, 8-14, 27-29.

[6] Lawrence A. Cremin, *American Education: The Colonial Experience, 1607-1783*, 1st ed. (New York: Harper, 1970), 9, 11, 16-21, 124-5, 28, 30, 77-85, 544-63; Howe, "Church," 12; Morgan, *Puritan*, 87-102; Morison, *Puritan*, 56, 61-63, 66-71, 73, 76-81; Notestein, *English People*, 116-17, 22.

[7] Notestein, *English People*, 171; Simpson, *Puritanism*, 103-06, 13.

[8] Howe, *What Hath God Wrought*, 136-37, 40; John C. Hudson, "North American Origins of Middlewestern Populations," *Annuals of the Association of American Geographers* 78, no. 3 (1988): 398-99, 404-08; Kenneth V. Lottich, *New England Transplanted, a Study of the Development of Educational and Other Cultural Agencies in the Connecticut Western Reserve in Their National and Philosophical Setting* (Dallas: Royal, 1964), 27-28, 94-95; Richard Lyle Power, *Planting Corn Belt Culture: The Impress of the Upland Southerner and Yankee in the Old Northwest* (Indianapolis: Indiana Historical Society, 1953), 2-3, 5-6, 10-11, 13-14; Richard K. Vedder and Lowell E. Gallaway, "Migration and the Old Northwest," in *Essays in 19th Century Economic History: The Old Northwest*, ed. David C. Klingaman and Richard K. Vedder (Athens: Ohio University, 1975), 161-62, 67, 72-73.

[9] Cayton, *Frontier*, 138; Cayton and Onuf, *Midwest*, 26-27, 29, 35-39, 47-50, 60; John P. Foote, *The Schools of Cincinnati and Its Vicinity* (New York: Arno Press, 1970; reprint, originally published in 1855), 35; Howe, *What Hath God Wrought*, 39, 629; Lottich, *New England*, 11-15, 52-54, 69, 71; Nye, *Cultural*, 118-19.

[10] Cremin, *National Experience*, 50-51, 378-88; Nathan O. Hatch, "The Second Great Awakening and the Market Revolution," in *Devising Liberty: Preserving and Creating Freedom in the New American Republic*, ed. David Thomas Konig (Palo Alto: Stanford Universisty, 1995), 244-46; Howe, *What Hath God Wrought*, 3, 6, 849, 51 ; Hutson, *Religion*, 100-01; Noll, *History*, 167-69; ————, *America's God*, 166-68, 79-86, 97; Nye, *Cultural*, 216-19.

[11] Cremin, *National Experience*, 53-56; Marshall William Fishwick, *Great Awakenings: Popular Religion and Popular Culture* (New York: Haworth, 1995), 23-24; Hatch, "Second," 245-46; Howe, *What Hath God Wrought*, 176-86; Hutson, *Religion*, 105-06; Noll, *History*, 171, 73, 78-79; ————, *America's God*, 195-96; Nye, *Cultural*, 230-31.

[12] Nathan O. Hatch, *The Democratization of American Christianity* (New Haven: Yale University, 1989), 171-73; Donald G. Mathews, "The Second Great Awakening as an Organizing Process, 1780-1830: An Hypothesis," *American Quarterly* 21, no. 1 (1969): 41-42; William Warren Sweet, *Religion in the Development of American Culture, 1765-1840* (New York: Scribner, 1952), 99-102, 99-201.

[13] Joyce Oldham Appleby, *Inheriting the Revolution: The First Generation of Americans* (Cambridge, MA: Belknap, 2000), 182-83; Fishwick, *Great*, 19-23;

Bridget Ford, "Beyond Cane Ridge: The "Great Western Rivivals" in Louisville and Cincinnati, 1828-1845," *Ohio Valley History* 8, no. 4 (2008): 17-24; Hatch, *Democratization*, 49-55; — — — —, "Second," 262; Sweet, *Religion*, 148-50, 53.

[14] Candy Gunther Brown, *The Word in the World: Evangelical Writing, Publishing, and Reading in America, 1789-1880* (Chapel Hill: University of North Carolina, 2004), 39-40; Cremin, *National Experience*, 57-63; Paul E. Johnson, *A Shopkeeper's Millennium: Society and Revivals in Rochester, New York, 1815-1837*, 1st ed. (New York: Hill and Wang, 1978), 5-6; Marsden, *Evangelical*, 14-16; Noll, *History*, 169; — — — —, *America's God*, 198-99; Sweet, *Religion*, 253-66, 71-72.

[15] Brown, *Word*, 1-2, 47, 51, 60-79, 81-105, 18-23, 54; Cremin, *National Experience*, 68-73; Hatch, *Democratization*, 125, 27, 41-46; Howe, *What Hath God Wrought*, 39, 230-31, 447; Marsden, *Religion*, 76-79, 85; R. Laurence Moore, *Selling God: American Religion in the Marketplace of Culture* (New York: Oxford University, 1994), 18-19; Nord, *Faith*, 5-7, 14-18, 63, 77, 81, 151.

[16] Howe, "Church," 23-24; — — — —, *What Hath God Wrought*, 459-63.

[17] Cremin, *National Experience*, 68; Hatch, *Democratization*, 5-6; Howe, "Church," 24; — — — —, *What Hath God Wrought*; King, *Ohio*, 341-42; Noll, *America's God*, 200-02; Mark A. Noll, *The Old Religion in a New World: The History of North American Christianity* (Grand Rapids, MI: Eerdmans, 2002), 86; Gregory H. Singleton, "Protestant Voluntary Organizations and the Shaping of Victorian America," in *Victorian America*, ed. Geoffrey Blodgett and Daniel Walker Howe (Philadelphia: University of Pennsylvania, 1976), 48, 52-53.

[18] Cayton and Onuf, *Midwest*, 47-49; Cremin, *National Experience*, 66-67; Howe, "Church"; Kaestle, *Pillars*, x-xi, 75-103; Marsden, *Evangelical*, 18; Mathews, "Second," 27, 40, 42-43; Noll, *America's God*, 194-95; Nye, *Cultural*, 220; Singleton, "Protestant," 51-52.

[19] Quote from Julia Perkins Cutler, *Life and Times of Ephraim Cutler* (New York: Arno Press, 1971; reprint, originally published in 1890), 8-9, 12; Ferris, *Dawes-Gates*, 221-22.

[20] Cutler, *Ephraim Cutler*, 13, 15-16, 31, 51, 74, 77; Lottich, *New England*, 68.

[21] Ohio Historical Society, "Constitution of the State of Ohio, 1802," *Ohio Fundamental Documents*, http://ww2.ohiohistory.org/onlinedoc/ohgovernment/constitution/cnst1802.html.

[22] Cutler, *Ephraim Cutler*, 74-77; Ohio Historical Society, "Constitution of the State of Ohio, 1802"; — — — —, "Ohio Constitutional Convention of 1802," *Ohio History Central*, http://www.ohiohistorycentral.org/entry.php?rec=523.

[23] Cutler, *Ephraim Cutler*, 89, 229-34, 67, 69.

[24] James Jesse Burns, *Educational History of Ohio: A History of Its Progress since the Formation of the State, Together with the Portraits and Biographies of Past and Present State Officials* (Columbus, OH: Historical, 1905), 409; Cutler, *Ephraim Cutler*, 43-44, 49-51, 56, 68, 77, 88, 113, 23

[25] *DAB*.

[26] Clement L. Martzolff, "Caleb Atwater," *Ohio Archaeological and Historical Publications* 14 (1905): 248-56; Henry C. Shetrone, "Caleb Atwater: Versatile Pioneer, a Re-Appraisal," *Ohio State Archaeological and Historical Quarterly* 54, no. 1 (1945): 79-85; Francis P. Weisenburger, "Caleb Atwater: Pioneer Politician and Historian," *The Ohio Historical Quarterly* 68, no. 1 (1959): 19, 23-27, 29-30, 36-37.

[27] *DAB*; Martzolff, "Atwater," 249, 57-58; Weisenburger, "Caleb Atwater," 20, 23.

[28] Caleb Atwater, *An Essay on Education* (Cincinnati, 1841), 15-17, 24-29, 33, 83, 119.

[29] Ibid., 19-24, 38-45, 57-65, 70-82.

[30] Ibid., 9-12; — — — —, *A History of the State of Ohio: Natural and Civil*, 1st ed. (Cincinnati, 1838), 3-4; Martzolff, "Atwater," 271; Shetrone, "Caleb Atwater," 88; Weisenburger, "Caleb Atwater," 37.

[31] Burns, *Educational*, 410; *DAB*.

[32] Burns, *Educational*, 410; William T. Coggeshall, "Nathan Guilford," *American Journal of Education* 9 (1860): 289-90; *DAB*.

[33] Burns, *Educational*, 410-11; Coggeshall, "Guilford," 289-94; *DAB*.

[34] *DAB*.

[35] Ibid; Burns, *Educational*, 410; Coggeshall, "Guilford," 290.

[36] Burns, *Educational*, 410. Guilford continued to fight for the schools and served as Cincinnati's first superintendent of schools. Unfortunately, his Unitarian views on the use of the Bible eventually led to his dismissal.

[37] James Edward Davis, *Frontier Illinois, A History of the Trans-Appalachian Frontier* (Bloomington: Indiana University, 1998), 175-76, 247-54; Robert P. Howard, *Illinois: A History of the Prairie State* (Grand Rapids, MI: Eerdmans, 1972), 173.

[38] *DAB*; Davis, *Frontier*, 171-72; Howard, *Illinois*, 174-75; Julia Kirby, *Biographical Sketch of Joseph Duncan, Fifth Governor of Illinois* (Chicago, 1888), 6-9.

[39] Kirby, *Biographical*, 9-15; Ohio Historical Society, "Fort Stephenson," *Ohio History Central*, http://www.ohiohistorycentral.org/entry.php?rec=717.

[40] *BDG*; *DAB*; Kirby, *Biographical*, 18-19, 26, 32-34;.

[41] *BDG*; Davis, *Frontier*, 185-87; Kirby, *Biographical*, 18-19, 32-34, 53-54, 65-66; Morison, *Puritan*, 7.

[42] Kirby, *Biographical*, 42-46, 49-54. Duncan freed his own slaves before migrating to Illinois and opposed violence against abolitionists, but he did not support the immediate abolition of slavery.

Chapter 6: Two Steps Forward, One Step Back

[1] Fletcher Harper Swift, *A History of Public Permanent Common School Funds in the United States, 1795-1905* (New York: Holt, 1911), 152. The governor's

home, now known as the Old Governor's Mansion, was built in 1798 and was completely renovated in 2004. It is reputed to be the oldest governor's residence still used for public purposes.

[2] Edgar Wallace Knight, *Education in the United States*, 3rd ed. (Boston: Ginn, 1951), 255-56; Swift, *History*, 11-12, 276-77; Tyack, James, and Benavot, *Law*, 38-39.

[3] A.D. Mayo, "The Development of the Common School in the Western States from 1830 to 1865," in *Report of the Commissioner of Education for the Year 1898-1899*, ed. Department of the Interior, US Bureau of Education (Washington, DC: GPO, 1900), 360, 63; Swift, *History*, 108, 15, 58-59; Tyack, James, and Benavot, *Law*, 39; William Thomas Utter, *The Frontier State, 1803-1825* (Columbus: Ohio State Archaeological and Historical Society, 1941), 5.

[4] Howard, *Illinois*, 95-96; Knepper, *Ohio*, 79-81; James H. Madison, *The Indiana Way: A State History* (Bloomington: Indiana University, 1986), 39, 44-45.

[5] Daniel Feller, *The Public Lands in Jacksonian Politics* (Madison: University of Wisconsin, 1984), 66-70; Francis Samuel Philbrick, *The Rise of the West, 1754-1830*, 1st ed. (New York: Harper, 1965), 294-96; Rohrbough, *Land Office*, 16-44.

[6] R. Carlyle Buley, *The Old Northwest: Pioneer Period, 1815-1840*, 2 vols. (Indianapolis: Indiana Historical Society, 1950), 1:124; Philbrick, *Rise*, 309; Rohrbough, *Land Office*, 78-101, 09-27.

[7] Rohrbough, *Land Office*, 130-32; Marshall Smelser, *The Democratic Republic, 1801-1815*, 1st ed. (New York: Harper, 1968), 35; Vedder and Gallaway, "Migration," 161-63; David Ward, *Cities and Immigrants: A Geography of Change in 19th-Century America* (New York: Oxford University, 1971), 7.

[8] Knight, *History*, 53-4, 61; Swift, *History*, 6-8, 23, 231-4; Tyack, James, and Benavot, *Law*, 34-38.

[9] Feller, Public, 180-82; Knight, *History*, 257; Rohrbough, *Land Office*, 200-49; Swift, *History*, 74-78.

[10] Knight, *History*, 43-54, 64-71, 77-79; Edward Alanson Miller, *The History of Educational Legislation in Ohio from 1803 to 1850* (Columbus: Heer, 1918), 62-74; Quote from Swift, *History*, 132, 374; Utter, *History*, 5.

[11] Cayton, *Frontier*, 112-20; Rohrbough, *Land Office*, 137, 302.

[12] Cayton, *Frontier*, 126-41; Howe, *What Hath God Wrought*, 142-47; Richard Patrick McCormick, *The Second American Party System; Party Formation in the Jacksonian Era* (Chapel Hill: University of North Carolina, 1966), 22-23; Samuel Rezneck, *Business Depressions and Financial Panics: Essays in American Business and Economic History* (New York: Greenwood, 1968), 53-72; Rohrbough, *Land Office*, 137-42.

[13] Urban and Wagoner, *American*, 96.

[14] R. Freeman Butts and Lawrence Arthur Cremin, *A History of Education in American Culture* (New York: Holt, 1953), 244; Cubberley, *Public*, 163.

[15] Edward W. Stevens, Jr., "Structural and Ideological Dimensions of Literacy and Education in the Old Northwest," in *Essays on the Economy of the Old North-*

west, ed. David C. Klingaman and Richard K. Vedder (Athens: Ohio University, 1987), 158.

[16] Appleby, *Inheriting*, 103, 22-3, 210; Wayne Edison Fuller, *The Old Country School: The Story of Rural Education in the Middle West* (Chicago: University of Chicago, 1982), 26-29; Kaestle, *Pillars*, 13-23, 27; Jack Larkin, *The Reshaping of Everyday Life, 1790-1840*, 1st ed. (New York: Harper, 1988), 3; Adolphe Erich Meyer, *An Educational History of the American People*, 2nd ed. (New York: McGraw-Hill, 1967), 118, 24-28; Rohrbough, *Trans-Appalachian*, 152-55; Stevens, "Structural," 168-69.

[17] Appleby, *Inheriting*, 91-103, 24-25; Larkin, *Reshaping*, 35-36; Smelser, *Democratic*, 29; Stevens, "Structural," 157; Paul Theobald, *Call School: Rural Education in the Midwest to 1918* (Carbondale: Southern Illinois University, 1995), 53. Several zealots developed severe vision problems as a result of reading in poor light.

[18] Cayton, *Frontier*, 126, 33-4, 41-43; Donald J. Ratcliffe, *The Politics of Long Division: The Birth of the Second Party System in Ohio, 1818-1828* (Columbus: Ohio State University, 2000), 21, 31-35; Richard C. Wade, *The Urban Frontier: The Rise of Western Cities, 1790-1830* (Cambridge: Harvard University, 1959), 157; Harry L. Watson, *Liberty and Power: The Politics of Jacksonian America*, 1st ed. (New York: Hill and Wang, 1990), 40-41.

[19] Cayton, *Frontier*, 138-41.

[20] Butts, *Public*, 49.

[21] Cayton and Onuf, *Midwest*, 60; Michael F. Holt, *The Rise and Fall of the American Whig Party: Jacksonian Politics and the Onset of the Civil War* (New York: Oxford University, 1999), xiii; Daniel Walker Howe, "Religion and Politics in the Antebellum North," in *Religion and American Politics: From the Colonial Period to the 1980s*, ed. Mark A. Noll (New York: Oxford University, 1990), 130-32.

[22] Holt, *Rise*, 3-7.

[23] Cayton, *Frontier*, 140-1, 48-49; Richard Terrence Farrell, "Cincinnati in the Early Jackson Era, 1816-1834: An Economic and Political Study" (PhD diss., Indiana University, 1967), 18; John Lauritz Larson, *Internal Improvement: National Public Works and the Promise of Popular Government in the Early United States* (Chapel Hill: University of North Carolina, 2001), 195-96; King, *Ohio*, 347; Philbrick, *Rise*, 328, 30, 36-7; Ratcliffe, *Politics*, 28.

[24] Burns, *Educational*, 409; Cutler, *Ephraim Cutler*, 113-16; Lottich, *New England*, 79; Utter, *History*, 322.

[25] Atwater, *History*, 254-59; Farrell, "Cincinnati," 107; Lottich, *New England*, 77-8; Martzolff, "Atwater," 249, 51-6; Ratcliffe, *Politics*, 68.

[26] Atwater, *History*, 260-4; Burns, *Educational*, 410; Coggeshall, "Guilford," 290; Cutler, *Ephraim Cutler*, 140-43; Larson, *Internal*, 197-200; Lottich, *New England*, 80; Martzolff, "Atwater," 256-58.

[27] Atwater, *History*, 264; Larson, *Internal*, 199; Lottich, *New England*, 81; Martzolff, "Atwater," 259; Donald J. Ratcliffe, "The Role of Voters and Issues in Party

Formation: Ohio, 1824," *The Journal of American History* 59, no. 4 (1973): 850; Ratcliffe, *Politics*, 40, 69, 79.

[28] Cayton and Onuf, *Midwest*, 39; King, *Ohio*, 348-9; Larson, *Internal*, 200-1; Ratcliffe, *Politics*, 69.

[29] Coggeshall, "Guilford," 291; Farrell, "Cincinnati," 108-9; Lottich, *New England*, 81-2; A.D. Mayo, "Education in the Northwest During the First Half Century of the Republic, 1790-1840," in *Report of the Commissioner of Education for the Year 1894-1895*, ed. Department of the Interior, US Bureau of Education (Washington, DC: GPO, 1896), 1532; Ratcliffe, *Politics*, 69; Utter, *History*, 322-24.

[30] Coggeshall, "Guilford," 291-93; Farrell, "Cincinnati," 168; Judith Spraul-Schmidt, "The Origins of Modern City Government: From Corporate Regulation to Municipal Corporation in New York, New Orleans and Cincinnati, 1785-1870" (PhD diss., University of Cincinnati, 1990), 123-27.

[31] Buley, *Old*, 2:351; King, *Ohio*, 352; Lottich, *New England*, 82; Mayo, "Education," 1532; Spraul-Schmidt, "Origins," 130; Wade, *Urban*, 243-46.

[32] Richard B. Drake, *A History of Appalachia* (Lexington: University of Kentucky, 2001), ix, 62-66, 119-30; Fischer, *Albion's*, 652-83, 91-702, 32-35, 40-47; Herman, *How the Scots*, 232, 35-36.

[33] Drake, *History*, 35-6; Fischer, *Albion's*, 618-22, 27, 34-35; Herman, *How the Scots*, 231-33; Barry Vann, *In Search of Ulster-Scots Land: The Birth and Geotheological Imagings of a Transatlantic People, 1603-1703* (Columbia: University of South Carolina, 2008), 25-26.

[34] Fischer, *Albion's*, 622-32, 50-51, 62-68, 749-50, 54-58.

[35] Ibid., 665-67, 760-63, 77-82; Herman, *How the Scots*, 232-35.

[36] Fischer, *Albion's*, 687-90, 703-08, 21-22.

[37] Drake, *History*, 33-36; Fischer, *Albion's*, 605-11, 28, 33-39, 55-62; Herman, *How the Scots*, 233-35.

[38] Larkin, *Reshaping*, 3; Philbrick, *Rise*, 303.

[39] Hudson, "North American," 396-405. Hudson creatively mapped this massive exodus by tediously reviewing the biographies of over 40,000 of the original settlers for more than three hundred counties in the Old Northwest and eight other states to its west. He recorded their place of birth and its latitude and then mapped the results showing both the sources and destinations of the great migration. Hudson concluded that "it is possible to predict with specified accuracy where a typical pioneer settler of a given county was born[,] simply on the basis of a county's location."

[40] Ibid.: 404-08; Power, *Planting*, 74, 82-84.

[41] Nicole Etcheson, *The Emerging Midwest: Upland Southerners and the Political Culture of the Old Northwest, 1787-1861* (Bloomington: Indiana University, 1996), 5, 7, 16, 17, 63-66; Howe, *What Hath God Wrought*, 138-39; Power, *Planting*, 116-18, 24; Vann, *In Search of Ulster-Scots Land*, 1603-1703, 137-8, 42-3. Religion is still important today in many areas populated by Appalachians,

like southern Indiana and southern Illinois, which are considered part of the Bible Belt. It is also a recurring theme in Bluegrass music.
[42] Paul Everett Belting, *The Development of the Free Public High School in Illinois to 1860* (New York: Arno Press, 1969; reprint, first published in 1919), 7-8; Buley, *Old*, 1:39-47; Davis, *Frontier*, 159, 249; Howard, *Illinois*, 75, 79; John D. Pulliam, "A History of the Struggle for a Free Common School System in Illinois from 1818 to the Civil War" (EdD diss., University of Illinois, 1965), 56; Rosenberry, *Expansion*, 206-7.
[43] Davis, *Frontier*, 227-8; Howard, *Illinois*, 117, 38-41; McCormick, *Second*, 277, 81.
[44] Buley, *Old*, 1:80-83, 89-90, 93; Fischer, *Albion's*, 642-46; Howard, *Illinois*, 97-102, 29-31, 35-37, 75.
[45] Buley, *Old*, 2:28; Vedder and Gallaway, "Migration," 162-64; Ward, *Cities*, 27.
[46] Belting, *Development*, 41-56; Pulliam, "History," 79-109, 34, 39.
[47] Belting, *Development*, 96-107; John Williston Cook, *Educational History of Illinois* (Chicago: Henry O. Shepard, 1912), 32-34; Howard, *Illinois*, 174-5; Pulliam, "History," 32-37. Some historians, including Belting, have attributed the passage of this law to Coles. While he and his paper certainly filled an important role, it was Duncan who introduced the bill and who directed it through the legislature.
[48] Robert G. Bone, "Education in Illinois before 1857," *Journal of the Illinois State Historical Society* 50, no. 1 (1957): 124-5; Cook, *Educational*, 35-39; Kirby, *Biographical*, 18-19; Pulliam, "History," 38-41, 62-3.
[49] James M. Bergquist, "Tracing the Origins of a Midwestern Culture: The Case of Central Indiana," *Indiana Magazine of History* 77, no. 1 (1981): 1-32; Carl Bode, *The American Lyceum: Town Meeting of the Mind* (New York: Oxford University, 1956), 90; Donald F. Carmony, *Indiana, 1816-1850: The Pioneer Era* (Indianapolis: Indiana Historical Bureau & Indiana Historical Society, 1998), 12-3; Madison, *Indiana*, 58-63, 100-04, 15; Richard Franklin Nation, *At Home in the Hoosier Hills: Agriculture, Politics, and Religion in Southern Indiana, 1810-1870* (Bloomington: Indiana University, 2005), 1-2, 14, 40, 128-9; Gregory S. Rose, "Upland Southerners: The County Origins of Southern Migrants to Indiana by 1850," *Indiana Magazine of History* 82, no. 3 (1986): 242-63; Rosenberry, *Expansion*, 197-98; L.C. Rudolph, *Hoosier Zion: The Presbyterians in Early Indiana* (New Haven: Yale University, 1963), 15-19, 20-22, 27, 47-50; Vedder and Gallaway, "Migration," 163-64; Ward, *Cities*, 27.
[50] Grover L. Hartman, "The Hoosier Sunday School: A Potent Religious/Cultural Force," *Indiana Magazine of History* 78, no. 3 (1982): 217-22; Madison, *Indiana*, 108-11; Rudolph, *Hoosier*, 159-69.
[51] Richard G. Boone, *A History of Education in Indiana* (New York: Appleton, 1892), 9-11; Madison, *Indiana*, 51-53.
[52] Boone, *Education in Indiana*, 13-14, 21-34; Carmony, *Indiana*, 366-68; Mayo, "Education," 1538-9; Otho Lionel Newman, "Development of the Common

Schools of Indiana to 1851," *Indiana Magazine of History* 22, no. 3 (1926): 239-57.

[53] Butts and Cremin, *History*, 250-1; Cubberley, *Public*, 22-24, 97; Howe, *What Hath God Wrought*, 452; Kaestle, *Pillars*, 192-217.
[54] Butts, *Public*, 49, 68-77.
[55] Butts and Cremin, *History*, 247-49; Lawrence Arthur Cremin, *The American Common School: An Historic Conception* (New York: Teachers College, 1951), 95-98; Cubberley, *Public*, 215; Cremin, *National Experience*, 151-53, 64-69.
[56] Cremin, *American Common*, 103-08; Cubberley, *Public*, 97, 101-02, 91-96; Kaestle, *Pillars*, 149, 64.
[57] Cremin, *National Experience*, 153-54; Cubberley, *Public*, 163; Cecil Branner Hayes, *The American Lyceum: Its History and Contribution to Education* (Washington, DC: GPO, 1932), 25-29; Lottich, *New England*, 70; Kaestle, *Pillars*, 184-5.

Chapter 7: Circuit Riders for the Public Schools

[1] Thomas W. Hagedorn, "In the Shadow of Horace Mann: The Forgotten Evangelical Leaders of the Common School Movement," unpublished paper presented at the *Annual Conference of the History of Education Society* (Cleveland, OH, 2007); Jonathan Messerli, Horace Mann: *A Biography*, 1st ed. (New York: Knopf, 1972), xi. The author's paper on Mann included a survey of twenty-two educational histories. It found that Mann was discussed on 553 pages, Barnard on 219 pages, but Lewis on only 51 lines of text.
[2] Burns, *Educational*; William G. W. Lewis, *Biography of Samuel Lewis, First Superintendent of Common Schools for the State of Ohio* (Cincinnati, 1857); Ohio State Teachers Association, *A History of Education in the State of Ohio: A Centennial Volume*, ed. E.E. White and T.W. Harvey (Columbus, OH: General Assembly, 1876); Sister Mary Loretta Petit, "Samuel Lewis: Educational Reformer Turned Abolitionist" (EdD diss., Western Reserve University, 1966), 151-52; James W. Taylor, *A Manual of the Ohio School System: Consisting of an Historical View of Its Progress, and a Republication of the School Laws in Force* (Cincinnati, 1857).
[3] Burns, *Educational*, 420; Lewis, *Samuel Lewis*, 13,16; Petit, "Samuel Lewis," 2-5.
[4] Burns, *Educational*, 420; Quote from Lewis, *Samuel Lewis*, 18; Petit, "Samuel Lewis," 4-6.
[5] Lewis, *Samuel Lewis*, 19-21.
[6] Petit, "Samuel Lewis," 6.
[7] Burns, *Educational*, 420-21; Lewis, *Samuel Lewis*, 22-29; Petit, "Samuel Lewis," 7-8.
[8] Burns, *Educational*, 421; Lewis, *Samuel Lewis*, 29-40, 42, 44-45, 50; Petit, "Samuel Lewis," 8-12.
[9] Lewis, *Samuel Lewis*, 39, 43-44,121, 323.

[10] Ibid., 50, 58, 123-24, 75-76, 244-45, 323, 409.

[11] Ibid., 25, 44-5, 50, 85, 89, 94, 124, 212, 44-45, 378, 81, 87, 409; Petit, "Samuel Lewis," 8, 16-17.

[12] Lewis, *Samuel Lewis*, 4, 16, 18, 26, 30, 292; Petit, "Samuel Lewis," 4, 6-7, 18-24.

[13] Lewis, *Samuel Lewis*, 36, 51-56.

[14] Ibid., 28, 59, 62-3, 282-83; Petit, "Samuel Lewis," 18-24.

[15] Lewis, *Samuel Lewis*, 47-49, 89-93, 360-61.

[16] Ibid., 282-83, 99, 300, 19-20.

[17] Ibid., 320-21.

[18] Ibid., 321-22.

[19] Louis Filler, *Crusade against Slavery: Friends, Foes, and Reforms, 1820-1860*, rev. ed., originally published in 1960 (Algonac, MI: Reference Publications, 1986), 40, 47; Edgar Allen Holt, "Party Politics in Ohio, 1840-1850, Part 2," *Ohio Archaeological and Historical Quarterly* 38, no. 1 (1929): 88, 126, 30-1, 35, 81; Lewis, *Samuel Lewis*, 67, 286-88, 92-5, 308, 15, 26, 29, 57, 65, 73, 78-415; John Niven, *Salmon P. Chase: A Biography* (New York: Oxford University, 1995), 66, 68, 102, 05; Petit, "Samuel Lewis," 111-35; Frederick Ray Ross, "A Portrait of Dedication: Samuel Lewis' Influence on the Abolitionist Movement in Ohio, 1840-1854" (MA thesis, Morehead State, 1970), 38, 43-44, 63, 86.

[20] Lewis, *Samuel Lewis*, 36.

[21] Burns, *Educational*, 421; Alton Ellis, "Samuel Lewis, Progressive Educator in the Early History of Ohio," *Ohio Archaeological and Historical Publications* 25 (1916): 79; Lewis, *Samuel Lewis*, 105-09; Ross, "Portrait," 19. It is hard to imagine that Lewis was not involved in the passage of Cincinnati's School Ordinance in 1929. He had been friends with Nathan Guilford, its champion, since his days as a law student.

[22] Lewis, *Samuel Lewis*, 121; Ohio State Teachers Association, *History*, 361-63.

[23] Quotes from Lewis, *Samuel Lewis*, 123; Ohio State Teachers Association, *History*, 333-34; Petit, "Samuel Lewis," 78-79.

[24] Lewis, *Samuel Lewis*, 111-16, 24-25, 259-61; Petit, "Samuel Lewis," 26-27, 95-96, 109-10.

[25] Lewis, *Samuel Lewis*, 116-17, 427.

[26] Burns, *Educational*, 421; Lewis, *Samuel Lewis*, 276; Petit, "Samuel Lewis," 152-54.

[27] *BDAE*; *DAB*.

[28] *DAB*; Messerli, *Horace Mann*, 126-35.

[29] Frederick M. Binder, *The Age of the Common School: 1830-1865* (New York: Wiley, 1974), 42-44; *DAB*; Horace Mann, *The Republic and the School: Horace Mann on the Education of Free Men*, ed. Lawrence Arthur Cremin (New York: Teachers College, 1957), 4; Messerli, *Horace Mann*, 3-13.

[30] *DAB*; Messerli, *Horace Mann*, 18-23; David B. Tyack and Elisabeth Hansot, *Managers of Virtue: Public School Leadership in America, 1820-1980* (New York: Basic Books, 1982), 57-58.

[31] Mann, "Republic," 4-5; Quote from Messerli, *Horace Mann*, 28-53.

[32] Messerli, *Horace Mann*, 41, 55-62, 69-72, 81-84.

[33] Raymond B. Culver, *Horace Mann and Religion in the Massachusetts Public Schools* (New Haven: Yale University, 1929), 215; *DAB*; Messerli, *Horace Mann*, 74-78, 84-85, 109, 422-24.

[34] Culver, *Horace Mann*, 230-31; *DAB*; Messerli, *Horace Mann*, 310-12, 416-17, 34.

[35] Messerli, *Horace Mann*, 160-81, 558. He retained his belief in God throughout his life. As the President of Antioch College near the end of his life he required daily chapel and often gave the sermons there.

[36] Culver, *Horace Mann*, 224-29; Merle Eugene Curti, *The Social Ideas of American Educators* (Paterson, NJ: Pageant, 1959; reprint, originally published in 1935), 101, 04; Dunn, *What Happened?*, 124-26; Newton Edwards and Herman G. Richey, *The School in the American Social Order: The Dynamics of American Education* (Boston: Houghton Mifflin, 1947), 346; Messerli, *Horace Mann*, 8-11, 18-20; Tyack and Hansot, *Managers*, 56-57. Only three Unitarians were involved in the leadership of the common school movement and all three experienced serious opposition from more religiously conservative reformers.

[37] Binder, *Age*, 43-45; Curti, *Social*, 102-05; Mann, "Republic," 4; Messerli, *Horace Mann*, 109-10, 14-35, 81, 83-85, 87, 200-06, 557, 68.

[38] Messerli, *Horace Mann*, 448-57, 88-91, 97-99, 506-21.

[39] Ibid., 109-10, 221-24.

[40] Culver, *Horace Mann*, 34-37; Mann, "Republic," 3; Messerli, *Horace Mann*, 241-46, 49-51.

[41] Culver, *Horace Mann*, 38; Messerli, *Horace Mann*, 251-51, 61, 67. While the vast majority of educational textbooks and surveys spend a great deal of time describing the educational thought of Rousseau, Voltaire, Paine, and Jefferson there is no evidence that Mann was influenced by them.

[42] Messerli, *Horace Mann*, 267-80, 89-91, 349.

[43] Mann, "Republic," 27; Messerli, *Horace Mann*, xi-xii.

[44] *DAB*; Edith Nye MacMullen, *In the Cause of True Education: Henry Barnard & 19th-Century School Reform* (New Haven: Yale University, 1991), x, 329.

[45] Henry Barnard and Vincent P. Lannie, *Henry Barnard, American Educator* (New York: Teachers College, 1974), 1-3; MacMullen, *Cause*, 1-2, 7, 10-13.

[46] Barnard and Lannie, *Henry Barnard*, 3-5; MacMullen, *Cause*, 14-23.

[47] Barnard and Lannie, *Henry Barnard*, 13; Curti, *Social*, 142-43; MacMullen, *Cause*, 16, 18-19; Barnard C Steiner, *Life of Henry Barnard: The First United States Commissioner of Education, 1867-1870*, ed. Department of Interior (Washington, DC: GPO, 1919), 36.

[48] Barnard and Lannie, *Henry Barnard*, 6, 7, 9-10; Curti, *Social*, 139-40; *DAB*; MacMullen, *Cause*, 32-34, 37-40, 83.

[49] Barnard and Lannie, *Henry Barnard*, 10-13; Curti, *Social*, 166; MacMullen, *Cause*, 60-61, 76, 97-98.

[50] Barnard and Lannie, *Henry Barnard*, 14-24; MacMullen, *Cause*, 106, 16-20, 41-42, 44-50, 53-4, 343; W. S. Monroe, *The Educational Labors of Henry Barnard: A Study in the History of American Pedagogy* (Syracuse, 1893), 15-17; Steiner, *Henry Barnard*, 56, 66.

[51] Barnard and Lannie, *Henry Barnard*, 21-23; MacMullen, *Cause*, 163-64, 68, 87, 92-93, 97-98, 204-05.

[52] Barnard and Lannie, *Henry Barnard*, 25-28, 31-32; MacMullen, *Cause*, 184, 217, 21-22, 28-31, 38-42; Steiner, *Henry Barnard*, 68, 89-92.

[53] Barnard and Lannie, *Henry Barnard*, 34-37, 143-45; MacMullen, *Cause*, 246-47, 59, 64-66, 76-78.

[54] Barnard and Lannie, *Henry Barnard*, ix, 10-12, 24, 36-39, 125-27 ; Nicholas Murray Butler, "The Barnard Relief Movement," *Educational Review* 3 (1892): 409-10; MacMullen, *Cause*, 284, 87, 89, 300, 04, 23-27, 32, 42, 44-46; Monroe, *Educational*, 33-34; Steiner, *Henry Barnard*, 33, 44, 49-50.

[55] Barnard and Lannie, *Henry Barnard*, 14; MacMullen, *Cause*, 345.

[56] Lewis, *Samuel Lewis*, 405, 09, 15, 25; Messerli, *Horace Mann*, 573, 77-82, 88; Petit, "Samuel Lewis," 145-48.

Chapter 8: The Perfect Moment

[1] Cremin, *National Experience*; Holt, *Rise*, 23-27, 61-63; Kaestle, *Pillars*; Donald Hugh Parkerson and Jo Ann Parkerson, *The Emergence of the Common School in the U.S. Countryside* (Lewiston, NY: Mellen, 1998), 5-20; Larry Schweikart and Michael Allen, *A Patriot's History of the United States: From Columbus's Great Discovery to the War on Terror* (New York: Sentinel, 2004), 216-17; Spring, *The American School*; Urban and Wagoner, *American*. Educational historians Cremin, Kaestle, Spring, and Urban and Wagner mention Massachusetts, Connecticut, and Ohio on 142, 58, and 25 pages, respectively. The Parkerson's provide an excellent critique of the eastern and urban dominance of the interpretations and explanations for the common school movement.

[2] Holt, *Rise*, 64, 75; Schweikart and Allen, *Patriot's History*, 231-32.

[3] Butts, *Public*, 90-91; Herbert Ershkowitz and William G. Shade, "Consensus or Conflict? Political Behavior in the State Legislatures During the Jacksonian Era," in *The Many-Faceted Jacksonian Era*, ed. Edward Pessen (Westport, CN: Greenwood, 1977), 212-41; Feller, *Public*, 175-79; Holt, *Rise*, 62, 64, 68-69, 75; Howe, *What Hath God Wrought*, 453-54; Rezneck, *Business*, 81-82, 86; Watson, *Liberty*, 196, 234, 36. Ershkowitz has demonstrated that Whigs favored education and Democrats opposed it in 13 out of 14 state legislative votes in this era.

[4] Holt, *Rise*, 64, 71, 74-75, 80; Donald J. Ratcliffe, "The Market Revolution and Party Alignments in Ohio, 1828-1840," in *The Pursuit of Public Power: Political Culture in Ohio*, 1787-1861, ed. Jeffrey Paul Brown and Andrew R. L. Cayton (Kent: Kent State University, 1994), 111, 15.

[5] Joseph Schweikert, "The Western Literary Institute and College of Professional Teachers: An Instrument in the Creation of a Profession" (PhD diss., University of Cincinnati, 1971), 62-66.

[6] *BDG*; Holt, *Rise*, 51-53, 80; Lewis, *Samuel Lewis*, 120; Miller, *History*, 11-13; Schweikert, "Western," 66-67.

[7] Knepper, *Ohio*, 156-60; Larson, *Internal*, 201-03; Ohio Historical Society, "Plunder Law," *Ohio History Central*, http://www.ohiohistorycentral.org/entry.php?rec=1445. Swift, *History*, 374-75. Ohio's debt would remain so problematic that it adopted a new constitution in 1851, at least in part to severely limit its ability to borrow. For that reason most major expansions of borrowing today require a constitutional amendment in order to circumvent those provisions.

[8] Lewis, *Samuel Lewis*, 121, 29-35, 37-38, 41, 46, 53, 69, 73-75; Mayo, "Development," 358-59; Miller, *History*, 23-24; Ohio State Teachers Association, *History*, 335; Schweikart and Allen, *Patriot's History*, 67.

[9] Mary L. Hinsdale, "A Legislative History of the Public School System of the State of Ohio," in *Report of the Commissioner of Education for the Year 1900-1901*, ed. Department of the Interior, US Bureau of Education (Washington, DC: GPO, 1902), 138-39; Holt, *Rise*, 74-75; Mayo, "Development," 360; Miller, *History*, 11-13; Ohio State Teachers Association, *History*, 333.

[10] *BDG*; Hinsdale, "Legislative," 140; Holt, *Rise*, 71, 74-75, 80; Lewis, *Samuel Lewis*, 184, 212; Ross, "Portrait," 22-23; Peter Temin, "The Jacksonian Economy," in *The Many-Faceted Jacksonian Era*, ed. Edward Pessen (Westport, CN: Greenwood, 1977), 109-10.

[11] Holt, *Rise*, 75, 80; Edgar Allen Holt, "Party Politics in Ohio, 1840-1850, Part 1," *Ohio Archaeological and Historical Quarterly* 37, no. 3 (1928): 452, 97-98, 501; Lewis, *Samuel Lewis*, 254, 59-61.

[12] *BDG*; Holt, *Rise*, 75-76; Temin, "Jacksonian," 110.

[13] Lewis, *Samuel Lewis*.

[14] William R. Hasselbrinck, "The Whigs of Indiana, 1834-1843" (PhD diss., Ball State University, 1985), 83-86, 92, 94-97; Larson, *Internal*, 209-15; Vedder and Gallaway, "Migration," 163-64.

[15] Howard, *Illinois*, 147-60, 76-77, 80; Larson, *Internal*, 218-19; Vedder and Gallaway, "Migration," 163-64.

[16] Mayo, "Development," 389-96; Vedder and Gallaway, "Migration," 163-64.

[17] Henry Barnard, "James G. Carter," *American Journal of Education* 5 (1858): 413-15; Thomas Dionysius Clark, *A History of Kentucky*, rev. ed. (Ashland, KY: The Jesse Stuart Foundation, 1992), 19-20; Cremin, *American Common*, 134-35; Culver, *Horace Mann*, 21-22; Kenneth V. Lottich, "Educational Leadership in Early Ohio," *History of Education Quarterly* 2, no. 1 (1962): 53; George H. Martin, *The Evolution of the Massachusetts Public School System* (New York: Appleton, 1894), 83-88, 92, 121-30, 46-47, 51.

[18] Barnard, "James G. Carter," 408-16; Sylvia Marie Clark, "James Gordon Carter: His Influence in Massachusetts Education, History, and Politics from 1820-1850" (EdD diss., Boston College, 1982), 21-22; Cremin, *American Common*, 139-

41; — — —, *National Experience*, 154; Culver, *Horace Mann*, 20-21; Keith R Hutchison, "James Gordon Carter: Education Reformer," *New England Quarterly* 16, no. 3 (1943): 381, 86-87; Martin, *Evolution*, 154; Messerli, *Horace Mann*, 17, 226.

[19] Barnard, "James G. Carter," 416; Messerli, *Horace Mann*, 224-26.

[20] Clark, "Carter," 56-58; Cremin, *American Common*, 142; Culver, *Horace Mann*, 30-31, 39-40; *DAB*; Hutchison, "Carter," 392-93; Martin, *Evolution*, 155-56; Messerli, *Horace Mann*, 239-40, 85-91.

[21] Clark, "Carter," 45-48, 58-60; Messerli, *Horace Mann*, 298-301.

[22] Ronald P. Formisano, *The Transformation of Political Culture: Massachusetts Parties, 1790s-1840s* (New York: Oxford University, 1983), 262-63; Holt, *Rise*, 71, 74-75, 82; Messerli, *Horace Mann*, 327-28.

[23] Cremin, *National Experience*, 155-56; Culver, *Horace Mann*, 31-32, 127-9, 34-41, 44-5; *DAB*; Formisano, *Transformation*, 275, 77; Messerli, *Horace Mann*, 328, 30. Since state control was more popular in Boston than the countryside, the outliers tended to be Whigs from the country and Democrats from Boston.

[24] Clark, "Carter," 113, 23-28; Holt, *Rise*, 74-75, 82.

[25] Culver, *Horace Mann*, 141; Messerli, *Horace Mann*, 335, 37.

[26] Binder, *Age*, 58; Robert L. Church and Michael W. Sedlak, *Education in the United States: An Interpretive History* (New York: Free Press, 1976), 89-90; Culver, *Horace Mann*, 3-9, 23-26, 55-72, 83-110, 81-97, 204-08; Dunn, *What Happened?*, 161-66, 68-74; Messerli, *Horace Mann*, 309-14, 32-33, 404-07, 09-11, 13-22, 31-34.

[27] Binder, *Age*, 85; Curti, *Social*, 107-08; Edwards and Richey, *School*, 349. While one has to be careful comparing statistics among the states, it appears that schools in Ohio in just three years had growth comparable to those in Massachusetts in twelve. Attendance figures collected from the US census seem to confirm this in Part IV.

[28] MacMullen, *Cause*, 46, 51, 58; Jarvis Means Morse, *A Neglected Period of Connecticut's History* (New Haven: Yale University, 1933), 121-23, 26-27.

[29] *DAB*; Albert Fishlow, "The American Common School Revival: Fact or Fancy?" in *Industrialization in Two Systems*, ed. Henry Rosovsky and Alexander Gerschenkron (New York: Wiley, 1966), 46-7; Orwin Bradford Griffin, *The Evolution of the Connecticut State School System* (New York: Teachers College, 1928), 59; Lottich, "Educational," 53, 54; MacMullen, *Cause*, 52-56, 60; Arthur Raymond Mead, *The Development of Free Schools in the United States as Illustrated by Connecticut and Michigan* (New York: Teachers College, 1918), 12-15, 20-22, 24-26; Morse, *Neglected*, 144-47.

[30] Griffin, *Evolution*, 61; MacMullen, *Cause*, 53, 58-64.

[31] *DAB*; Holt, *Rise*, 75; Lottich, "Educational," 54; MacMullen, *Cause*, 53, 66, 68-70, 75-78; Mead, *Development*, 29-31, 46; Steiner, *Henry Barnard*, 42, 44-46.

[32] Holt, *Rise*, 75, 121-24, 34, 54; MacMullen, *Cause*, 48-49.

[33] Griffin, *Evolution*, 72-73; MacMullen, *Cause*, 79-83, 96-98; Mead, *Development*, 16; Steiner, *Henry Barnard*, 33.

[34] Lottich, "Educational," 53-55; Steiner, *Henry Barnard*, 51.

[35] Fishlow, "American," 44, 49-51, 57; Kaestle, *Pillars*, 182, 84-85, 88-89, 92; MacMullen, *Cause*, 341-42; Petit, "Samuel Lewis," 37, 75n; Schweikert, "Western," 70. Histories up to the 1980s credited New England, Mann, and Barnard almost exclusively for the common school movement. Since then the Midwest has received more attention from scholars, but that still pales in comparison to their treatment of New England.

[36] Messerli, *Horace Mann*, 336.

[37] Barnard and Lannie, *Henry Barnard*, 99-101; Binder, *Age*, 48; Cremin, *National Experience*, 140; Lewis, *Samuel Lewis*, 131-32.

[38] Curti, *Social*, 112-13; Lewis, *Samuel Lewis*, 131.

[39] Barnard and Lannie, *Henry Barnard*, 100; Lewis, *Samuel Lewis*, 132.

[40] Binder, *Age*, 61; Kaestle, *Pillars*, 100; Lewis, *Samuel Lewis*, 89, 132; MacMullen, *Cause*, 77; Horace Mann, *On the Crisis in Education*, ed. Louis Filler (Yellow Springs: Antioch, 1965), ix, xi, 87-88; William J. Reese, *America's Public Schools: From the Common School to"No Child Left Behind"* (Baltimore, MD: Johns Hopkins University, 2005), 13, 33-34.

[41] Mann, "Republic," 21.

[42] Butts and Cremin, *History*, 215-16; Culver, *Horace Mann*, 208, 19, 35; Dunn, *What Happened?*, 143-44, 82, 87.

[43] Church and Sedlak, *Education*, 89, 95-103; Curti, *Social*, 123-24; Mann, "Republic," 16.

[44] Kaestle, *Pillars*, 200-02.

[45] Clark, *History*, 224-25; Barksdale Hamlett, *History of Education in Kentucky* (Frankfort: Kentucky Dept. of Education, 1914), 7-8, 11-12, 21-23; Moses E. Ligon, "A History of Public Education in Kentucky," *Bulletin of the Bureau of School Service, College of Education, University of Kentucky* 14, no. 4 (1942): 77-78; Perry McCandless, *A History of Missouri, 1820 to 1860* (Columbia: University of Missouri, 1972), 190-93; Claude Anderson Phillips, *A History of Education in Missouri: The Essential Facts Concerning the History and Organization of Missouri's Schools* (Jefferson City, MO: Hugh Stephens Printing, 1911), 9-10, 124.

[46] Butts and Cremin, *History*, 247-49; Cubberley, *Public*, 192-96; Kaestle, *Pillars*, 149.

Chapter 9: Greenhouse of the Public Schools

[1] Lyman Beecher and Charles Beecher, *Autobiography, Correspondence, Etc*, 2 vols. (New York: Harper, 1864), 1:13, 17, 25, 28, 32, 34, 36, 38; *DAB*.

[2] Bainton, *Yale*, 127-28, 32; Beecher and Beecher, *Autobiography*, 1:16, 43, 45-48, 70-71, 330-31; Fitzmier, *Timothy Dwight*, 18, 44, 98, 100, 77, 81; James W. Fraser, *Pedagogue for God's Kingdom: Lyman Beecher and the Second Great*

Awakening (Lanham: University Press of America, 1985), 11-13; Vincent Harding, "Lyman Beecher and the Transformation of American Protestantism, 1775-1863" (PhD diss., University of Chicago, 1965), 2, 24-25, 35-36, 116; Stuart C. Henry, *Unvanquished Puritan: A Portrait of Lyman Beecher* (Grand Rapids, MI: Eerdmans, 1973), 21-22; Daniel Walker Howe, *The Political Culture of the American Whigs* (Chicago: University of Chicago, 1979), 152-53; Marsden, *Evangelical*, 56-57.

[3] Beecher and Beecher, *Autobiography*, 2:52-56, 274-76; *DAB*; Fraser, *Pedagogue*, 17-21; Harding, "Beecher," 104-08, 10-14, 297, 416.

[4] Fraser, *Pedagogue*, 44; Harding, "Beecher," 270-76, 373-90, 98, 438; Henry, *Lyman Beecher*, 18-19.

[5] Quotes from Lyman Beecher, *A Plea for the West*, 2nd ed. (Cincinnati, 1835), 7, 9-13, 24, 32-34; Beecher and Beecher, *Autobiography*, 2:333; Fraser, *Pedagogue*, 3; Harding, "Beecher," 563; Howe, *Political*, 161. Beecher was trying to raise funds for Lane Seminary at the time, but there is little reason to doubt his sincerity about the need for seminaries in general.

[6] Charles Chester Cole, *The Social Ideas of the Northern Evangelists, 1826-1860* (New York: Coumbia University, 1954), 117-19; Charles I. Foster, *An Errand of Mercy: The Evangelical United Front, 1790-1837* (Chapel Hill: University of North Carolina, 1960), 189-92; Fraser, *Pedagogue*, 37-44, 99, 101.

[7] Cole, *Social*, 4, 100; Fraser, *Pedagogue*, 25-36, 181-2; Harding, "Beecher," 60-65, 70-77, 104-08, 10-14; Noll, *History*, 169-70; John H. Westerhoff, *McGuffey and His Readers: Piety, Morality, and Education in 19th-Century America* (Nashville, TN: Abingdon, 1978), 53.

[8] Fraser, *Pedagogue*, 182-84, 86-88; Schweikert, "Western," 24, 27-29, 53-54. Western Literary Institute, *The Annual Register of the Proceedings of the Western Literary Institute and College of Professional Teachers*, 5 vols. (Cincinnati, 1834-1838). The author's review of the list of delegates from just five states revealed that at least forty members were ordained ministers. It is likely that many more of the 130 delegates were clergy, since the minister's title is often not recorded in the minutes.

[9] Allen Oscar Hansen, *Early Educational Leadership in the Ohio Valley: A Study of Educational Reconstruction through the Western Literary Institute and College of Professional Teachers, 1829-1841* (Bloomington, IL: Public School Publishing, 1923), 15, 16; Ohio State Teachers Association, *History*, 362; Schweikert, "Western," 31, 36-37, 41-48, 51.

[10] Hansen, *Early*, 52-56, 101-04, 08-09; Ohio State Teachers Association, *History*, 363; Schweikert, "Western," 51, 55-56.

[11] *WLI* (1834, 3rd meeting), 11, 12.

[12] *WLI* (1835, 4th meeting), 22, 30.

[13] Ibid., 13.

[14] Hansen, *Early*, 52-56; Schweikert, "Western," 51; *WLI* (1836, 5th meeting), 18; *WLI* (1838, 7th meeting), 129-136.

[15] Schweikert, "Western," 40-41; *WLI* (1834, 3rd meeting), 10.

[16] Marsden, *Religion*, 60; *WLI* (1835, 4th meeting), 10, 12.

[17] *WLI* (1835, 4th meeting), 4, 5, 30; *WLI* (1837, 6th meeting), 31; *WLI* (1838, 7th meeting), 29.

[18] Bernard Mandel, "Religion and the Public Schools of Ohio," *Ohio State Archaeological and Historical Quarterly* 58 (1949): 188-89; *WLI* (1838, 7th meeting), 39, 98, 190-98.

[19] *BDAE*; Cremin, *American Common*, 49-51; *DAB*; Schweikert, "Western," 3-4; *WLI*.

[20] Aaron, *Cincinnati*, 213-17; Hansen, *Early*, 110-11; Paul H. Mattingly, *The Classless Profession: American Schoolmen in the 19th Century* (New York: New York University, 1975), 99, 176; Ohio State Teachers Association, *History*, 108-09, 363; Schweikert, "Western," 3-4.

[21] *DAB*; Hansen, *Early*, 110; Schweikert, "Western," 53.

[22] Bainton, *Yale*, 133; *BDAE*; Arthur Charles Cole, *The Era of the Civil War, 1848-1878* (Springfield: Illinois Centennial Commission, 1919), 230-37, 430-37; *DAB*; Howard, *Illinois*, 177, 274, 77; Beecher Hall has survived into the 21st century and is still in use at Illinois College.

[23] *BDAE; DAB*.

[24] *BDAE; DAB*; Hansen, *Early*, 110; Schweikert, "Western," 53.

[25] *BDAE; DAB*; Howe, *What Hath God Wrought*, 459-62; Timothy L. Smith, "Protestant Schooling and American Nationality, 1800-1850," *Journal of American History* 53 (1967): 694.

[26] Sheldon Emmor Davis, *Educational Periodicals During the 19th Century* (Metuchen, NJ: Scarecrow, 1970; reprint, originally published in 1919), 12, 22-28, 45, 51, 68, 83-84.

[27] Bode, *American*, 10-12, 22-25, 28, 31, 92, 113-15; Hayes, *American*, vii-viii, 7-8, 18, 20, 36-37, 39, 41, 45-49, 50-51.

[28] *WLI* (1836, 5th meeting), 131-35, 38, 40-42, 46.

[29] *DAB*; William Holmes McGuffey, *The McGuffey Readers: Selections from the 1879 Edition*, ed. Elliott J. Gorn (Boston: Bedford/St. Martin's, 1998), 3-5; Harvey C. Minnich, *William Holmes McGuffey and His Readers* (New York: American Book Company, 1936), 8-13; Westerhoff, *McGuffey*, 28-35.

[30] *DAB*; McGuffey, *McGuffey Readers*, 4-10; Westerhoff, *McGuffey*, 34-37, 40-43. McGuffey completed his career at the University of Virginia and those years illustrate the total failure of Jefferson's dream of establishing a secular university. McGuffey and his fellow faculty members made Christianity an integral part of Virginia, just like the other Calvinist-dominated institutions during this era.

[31] Charles H. Carpenter, *History of American Schoolbooks* (Philadelphia: University of Pennsylvania, 1963), 80-81, 85-6; McGuffey, *McGuffey Readers*, 2, 14, 16; Minnich, *William Holmes McGuffey*, 31-32; John A. Nietz, *Old Textbooks: Spelling, Grammar, Reading, Arithmetic, Geography, American History, Civil Government, Physiology, Penmanship, Art, Music, as Taught in the Common*

Schools from Colonial Days to 1900 (Pittsburgh: University of Pittsburgh, 1961), 72-74; Westerhoff, *McGuffey*, 15-16, 53.
[32] McGuffey, *McGuffey Readers*, vii; Minnich, *William Holmes McGuffey*, 88; Richard David Mosier, *Making the American Mind: Social and Moral Ideas in the McGuffey Readers* (New York: Russell & Russell, 1965), 167, 69; Nietz, *Old Textbooks*, 70, 76-79; Westerhoff, *McGuffey*, 15-16.
[33] Ruth Miller Elson, *Guardians of Tradition: American Schoolbooks of the 19th Century* (Lincoln: University of Nebraska, 1964), 8, 9; Nietz, *Old Textbooks*, 1; David B. Tyack, *Turning Points in American Educational History* (Waltham, MA: Blaisdell, 1967), 178.
[34] Elson, *Guardians*, vii; Nietz, *Old Textbooks*, 76, 77.
[35] Carpenter, *History*, 85-86; McGuffey, *McGuffey Readers*, 17; Nietz, *Old Textbooks*, 52-54, 56; Smith, "Protestant Schooling," 695; Westerhoff, *McGuffey*, 18, 37.
[36] McGuffey, *McGuffey Readers*, 11, 114-26; Minnich, *William Holmes McGuffey*, 29, 37, 50, 56, 82; Mosier, *Making*, 57, 59, 66, 124-52; Westerhoff, *McGuffey*, 61-62, 75-86.
[37] Mosier, *Making*, 1-32, 57, 66-69, 71, 154-57.
[38] McGuffey, *McGuffey Readers*, 11-12, 127-42; Mosier, *Making*, 66, 73-74, 156.
[39] *BDAE; DAB.*
[40] *BDAE; DAB.*
[41] *BDAE;* Cubberley, *Public*, 359; *DAB;* C. E. Stowe, *The Prussian System of Public Instruction, and Its Applicability to the United States* (Cincinnati, 1836); C. E Stowe, *Report on Elementary Public Instruction in Europe, Made to the Thirty-Sixth General Assembly of the State of Ohio, December 19, 1837* (Columbus: Ohio General Assembly, 1838).
[42] Cubberley, *Public*, 359; Stowe, *Prussian*, 19-20, 22-23.
[43] Gutek, *History*, 393-94; Stowe, *Prussian*, 30-32, 34, 37-40, 45, 73.
[44] Stowe, *Prussian*, 24-30.
[45] Cubberley, *Public*, 169-70; Knight, *Education*, 195-202; Meyer, *Educational*, 177-79. Barnard attributed Stowe's report with "not a little of the advancement of the common school during the next twenty years."

Chapter 10: Topping-out Ceremonies

[1] Fishlow, "American," 56; Larkin, *Reshaping*, 53-54.
[2] Cubberley, *Public*, 22-25; Kaestle, *Pillars*, 195-96, 205, 12; Notestein, *English People*, 27-29; Urban and Wagoner, *American*, 119-20, 23-24.
[3] Cubberley, *Public*, 408-09, 22; Kaestle, *Pillars*, 203-04; Urban and Wagoner, *American*, 117, 20.
[4] Cubberley, *Public*, 411-14, 16-21; John K. Folger and Charles B. Nam, *Education of the American Population* (Washington, DC: US Dept. of Commerce, Bureau of the Census, 1967), 18; Kaestle, *Pillars*, 200, 03.

[5] Cubberley, *Public*, 408, 21-25; Kaestle, *Pillars*, 193-94, 98; Urban and Wagoner, *American*, 117, 21.

[6] Hudson, "North American," 400-02; McCandless, *History*, 37; Phillips, *History*, 124.

[7] Cubberley, *Public*, 101-02, 409-10, 15, 19.

[8] Patricia Kelly Hall and Steven Ruggles, "'Restless in the Midst of Their Prosperity': New Evidence on the Internal Migration of Americans, 1850-2000," *The Journal of American History* 91, no. 3 (2004): 835, 37-39, 45; Hudson, "North American." In the 1830s the Midwest grabbed the balance of power in American government as a result of this population shift. So beginning with Lincoln's victory in 1860, candidates from Ohio and Illinois won ten of the next sixteen presidential contests (1860-1920). Interestingly, American's great migration—to the South and West in the 20th century—produced a similar effect. In the sixteen elections since 1952, six were won by Texans (including George H.W. Bush), four by Californians (including Reagan), three by Democrats from the South and only three by Northerners (Kennedy and Obama), who both benefited from a strong political tailwind as a result of their affiliation with a minority group.

[9] Ian R. Tyrrell, *Sobering Up: From Temperance to Prohibition in Antebellum America, 1800-1860* (Westport, CN: Greenwood, 1979), 3.

[10] Jack S. Blocker, *American Temperance Movements: Cycles of Reform* (Boston: Twayne, 1989), 9; Bruce Dorsey, *Reforming Men and Women: Gender in the Antebellum City* (Ithaca: Cornell University, 2002), 90-91; Russel Blaine Nye, *Society and Culture in America, 1830-1860*, 1st ed. (New York: Harper, 1974), 48; W. J. Rorabaugh, *The Alcoholic Republic, an American Tradition* (New York: Oxford University, 1979), 14-16, 20-21, 78-80, 145.

[11] Blocker, *American*, 12-24, 26, 34; Dorsey, *Reforming*, 116; Nye, *Society*, 48-50; Rorabaugh, *Alcoholic*, 8-9, 187, 96-202, 04-10; Tyrrell, *Sobering*, 4, 7, 54-56, 70, 87-88. The reader might recall Samuel Lewis's letter that questioned a fellow attorney's drinking habits, which illustrates the boldness that was typical of many temperance advocates.

[12] Blocker, *American*, 26-27, 56-57; Ershkowitz and Shade, "Consensus," 223; Tyrrell, *Sobering*, 237-39, 61, 97-304.

[13] Blocker, *American*, 33, 54-58; Tyrrell, *Sobering*, 239-40, 43-44, 53, 60-62.

[14] Filler, *Crusade*, 70-73, 87-88, 97-98, 100-05, 13, 23-26; Nye, *Society*, 61.

[15] Ershkowitz and Shade, "Consensus," 225; Filler, *Crusade*, 60-64, 154-9, 87, 89, 210-11, 15, 28-30, 40-43, 50-54, 66; Edwin S. Gaustad and Leigh Eric Schmidt, *The Religious History of America*, rev. ed. (San Francisco: Harper, 2002), 189-96; Holt, *Rise*, 156-57, 208-09, 368, 72-73, 799, 826; Nye, Society, 61; David Morris Potter and Don Edward Fehrenbacher, *The Impending Crisis, 1848-1861*, 1st ed. (New York: Harper, 1976), 90, 113-35, 40, 63-73, 75-99, 226-29.

[16] Ray Allen Billington, *The Protestant Crusade, 1800-1860: A Study of the Origins of American Nativism* (Chicago: Quadrangle, 1964), 381, 87; Holt, *Rise*, 117, 805; Potter and Fehrenbacher, *Impending*, 241-42, 45.

[17] Billington, *Protestant*, 387-88, 407; Potter and Fehrenbacher, *Impending*, 250-51; US House of Representatives, "Institutution," *History, Art and Archives*, http://artandhistory.house.gov/house_history/index.aspx. Go to 33rd and 34th Congresses in "Congressional Profiles."

[18] Billington, *Protestant*, 390; Filler, *Crusade*, 56-60, 271-75; Holt, *Rise*, 838; Potter and Fehrenbacher, *Impending*, 240, 47-49.

[19] Stephen C. Fox, *The Group Bases of Ohio Political Behavior, 1803-1848* (New York: Garland, 1989), 158-61; Holt, "Party Politics in Ohio, 1840-1850, Part 2," 77-78, 80, 138,80; Hudson, "North American," 402-06; Eugene Holloway Roseboom, *The Civil War Era, 1850-1873* (Columbus: Ohio State Archaeological and Historical Society, 1941), 212,19.

[20] *BDAE*; *DAB*; F.L. Shoemaker, "Samuel Galloway: An Educational Statesman of First Rank," *History of Education Journal* 5, no. 4 (1954): 105-12, 15-6; Taylor, *Manual*, 174-5, 86.

[21] Lottich, "Educational," 56-59; — — — —, *New England*, 55-58, 202-04; Miller, *History*, 26-27; Spraul-Schmidt, "Origins," 132; Francis P. Weisenburger, *The Passing of the Frontier, 1825-1850* (Columbus: Ohio State Archaeological and Historical Society, 1941), 171-72, 415, 20, 28, 30, 32.

[22] Lewis, *Samuel Lewis*, 270.

[23] Leonard Erickson, "Politics and Repeal of Ohio's Black Laws, 1837-1849," *Ohio History* 82, no. 3 (1973): 171-73; Holt, "Party Politics in Ohio, 1840-1850, Part 2," 130-31; Holt, *Rise*, 399-401, 52, 571; Stephen E. Maizlish, "Ohio and the Rise of Sectional Politics," in *The Pursuit of Public Power: Political Culture in Ohio, 1787-1861*, ed. Jeffrey Paul Brown and Andrew R. L. Cayton (Kent: Kent State University, 1994), 130-33; Weisenburger, *Passing*, 467-68, 70-71, 77.

[24] Miller, *History*, 27; Eugene Holloway Roseboom and Francis P. Weisenburger, *A History of Ohio* (Columbus: Ohio State Archaeological and Historical Society, 1953), 163-64; Spraul-Schmidt, "Origins," 133-34; Taylor, *Manual*, 215; Weisenburger, *Passing*, 478-79.

[25] *BDG*; Lewis, *Samuel Lewis*, 272, 74-75; Roseboom, *Civil War*, 176, 93-94. True to their beliefs, the zealots included provisions for the schooling of blacks, though there was no mention of intergration.

[26] Holt, *Rise*, 782-3, 99, 803, 05; Maizlish, "Ohio," 135-6; Roseboom, *Civil War*, 177-80, 219, 22-5, 76.

[27] Maizlish, "Ohio," 136-39; Roseboom, *Civil War*, 282-86, 88-89, 93, 95, 311.

[28] Boone, *Education in Indiana*, 87; Carmony, *Indiana*, 369; Hudson, "North American," 401-04; Madison, *Indiana*, 83; Nation, *At Home*, 159-60, 79-82; Maureen Anne Reynolds, "Politics and Indiana's Public Schools During the Civil War Era, 1850-1875" (PhD diss., Indiana University, 1997), 3-4, 11; Roger H. Van Bolt, "The Indiana Scene in the 1840s," *Indiana Magazine of History* 47, no. 4 (1951): 333, 38-39; — — — —, "The Hoosier Politician of the 1940s," *Indiana Magazine of History* 48, no. 1 (1952): 24; Vedder and Gallaway, "Migration," 163-4. A typical attitude towards education was expressed by a state representa-

tive in 1837: "When I die I want my epitaph written: Here lies an enemy to free schools."

[29] Carmony, *Indiana*, 373-77, 89. Caleb Mills, "An Address to the Legislature of Indiana," in *Caleb Mills and the Indiana School System*, ed. Charles W. Moores (Indianapolis, IN: Wood-Weaver Printing Company, 1905), 382; Andrew A. Sherockman, "Caleb Mills: Pioneer Educator in Indiana" (PhD diss., University of Pittsburgh, 1955), 29, 32-41, 44, 47, 51-55, 69, 74-77, 84, 87-88, 92-95. Like so many other Calvinists, Mills felt that the teaching of religion and morality were important goals for the schools.

[30] *BDAE*; Boone, *Education in Indiana*, 141; Mills, "Address," preface.

[31] Boone, *Education in Indiana*, 88-89, 93, 95, 97-108, 12-28; Carmony, *Indiana*, 392-93, 87-91; Cubberley, *Public*, 185-86; Mills, "Address," 364-69; Newman, "Development," 266-69; Reynolds, "Politics," 4, 6, 8.

[32] Boone, *Education in Indiana*, 129-39, 41-50, 213-15; *DAB*; Holt, *Rise*, 402, 41-42; Indiana University School of Law, "Constitution of the State of Indiana," http://www.law.indiana.edu/uslawdocs/inconst.html - education. See Article 8; Reynolds, "Politics," 11-32, 35-6, 43-47, 56-61, 66-7; Roger H. Van Bolt, "Hoosiers and the Eternal Agitation, 1848-1850," *Indiana Magazine of History* 48, no. 4 (1952): 342-48; Van Bolt, "Politician," 35.

[33] *BDAE*; Boone, *Education in Indiana*, 150, 213-15; Madison, *Indiana*, 180-1; Nation, *At Home*, 186; Reynolds, "Politics" 72, 76, 82-84; Emma Lou Thornbrough, *Indiana in the Civil War Era, 1850-1880* (Indianapolis: Indiana Historical Bureau, 1965), 465-68. Oddly enough, Mills agreed with both Supreme Court decisions, based upon his belief that the schools should find other sources of revenue.

[34] Davis, *Frontier*, 227-28, 47-54; Howard, *Illinois*, 237-41, 43-47, 55-58; Hudson, "North American," 401-04; Rosenberry, *Expansion*, 217; Vedder and Gallaway, "Migration," 163-64.

[35] *BDAE*; *DAB*; Sweet, *Religion*, 268.

[36] *BDG*; Cook, *Educational*, 44; Howard, *Illinois*, 232; Pulliam, "History," 79-81, 212-14.

[37] Bone, "Education," 133-4; Cole, *Era*, 133, 37, 209; Cook, *Educational*, 45-53, 56-58; Stephen L. Hansen, *The Making of the Third Party System: Voters and Parties in Illinois, 1850-1876* (Ann Arbor, MI: UMI Research, 1980), 1-11, 37-51, 59, 62-66, 69, 74; Howard, *Illinois*, 275-6, 83, 87; Mayo, "Development," 383-84; Pulliam, "History," 178, 81-2.

[38] Belting, *Development*, 146-53; Bone, "Education," 136-37; Cole, *Era*, 233; Cook, *Educational*, 55-56; Howard, *Illinois*, 277, 91; Daniel W. Kucera, *Church-State Relationships in Education in Illinois* (Washington: Catholic University, 1955), 73; Mayo, "Development," 383-84; Pulliam, "History," 196-97.

[39] *DAB*; Willis Frederick Dunbar and George S. May, *Michigan, a History of the Wolverine State*, rev. ed. (Grand Rapids: Eerdmans, 1980), 288-89; Hudson, "North American," 404-08; Mead, *Development*, 128-30, 84; Rosenberry, *Expan-*

sion, 226-35; J. Harold Stevens, "The Influence of New England in Michigan," *Michigan History Magazine* 19 (1935): 325-28, 30-34, 42, 46-49.

[40] Dunbar and May, *History of the Wolverine State*, 194-95, 287; Charles R. Starring and James Owen Knauss, *The Michigan Search for Educational Standards* (Lansing: Michigan Historical Commission, 1969), 1; Vedder and Gallaway, "Migration," 162-64.

[41] *BDAE*; *DAB*; Charles Oliver Hoyt and R. Clyde Ford, John D. Pierce, *Founder of the Michigan School System: A Study of Education in the Northwest* (Ypsilanti, MI: Scharf Tag, Label & Box Co., 1905), 56-61, 73, 76-77, 79, 81-84, 89-102; Quote from Andrew Cunningham McLaughlin, *History of Higher Education in Michigan* (Washington, DC: Department of Interior, Bureau of Education, 1891), 35; *WLI*.

[42] F. Clever Bald, *Michigan in Four Centuries*, 1st ed. (New York: Harper, 1954), 197, 208, 12-21; Quote from Harold C. Brooks, "Founding of the Michigan Public School System," *Michigan History* 33, no. 4 (1949): 303; Floyd Russell Dain, *Education in the Wilderness* (Lansing: Michigan Historical Commission, 1968), 206-10, 20, 23-38; Dunbar and May, *History of the Wolverine State*, 337; Martin J. Hershock, *The Paradox of Progress: Economic Change, Individual Enterprise, and Political Culture in Michigan, 1837-1878* (Athens: Ohio University, 2003), 4; Tyack, James, and Benavot, *Law*, 80-84.

[43] Bald, *Michigan*, 255-58; Dunbar and May, *History of the Wolverine State*, 350, 52-53, 58-59, 63, 66-7; Holt, *Rise*, 210, 13; Mead, *Development*, 96-119; Daniel Putnam, *The Development of Primary and Secondary Public Education in Michigan: A Historical Sketch* (Ann Arbor, MI: G. Wahr, 1904), 25-34; Starring and Knauss, *Michigan*, 5-6, 9-10, 12, 49-50, 57-67; Stevens, "Influence," 347-49.

[44] Edward P. Alexander, "Wisconsin, New York's Daughter State," *Wisconsin Magazine of History* 30, no. 1 (1946): 11-30; Richard N. Current, *The Civil War Era, 1848-1873* (Madison: State Historical Society of Wisconsin, 1976), 60-78; Hudson, "North American," 406-08; Rosenberry, *Expansion*, 237, 39, 43-46; Quote from Alice E. Smith, *From Exploration to Statehood* (Madison: State Historical Society of Wisconsin, 1973), 250, 465, 68-69, 71, 575; Vedder and Gallaway, "Migration," 162-64.

[45] *BDAE*; Michael Frank and Ernest St. Aubin, "The Autobiography of Michael Frank," *Wisconsin Magazine of History* 30, no. 4 (1947): 441-42, 52-53, 56, 58-59.

[46] Alexander, "Wisconsin, New York's Daughter State," 24-25; *BDAE*; *BDG*; Current, *Civil*, 162, 65; *DAB*; Jorgenson, *Founding*, 115-6, 22-4; Rosenberry, *Expansion*, 244-46; Joseph Schafer, "Origin of Wisconsin's Free School System," *Wisconsin Magazine of History* 9, no. 1 (1925): 27.

[47] Current, *Civil*, 161-63; Jorgenson, *Founding*, 53-69, 74, 90-99; Quote from Mayo, "Development," 413-15, 19; Conrad E. Patzer, *Public Education in Wisconsin* (Madison, WI: Wisconsin Department of Public Instruction, 1925), 12-15, 17-19, 21-29, 31-35, 37-39; Schafer, "Origin," 34-43; Smith, *Exploration*, 581-86, 665.

[48] Current, *Civil*, 162-65; Jorgenson, *Founding*, 111-15, 25-27; Patzer, *Public*, 72.

[49] Current, *Civil*, 197, 200, 02-04, 13-21.

[50] Binder, *Age*, 88-90; Butts and Cremin, *History*, 247; Cubberley, *Public*, 205, 15.

[51] Binder, *Age*, 99; Butts and Cremin, *History*, 246-47; Cremin, *American Common*, 176; Holt, *Rise*, 210, 25, 38.

[52] Formisano, *Transformation*, 330-32; John R. Mulkern, *The Know-Nothing Party in Massachusetts: The Rise and Fall of a People's Movement* (Boston: Northeastern University, 1990), 40-55, 61-63, 66, 69.

[53] *BDG*; Billington, *Protestant*, 388-90; Formisano, *Transformation*, 332; Holt, *Rise*, 878, 92; Mulkern, *Know Nothing*, 76, 87.

[54] Billington, *Protestant*, 413; Formisano, *Transformation*, 333; Mulkern, *Know Nothing*, 87, 89, 101.

[55] Billington, *Protestant*, 413; Formisano, *Transformation*, 332-33; Mulkern, *Know Nothing*, 102, 07-11.

[56] Fishlow, "American," 49-51, 57; Folger and Nam, *Education of the American Population*, 3-4; Larkin, *Reshaping*, 53-54.

[57] Current, *Civil*, 221-36; Dunbar and May, *History of the Wolverine State*, 363; Howard, *Illinois*, 289-91; Maizlish, "Ohio," 140.

[58] Cubberley, *Public*, 140, 312-15, 563-65, 627-32.

Chapter 11: The Mission Expands to the New Frontier

[1] Stevens, "Structural," 158.

[2] Randolph B. Campbell, *Gone to Texas: A History of the Lone Star State* (New York: Oxford University, 2003), 219, 27-28.

[3] Ray Allen Billington, *The Far Western Frontier, 1830-1860*, 1st ed. (New York: Harper, 1956), 119-33, 36; Robert A. Calvert and Arnoldo De Leâon, *The History of Texas* (Arlington Heights, IL: H. Davidson, 1990), 59, 78, 88; Campbell, *Gone*, 228; Frederick Eby, *The Development of Education in Texas* (New York: Macmillan, 1925), 66-79, 83-84, 87-88, 91-94, 102; Victoria-Marâia MacDonald, *Latino Education in U.S. History, 1513-2000* (New York: Palgrave Macmillan, 2004), 31-32, 36; Schweikart and Allen, *Patriot's History*, 237-38.

[4] Billington, *Far Western*, 134-5, 43-45, 48-54; Calvert and De Leâon, *History*, 111; Campbell, *Gone*, 228; Eby, *Development*, 104-09; Colin Brummitt Goodykoontz, *Home Missions on the American Frontier, with Particular Reference to the American Home Missionary Society* (Caldwell, ID: Caxton, 1939), 271-72, 76-77; Schweikart and Allen, *Patriot's History*, 237-40.

[5] Eby, *Development*, 110-12.

[6] *BDG*; *DAB*; Eby, *Development*, 112.

[7] Calvert and De Leâon, *History*, 111; Campbell, *Gone*, 228-30; Eby, *Development*, 93, 116-20, 25, 28; T. R. Fehrenbach, *Lone Star: A History of Texas and the Texans*, 1st ed. (New York: Da Capo, 2000), 303.

[8] Calvert and De Leâon, *History*, 112; Campbell, *Gone*, 228; Eby, *Development*, 87-88, 119, 30, 43; Fehrenbach, *Lone*, 303-4; Glen E. Lich, *The German Texans*, 1st ed. (San Antonio: University of Texas, San Antonio, 1981), 47, 53, 64-65, 124, 26, 29.

[9] Calvert and De Leâon, *History*, 100; Campbell, *Gone*, 214, 19, 27-28; Catholic Diocese of Galveston-Houston, *Recall, Rejoice, Renew: Diocese of Galveston-Houston, 1847-1997* (Dallas: Taylor Publishing, 1997), 24-25; Eby, *Development*, 92; Lich, *German Texans*, 91,94, 97; James T. Moore, *Through Fire and Flood: The Catholic Church in Frontier Texas, 1836-1900*, 1st ed. (College Station: Texas A&M University, 1992), 121-22.

[10] Calvert and De Leâon, *History*, 115-17; Campbell, *Gone*, 232-33.

[11] Calvert and De Leâon, *History*, 116; Campbell, *Gone*, 236-37; L.V. Jacks, *Claude Dubuis, Bishop of Galveston* (St. Louis: B. Herder, 1947), 136-39; Moore, *Through Fire*, 111-13.

[12] Cremin, *National Experience*, 182-85; Fehrenbach, *Lone*, 303.

[13] Mayo, "Development," 443; Kevin Starr, *Americans and the California Dream, 1850-1915* (New York: Oxford University, 1973), 87.

[14] Walton Bean, *California: An Interpretive History*, 2nd ed. (New York: McGraw-Hill, 1973), 57-58; J. Andrew Ewing, "Education in California During the Pre-Statehood Period," *Annual Publications of the Historical Society of Southern California* 11 (1918): 51-56, 59; Charles John Falk, *The Development and Organization of Education in California* (New York: Harcourt, 1968), 11-14; Mayo, "Development," 442; MacDonald, *Latino*, 41-44.

[15] Bean, *California*, 158; Billington, *Far Western*, 218-42; John Walton Caughey, *California* (New York: Prentice-Hall, 1940), 260; Falk, *Development*, 62-3; William Hanchett, "The Question of Religion and the Taming California, 1849-1854," *California Historical Society Quarterly* 32 (1953): 119, 29-30, 37; Mayo, "Development," 443; Starr, *Americans*, 69-70, 77-78, 85-92, 107. Interestingly, almost half the ships that arrived in San Francisco in 1849 originated in New England.

[16] Bean, *California*, 158; Falk, *Development*, 14-15, 17-21, 61; David Frederic Ferris, *Judge Marvin and the Founding of the California Public School System* (Berkeley: University of California, 1962), 70-72; Quote from Mayo, "Development," 445; Ernest Moore, "California's Educators," *The Historical Society of Southern California Quarterly* 31 (1949): 173-74.

[17] *BDAE*; Ferris, *Judge Marvin*, 1-6.

[18] Bean, *California*, 158; Falk, *Development*, 24-5; Ferris, *Judge Marvin*, 49, 78-81, 102, 07-09; Quote from Mayo, "Development," 446-47; Tyack, James, and Benavot, *Law*, 88-89.

[19] Bean, *California*, 158; Ferris, *Judge Marvin*, 102, 07-09.

[20] Bean, *California*, 111; Caughey, *California*, 334-35; Mayo, "Development," 443, 45; Andrew F. Rolle, *California: A History* (New York: Crowell, 1963), 309-11.

[21] Bean, *California*, 113-14, 23-30; Caughey, *California*, 334-6; John Bernard McGloin, *California's First Archbishop: The Life of Joseph Sadoc Alemany,*

1814-1888 (New York: Herder and Herder, 1966), 163; Rolle, *California*, 311-15; Starr, *Americans*, 93-95; Tyack, James, and Benavot, *Law*, 91.

[22] *BDAE*; *DAB*; Falk, *Development*, 26-27; John Swett, *Public Education in California Its Origin and Development, with Personal Reminiscences of Half a Century* (New York: American Book, 1911), 118, 22.

[23] *BDAE*; *DAB*; Moore, "*California*'s," 171; Nicholas C. Polos, *John Swett: California's Frontier Schoolmaster* (Washington: University Press of America, 1978), 1-6, 8-9, 24-25, 121, 23, 25; Starr, *Americans*, 88.

[24] Moore, "California's," 171-2; Polos, *Swett*, 15-17; Quote from Swett, *Public*, 9-23.

[25] *DAB*; Moore, "California's," 172; Polos, *Swett*, 35-36, 51-52; Rolle, *California*, 317, 19-20; Swett, *Public*, 140-45. Stanford was one of the four partners in the Central Pacific Railroad and was the founder and first benefactor of Stanford University.

[26] *BDAE*; *DAB*; Moore, "California's," 174-75; Polos, *Swett*, 42-43, 76-82; Starr, *Americans*, 87-88; Swett, *Public*, 153, 63-67; Tyack, James, and Benavot, *Law*, 92.

[27] *BDAE*; *DAB*; Falk, *Development*, 27; Mayo, "Development," 449-50; Moore, "California's," 172-3, 75-76; Polos, *Swett*, 46, 52-54, 56-61; Swett, *Public*, 154-55, 63-67, 74-77, 82-87; Tyack, James, and Benavot, *Law*, 93-4.

[28] Bean, *California*, 159; Swett, *Public*, 178, 85.

[29] Polos, *Swett*, 38, 76, 91-93; Swett, *Public*, 115, 88-89, 96; Tyack, James, and Benavot, *Law*.

[30] Cremin, *National Experience*, 184.

[31] Gordon B. Dodds, *Oregon: A Bicentennial History* (New York: Norton, 1977), 89; William G. Robbins, *Oregon: This Storied Land* (Portland: Oregon Historical Society, 2005), 159-60.

[32] Billington, *Far Western*, 79-85; Charles Henry Carey, *History of Oregon* (Chicago: Pioneer Historical, 1922), 324, 29-30, 33-34, 38, 51-64; *DAB*; Dodds, *Oregon*, 54-56, 59-60; Robbins, *Oregon*, 39, 41-42, 47.

[33] Carey, *History*, 323-24, 33-34, 36, 40, 50; Dodds, *Oregon*, 88, 92; Alan Frederick Quick, "The History and Development of Common School Education in Oregon, 1849-1872" (EdD diss., University of Oregon, 1963), 28; Robbins, *Oregon*, 43, 45, 158; Tyack, "Kingdom," 458-61.

[34] Carey, *History*, 349-50, 83, 711; Dodds, *Oregon*, 61, 71-72, 86-7, 105; Goodykoontz, *Home*, 276-7; Ira W. Lewis, "Education in the Oregon Constitutional Convention," *The Quarterly of the Oregon Historical Society* 23 (1922): 220-21; Quick, "History," 44-45, 73.

[35] *BDAE*; *DAB*; Quick, "History," 61; Tyack, "Kingdom," 456.

[36] *DAB*; Quotes from Tyack, "Kingdom," 457-59.

[37] Quotes from Nancy Bates Atkinson and Myron Eells, *Biography of Rev. G. H. Atkinson . . . Journal of Sea Voyage to Oregon in 1848, and Selected Addresses and Printed Articles, and a Particular Account of His Church Work in the Pacific*

Northwest (Portland, OR, 1893), 229-39; *DAB*; Dodds, *Oregon*, 106-7; Tyack, "Kingdom," 456, 59.
[38] Carey, *History*, 712, 15-6; *DAB*; Quick, "History," 54, 63-66, 68-70, 74-78; Tyack, "Kingdom," 456.
[39] *BDAE*; Carey, *History*, 719-3, 27-8; Dodds, *Oregon*, 105; Quick, "History," 82; Tyack, "Kingdom," 447, 59-68.
[40] Carey, *History*, 534; Lewis, "Education," 222-28; Quick, "History," 87-88, 111-12, 27-33; Robbins, *Oregon*, 55.
[41] Carey, *History*, 528-30, 631, 45-47, 55-56; *DAB*; Dodds, *Oregon*, 100-03; Lewis, "Education," 228; Quick, "History," 112, 14, 16-18; Robbins, *Oregon*, 54-55, 163.
[42] *BDG*; Carey, *History*, 655-56; Dodds, *Oregon*, 74; Quick, "History," 123-26, 61-62, 71, 77-83.
[43] Cremin, *National Experience*, 184-85.

Epilogue

[1] Ibid., 536n; Smith, "Protestant Schooling," 695; Tyack, "Kingdom," 468-69.
[2] Henry Barnard, *American Journal of Education*; Richard G. Boone, *Education in the United States* (New York: Appleton, 1889), xii, 103-07; Lawrence Arthur Cremin, *The Wonderful World of Ellwood Patterson Cubberley: An Essay on the Historiography of American Education* (New York: Teachers College, 1965), 7-8; Hagedorn, "In the Shadow of Horace Mann: The Forgotten Evangelical Leaders of the Common School Movement"; Messerli, *Horace Mann*, 491. Boone wrote the first comprehensive history of the American public schools and he relied heavily upon Barnard's *American Journal of Education*.
[3] Cremin, *Wonderful*, 15-17, 24-25, 33.
[4] Sol Cohen, "The History of the History of American Education, 1900-1965: The Uses of the Past," *Harvard Education Review* 46, no. 2 (1976): 307; Milton Gaither, *American Educational History Revisited: A Critique of Progress* (New York: Teachers College, 2003), 97-102; Gerald Lee Gutek, *Education and Schooling in America*, 3rd ed. (Boston: Allyn and Bacon, 1992), 85-87, 120-22.
[5] Timothy J. Curry, Robert M. Jiobu, and Kent P. Schwirian, *Sociology for the 21st Century*, 2nd ed. (Upper Saddle River, NJ: Prentice Hall, 1999), 8, 17-18; Hatch, "Second," 248; Spring, *The American School*, 3.
[6] Martin Carnoy, "Marxism and Education," in *The Left Academy: Marxist Scholarship on American Campuses*, ed. Bertell Ollman and Edward Vernoff (New York: Praeger, 1984), ix, 79-98; Isaac Gottesman, "The Critical Turn in Education: Marxist Thought and the Rise of an Academic Left from the 1960s to the 1980s" (PhD diss., University of Washington, 2009), 1, 3, 11-12, 18, 23, 27, 44-45, 86-87, 96, 100-01, 11, 15, 80, 94; Rita Kramer, *Ed School Follies: The Miseducation of America's Teachers* (New York: Free Press, 1991), 8; Stanley Rothman, S. Robert Lichter, and Neil Nevitte, "Politics and Professional Advancement among

College Faculty," *The Forum* 3, no. 1 (2005): 4,6,7; Gary Allen Tobin and Aryeh K. Weinberg, *Religious Beliefs and Behavior of College Faculty* (San Francisco, CA: Institute for Jewish & Community Research, 2007), 6.

[7] Curry, Jiobu, and Schwirian, *Sociology for the 21st Century*, 364-65; Neil Gross and Solon Simmons, "The Religiosity of American College and University Professors," *Sociology of Religion* 70, no. 2 (2009): 106, 13-14. Hatch, "Second," 247-49; Howe, "Religion," 121-25; George M. Marsden, *The Soul of the American University: From Protestant Establishment to Established Nonbelief* (New York: Oxford University, 1994). Gross and Simmons found that professors are three times as likely as the general populace to be a religious skeptic and the ratio is even higher at elite institutions. With respect to Marxist influences among college faculty, Marx himself famously called religion the "opiate of the masses," so it is not surprising to find that many faculty have a very negative stance towards religion. Some of Marx's followers, of course, have shown astonishing brutality in repressing religion and its adherents.

[8] George M. Marsden, *The Outrageous Idea of Christian Scholarship* (New York: Oxford University, 1997), 23-24; Rothman, Lichter, and Nevitte, "Politics," 6; Tobin and Weinberg, *Religious Beliefs*, 2,46.

[9] Gross and Simmons, "Religiosity," 115, 18-19; Rothman, Lichter, and Nevitte, "Politics," 10-11; Tobin and Weinberg, *Religious Beliefs*, 1, 3, 19-20.

[10] Jon Butler, "Jack-in-the-Box Faith: The Religion Problem in Modern American History," *The Journal of American History* 90, no. 4 (2004): 1357-59; James H. Hutson, *Forgotten Features of the Founding: The Recovery of Religious Themes in the Early American Republic* (Lanham, MD: Lexington, 2003), ix; George M. Marsden, "Can Jonathan Edwards (and His Heirs) Be Integrated into the American History Narrative?" *Historically Speaking* 5, no. 6 (2004): 14; David B. Tyack, "Onward Christian Soldiers: Religion in the American Common School," in *History and Education: The Educational Uses of the Past*, ed. Paul Nash (New York: Random House, 1970), 214-15.

[11] Richard J. Altenbaugh, *The American People and Their Education: A Social History*, 1st ed. (Upper Saddle River, NJ: Merrill/Prentice Hall, 2003); Binder, *Age*; Boone, *Education in the United States*; Butts, *Public*; Butts and Cremin, *History*; Frank Tracey Carlton, *Economic Influences Upon Educational Progress in the United States, 1820-1850* (Madison: University of Wisconson, 1908; reprint, first published in 1906); Church and Sedlak, *Education*; Cremin, *American Common*; — — — , *National Experience*; Cubberley, *Public*; Curti, *Social*; William E. Drake, *The American School in Transition* (New York: Prentice-Hall, 1955); Edwards and Richey, *School*; Fuller, *Old*; Gutek, *Historical*; Kaestle, *Pillars*; Knight, *Education*; Meyer, *Educational*; Paul Monroe, *Founding of the American Public School System: A History of Education in the United States, from the Early Settlements to the Close of the Civil War Period* (New York: Hafner, 1971; reprint, originally published in 1940); Parkerson and Parkerson, *Emergence*; John D. Pulliam and James J. Van Patten, *History of Education in America*, 8th ed. (Upper Saddle River, NJ: Merrill, 2003); Reese, *America's Public Schools*;

John L. Rury, *Education and Social Change: Themes in the History of American Schooling* (Mahwah, NJ: L. Erlbaum, 2002); Spring, *The American School*; Theobald, *Call School*; Tyack and Hansot, *Managers*; Urban and Wagoner, *American*; Rush Welter, *Popular Education and Democratic Thought in America* (New York: Columbia University, 1962). See pages 67-68 of Cremin's *National Experience* for his critique of those who attribute the movement to secular forces. Tyack has been writing since the late 1960s on the inadequate treatment of evangelicals in the common school movement. It is important to note that the terms "Christian" and "Protestant" describe so many different sects that they fail to tell us much about the spiritual beliefs of the founders of the common schools.

[12] Hagedorn, "In the Shadow of Horace Mann: The Forgotten Evangelical Leaders of the Common School Movement."

[13] Carnoy, "Marxism," xv, 79-80, 82-84; Hatch, "Second," 247-48; Howe, "Religion," 127-28; Noll, *America's God*, 188; Parkerson and Parkerson, *Emergence*, 20. Noll explains that Marxist analysis claims that evangelicalism was used by industrialists during the Second Great Awakening to further their interests;

[14] David Hackett Fischer, *Historians' Fallacies: Toward a Logic of Historical Thought*, 1st ed. (New York: Harper, 1970), 25-27; Kaestle, *Pillars*. Most scholars (Kaestle, for example) also attributed the rise of the movement to the desire to educate the next generation of citizens for their role in a democracy—what some call civic education. Most of the zealots, however, treat this as a secondary goal, which is secondary to the spiritual.

[15] Fishlow, "American," 49-65; Folger and Nam, *Education of the American Population*, 3, 4, 18; William C. Russell, "Education and the Working Class: The Expansion of Public Education During the Transition to Capitalism" (PhD diss., University of Cincinnati, 1981), 323-24.

[16] Jay M. Pawa, "Workingmen and Free Schools in the 19th Century: A Comment on the Labor-Education Thesis," *History of Education Quarterly* 11, no. 3 (1971).

[17] Lois W. Banner, "Religious Benevolence as a Social Control: A Critique of an Interpretation," in *The Many-Faceted Jacksonian Era: New Interpretations*, ed. Edward Pessen (Westport, CN: Greenwood, 1977), 302-21; John R. Bodo, *The Protestant Clergy and Public Issues, 1812-1848* (Princeton: Princeton University, 1954); Church and Sedlak, *Education*, 58-59, 62, 65-72, 79; Cole, *Social*, 68-69, 75-85, 95; Drake, *American*, 207-08; Edwards and Richey, *School*, 223-29, 98, 301, 03-05; Foster, *Errand*; Kaestle, *Pillars*, 63-67, 69, 75-103; Spring, *The American School*, 128-30.

[18] Marsden, "Jonathan Edwards," 13; Gordon S. Wood, "The Purpose of the Past: Reflections on the Uses of History," *Historically Speaking* 10, no. 1 (2009): 1-3. From 2007 through 2011 40% of the articles in the most prestigious journal in the discipline, the *History of Education Quarterly*, dealt with race or gender.

[19] Filler, *Crusade*, 6-15. Robert B. Townsend, "What's in a Label? Changing Patterns of Faculty Specialization since 1975," *Perspectives* (2007): 7; Wood, "Purpose," 4. For example, Filler claims that the mostly white male antislavery activists were not given their proper due in interpretations of their movement. It

appears that the same oversight has occurred with respect to the white male education reformers.

[20] Cohen, "History," 308-12, 26-28; Fischer, *Historians,'* 313-14; Gaither, *American*, 3, 98-100, 63; Wood, "Purpose," 4-5.

[21] *History of Education Quarterly*, Volumes 47-51.

[22] Tobin and Weinberg, *Religious Beliefs*, 2, 6, 10, 12, 71-72, 81, 83; George A. Yancey, *Compromising Scholarship: Religious and Political Bias in American Higher Education* (Waco, TX: Baylor University, 2011), 115-17, 35. While the terms "evangelical" and "fundamentalist" are different, many people use them interchangably.

[23] Richard Rorty, "Universality and Truth," in *Rorty and His Critics*, ed. Robert Brandom (Malden, MA: Blackwell, 2000), 17-22.

[24] Gross and Simmons, "Religiosity," 118; Tobin and Weinberg, *Religious Beliefs*, 3.

[25] Paul Boyer, "In Search of the Fourth "R": The Treatment of Religion in American History Textbooks and Survey Courses," in *Religious Advocacy and American History*, ed. Bruce Kuklick and D. G. Hart (Grand Rapids, MI: Eerdmans, 1997), 112-36; Bruce Kuklick and D. G. Hart, "Introduction," in *Religious Advocacy and American History*, ed. Bruce Kuklick and D. G. Hart (Grand Rapids, MI: Eerdmans, 1997), x-xii, xvii; Marsden, *Outrageous*, 52; Yancey, *Compromising*, 135-36, 51-52, 62-63.

[26] Wood, "Purpose," 5. Of course, the discrimination perpetrated against women and blacks during those times was quite unjust, but to intentionally seek to research and include members of those groups into one's narrative would not be the conduct of research, it would be the collection of propaganda.

[27] Marsden, *Outrageous*, 60-68.

[28] "The Shame of America's One-Party Campuses," *The American Enterprise* 2002, 18-25. One could argue that a professor should try to keep his personal beliefs out of classroom discussions. That is probably not a good idea, but in any event it is not possible. A better course would be to have ideological diversity among the faculty.

Bibliography

Aaron, Daniel. Cincinnati, *Queen City of the West, 1819-1838*. Columbus: Ohio State University, 1992.

Alexander, Edward P. "Wisconsin, New York's Daughter State." *Wisconsin Magazine of History* 30, no. 1 (1946): 11-30.

Altenbaugh, Richard J. *The American People and Their Education: A Social History*. 1st ed. Upper Saddle River, NJ: Merrill/Prentice Hall, 2003.

American Enterprise. "The Shame of America's One-Party Campuses." September 2002.

Appleby, Joyce Oldham. *Inheriting the Revolution: The First Generation of Americans*. Cambridge, MA: Belknap, 2000.

Atkinson, Nancy Bates, and Myron Eells. *Biography of Rev. G. H. Atkinson . . . Journal of Sea Voyage to Oregon in 1848, and Selected Addresses and Printed Articles, and a Particular Account of His Church Work in the Pacific Northwest*. Portland, OR, 1893.

Atwater, Caleb. *An Essay on Education*. Cincinnati, 1841.

————. *A History of the State of Ohio: Natural and Civil*. 1st ed. Cincinnati, 1838.

Bainton, Roland Herbert. *Yale and the Ministry: A History of Education for the Christian Ministry at Yale from the Founding in 1701*. 1st ed. New York: Harper, 1957.

Bald, F. Clever. *Michigan in Four Centuries*. 1st ed. New York: Harper, 1954.

Banner, Lois W. "Religious Benevolence as a Social Control: A Critique of an Interpretation." In *The Many-Faceted Jacksonian Era: New Interpretations*, edited by Edward Pessen, 302-321. Westport, CN: Greenwood, 1977.

Barnard, Henry. "James G. Carter." *American Journal of Education* 5 (1858): 407-16.

Barnard, Henry, and Vincent P. Lannie. *Henry Barnard, American Educator*. New York: Teachers College, 1974.

Bean, Walton. *California: An Interpretive History*. 2nd ed. New York: McGraw-Hill, 1973.

Becker, Robert A. "Currency, Taxation, and Finance, 1775-1787." In *A Companion to the American Revolution*, edited by Jack P. Greene and J. R. Pole, 388-397. Malden, MA: Blackwell, 2000.

Beecher, Lyman. *A Plea for the West*. 2nd ed. Cincinnati, 1835.

Beecher, Lyman, and Charles Beecher. *Autobiography, Correspondence, Etc.* 2 vols. New York: Harper, 1864.

Belting, Paul Everett. *The Development of the Free Public High School in Illinois to 1860*. New York: Arno Press, 1969. Reprint, first published in 1919.

Bergquist, James M. "Tracing the Origins of a Midwestern Culture: The Case of Central Indiana." *Indiana Magazine of History* 77, no. 1 (1981): 1-32.

Billington, Ray Allen. *The Far Western Frontier, 1830-1860*. 1st ed. New York: Harper, 1956.

—————. *The Protestant Crusade, 1800-1860: A Study of the Origins of American Nativism*. Chicago: Quadrangle, 1964. Reprint, first published in 1938.

Binder, Frederick M. *The Age of the Common School: 1830-1865*. New York: Wiley, 1974.

Blocker, Jack S. *American Temperance Movements: Cycles of Reform*. Boston: Twayne, 1989.

Bode, Carl. *The American Lyceum: Town Meeting of the Mind*. New York: Oxford University, 1956.

Bodo, John R. *The Protestant Clergy and Public Issues, 1812-1848*. Princeton: Princeton University, 1954.

Bone, Robert G. "Education in Illinois before 1857." *Journal of the Illinois State Historical Society* 50, no. 1 (1957): 119-40.

Boone, Richard G. *Education in the United States*. New York: Appleton, 1889.

—————. *A History of Education in Indiana*. New York: Appleton, 1892.

Boyer, Paul. "In Search of the Fourth 'R': The Treatment of Religion in American History Textbooks and Survey Courses." In *Religious Advocacy and American History*, edited by Bruce Kuklick and D. G. Hart, 112-136. Grand Rapids, MI: Eerdmans, 1997.

Broadie, Alexander. "Reid in Context." In *The Cambridge Companion to Thomas Reid*, edited by Terence Cuneo and Renâe van Woudenberg, 31-52. New York: Cambridge University, 2004.

Brooks, Harold C. "Founding of the Michigan Public School System." *Michigan History* 33, no. 4 (1949): 291-306.

Brown, Candy Gunther. *The Word in the World: Evangelical Writing, Publishing, and Reading in America, 1789-1880*. Chapel Hill: University of North Carolina, 2004.

Buley, R. Carlyle. *The Old Northwest: Pioneer Period, 1815-1840*. 2 vols. Indianapolis: Indiana Historical Society, 1950.

Burns, James Jesse. *Educational History of Ohio: A History of Its Progress since the Formation of the State, Together with the Portraits and Biographies of Past and Present State Officials*. Columbus, OH: Historical, 1905.

Butler, Jon. "Jack-in-the-Box Faith: The Religion Problem in Modern American History." *The Journal of American History* 90, no. 4 (2004): 1357-78.

Butler, Nicholas Murray. "The Barnard Relief Movement." *Educational Review* 3 (1892): 409-10.

Butts, R. Freeman. *Public Education in the United States: From Revolution to Reform*. New York: Holt, 1978.

Butts, R. Freeman, and Lawrence Arthur Cremin. *A History of Education in American Culture*. New York: Holt, 1953.

Calvert, Robert A., and Arnoldo De Leâon. *The History of Texas*. Arlington Heights, IL: H. Davidson, 1990.

Campbell, Randolph B. *Gone to Texas: A History of the Lone Star State*. New York: Oxford University, 2003.

Carey, Charles Henry. *History of Oregon*. Chicago: Pioneer Historical, 1922.

Carlton, Frank Tracey. *Economic Influences Upon Educational Progress in the United States, 1820-1850*. Madison: University of Wisconson, 1908. Reprint, first published in 1906.

Carmony, Donald F. *Indiana, 1816-1850: The Pioneer Era*. Indianapolis: Indiana Historical Bureau & Indiana Historical Society, 1998.

Carnoy, Martin. "Marxism and Education." In *The Left Academy: Marxist Scholarship on American Campuses*, edited by Bertell Ollman and Edward Vernoff, 79-98. New York: Praeger, 1984.

Carpenter, Charles H. *History of American Schoolbooks*. Philadelphia: University of Pennsylvania, 1963.

319

Catholic Diocese of Galveston-Houston. *Recall, Rejoice, Renew: Diocese of Galveston-Houston, 1847-1997.* Dallas: Taylor Publishing, 1997.

Caughey, John Walton. *California.* New York: Prentice-Hall, 1940.

Cayton, Andrew R. L. *The Frontier Republic: Ideology and Politics in the Ohio Country, 1780-1825.* Kent: Kent State, 1986.

Cayton, Andrew R. L., and Peter S. Onuf. *The Midwest and the Nation: Rethinking the History of an American Region.* Bloomington: Indiana University, 1990.

Church, Robert L., and Michael W. Sedlak. *Education in the United States: An Interpretive History.* New York: Free Press, 1976.

Clark, Sylvia Marie. "James Gordon Carter: His Influence in Massachusetts Education, History, and Politics from 1820-1850." EdD diss., Boston College, 1982.

Clark, Thomas Dionysius. *A History of Kentucky.* Rev. ed. Ashland, KY: The Jesse Stuart Foundation, 1992.

Coggeshall, William T. "Nathan Guilford." *American Journal of Education* 9 (1860): 289-294.

Cohen, Sol. "The History of the History of American Education, 1900-1965: The Uses of the Past." *Harvard Education Review* 46, no. 2 (1976): 298-330.

Cole, Arthur Charles. *The Era of the Civil War, 1848-1878.* Springfield: Illinois Centennial Commission, 1919.

Cole, Charles Chester. *The Social Ideas of the Northern Evangelists, 1826-1860.* New York: Columbia University, 1954.

Commager, Henry Steele, and Milton Cantor. *Documents of American History.* 10th ed. 2 vols. Englewood Cliffs, NJ: Prentice Hall, 1988.

Cook, John Williston. *Educational History of Illinois.* Chicago: Henry O. Shepard, 1912.

Cremin, Lawrence A. *American Education: The Colonial Experience, 1607-1783.* 1st ed. New York: Harper, 1970.

————. *The American Common School: An Historic Conception.* New York: Teachers College, 1951.

————. *American Education: The National Experience, 1783-1876.* 1st ed. New York: Harper, 1980.

————. *The Wonderful World of Ellwood Patterson Cubberley: An Essay on the Historiography of American Education.* New York: Teachers College, 1965.

Cubberley, Ellwood Patterson. *Public Education in the United States, a Study and Interpretation of American Educational History*. Rev. and enl. ed. Boston: Houghton Mifflin, 1934.

Culver, Raymond B. *Horace Mann and Religion in the Massachusetts Public Schools*. New Haven: Yale University, 1929.

Current, Richard N. *The Civil War Era, 1848-1873*. Madison: State Historical Society of Wisconsin, 1976.

Curry, Timothy J., Robert M. Jiobu, and Kent P. Schwirian. *Sociology for the 21st Century*. 2nd ed. Upper Saddle River, NJ: Prentice Hall, 1999.

Curti, Merle Eugene. *The Social Ideas of American Educators*. Paterson, NJ: Pageant, 1959. Reprint, first published in 1935.

Cutler, Julia Perkins. *Life and Times of Ephraim Cutler*. New York: Arno Press, 1971. Reprint, first published in 1890.

Cutler, Manasseh. "Manasseh Cutler Sermons." Special Collections, Dawes Memorial Library, Marietta College, Marietta, OH.

Dain, Floyd Russell. *Education in the Wilderness*. Lansing: Michigan Historical Commission, 1968.

Davis, James Edward. *Frontier Illinois*. Bloomington: Indiana University, 1998.

Davis, Sheldon Emmor. *Educational Periodicals During the 19th Century*. Metuchen, NJ: Scarecrow, 1970. Reprint, with foreword by Francesco Cordasco, first published in 1919.

Dodds, Gordon B. *Oregon: A Bicentennial History*. New York: Norton, 1977.

Dorsey, Bruce. *Reforming Men and Women: Gender in the Antebellum City*. Ithaca: Cornell University, 2002.

Drake, Richard B. *A History of Appalachia*. Lexington: University of Kentucky, 2001.

Drake, William E. *The American School in Transition*. New York: Prentice-Hall, 1955.

Dunbar, Willis Frederick, and George S. May. *Michigan, a History of the Wolverine State*. Rev. ed. Grand Rapids: Eerdmans, 1980.

Dunn, William Kailer. *What Happened to Religious Education? The Decline of Religious Teaching in the Public Elementary School, 1776-1861*. Baltimore: Johns Hopkins, 1958.

Eblen, Jack Ericson. *The First and Second United States Empires: Governors and Territorial Government, 1784-1912*. Pittsburgh: University of Pittsburgh, 1968.

Eby, Frederick. *The Development of Education in Texas*. New York: Macmillan, 1925.

— — — — . *Early Protestant Educators*. New York: McGraw-Hill, 1931.

Edwards, Newton, and Herman G. Richey. *The School in the American Social Order: The Dynamics of American Education*. Boston: Houghton Mifflin, 1947.

Ellis, Alton. "Samuel Lewis, Progressive Educator in the Early History of Ohio." *Ohio Archaeological and Historical Publications* 25 (1916).

Elson, Ruth Miller. *Guardians of Tradition: American Schoolbooks of the 19th Century*. Lincoln: University of Nebraska, 1964.

Emerson, Roger. "The Contexts of the Scottish Enlightenment." In *The Cambridge Companion to the Scottish Enlightenment*, edited by Alexander Broadie, 9-30. Cambridge, UK: Cambridge University, 2003.

Erickson, Leonard. "Politics and Repeal of Ohio's Black Laws, 1837-1849." *Ohio History* 82, no. 3 (1973): 154-75.

Ershkowitz, Herbert, and William G. Shade. "Consensus or Conflict? Political Behavior in the State Legislatures During the Jacksonian Era." In *The Many-Faceted Jacksonian Era: New Interpretations*, edited by Edward Pessen, 212-241. Westport, CN: Greenwood, 1977.

Etcheson, Nicole. *The Emerging Midwest: Upland Southerners and the Political Culture of the Old Northwest, 1787-1861*. Bloomington: Indiana University, 1996.

Ewing, J. Andrew. "Education in California During the Pre-Statehood Period." *Annual Publications of the Historical Society of Southern California* 11 (1918): 51-59.

Falk, Charles John. *The Development and Organization of Education in California*. New York: Harcourt, 1968.

Faragher, John Mack. *The Encyclopedia of Colonial and Revolutionary America*. New York: Facts on File, 1990.

Farrell, Richard Terrence. "Cincinnati in the Early Jackson Era, 1816-1834: An Economic and Political Study." PhD diss., Indiana University, 1967.

Fehrenbach, T. R. *Lone Star: A History of Texas and the Texans*. 1st ed. New York: Da Capo, 2000.

Feller, Daniel. *The Public Lands in Jacksonian Politics*. Madison: University of Wisconsin, 1984.

Ferris, David Frederic. *Judge Marvin and the Founding of the California Public School System*. Berkeley: University of California, 1962.

Ferris, Mary Walton. *Dawes-Gates Ancestral Lines: The American Ancestry of Rufus R. Dawes*. Milwaukee, WI: Cuneo, 1943.

Filler, Louis. *Crusade against Slavery: Friends, Foes, and Reforms, 1820-1860*. Rev. ed., first published in 1960. Algonac, MI: Reference Publications, 1986.

Finkelman, Paul. "Slavery and the Northwest Ordinance: A Study in Ambiguity." *Journal of the Early Republic* 6, no. 4 (1986): 343-70.

Fischer, David Hackett. *Albion's Seed: Four British Folkways in America*. New York: Oxford University, 1989.

————. *Historians' Fallacies: Toward a Logic of Historical Thought*. 1st ed. New York: Harper, 1970.

————. *Paul Revere's Ride*. New York: Oxford University, 1994.

Fishlow, Albert. "The American Common School Revival: Fact or Fancy?" In *Industrialization in Two Systems*, edited by Henry Rosovsky and Alexander Gerschenkron, 40-65. New York: Wiley, 1966.

Fishwick, Marshall William. *Great Awakenings: Popular Religion and Popular Culture*. New York: Haworth, 1995.

Fitzmier, John R. *New England's Moral Legislator: Timothy Dwight, 1752-1817*. Bloomington: Indiana University, 1998.

Fleischhacker, Samuel. "The Impact on America: Scottish Philosophy and the American Founding." In *The Cambridge Companion to the Scottish Enlightenment*, edited by Alexander Broadie, 316-337. Cambridge, UK: Cambridge University, 2003.

Folger, John K., and Charles B. Nam. *Education of the American Population*. Washington, DC: US Dept. of Commerce, Bureau of the Census, 1967.

Foote, John P. *The Schools of Cincinnati and Its Vicinity*. Reprint, first published in 1855. New York: Arno Press, 1970.

Ford, Bridget. "Beyond Cane Ridge: The 'Great Western Rivivals' in Louisville and Cincinnati, 1828-1845." *Ohio Valley History* 8, no. 4 (2008): 17-37.

Formisano, Ronald P. *The Transformation of Political Culture: Massachusetts Parties, 1790s-1840s*. New York: Oxford University, 1983.

Foster, Charles I. *An Errand of Mercy: The Evangelical United Front, 1790-1837*. Chapel Hill: University of North Carolina, 1960.

Fox, Stephen C. *The Group Bases of Ohio Political Behavior, 1803-1848*. New York: Garland, 1989.

Frank, Michael, and Ernest St. Aubin. "The Autobiography of Michael Frank." *Wisconsin Magazine of History* 30, no. 4 (1947): 441-81.

Fraser, James W. *Pedagogue for God's Kingdom: Lyman Beecher and the Second Great Awakening*. Lanham: University Press of America, 1985.

Fuller, Wayne Edison. *The Old Country School: The Story of Rural Education in the Middle West*. Chicago: University of Chicago, 1982.

Gabriel, Ralph Henry. *Religion and Learning at Yale: The Church of Christ in the College and University, 1757-1957*. New Haven: Yale University, 1958.

Gaither, Milton. *American Educational History Revisited: A Critique of Progress*. New York: Teachers College, 2003.

Gaustad, Edwin S., and Leigh Eric Schmidt. *The Religious History of America*. Rev. ed. San Francisco: Harper, 2002.

Goodykoontz, Colin Brummitt. *Home Missions on the American Frontier, with Particular Reference to the American Home Missionary Society*. Caldwell, ID: Caxton, 1939.

Gottesman, Isaac. "The Critical Turn in Education: Marxist Thought and the Rise of an Academic Left from the 1960s to the 1980s." PhD diss., University of Washington, 2009.

Greene, Jack P. *The Reinterpretation of the American Revolution, 1763-1789*. New York: Harper, 1968.

Griffin, Orwin Bradford. *The Evolution of the Connecticut State School System*. New York: Teachers College, 1928.

Gross, Neil, and Solon Simmons. "The Religiosity of American College and University Professors." *Sociology of Religion* 70, no. 2 (2009): 101-29.

Gutek, Gerald Lee. *Education and Schooling in America*. 3rd ed. Boston: Allyn and Bacon, 1992.

————. *An Historical Introduction to American Education*. 2nd ed. Prospect Heights, IL: Waveland, 1991.

————. *A History of the Western Educational Experience*. 2nd ed. Prospect Heights, IL: Waveland, 1995.

Hagedorn, Thomas W. "In the Shadow of Horace Mann: The Forgotten Evangelical Leaders of the Common School Movement." Unpublished paper presented at the *Annual Conference of the History of Education Society*. Cleveland, OH: 2007.

————. "The Strange History of the Origins of the Public School: What Happened to the Ministers?" Unpublished paper presented at the

Christianity and American History Conference. Lynchburg, VA: 2007.

Hall, Patricia Kelly, and Steven Ruggles. ""Restless in the Midst of Their Prosperity": New Evidence on the Internal Migration of Americans, 1850-2000." *The Journal of American History* 91, no. 3 (2004): 829-46.

Hamlett, Barksdale. *History of Education in Kentucky*. Frankfort: Kentucky Dept. of Education, 1914.

Hanchett, William. "The Question of Religion and the Taming California, 1849-1854." *California Historical Society Quarterly* 32 (1953): 119-44.

Hansen, Allen Oscar. *Early Educational Leadership in the Ohio Valley: A Study of Educational Reconstruction through the Western Literary Institute and College of Professional Teachers, 1829-1841*. Bloomington, IL: Public School Publishing, 1923.

Hansen, Stephen L. *The Making of the Third Party System: Voters and Parties in Illinois, 1850-1876*. Ann Arbor, MI: UMI Research, 1980.

Harding, Vincent. "Lyman Beecher and the Transformation of American Protestantism, 1775-1863." PhD diss., University of Chicago, 1965.

Hartman, Grover L. "The Hoosier Sunday School: A Potent Religious/ Cultural Force." *Indiana Magazine of History* 78, no. 3 (1982): 215-41.

Hasselbrinck, William R. "The Whigs of Indiana, 1834-1843." PhD diss., Ball State University, 1985.

Hatch, Nathan O. *The Democratization of American Christianity*. New Haven: Yale University, 1989.

————. "The Second Great Awakening and the Market Revolution." In *Devising Liberty: Preserving and Creating Freedom in the New American Republic*, edited by David Thomas Konig, 243-264. Palo Alto: Stanford Universisty, 1995.

Hawke, David Freeman. *Benjamin Rush: Evolutionary Gadfly*. Indianapolis: Bobbs-Merrill, 1971.

Hayes, Cecil Branner. *The American Lyceum: Its History and Contribution to Education*. Washington, DC: GPO, 1932.

Heimert, Alan. *Religion and the American Mind, from the Great Awakening to the Revolution*. Cambridge: Harvard University, 1966.

Henry, Stuart C. *Unvanquished Puritan: A Portrait of Lyman Beecher*. Grand Rapids, MI: Eerdmans, 1973.

Herman, Arthur. *How the Scots Invented the Modern World: The True Story of How Western Europe's Poorest Nation Created Our World & Everything in It.* 1st ed. New York: Crown, 2001.

Hershock, Martin J. *The Paradox of Progress: Economic Change, Individual Enterprise, and Political Culture in Michigan, 1837-1878.* Athens: Ohio University, 2003.

Hinsdale, Mary L. "A Legislative History of the Public School System of the State of Ohio." In *Report of the Commissioner of Education for the Year 1900-1901*, edited by Department of the Interior, US Bureau of Education, 129-150. Washington, DC: GPO, 1902.

Holifield, E. Brooks. *Theology in America: Christian Thought from the Age of the Puritans to the Civil War.* New Haven, CT: Yale University, 2003.

Holt, Edgar Allen. "Party Politics in Ohio, 1840-1850, Part 1." *Ohio Archaeological and Historical Quarterly* 37, no. 3 (1928): 439-591.

— — — —. "Party Politics in Ohio, 1840-1850, Part 2." *Ohio Archaeological and Historical Quarterly* 38, no. 1 (1929): 47-182.

Holt, Michael F. *The Rise and Fall of the American Whig Party: Jacksonian Politics and the Onset of the Civil War.* New York: Oxford University, 1999.

Howard, Robert P. *Illinois: A History of the Prairie State.* Grand Rapids, MI: Eerdmans, 1972.

Howe, Daniel Walker. "Church, State, and Education in the Young American Republic." *Journal of the Early Republic* 22, no. 1 (2002): 1-24.

— — — —. *Making the American Self: Jonathan Edwards to Abraham Lincoln.* Cambridge, Mass.: Harvard University, 1997.

— — — —. *The Political Culture of the American Whigs.* Chicago: University of Chicago, 1979.

— — — —. "Religion and Politics in the Antebellum North." In *Religion and American Politics: From the Colonial Period to the 1980s*, edited by Mark A. Noll. New York: Oxford University, 1990.

— — — —. *What Hath God Wrought: The Transformation of America, 1815-1848.* New York: Oxford University, 2007.

Hoyt, Charles Oliver, and R. Clyde Ford. *John D. Pierce, Founder of the Michigan School System: A Study of Education in the Northwest.* Ypsilanti, MI: Scharf Tag, Label & Box Co., 1905.

Hudson, John C. "North American Origins of Middlewestern Popula-tions." *Annuals of the Association of American Geographers* 78, no. 3 (1988): 395-413.

Hutchison, Keith R. "James Gordon Carter: Education Reformer." *New England Quarterly* 16, no. 3 (1943): 376-96.

Hutson, James H. *Forgotten Features of the Founding: The Recovery of Religious Themes in the Early American Republic*. Lanham, MD: Lexington, 2003.

————. *Religion and the Founding of the American Republic*. Washington, DC: Library of Congress, 1998.

Indiana Historical Bureau. "The Virginia Cession." http://www.in.gov/history/2898.htm.

Indiana University School of Law. "Constitution of the State of Indiana." http://www.law.indiana.edu/uslawdocs/inconst.html - education.

Jacks, L.V. *Claude Dubuis, Bishop of Galveston*. St. Louis: B. Herder, 1947.

Johnson, Paul E. *A Shopkeeper's Millennium: Society and Revivals in Rochester, New York, 1815-1837*. 1st ed. New York: Hill and Wang, 1978.

Jones, Lindsay. *Encyclopedia of Religion*. 2nd ed. Detroit: Macmillan, 2005.

Jorgenson, Lloyd P. *The Founding of Public Education in Wisconsin*. Madison: State Historical Society of Wisconsin, 1956.

Kaestle, Carl F. "The Development of Common School Systems in the States of the Old Northwest." In *"—Schools and the Means of Education Shall Forever Be Encouraged": A History of Education in the Old Northwest, 1787-1880*, edited by Paul H. Mattingly and Edward W. Stevens, Jr., 31-42 Athens: Ohio University, 1987.

————. *Pillars of the Republic: Common Schools and American Society, 1780-1860*. 1st ed. New York: Hill and Wang, 1983.

Kelley, Brooks Mather. *Yale: A History*. New Haven: Yale University, 1974.

King, Rufus. *Ohio: First Fruits of the Ordinance of 1787*. Boston, 1888.

Kirby, Julia. *Biographical Sketch of Joseph Duncan, Fifth Governor of Illinois*. Chicago, 1888.

Knepper, George W. *Ohio and Its People*. 2nd ed. Kent, OH: Kent State University, 1997.

Knight, Edgar Wallace. *Education in the United States*. 3rd ed. Boston: Ginn, 1951.

Knight, George Wells. *History and Management of Land Grants for Education in the Northwest Territory (Ohio, Indiana, Illinois, Michigan, Wisconsin)*. New York, 1885.

Kohn, Richard H. *Eagle and Sword: The Federalists and the Creation of the Military Establishment in America, 1783-1802*. New York: Free Press, 1975.

— — — —. "The Inside History of the Newburgh Conspiracy: America and the Coup D'etat." *The William and Mary Quarterly* 27, no. 2 (1970): 187-220.

Kors, Alan Charles. *Encyclopedia of the Enlightenment*. New York: Oxford University Press, 2003.

Kramer, Rita. *Ed School Follies: The Miseducation of America's Teachers*. New York: Free Press, 1991.

Kucera, Daniel W. *Church-State Relationships in Education in Illinois*. Washington, DC: Catholic University of America, 1955.

Kuklick, Bruce. *A History of Philosophy in America, 1720-2000*. Oxford: Clarendon, 2001.

Kuklick, Bruce, and D. G. Hart. "Introduction." In *Religious Advocacy and American History*, edited by Bruce Kuklick and D. G. Hart, x-xx. Grand Rapids, MI: Eerdmans, 1997.

Larkin, Jack. *The Reshaping of Everyday Life, 1790-1840*. 1st ed. New York: Harper, 1988.

Larson, John Lauritz. *Internal Improvement: National Public Works and the Promise of Popular Government in the Early United States*. Chapel Hill: University of North Carolina, 2001.

Lewis, Ira W. "Education in the Oregon Constitutional Convention." *The Quarterly of the Oregon Historical Society* 23 (1922): 220-29.

Lewis, William G. W. *Biography of Samuel Lewis, First Superintendent of Common Schools for the State of Ohio*. Cincinnati, 1857.

Library of Congress. "Journals of the Continental Congress, 1774-1789." *American Memory*, http://memory.loc.gov/ammem/amlaw/lwj-clink.html.

— — — —. "The Newburgh Conspiracy." *American Memory*, http://www.loc.gov/teachers/classroommaterials/presentationsandactivities/presentations/timeline/amrev/peace/newburgh.html.

Lich, Glen E. *The German Texans*. 1st ed. San Antonio: University of Texas, San Antonio, 1981.

Ligon, Moses E. "A History of Public Education in Kentucky." *Bulletin of the Bureau of School Service, College of Education, University of Kentucky* 14, no. 4 (1942): 53-104.

Linklater, Andro. *Measuring America: How an Untamed Wilderness Shaped the United States and Fulfilled the Promise of Democracy.* Reprint, first published in 2002 by Walker. New York: Plume, 2003.

Lottich, Kenneth V. "Educational Leadership in Early Ohio." *History of Education Quarterly* 2, no. 1 (1962): 52-61.

————. *New England Transplanted, a Study of the Development of Educational and Other Cultural Agencies in the Connecticut Western Reserve in Their National and Philosophical Setting.* Dallas: Royal, 1964.

MacCulloch, Diarmaid. *The Reformation.* 1st ed. New York: Viking, 2004.

MacDonald, Victoria-Marâia. *Latino Education in U.S. History, 1513-2000.* New York: Palgrave Macmillan, 2004.

MacMullen, Edith Nye. *In the Cause of True Education: Henry Barnard & 19th-Century School Reform.* New Haven: Yale University, 1991.

Madison, James H. *The Indiana Way: A State History.* Bloomington: Indiana University, 1986.

Maizlish, Stephen E. "Ohio and the Rise of Sectional Politics." In *The Pursuit of Public Power: Political Culture in Ohio, 1787-1861,* edited by Jeffrey Paul Brown and Andrew R. L. Cayton, 117-143. Kent: Kent State University, 1994.

Mandel, Bernard. "Religion and the Public Schools of Ohio." *Ohio State Archaeological and Historical Quarterly* 58 (1949): 185-192.

Mann, Horace. *The Republic and the School: Horace Mann on the Education of Free Men.* Edited by Lawrence Arthur Cremin. New York: Teachers College, 1957.

Mann, Horace. *On the Crisis in Education.* Edited by Louis Filler. Yellow Springs: Antioch, 1965.

Marsden, George M. "Can Jonathan Edwards (and His Heirs) Be Integrated into the American History Narrative?" *Historically Speaking* 5, no. 6 (2004): 13-15.

————. *The Evangelical Mind and the New School Presbyterian Experience: A Case Study of Thought and Theology in 19th-Century America.* New Haven: Yale University, 1970.

————. *The Outrageous Idea of Christian Scholarship.* New York: Oxford University, 1997.

————. *Religion and American Culture.* San Diego: Harcourt Brace Jovanovich, 1990.

— — — —. *The Soul of the American University: From Protestant Estab-lishment to Established Nonbelief.* New York: Oxford University, 1994.

Martin, George H. *The Evolution of the Massachusetts Public School System.* New York: Appleton, 1894.

Martzolff, Clement L. "Caleb Atwater." *Ohio Archaeological and Historical Publications* 14 (1905): 247-271.

Mather, Cotton. *The Christian Philosopher.* Edited, with introduction and notes by Winton U. Solberg. Reprint, first published in 1721. Urbana: University of Illinois, 1994.

Mathews, Donald G. "The Second Great Awakening as an Organizing Process, 1780-1830: An Hypothesis." *American Quarterly* 21, no. 1 (1969): 23-43.

Matthew, H. C. G., Brian Howard Harrison, and the British Academy. *Oxford Dictionary of National Biography.* New York: Oxford University Press, 2004.

Mattingly, Paul H. "American School Teachers Before and After the Northwest Ordinance." In *"—Schools and the Means of Education Shall Forever Be Encouraged": A History of Education in the Old Northwest, 1787-1880,* edited by Paul H. Mattingly and Edward W. Stevens, Jr., 45-51. Athens: Ohio University, 1987.

— — — —. *The Classless Profession: American Schoolmen in the 19th Century.* New York: New York University, 1975.

May, Henry Farnham. *The Enlightenment in America.* New York: Oxford University, 1976.

Mayo, A.D. "The Development of the Common School in the Western States from 1830 to 1865." In *Report of the Commissioner of Education for the Year 1898-1899,* edited by Department of the Interior, US Bureau of Education, 357-450. Washington, DC: GPO, 1900.

— — — —. "Education in the Northwest During the First Half Century of the Republic, 1790-1840." In *Report of the Commissioner of Education for the Year 1894-1895,* edited by Department of the Interior, US Bureau of Education, 1513-1550. Washington, DC: GPO, 1896.

McCandless, Perry. *A History of Missouri, 1820 to 1860.* Columbia: University of Missouri, 1972.

McClellan, B. Edward. *Moral Education in America: Schools and the Shaping of Character from Colonial Times to the Present.* New York: Teachers College, 1999.

McCormick, Richard Patrick. *The Second American Party System; Party Formation in the Jacksonian Era.* Chapel Hill: University of North Carolina, 1966.

McDonald, Forrest. *E Pluribus Unum: The Formation of the American Republic, 1776-1790.* Boston: Houghton Mifflin, 1965.

————. *Novus Ordo Seclorum: The Intellectual Origins of the Constitution.* Lawrence: University Press of Kansas, 1985.

McGloin, John Bernard. *California's First Archbishop: The Life of Joseph Sadoc Alemany, 1814-1888.* New York: Herder, 1966.

McGuffey, William Holmes. *The McGuffey Readers: Selections from the 1879 Edition.* Edited by Elliott J.Gorn. Boston: Bedford/St. Martin's, 1998.

McLaughlin, Andrew Cunningham. *History of Higher Education in Michigan.* Washington, DC: Department of Interior, US Bureau of Education, 1891.

Mead, Arthur Raymond. *The Development of Free Schools in the United States as Illustrated by Connecticut and Michigan.* New York: Teachers College, 1918.

Messerli, Jonathan. *Horace Mann: A Biography.* 1st ed. New York: Knopf, 1972.

Meyer, Adolphe Erich. *An Educational History of the American People.* 2nd ed. New York: McGraw-Hill, 1967.

Miller, Edward Alanson. *The History of Educational Legislation in Ohio from 1803 to 1850.* Columbus: Heer, 1918.

Mills, Caleb. "An Address to the Legislature of Indiana." In *Caleb Mills and the Indiana School System,* edited by Charles W. Moores, 363-638. Indianapolis, IN: Wood-Weaver Printing Company, 1905.

Minnich, Harvey C. *William Holmes McGuffey and His Readers.* New York: American Book Company, 1936.

Miyakawa, Tetsuo Scott. *Protestants and Pioneers: Individualism and Conformity on the American Frontier.* Chicago: University of Chicago, 1964.

Monroe, Paul. *Founding of the American Public School System: A History of Education in the United States, from the Early Settlements to the Close of the Civil War Period.* Reprint, first published in 1940. New York: Hafner, 1971.

Monroe, W. S. *The Educational Labors of Henry Barnard: A Study in the History of American Pedagogy.* Syracuse, 1893.

Moore, Ernest. "California's Educators." *The Historical Society of Southern California Quarterly* 31 (1949): 169-77.

Moore, James T. *Through Fire and Flood: The Catholic Church in Frontier Texas, 1836-1900.* 1st ed. College Station: Texas A&M University, 1992.

Moore, R. Laurence. *Selling God: American Religion in the Marketplace of Culture.* New York: Oxford University, 1994.

Morgan, Edmund Sears. *The Puritan Family: Religion & Domestic Relations in 17th-Century New England.* Westport, CN: Greenwood, 1980.

Morison, Samuel Eliot. *The Puritan Pronaos: Studies in the Intellectual Life of New England in the 17th Century.* New York: New York University, 1936.

Morse, Jarvis Means. *A Neglected Period of Connecticut's History.* New Haven: Yale University, 1933.

Mosier, Richard David. *Making the American Mind: Social and Moral Ideas in the McGuffey Readers.* New York: Russell & Russell, 1965.

Mulkern, John R. *The Know-Nothing Party in Massachusetts: The Rise and Fall of a People's Movement.* Boston: Northeastern University, 1990.

Nation, Richard Franklin. *At Home in the Hoosier Hills: Agriculture, Politics, and Religion in Southern Indiana, 1810-1870.* Bloomington: Indiana University, 2005.

National Humanities Institute. "Constitution of Massachusetts, 1780." *Who We Are: The Story of America's Constitution*, http://www.nhinet.org/ccs/docs/ma-1780.htm.

Nelson, Paul David. "Horatio Gates at Newburgh, 1783: A Misunderstood Role." *The William and Mary Quarterly* 29, no. 1 (1972): 143-58.

Newcomer, Lee Nathaniel. "The Big World of Mannaseh Cutler." *The New-England Galaxy* 4 (1962): 29-37.

————. "Manasseh Cutler's Writings: A Note on Editorial Practice." *The Mississippi Valley Historical Review* 47, no. 1 (1960): 88-101.

Newman, Otho Lionel. "Development of the Common Schools of Indiana to 1851." *Indiana Magazine of History* 22, no. 3 (1926): 229-76.

Nietz, John A. *Old Textbooks: Spelling, Grammar, Reading, Arithmetic, Geography, American History, Civil Government, Physiology, Penmanship, Art, Music, as Taught in the Common Schools from Colonial Days to 1900.* Pittsburgh: University of Pittsburgh, 1961.

Niven, John. *Salmon P. Chase: A Biography.* New York: Oxford University, 1995.

Noll, Mark A. *America's God: From Jonathan Edwards to Abraham Lincoln*. New York: Oxford University, 2002.

————. *A History of Christianity in the United States and Canada*. Grand Rapids, MI: Eerdmans, 1992.

————. *The Old Religion in a New World: The History of North American Christianity*. Grand Rapids, MI: Eerdmans, 2002.

————. *Princeton and the Republic, 1768-1822: The Search for a Christian Enlightenment in the Era of Samuel Stanhope Smith*. Princeton: Princeton University, 1989.

Nord, David Paul. *Faith in Reading: Religious Publishing and the Birth of Mass Media in America*. New York: Oxford University, 2004.

Notestein, Wallace. *The English People on the Eve of Colonization, 1603-1630*. 1st ed. New York: Harper, 1954.

Nye, Russel Blaine. *The Cultural Life of the New Nation, 1776-1830*. 1st ed. New York: Harper, 1960.

————. *Society and Culture in America, 1830-1860*. 1st ed. New York: Harper, 1974.

Ohio Company. *The Records of the Original Proceedings of the Ohio Company (1786-1796)*. Edited with introduction by Archer Butler Hulbert. Marietta, OH: Marietta Historical Commission, 1917.

Ohio Historical Society. "Constitution of the State of Ohio, 1802." *Ohio Fundamental Documents*, http://ww2.ohiohistory.org/onlinedoc/ohgovernment/constitution/cnst1802.html.

————. "Fort Stephenson." *Ohio History Central*, http://www.ohiohistorycentral.org/entry.php?rec=717.

————. "Ohio Constitutional Convention of 1802." *Ohio History Central*, http://www.ohiohistorycentral.org/entry.php?rec=523.

————. "Plunder Law." *Ohio History Central*, http://www.ohiohistorycentral.org/entry.php?rec=1445.

Ohio State Teachers Association. *A History of Education in the State of Ohio: A Centennial Volume*. Edited by E.E. White and T.W. Harvey. Columbus, Ohio: Ohio General Assembly, 1876.

Onuf, Peter S. "The Founder's Vision: Education in the Development of the Old Northwest." In *"—Schools and the Means of Education Shall Forever Be Encouraged": A History of Education in the Old Northwest, 1787-1880*, edited by Paul H. Mattingly and Edward W. Stevens, Jr., 5-13. Athens: Ohio University, 1987.

————. *Statehood and Union: A History of the Northwest Ordinance*. Bloomington: Indiana University, 1987.

Parkerson, Donald Hugh, and Jo Ann Parkerson. *The Emergence of the Common School in the U.S. Countryside*. Lewiston, NY: Mellen, 1998.

Patzer, Conrad E. *Public Education in Wisconsin*. Madison, WI: Wisconsin Department of Public Instruction, 1925.

Pawa, Jay M. "Workingmen and Free Schools in the 19th Century: A Comment on the Labor-Education Thesis." *History of Education Quarterly* 11, no. 3 (1971): 287-302.

Petit, Sister Mary Loretta. "Samuel Lewis: Educational Reformer Turned Abolitionist." EdD diss., Western Reserve University, 1966.

Philbrick, Francis Samuel. *The Rise of the West, 1754-1830*. 1st ed. New York: Harper, 1965.

Phillips, Claude Anderson. *A History of Education in Missouri: The Essential Facts Concerning the History and Organization of Missouri's Schools*. Jefferson City, MO: Hugh Stephens Printing, 1911.

Polos, Nicholas C. *John Swett: California's Frontier Schoolmaster*. Washington, DC: University Press of America, 1978.

Poole, William Frederick. *The Ordinance of 1787, and Dr. Manasseh Cutler as an Agent in Its Formation*. Cambridge, MA, 1876.

Potter, David Morris, and Don Edward Fehrenbacher. *The Impending Crisis, 1848-1861*. 1st ed. New York: Harper, 1976.

Potts, Louis W. "Manasseh Cutler, Lobbyist." *Ohio History* 96 (1987): 101-23.

————. "Visions of America, 1787-1788: The Ohio of Reverend Manasseh Cutler." *Ohio History* 111 (2002): 101-20.

Power, Richard Lyle. *Planting Corn Belt Culture: The Impress of the Upland Southerner and Yankee in the Old Northwest*. Indianapolis: Indiana Historical Society, 1953.

Pulliam, John D. "A History of the Struggle for a Free Common School System in Illinois from 1818 to the Civil War." EdD diss., University of Illinois, 1965.

Pulliam, John D., and James J. Van Patten. *History of Education in America*. 8th ed. Upper Saddle River, NJ: Merrill, 2003.

Putnam, Daniel. *The Development of Primary and Secondary Public Education in Michigan: A Historical Sketch*. Ann Arbor, MI: G. Wahr, 1904.

Quick, Alan Frederick. "The History and Development of Common School Education in Oregon, 1849-1872." EdD diss., University of Oregon, 1963.

Rakove, Jack N. *The Beginnings of National Politics: An Interpretive History of the Continental Congress.* 1st ed. New York: Knopf, 1979.

Ratcliffe, Donald J. "The Market Revolution and Party Alignments in Ohio, 1828-1840." In *The Pursuit of Public Power: Political Culture in Ohio, 1787-1861,* edited by Jeffrey Paul Brown and Andrew R. L. Cayton, 99-116. Kent: Kent State University, 1994.

— — — —. *The Politics of Long Division: The Birth of the Second Party System in Ohio, 1818-1828.* Columbus: Ohio State University, 2000.

— — — —. "The Role of Voters and Issues in Party Formation: Ohio, 1824." *The Journal of American History* 59, no. 4 (1973): 847-70.

Redekop, Benjamin W. "Reid's Influence in Britain, Germany, France and America." In *The Cambridge Companion to Thomas Reid,* edited by Terence Cuneo and Renâe van Woudenberg, 323-335. New York: Cambridge University, 2004.

Reese, William J. *America's Public Schools: From the Common School To "No Child Left Behind."* Baltimore: Johns Hopkins University, 2011.

Reynolds, Maureen Anne. "Politics and Indiana's Public Schools During the Civil War Era, 1850-1875." PhD diss., Indiana University, 1997.

Rezneck, Samuel. *Business Depressions and Financial Panics: Essays in American Business and Economic History.* New York: Greenwood, 1968.

Robbins, William G. *Oregon: This Storied Land.* Portland: Oregon Historical Society, 2005.

Rohrbough, Malcolm J. *The Land Office Business: The Settlement and Administration of American Public Lands, 1789-1837.* New York: Oxford University, 1968.

— — — —. *The Trans-Appalachian Frontier: People, Societies, and Institutions, 1775-1850.* New York: Oxford University, 1978.

Rolle, Andrew F. *California: A History.* New York: Crowell, 1963.

Rorabaugh, W. J. *The Alcoholic Republic, an American Tradition.* New York: Oxford University, 1979.

Rorty, Richard. "Universality and Truth." In *Rorty and His Critics,* edited by Robert Brandom. Malden, MA: Blackwell, 2000.

Rose, Gregory S. "Upland Southerners: The County Origins of Southern Migrants to Indiana by 1850." *Indiana Magazine of History* 82, no. 3 (1986): 242-63.

Roseboom, Eugene Holloway. *The Civil War Era, 1850-1873*. Columbus: Ohio State Archaeological and Historical Society, 1941.

Roseboom, Eugene Holloway, and Francis P. Weisenburger. *A History of Ohio*. Columbus: Ohio State Archaeological and Historical Society, 1953.

Rosenberry, Lois Mathews. *The Expansion of New England*. Boston: Houghton Mifflin, 1909.

Ross, Frederick Ray. "A Portrait of Dedication: Samuel Lewis' Influence on the Abolitionist Movement in Ohio, 1840-1854." MA thesis, Morehead State, 1970.

Rothman, Stanley, S. Robert Lichter, and Neil Nevitte. "Politics and Professional Advancement among College Faculty." *The Forum* 3, no. 1 (2005).

Rudolph, L.C. *Hoosier Zion: The Presbyterians in Early Indiana*. New Haven: Yale University, 1963.

Rury, John L. *Education and Social Change: Themes in the History of American Schooling*. Mahwah, NJ: Erlbaum, 2002.

Russell, William C. "Education and the Working Class: The Expansion of Public Education During the Transition to Capitalism." PhD diss., University of Cincinnati, 1981.

Schafer, Joseph. "Origin of Wisconsin's Free School System." *Wisconsin Magazine of History* 9, no. 1 (1925): 27-46.

Schweikart, Larry, and Michael Allen. *A Patriot's History of the United States: From Columbus's Great Discovery to the War on Terror*. New York: Sentinel, 2004.

Schweikert, Joseph. "The Western Literary Institute and College of Professional Teachers: An Instrument in the Creation of a Profession." PhD diss., University of Cincinnati, 1971.

Schweitzer, Mary M. "The Economic and Demographic Consequences of the Revolution." In *A Companion to the American Revolution*, edited by Jack P. Greene and J. R. Pole, 559-578. Malden, MA: Blackwell, 2000.

Sherockman, Andrew A. "Caleb Mills: Pioneer Educator in Indiana." PhD diss., University of Pittsburgh, 1955.

Shetrone, Henry C. "Caleb Atwater: Versatile Pioneer, a Re-Appraisal." *Ohio State Archaeological and Historical Quarterly* 54, no. 1 (1945): 79-88.

Shoemaker, F.L. "Samuel Galloway: An Educational Statesman of First Rank." *History of Education Journal* 5, no. 4 (1954): 105-17.

Simpson, Alan. *Puritanism in Old and New England*. Chicago: University of Chicago, 1955.

Singleton, Gregory H. "Protestant Voluntary Organizations and the Shaping of Victorian America." In *Victorian America*, edited by Geoffrey Blodgett and Daniel Walker Howe, 47-58. Philadelphia: University of Pennsylvania, 1976.

Skeen, C. Edward. "The Newburgh Conspiracy Reconsidered." *The William and Mary Quarterly* 31, no. 2 (1974): 273-98.

Sloan, Douglas. *The Scottish Enlightenment and the American College Ideal*. New York: Teachers College, 1971.

Smelser, Marshall. *The Democratic Republic, 1801-1815*. 1st ed. New York: Harper, 1968.

Smith, Alice E. *From Exploration to Statehood*. Madison: State Historical Society of Wisconsin, 1973.

Smith, Timothy L. "Protestant Schooling and American Nationality, 1800-1850." *Journal of American History* 53 (1967): 679-795.

Spraul-Schmidt, Judith. "The Origins of Modern City Government: From Corporate Regulation to Municipal Corporation in New York, New Orleans and Cincinnati, 1785-1870." PhD diss., University of Cincinnati, 1990.

Spring, Joel H. *The American School, 1642-2004*. 6th ed. Boston: McGraw-Hill, 2005.

Starr, Kevin. *Americans and the California Dream, 1850-1915*. New York: Oxford University, 1973.

Starring, Charles R., and James Owen Knauss. *The Michigan Search for Educational Standards*. Lansing: Michigan Historical Commission, 1969.

Steiner, Barnard C. *Life of Henry Barnard: The First United States Commissioner of Education, 1867-1870*. Washington, DC: GPO, 1919.

Stevens, J. Harold. "The Influence of New England in Michigan." *Michigan History Magazine* 19 (1935): 321-53.

Stevens, Jr., Edward W. "Structural and Ideological Dimensions of Literacy and Education in the Old Northwest." In *Essays on the Economy of the Old Northwest*, edited by David C. Klingaman and Richard K. Vedder, 157-177. Athens: Ohio University, 1987.

Stewart, M.A. "Religion and Rational Theology." In *The Cambridge Companion to the Scottish Enlightenment*, edited by Alexander Broadie, 31-59. Cambridge, UK: Cambridge University, 2003.

Stowe, C. E. *Report on Elementary Public Instruction in Europe, Made to the Thirty-Sixth General Assembly of the State of Ohio, December 19, 1837.* Columbus: Ohio General Assembly, 1838.

————. *The Prussian System of Public Instruction, and Its Applicability to the United States.* Cincinnati, 1836.

Sweet, William Warren. *Religion in the Development of American Culture, 1765-1840.* New York: Scribner, 1952.

Swett, John. *Public Education in California: Its Origin and Development, with Personal Reminiscences of Half a Century.* New York: American Book, 1911.

Swift, Fletcher Harper. *A History of Public Permanent Common School Funds in the United States, 1795-1905.* New York: Holt, 1911.

Taylor, Howard Cromwell. *The Educational Significance of the Early Federal Land Ordinances.* New York: Teachers College, 1922.

Taylor, James W. *A Manual of the Ohio School System: Consisting of an Historical View of Its Progress, and a Republication of the School Laws in Force.* Cincinnati, 1857.

Temin, Peter. "The Jacksonian Economy." In *The Many-Faceted Jacksonian Era: New Interpretations*, edited by Edward Pessen, 101-113. Westport, CN: Greenwood, 1977.

Theobald, Paul. *Call School: Rural Education in the Midwest to 1918.* Carbondale: Southern Illinois University, 1995.

Thornbrough, Emma Lou. *Indiana in the Civil War Era, 1850-1880.* Indianapolis: Indiana Historical Bureau, 1965.

Tobin, Gary Allen, and Aryeh K. Weinberg. *Religious Beliefs and Behavior of College Faculty.* San Francisco, CA: Institute for Jewish & Community Research, 2007.

Townsend, Robert B. "What's in a Label? Changing Patterns of Faculty Specialization since 1975." *Perspectives*, January 2007, 7-10.

Tuggy, Dale. "Reid's Philosophy of Religion." In *The Cambridge Companion to Thomas Reid*, edited by Terence Cuneo and Renâe van Woudenberg, 289-312. New York: Cambridge University, 2004.

Turco, Luigi. "Moral Sense and the Foundations of Morals." In *The Cambridge Companion to the Scottish Enlightenment*, edited by Alexander Broadie. Cambridge, UK: Cambridge University, 2003.

Tyack, David B. "Forming Schools, Forming States: Education in a Nation of Republics." In *"—Schools and the Means of Education Shall Forever Be Encouraged": A History of Education in the Old Northwest, 1787-1880*, edited by Paul H. Mattingly and Edward Stevens, Jr., 17-27. Athens: Ohio University, 1987.

————. "The Kingdom of God and the Common Schools." *Harvard Education Review* 36, no. 4 (1966): 447-469.

————. "Onward Christian Soldiers: Religion in the American Common School." In *History and Education: The Educational Uses of the Past*, edited by Paul Nash, 212-255. New York: Random House, 1970.

————. *Turning Points in American Educational History.* Waltham, MA: Blaisdell, 1967.

Tyack, David B., and Elisabeth Hansot. *Managers of Virtue: Public School Leadership in America, 1820-1980.* New York: Basic Books, 1982.

Tyack, David B., Thomas James, and Aaron Benavot. *Law and the Shaping of Public Education, 1785-1954.* Madison: University of Wisconsin, 1987.

Tyrrell, Ian R. *Sobering Up: From Temperance to Prohibition in Antebellum America, 1800-1860.* Westport, CN: Greenwood, 1979.

Ulrich, Dennis Nicholas. "Manasseh Cutler: Early American Scientist." MA thesis, Miami University, 1974.

Urban, Wayne J., and Jennings L. Wagoner. *American Education: A History.* 2nd ed. Boston: McGraw-Hill, 2000.

US House of Representatives, Office of the Clerk. "Congress Overview." *House History*, http://artandhistory.house.gov/house_history/index.aspx.

Utter, William Thomas. *The Frontier State, 1803-1825.* Columbus: Ohio State Archaeological and Historical Society, 1941.

Van Bolt, Roger H. "The Hoosier Politician of the 1940s." *Indiana Magazine of History* 48, no. 1 (1952): 23-36.

————. "Hoosiers and the Eternal Agitation, 1848-1850." *Indiana Magazine of History* 48, no. 4 (1952): 331-68.

————. "The Indiana Scene in the 1840s." *Indiana Magazine of History* 47, no. 4 (1951): 333-56.

Vann, Barry. *In Search of Ulster-Scots Land: The Birth and Geotheological Imagings of a Transatlantic People, 1603-1703.* Columbia: University of South Carolina, 2008.

Vedder, Richard K., and Lowell E. Gallaway. "Migration and the Old Northwest." In *Essays in 19th Century Economic History: The Old Northwest*, edited by David C. Klingaman and Richard K. Vedder, 159-174. Athens: Ohio University, 1975.

Wade, Richard C. *The Urban Frontier: The Rise of Western Cities, 1790-1830.* Cambridge: Harvard University, 1959.

Ward, David. *Cities and Immigrants: A Geography of Change in 19th-Century America*. New York: Oxford University, 1971.

Ward, Harry M. *The American Revolution: Nationhood Achieved, 1763-1788*. New York: St. Martin's, 1995.

Watson, Harry L. *Liberty and Power: The Politics of Jacksonian America*. 1st ed. New York: Hill and Wang, 1990.

Weigley, Russell Frank. *History of the United States Army*. Enl. ed. Bloomington: Indiana University, 1984.

Weisenburger, Francis P. "Caleb Atwater: Pioneer Politician and Historian." *The Ohio Historical Quarterly* 68, no. 1 (1959): 18-37.

———. *The Passing of the Frontier, 1825-1850*. Columbus: Ohio State Archaeological and Historical Society, 1941.

Welter, Rush. *Popular Education and Democratic Thought in America*. New York: Columbia University, 1962.

Westerhoff, John H. *McGuffey and His Readers: Piety, Morality, and Education in 19th-Century America*. Nashville, TN: Abingdon, 1978.

Wolterstorff, Nicholas. "Reid on Common Sense." In *The Cambridge Companion to Thomas Reid*, edited by Terence Cuneo and Renâe van Woudenberg, 77-100. New York: Cambridge University, 2004.

Wood, Gordon S. *The Creation of the American Republic, 1776-1787*. Chapel Hill: University of North Carolina, 1998.

———. "The Purpose of the Past: Reflections on the Uses of History." *Historically Speaking* 10, no. 1 (2009).

Wood, Paul. "Science in the Scottish Enlightenment." In *The Cambridge Companion to the Scottish Enlightenment*, edited by Alexander Broadie. Cambridge, UK: Cambridge University, 2003.

Yancey, George A. *Compromising Scholarship: Religious and Political Bias in American Higher Education*. Waco, TX: Baylor University, 2011.

Index

military conspiracy, 3–6
surveying systems, 6–7, 19–20
Public Education in the United States
(Cubberley), 256–257
Puritans, cultural traditions of, 79-82
Putnam, Rufus
Army Plan of, 8–9
Marietta burial place of, 56
in Ohio Company of Associates,
40–41, 44–45

Rational belief system (Dewey), 258
Read, Daniel, 215
Readers (McGuffey), 86, 138, 192–195
Rectangular surveying system, 6
Reese, William, 259
Reeve, Tapping, 141, 178
Reformation, 59–60, 197
Reid, Thomas, 64–66, 70, 75
Religion. *See also* Moral education
land grants for support of, 8-9, 14-
17, 47, 51-52, 55–56
Land Ordnance failure to support,
20
public office tests on, 16
role of in schools, 164
township lots for, 15–16
Report of Government for the Western
Territory of 1784, 13
Report on Creating State Departments
of Public Instruction
(Campbell), 184
Report on Elementary Education in
Europe (Stowe), 196
Republicanism, 58
Reverse discrimination, 266
Rhode Island, education developments
in, 226–227
Rhode Island Campaign of 1777, 30, 37
Rincon School (San Francisco, CA),
242
Rittenhouse, David, 46
Robinson, John, 128
Rockefeller, John D., 195
Rorty, Richard, 264
Rothman, Stanley S., 257–259
Rousmaniere, Kate, 356
Rousseau, Henri, 59, 172, 260

Rush, Benjamin, 47, 57–58, 66
Rush Medical College, 96
Russell, William, 145, 190, 241
Rutgers University, 68

Sargent, Winthrop, 44, 47, 50
Schlesinger, Arthur M., 261
School attendance, 1850, 272–273
School Code of Wurttemberg
(Melancthon), 60
School Law of 1837 (Ohio), 145, 155
School Law of 1854 (TX), 234
Schools, *See* Public education
Schweikart, Larry, 356
Scioto Company, 50–51, 53–54
Scottish Common Sense Realism, 63-
75
Appalachian resistance to, 114
in Atwater theory of education, 92
in Congregationalist and
Presbyterian college
curricula, 87
as evangelical philosophy, 259
Horace Mann and, 141
John Pierce influenced by, 220
McGuffey's Eclectic Readers and,
195
public education influenced by,
66–67, 74–75
Yale University influenced by, 147
Second Great Awakening
Benevolent Empire foundation and,
64
college growth in, 189
education influenced by, 57–59
religious unity forged by, 122
spread of, 180
zealots and, 84–85
Secular humanism, 258
Secularism in academia, 256–258
Separation of powers concept, 67
Seven Ranges project
description of, 18–19
education land grant pattern of, 52
failure of, 49
Tupper survey of, 39–40
Shays' Rebellion, 20, 37, 41, 58–59
Sherman, Roger, 47

Acknowledgements

$\mathcal{A}$t the end of a twenty-year project there are just too many people to adequately thank each and every one of them. In any event my memory would not be up to the task, so consequently I will keep these comments brief. Of course, I first have to include the perfunctory but necessary boilerplate. This book is fully my responsibility and none of those mentioned below are to blame for any of its shortcomings, errors, or omissions.

First, I visited many libraries over the years, but two were essential to the success of my project. In fact, its very inspiration came to me after more than a year of diving into the archives almost every Saturday at the Cincinnati History Library at the Museum Center. Once I began work on my manuscript in earnest, the research library of my alma mater, the University of Cincinnati, proved to be an invaluable resource. In addition to its own excellent collection it also provided me access to almost every book held in college and university libraries throughout Ohio. Almost without exception I found the librarians at these two libraries and elsewhere to be extremely helpful.

Second, I owe a debt of gratitude to many historians—both those that I simply read and those with whom I communicated directly. With respect to the first group, since this book spans so many states and so many years, it had to be largely a work of synthesis. So, I read the works of many other historians, digested them, and then decided how they related to the story I was trying to tell. Several historians stood out, as types representing the dedication and professionalism

355

that embodies the best of their discipline. Lawrence Cremin's three volumes on *American Education* exhibit the depth and breadth of scholarship that only a senior scholar can bring to bear on a topic to which he has devoted a lifetime. Daniel Walker Howe's *What Hath God Wrought* exemplifies the same virtues for a historic period of time. Finally, the preface of Michael Holt's *The Rise and Fall of the American Whig Party*—which took two decades to complete—is a glimpse into the incredible persistence necessary to complete any attempt to explain a complex subject.

With respect to the historians with whom I have communicated over the years, several stand out. The following historians were very generous of their time, either on the phone, on the internet, or in person: James Carper, Andrew Cayton, Milton Gaither, Glenn Lauzon, George Marsden, Kate Rousmaniere, Larry Schweikart, and David Tyack. These are all very busy people with many responsibilities, yet they graciously made time for my questions. Every one of them made valuable suggestions and comments, although I did not agree with or use all of them. Further, I do not want to leave the impression that they agree with the issues raised in the Epilogue, nor do I want to imply by their listing here that they necessarily agreed with the interpretations implicit in *Founding Zealots*.

Lastly, I want to thank Dr. John Tallmadge, who provided literary coaching and developmental editing services during the latter stages of this project. His wise counsel allowed me to develop this topic with much more clarity. Further, his thorough editing helped me develop my style and improve my writing dramatically.

CPSIA information can be obtained at www.ICGtesting.com
Printed in the USA
BVOW002312190513

321049BV00002B/6/P